Edmund Wilson, the Man in Letters

Edmund Wilson, the Man in Letters

Edited and Introduced
by
David Castronovo and Janet Groth

Ohio University Press
ATHENS

Ohio University Press, Athens, Ohio 45701

Ohio University Press books are printed on acid-free paper ∞™

10 09 08 07 06 05 04 03 02 01   5 4 3 2 1

Library of Congress Cataloging-in-Publication Data

Wilson, Edmund, 1895–1972.
    Edmund Wilson, the man in letters / edited and introduced by David Castronovo
and Janet Groth.
    p. cm.
    Includes bibliographical references and index.
    ISBN 0-8214-1420-8 (cloth : alk. paper)
    1. Wilson, Edmund, 1895–1972—Correspondence.   2. Authors, American—
20th century—Correspondence.   3. Critics—United States—Correspondence.
I. Castronovo, David.   II. Groth, Janet.   III. Title.

PS3545.I6245 Z48 2001
818'.5209—dc21
[B]   2001036075

This book is dedicated to the memory of Leon Edel.

Reproduction of a May 29, 1957, letter to Dawn Powell's friend and patron Margaret de Silver. The marginal note is in Margaret de Silver's handwriting—or perhaps that of Dawn Powell: the letter was found among the papers of Dawn Powell at the Columbia University Rare Book and Manuscript Library.

I was startled to realize one day that I was imitating my father's signature—my name was the same as his—which, like his writing in general, was completely illegible but quite beautiful in a graphic way, as if he had invented a calligraphy in order to conceal his meaning from everyone but himself. This handwriting had thus also its arrogance as well as its curious elegance and I found myself emulating these. (*A Piece of My Mind*, 159–60)

Letter to Margaret de Silver (transcription of holograph letter on facing page)

May 29, 1957 / Talcottville

Darling Margaret: I am just recovering from an attack of gout, which has had me more or less helpless for a week—hence my wobbly writing.—I am going down to New York the 5th, Reuel flies from New York the 17th, and Rosalind [?] a day or two afterwards. I shall come back here from Wellfleet. It would be absolutely divine if you could come up here soon after that—that is, from, say, the 21st on. My cousins will be here then—not in this house, but next door—and make life a little more entertaining, in case I am not the entertainer I was. Do take this seriously; fix on a date and let me know about it.

Love as ever, / Bunny

Marginal note: I love blaming "wobbly writing" on gout. It's <u>always</u> wobbly—in fact, this is less so!

CONTENTS

INTRODUCTION

This book will complete the picture of Edmund Wilson, the writer whose candor, range, flintiness, and erudition have made him a major intellectual and moral resource for literary critics and scholars, social historians, and general readers since the 1920s when he first set up shop. His letters are part of the life blood of his achievement, a steady current of reactions that contain the ideas and emotions of a career. Elena Wilson's 1977 volume *Letters on Literature and Politics, 1912–1972,* with an introduction by Daniel Aaron and a foreword by Leon Edel, gave readers their first sense of Wilson the correspondent, but, in the main, it avoided the personal; this volume is rooted in the personal, the life of the man as son, lover, romantic mentor, husband, friend, neighbor, and day-to-day worker always about the business of using his talent. The letters that follow constitute the unguarded account of a writer's convictions and passions, tastes and prejudices, as they were registered from the late 1910s until the year of his death.

Wilson's famous journal—that decade-by-decade storehouse of impressions—planned; these letters are the spontaneous outpourings of a man in the midst of huge writing projects, overlapping love affairs, and new and long-standing friendships. They contain an atypical American literary success story: the narrative of a writer who transcended the distractions of the marketplace and mass culture and did his thousands of days' work despite the demons of drink, neurosis, and debt. Wilson's relentless schedule, kept up until he was well into his sixties, calls to mind Lionel Trilling's remark about Dickens's social life: the mere listing of its contents was exhausting. Just reading about Wilson's writing regimen and after-hours plans is enough to flatten most of us. And after all the planning and writing and romancing and talking and traveling, he found time to write pithy and forthright letters about what he had done—often exhorting his correspondent to engage in similar literary and social games of endurance. A note of patrician confidence is sustained throughout, a sense that one is entitled to firm positions, promising life chances, solid achievements, and stubborn resistances. Some of this could be overbearing and arrogant, but most of it seems invigorating in our age of victims and excuse-makers. Wilson's passion for reading and writing and for vigorous exchange with friends never let up. Wherever he was—New York or London, Rome or Tel Aviv, Wellfleet or Talcottville—he got to work and also got out and about to observe and talk.

The contents of the present volume reflect what we least expect in American writers' careers—the second act that Fitzgerald said was most often missing. Wilson's work and life had the spaciousness and coherence of a European career, more like that of V. S. Pritchett or André Malraux than of Fitzgerald himself. Wilson's identity as revealed in the letters rests firmly on his habit of reflection and planning rather than on impulses and exigencies. His work—and the life that was given a measure of stability by the discipline of the work—represents a gradual maturation and clarity of purpose uncharacteristic of his American contemporaries.

This book consists almost entirely of material that Elena Wilson omitted from her edition; the exceptions are the restoration of the complete texts of letters where significant personal material was formerly elided. The sheer magnitude of the Wilson hoard—some 70,000 letters extant, of which a mere 800 or so have seen print, mainly in Mrs. Wilson's volume and in the Nabokov-Wilson correspondence edited by Simon Karlinsky—has required hard and often painful choices on the part of the editors. From the mountainous record remaining to be drawn upon, we have been able to reject notes about business matters and routines that do not resonate. Our decision has been to omit good letters—be they early, middle, or late—to correspondents who are well or better represented elsewhere. We have used flavor or substance or uniqueness as our standards.

And by the last of these criteria this unpublished correspondence does not merely supplement and parallel the letters in previous volumes; the new letters provide fresh evidence about Wilson's more private self. The best evidence of this Wilson has been unavailable to the general public. The fragmentary quotations in biographies and critical studies can never quite provide the authentic experience of Wilson to be gained by reading the letters themselves. We print here for the first time letters to Wilson's parents; his third wife, Mary McCarthy; Lionel Trilling; his English pals Cyril Connolly and Isaiah Berlin; and a less famous friend, Clelia Carroll. Also now included are valuable personal letters to major correspondents such as Elena Mumm Thornton, Morton Dauwen Zabel, and Upstate neighbors of his later years: Dick and Jo Costa, Mary Pcolar, and Glyn and Gladys Morris. His letters about literary business to William Shawn and Roger Straus are often memorable amalgams of hard-headed negotiation and abrasive or friendly banter. Taken altogether, in development, texture, and tone, these letters constitute a kind of autobiography.

ACKNOWLEDGMENTS

No book of this kind can be realized without the help of the subject's family, the courtesies of publishers, the good offices of staff members at research institutions and the collective support of colleagues, scholars and friends. In particular, we wish to express our gratitude to Reuel Wilson, Helen Miranda Wilson, and the late Rosalind Wilson for their kind assistance. In addition, we are indebted to Roger Straus, Erica Seidman, and Victoria Fox at Farrar, Straus and Giroux.

Our thanks also to the library at Amherst College for letters to Louise Bogan; the Beinecke Library of Rare Books and Manuscripts—where Wilson's papers reside—for letters to his mother and father, Elena Mumm Wilson, John Berryman, Henry D. Blumberg, Richard and Jo Costa, Norman Gottwald, John Lester, Mary Pcolar, Stephen Spender, and Fredric Warburg; the Boston Public Library for a letter to Rosalind Wilson; the Bryn Mawr College Library for a letter to Katharine S. White; Columbia University for letters to Dawn Powell and Lionel Trilling; the Edward Gorey estate and especially curator Andreas Brown of the Gotham Book Mart for annotated letters to Edward Gorey; the Harvard Theatre Collection, Houghton Library, for a letter to Elmer Rice; the Houghton Library, Harvard University, for a letter to William James Jr.; the estate of Jacob Landau for the letters to Jacob Landau; the Pierpont Morgan Library for letters to Clelia Carey (Carroll); the Newberry Library for letters to Morton Dauwen Zabel; the Berg Collection at the New York Public Library for letters to V. S. Pritchett and Frances Steloff; the New York Public Library collections of rare books and manuscripts for letters to S. N. Behrman, William Shawn, and Roger Straus; the University of Oregon Library for a letter to Robert Cantwell; Henry Hardy at Wolfson College, Oxford University, for letters to Isaiah Berlin; Princeton University for letters to Helen Muchnic, Glyn Morris, Margaret Rullman, Allen Tate, and John Hall Wheelock; the University of Pennsylvania for letters to Burton and Hazel Rascoe; Syracuse University for a letter to William Van O'Connor; the library at the University of Tulsa for letters to Cyril Connolly, Betty Huling, and Ken McCormick; Vassar College for letters to Mary McCarthy; and the University of Virginia for letters to John Dos Passos.

Christine Nelson of the Morgan Library provided special help with the Clelia Carey (Carroll) collection; Mrs. Barbara Morris very kindly let us read the unpublished memoir of the late Glyn Morris; Professor Emeritus Francis Bethlen of Plattsburgh State University provided translation from the Hungarian; Michael Kimmage provided translation from the Russian; Professor Fred Weidman of the Union Theological Seminary provided translation from Greek and Hebrew; and the research librarians at Feinberg Library, the British Library, and the Cambridge University Library all offered valuable assistance. We wish to thank English Department Chairman Sherman Raskin of Pace University, Gail Dinter-Gottlieb, Dean of Dyson College of Pace University, and the Scholarly Research Committee of Pace University. At Plattsburgh State University our thanks to English Department Chairman Paul Johnson and the Office of Scholarly Support for research assistance from Nathaniel Johnson and graduate student Marissa Dandrow; also deserving our gratitude are Plattsburgh State University students Michael Apple, Alison Daly, Nicole diDomenico, Joseph Laurenzi, Gregory Marano, Keri O'Connor, Joshua Pokotilow, Christopher Shortt, and Katherine Stathis for their help in transcribing and word processing the letters.

Our friend Foster Hirsch took an active interest in the book from the beginning; Anne Whitehouse and Rebecca Landau provided valuable annotation for the Jacob Landau letters, and Burton Besen, Jane Boutwell, Paul Collet, Carl and Margaret Engelhart, Jurgen Kleist, Sid Levinson, Alexis Levitin, Eunice and Alan Musk, Gretchen Shine, and Peter and Winifred Wroe helped with the manuscript or in countless other ways lent support to the editors.

A NOTE ABOUT THE EDITING

Wilson of course deplored ponderous footnotes, elaborate emendations, and other scholarly flummery that can render a volume unattractive and inaccessible to the general reader. In the spirit of his convictions, we have used editing techniques that are precise but not obtrusive. Notes are indicated by superscript numerals in the text and immediately follow each letter. They are as sparse as possible, providing the reader with information about personalities, works, and historical and social allusions necessary for understanding. We have silently cleaned up punctuation matters and small grammatical glitches according to Wilson's directives to Leon Edel to edit his writing "not in the ways of scholarship, but as if you were preparing a living manuscript for a publisher." Any editorial intrusions of our own are indicated by brackets.

I. The Young Man and the Great War

After graduating from Princeton in June 1916, Wilson spent the summer at a military preparedness camp in Plattsburgh, New York. The results did not suggest that he had the makings of an officer. In the fall he started to work as a reporter for the *Evening Sun,* without much sense that this day-to-day journalism—the covering of local news—was his vocation. On enlistment in the army, Wilson began a soldier's itinerary—rough passage from Detroit to Halifax to Southampton, England, to various parts of France. He immediately came in contact with old friends and Ivy Leaguers as well as with many men and women from outside his sheltered world of privilege. The letters in this section introduce a cast of characters—shadowy fellow soldiers, vividly depicted comrades, new friends, and glancing looks at the officers. Wilson's reactions range from standoffishness and snobbery to sympathetic fellow feeling. They suggest that he did not become a seasoned, tolerant citizen of the world overnight. Wilson's socialist convictions, especially his growing contempt for the American power drive, began to reveal themselves in this period; yet his complexity and ambivalence keep him from ignoring Woodrow Wilson's idealism. He could write the two scathing indictments of army life—"Lieutenant Franklin" and "The Death of a Soldier" in *A Prelude*—and also a protest manifesto for an army paper that aroused the anger of the officers; yet he maintained his stance as a humanistic critic of war rather than an E. E. Cummings radical.

TO MOTHER / FATHER

August 26, 1917 / Detroit, Mich.

Dear Mother:

The second day of camp David[1] and I were detailed to help in the mess-shack—one of the most unpleasant jobs in the whole set of unpleasant jobs. We had to help get the food ready, set the tables, wait on the men, and finally wash and dry the dishes (with the same dish cloths which we had been using to kill and drive out the flies a little while before). It is an endless performance: by the time the breakfast things have been finished, it is nearly time for lunch, etc.—and the regular men who work in the mess are a fairly tough bunch, of course. David, not having ever had to do any sort of army work before, minded it. He minded much more than I did, although, I assure you, it was the worst drudgery I have ever had to do. We fell victims to one of the mistakes of mismanagement which is bound to occur before a [blank spaces here] affair like this has been fully organized, and at one time it looked as if we might have to wait on table indefinitely: but David appealed to Dr. Mc-Graw, the captain, and we were relieved of mess duty the morning after, in spite of the fact that the messmen made an attempt to keep us.

In the evenings we have been going to the Hamiltons, who sent the automobile for us, and of course we enjoy it intensely for having had to put up with the camp life in the daytime. It is cold sleeping in tents these days: your sweater will be useful. We have such fun when we come back in the evenings telling about working in the mess, etc. Elizabeth's husband has warmed up a little and although I do think he is a snob, I admit that he is amusing. (He is at present rummaging for his army overcoat, which he is going to offer to sell me if they will allow me to wear it. He had it at Fort Sheridan, where he was training before they discharged him on account of his eyes.) The Hamilton family are really great fun when they are all together;[2] and, in contrast to the stupid routine of the day, evening here is hilarious entertainment.

We got off yesterday afternoon for all Sunday till twelve tonight (except an hour, when we had to report and go to mess at noon). This morning we slept until about ten, and in the afternoon, Shorty[3] slept some more, while I finished typewriting one of my manuscripts. Mary[4] offered to dictate it to me, after I had started, and did, while I sat on the grass and worked the typewriter, Mary is so unsophisticated for an American girl of her age and intelligence; it is one of the anomalies of the family.—But I will say they are about the most wonderfully dressed girls I have ever seen and they always look perfectly fresh and neat. I like Mrs. Hamilton better than I did. There is something rather fine about her, in spite of the way she has run the children, and she has certainly gone out of her way to do things for me.

The personnel of the unit is distinctly mediocre on the whole; there are a few nice fellows, but they haven't been sifted out from the others yet. Mess is usually a riot. The climax comes when somebody breaks a plate; then everybody else screams with laughter. I have an intimate knowledge of mess now and can never again have the same simple trust in the food and knives and forks that I used to have. All the kitchen hands dreaded the washing of the knives, forks, and spoons. We would collect them in a basket, throw them into a kind of lobster pot, dowse them a couple of times in the dishwater which had been used for all the plates and then dry them with lightning rapidity on the dishtowels which I have already mentioned. Of course, mess duty is something which is done by turns, so I suppose we are just as fortunate to have had it over with at once. I think that David will recover after he gets a little more used to military life. Capt. McGraw is planning to make him the photographer for the unit, in which capacity he will take official pictures of the camp, assist the X-ray man in France, etc. I hope he can make me his assistant or something. Nothing is very well managed as yet. Men are made to do guard duty two nights running sometimes and similar accidents occur.

I am glad you wrote me about Earl Osborn; I hadn't seen it, of course, in the Detroit papers. Bill told me that Earl was about to go into the French artillery. I'm told that the ambulance drivers are having a harder time of it now that the United States has entered the war, and that the French officers no longer spare them any risks, but send them everywhere. Shorty has a friend in the ambulance [corps] who wrote him this.

Shorty, as I have mentioned before, has charge of a tent and has had to pretend to be an oracle on all military matters, although he has never had anything to do with them before. Thursday night a gang of mess men came into his tent when the regular occupants were away. They were a rough bunch, with tattooed arms, and they kept him up all night with conversation[5] which he would rather not have listened to under any circumstances. He had not then realized his authority sufficiently to get rid of them.

Give my best love to Aunt Laura[6] and tell her that her mirror is a perfect success and a great improvement upon the little shaving mirror with which the Government supplies us.

We are going back to camp very soon now, so good-bye for the present.

Yours lovingly, / Edmund

[Postscript] Will you give the Kimballs' New York number in your next letter. I always forget the street number. I sent Esther a check and am now afraid it may have gone wrong.

[1]David Hamilton, Yale-educated friend with whom Wilson spent the summer of 1914 in England.

[2]In *Edmund Wilson: A Biography* by Jeffrey Meyers, Meyers points out that when Wilson wrote of the Hamiltons to his friend Stanley Dell he is less complimentary, confessing that he found them boring as well as pleasant and refined.

[3]Shorty: an unidentified Army buddy of Wilson's and David Hamilton's.

[4]Mary: presumably, one of David Hamilton's sisters.

[5]conversation: see *A Prelude: Landscapes, Characters, and Conversations from the Earlier Years of My Life* (1967). "I had here my first experience of how maddeningly monotonous the profanity and obscenity of the army can be."

[6]Laura Kimball, one of Mrs. Wilson's sisters: "She was by far the most literary of the Kimball children and one of my favorite relatives," Wilson writes of her in *A Prelude.*

Dear Mother:

I was unable to send the note I wrote in New York and will add this and send it from [blank spaces here] if they let us mail things from there. We didn't get our quarters changed, because it appeared that, although our commanding officer [out]ranks all the other commanding officers, the commander of the ship has orders from Washington not to change the troops once the boat has sailed. Consequently, while those other organizations are well taken care of in second-class quarters and while there are a number of first- and second-class staterooms unoccupied, we are supposed to sleep in the steerage, half in little staterooms (four to a room) and half (including myself) in an unventilated hold infested with rats and bedding so filthy that it makes you seasick ever to go down there. I have, therefore, refused to sleep in it and spent the first night on the benches on deck and last night in David's berth with him, lying sardine-fashion, with our feet in each other's faces, so tight that, once settled, we can scarcely move. Everybody is very sore— especially since we have learned that the "bug-pen" was never intended for even steerage-passengers to sleep in, but was simply a storeroom for baggage, before this steamer was made into a troopship. And one of the worst features of all is the absence of any place where we can sit and read or write. There is nothing but a little smoking room, which doesn't hold very many and, in the meantime, the whole interior of the ship is given over to the officers and nurses, so that the men have either to spend their time on deck, which is extremely cold, or down in their bunks, which, for most of them, is impossible.

David has been sick nearly all the time, but I have had barely a qualm so far. I have wisely refrained from going to meals and have been subsisting entirely on crackers and fruit bought of the canteen. Our voyage has been very smooth. Yesterday, Major Phillips explained to us that he had done everything possible about our quarters, but that it was impossible to change them. It seems we are to have life-boat drill. [. . .] A man comes and fastens down all the portholes, late in the afternoon, which doesn't help the ventilation much, although all the doors are left open here below and there is more air than you might expect.

I have at last received an overcoat, but it is only a short one made of inferior material (they never got the ones they expected in New York and had to do with a makeshift at the last moment), so Father had better send me a good one from Eisner's in France—full-length if possible, and of heavy material.

As for the [blank spaces here] which are with us, it was said by somebody that, beside them, the worst of our bunch looked like gentlemen, which is probably true, in the main, although I have seen some nice faces among them. The [blank spaces here] are only privates or helpers—not genuine [blank spaces here]

This, I am afraid, is the last you will hear from me until we land on the other side.

Yours lovingly, / Edmund

Oct. 30, 1917

Dear Mother:

This is just a note to tell you that David, two Harvard men, and some others and I have been organized by the Chaplain, Dr. Mason, for a Dramatic Association and a weekly magazine, to be called "Reveille," of which I am to be editorial writer. David is at the head of the Dramatic Association. For this we have permanent passes to the second-class salon, and are consequently much more comfortable with something to do and somewhere to go.

We have been for a day now off a city of which I am not allowed to tell you the name; my references to it in other letters have probably been censored. I think we are soon to leave. Each man has been assigned to a lifeboat and occasionally we have life-boat drill.

I am very happy at starting this magazine. It is so long since I have had anything intelligent to do.

Yours lovingly, / and in great haste / Edmund.

On board ship / Nov. 4, 1917

Dear Mother:

The censorship forbids me to tell so many things that I will not even try to describe how we left America or what ships are with us. I am afraid that much of the letters I mailed from the last port where we stopped will have been suppressed before they reach you. Life on board this ship is about as unpleasant as possible and yet I don't mind it particularly—partly, I think, because I have never yet had anything worse than the first qualm of seasickness. David, on the other hand, spends most of his time sitting on the deck, pale and silent. The food is vile and consequently he and I never go to mess but live on stuff bought at the canteen. We have been keeping ourselves alive on surprisingly little: chiefly fruit and chocolate. The crackers have given out.

For a time, we got tea at four, when we were working in the second-class cabin: but the commanding officer of the boat, who is only a lieutenant, apparently, the product of an officers' training camp, and has enraged our unit from first to last, drove all the officers out of the second-class rooms and not only was our magazine expelled but even Captain McGraw's office was compelled to move into staterooms. Just now we are working in one of the men's dining-rooms, which smells like the deuce, and overcomes David so that he can't stay there. There is no place to sit except a little smoking-room on deck, filled with men, tobacco smoke, and spittoons, and you were always being driven out of that so that they can sweep it. There are a few steamer-chairs and sometimes you can sit in them, when the guard has happened not to receive orders to keep people out—I am told that complaints upon the character of our quarters, food, etc. are not to be passed by the censor, so I dare say that my letters from shipboard may arrive with all the most vital portions removed.

I sleep in an upper berth with David. It is very close quarters and we are both cramped but it is infinitely better than trying to sleep in the "rat-hole" to which I was assigned and in which hardly any of the men ever sleep; (they go on deck or double up with somebody as I've done). I like the three men in David's stateroom. They are really three of the most decent men in the unit and have taken me in with great generosity, considering that it crowds them badly with five men in a room that is not as large as an ordinary clothes closet.

Nov. 7

Since writing the above we have had a spell of very rough weather. The ship is quite a small one and rocked terribly, so that the decks were lashed across with waves from either side. I don't remember ever to have been out in such a sea; at any rate, if I have, it was in a large boat. David was sick and spent the day in bed. I was also a little sick until I lay down in a bunk.

The paper has gone to press now and is being set up by a master printer named Madcalfe from our unit, formerly of the Detroit papers. It appears that he has had a printing-press and outfit sent to France with our supplies and that this paper is really largely indebted to him for its existence. He may be a master printer, but he is no journalist, and our meetings are much broken into by his arguments to persuade us to do impossible things. I'll send you copies as we print it. It has to be strictly censored and so won't tell you much that is particularly interesting. Rabette, a Harvard man, is managing editor: he and I and a man named Roy Gamble[1] do most of the work on it. I like Gamble especially. He is an artist and a very simple sort of fellow, with little education except artistic education. He hates the military life and spends a good deal of time sketching the gulls and the men. They put him on fatigue duty the other day (sweeping decks and other disagreeable work) for being late to some formation and it put him out so that we had to cajole him into making us a woodcut for the title of the paper ("Reveille"). Today is the first day in the danger zone and we have to carry our life preservers with us wherever we go. British destroyers are expected to turn up any moment for the purpose of convoying us. They say that we should sight land tomorrow. If we have a few days' "Liberty," when we get to the city where we are said to be going first (after we leave port) and which I am not supposed to mention to you, the first thing I shall do will be to look up the Kemp Smith[2] family. I feel a need for seeing somebody I know under civilized conditions. [. . .]

The talk is beginning to consist almost entirely of remarks about the good dinners we expect to have when we get ashore. The food is absolutely vile that they have been giving us and is, they tell me, beginning to give out. I am tired of living on oranges and peanut brittle, which, however, has not yet had any injurious effect upon my health. [. . .]

[1]Roy Gamble: Wilson army comrade, the painter in his unit. Notable for witticisms quoted in *A Prelude*.
[2]Norman Kemp Smith (1872–1958): head of the philosophy department at Princeton in Wilson's undergraduate years.

Nov. 9

We have had land in sight all morning, and the submarine-destroyers are with us now. They are little bits of things that lie very low in the water. I hope we may land tonight.

November 12, 1917

Dear Mother:

We were put on trains immediately at the western port.[1] [. . .] In the afternoon they let us go into the town, where David and two other men and

I got an excellent English tea of [blank spaces here] salad, oysters, cold veal, tea, and bread and butter and marmalade. It came to 1[pound] 8s. and some pence, but it was worth it, the first decent meal we had had since leaving America. And I got my shoes dry, for the first time in many days, over the fire in the tea-room. The town is delightful and life is extremely interesting with the mixture of every kind of English and American soldier. At night we walked in the darkened streets, which are doubly curious with all the shops screened in front, so that you don't know what is in them till you are right on top of them. On the other hand, the streets are full of pickpockets and the amount of prostitution is appalling. I mention this last, because it seems to be one of the worst and most serious results of war times among the civilian towns and cities. We have been warned of the conditions over here every time our Major has talked to us, since we started. On the way back from town, in the tram, we fell in with an English soldier who gave us the most amusing line of talk about the war. He had been to the front and came back slightly wounded and said he never wanted to go again. His cockney description of the way things were done beats anything I have ever seen in Kipling, possibly because he had none of the gusto for war which Kipling always attributes to his Tommies, and which, at least at this stage of the game, few Tommies ever really feel. In fact, all the soldiers I have talked to were strikingly frank about things, and had none of the rhetoric of civilians.

There is a German prison camp very near here, and today they brought some of them out to our camp to dig a ditch. They are nice-looking men, apparently well cared for, dressed in the remains of their German uniforms, with long patches of red and blue sewed on the back of the coat and on one of the knees, apparently so that if they shall escape, the bright spot would make an easy mark to shoot at. They are guarded by British soldiers with bayonets and a German sergeant, a nice-looking young man, evidently a better-class German, oversees the work. They have been nearly three years in England and work amiably but listlessly.

I just ran into Charley Jones, who was in my class at school, and is now in the aviation business. He is not particularly interesting in himself, but tells me that there are several Princeton men in his organization. I shall drop around later and find out who they are. As you probably know, the women are running the trams and doing almost every other kind of work over here. The YMCA building in which I am writing this letter is managed entirely by women.

I have just begun to enjoy life again since we have got to England, and would be content to spend some time here if it were not for the fact that, because they didn't warn us, not knowing themselves, that we would have to stay here, we have with us neither tooth brushes, clothes, nor anything else (we have been here since early (very early) Saturday morning) and are obliged to sleep on hard boards. We will, however, probably be moved out tonight or tomorrow, and sail from here for France. I may mention that I have not had a bath since one of the first days on the boat; but perhaps, if they let us leave camp again, I can get one in town. Our food is good, course stuff, almost entirely unseasoned and eaten out of doors, which I much prefer to eating in mess shacks—a great relief altogether from the stale scraps they gave us coming over.

I shall write to Father soon and when I get a chance. Thank the various people who have sent me things.

Lovingly, / Edmund

¹Western port: Southampton—see *A Prelude*.

Nov. 19, 1917 / France

Dear Mother:

Very soon after I wrote to you from the French port where we landed, we received orders that we were to move at three o'clock the next morning. So most of us went to bed at once in the dirty old bunks, which had evidently been in use since the beginning of the war, to try for a little sleep. But the men were coughing like consumptives and swearing like pirates and nobody got much rest. I found when they waked us up to go that the irregularities of my recent diet had finally begun to tell on me, because I had a splitting headache and could only stagger along with my blanket roll. (On the channel steamer, they had given us nothing but hardtack, exactly like dog biscuits in flavor and appearance, but a little softer, though several men broke their teeth on them, and "bully beef," which is a kind of coarse canned corned beef.) They marched us a considerable distance along the railroad tracks. And while we were on the way, the lights of the camp suddenly went out, and we could hear the sound of guns and see the searchlights feeling among the clouds for Zeppelins. There seemed to be an air raid taking place, but we never heard anything further about it. [. . .] They pulled us up at a waiting train in the dark at about 5 and packed us into box cars from 35 to 40 men in each. We were supposed to sit on rough seats that were fitted in the cars lengthwise. The officers and nurses had regular day coaches on the same train. I was feeling so miserable and was in with such a terrible bunch of men that I hardly took the trouble to look out the door at first, but sat in the dark corner in a kind of stupor. [. . .]

I went to sleep on blanket rolls under one of the seats, a narrow space, but the only one where it was possible to stretch one's self at all. But finally had to give it up when people began kicking me with their heels and occasionally stepping on my face. All night the train would proceed a little way and then back up for about the same distance. The next day we alternately spent the time looking out the door and dozing in our seats. It was terribly cold and whenever the train stopped, which was often, we got out and pranced up and down to warm our feet. We were going all the way across France and didn't know when we would be able to get away from those confounded box cars, which, by this time, were strewn with fragments of food, "bully beef," tins, and empty wine bottles. At last, late in the afternoon of the second day, we found ourselves in the most beautiful country along the Marne, where we could look down on the green river and narrow canals planted with lines of the tallest poplars I have ever seen; and about midnight we pulled up at our destination and were put to bed in a great garage, once the adjunct of a hotel, where clean beds and blankets had been provided for us. We were dirty beyond belief and more or less wrecks for want of sleep and raised a great cry of joy at the sight of real mattresses. We had had no decent place to sleep since we left Detroit nearly a month ago. [. . .]

I haven' t written to you before, because I have had absolutely no chance. I started this letter last night, but had to go back to camp (at nine) and am finishing it tonight. In time I hope we shall have somewhere to read and write. The cafes are delightful, but not ideal homes. We are, however, enjoying life in spite of the fact that the weariness of the war is evident everywhere. We can hear very clearly the sound of the guns at the front.

Your loving / Edmund

Dec. 5, 1917 / France.

Dear Mother:

Our mail has just begun to arrive and I have had five letters from you (almost in the order inverse to that in which you evidently wrote them, beginning with the latest and ending with a note written just after you left Detroit), and other letters from Father, Ralph, Stan, Larry and Robert Jackson,[1] who is only a few miles away from us with the Roosevelt Hospital Unit and spent the summer in Vittel. Twenty-five of our men were sent to help temporarily with their (the other unit's) work, but I was not among them and am just as glad. You mustn't be afraid of my not getting your letters; judging by the latest, I think that I have had all you have written up to the last-dated.

I have lately been doing regular detail work. An order has been received to put two hospitals in shape at once and, for a while, we worked day and night putting the beds in. The French shoes they issued are a little too large for me and, when I climb upstairs, with a bed on my back, every now and then slipping on the steps, I think I must look exactly like Charlie Chaplin. Today, however, I am on guard at the barracks and have a pretty easy time of it. It occurred to me the other day that there was no reason why several men who don't know as much French as I do should be interpreters, which I am not, so I spoke to one of the men in the office about it and was today notified that, for the time, I should be a regular interpreter at Headquarters and am going to begin my duties there tomorrow morning at nine-o'clock. I think that this will be a great improvement on anything I have hitherto done. Later I hope to be an X-ray assistant with David, who is still making plans of the hospitals with Roy Gamble. Roy finds it necessary about every other day to walk to a neighboring town and buy thumb tacks; and he hopes in time to get to Paris, avowedly for the purpose of buying the proper apparatus for the surgical dressing which he is supposed to do later. The secret of the army seems to be that, if you are clever enough, you can usually do as you please; but after a while, other people find out how these things are done, and before long, everybody is doing it: then the Commanding Officer finds out about it and puts a stop to it by very severe measures, which are, in turn, first evaded and then generally disregarded until another set of rules becomes necessary. And we have the most cautious Commanding Officer and Adjutant in the world. I have told you how the only accessible cafes have been closed to us one by one (though they have provided a recreation room now and we have our own mess, instead of the French mess, which as I think I told you, was convalescence rations; our breakfast was supposed to consist of black bread and a mixture of cognac and coffee). And they tell me that Roy's request to go to Paris created a panic at Headquarters.

We have been paid, at last, for the last two months and, the night after, three-fourths of the unit was drunk, including the sergeants, the military po-lice, and some of the officers. I have taken a Liberty Bond, and hereafter will not get as much of my pay as I otherwise would.

Last Sunday, David and I hired bicycles and rode to a large town about fifteen miles away, an older place than this, and not a summer resort. Our prime purpose was to buy for Christmas presents some of the lace for which this part of France is famous and much of which is made in that particular town, but we found the shops were closed on Sunday afternoon, and so will have to go again. [. . .]

Tonight, because I have to go on guard at 7, David and I are going to give up dinner at the Hôtel de France, which has become our regular place, and have a quicker meal at a café, which has a unique attraction in the daughter of the proprietor, a very pretty girl, very young, who goes to school in the south of France (or used to) and is obviously educated very much above the majority of her class.

She speaks English, for instance, with an excellent accent and is able to explain to us the meaning of the French words we don't know in the books we are reading—except when they turn out to be improper for "une jeune fille" to explain, in which case, she shakes her head and hides her face in her hands. The high tone of the proprietor's family appears also in the prices: it seems that we have to pay extra for Ninette's education and aristocratic complexion (which is beautifully white and clear and unlike that of most of the country girls). At any rate, it is the most expensive place in town, although we continue stupidly to go there, regardless of the fact that the prices amount to robbery, so powerful a fascination does Ninette exercise. We—that is, we four—usually call it "Ninette's place."

I am making rapid progress in speaking French and go every night to the station where the woman who keeps the book and paper stand holds a sort of salon for the French soldiers and the ladies in the town. They congregate there to get the papers, which arrive on the 8:30 train, but, as the train is always from half an hour to an hour late, the station takes on some of the character of the general store at Talcottville,[2] I engage in the conversation with some success, although there is one old rustic who is always making puns that have to be explained to me. All the soldiers—officers and all—are very genial, and, of course, a thousand times politer and more intelligent in conversation than American ones.

The damp and fog have disappeared and, since Sunday, the weather has been fine, very cold, with snow and ice. This morning in barracks, the bugle froze during the night and, having nothing to wake us up, we all overslept. It was finally thawed out in time to call us to breakfast. I must go to my guard.

Yours lovingly, / Edmund

[1]Robert Jackson: friend from Princeton; Wilson looked him up.
[2]Talcottville: location of the family's summer home in upstate New York.

Dear Mother:

I am still night orderly at the Central. Many of the patients are gone from my floor now and those that are left are not sick enough to be confined to their beds, for the most part, so I have nothing to do except keep two stoves going and sit up all night in the office. So, you see, my life is pretty uneventful, though it has, at least, the advantages of relieving me from the society of everyone else except the two or three nurses with whom I am associated and giving me a great deal of time to myself, during which I read, write letters, or carry on long conversations with the little Dane[1] I have told you about. He has told me recently something about his life. It seems that he has been fairly poor and obligated to spend most of his life in America (he is 37) working on farms and in factories, when all his real interests are intellectual. He tells me that he has at last saved up quite a little money and is now thinking of going to a university and studying to teach history, a subject that he has spent all his spare time reading up. He is handicapped for this, because he has never been even to school, he says, for much more than a year and it is difficult for a man without any sort of degree to get very far at a university. I asked Lieutenant Crandall, however, what a man could do in his circumstances, and he recommended Columbia and told me how Andersen ought to go about persuading them to give him a degree. I am anxious to see more of him and find out what he does when we get back to America.[2] Altogether, he is a most unusual, most intelligent man. In the course of the discharge of his function of coal carrier, he visits us in here every night, and, sitting on the edge of the coal box, like a gnome, he argues with me on every subject under the sun. The nurse listens and occasionally joins the conversation. I don't think that I have had a chance before to talk in a leisurely fashion since I first went into camp with this Unit.

Lieutenant Crandall has left. I didn't know he was going and didn't get a chance to say good-bye to him; but I suppose he will let me know if anything comes of his letter to his friend in the Adjutant General's office. (Please excuse all this spilt ink; there is so much junk on this table that I usually upset something every night.) Crandall has returned to his company, they tell me; but apparently he is disqualified by his rheumatism for active line service. Ninette has gone too. She started for Cannes yesterday, and I miss her very much. She may be back in April. Before she went, I found her here in the hospital late one afternoon, calling to be treated by Major Shurley, and offered to walk home with her. She said she wanted to say good-bye to one of the nurses, so

I went with her to the villa where the nurse lived and waited outside, while she went in. I continued to wait for the best part of an hour and was finally driven to make inquiries at the villa, when I learned that Ninette had gone. When I got to the café I found the old man scolding her for having stayed out so late. It appeared that two of the nurses had offered to walk home with her and that she, supposing that it was considered improper by Americans, as it is by the French, for girls and men to walk together after dark, had been afraid to tell the nurses I was waiting, and, in great embarrassment and confusion, had allowed them to take her back by another way than the one where I was posted. I explained to her that the nurses would probably not have been shocked if she had told them that I was walking home with her and, with apologies, she explained that, among respectable people in France, girls and young men were not supposed to be out alone together. I think she is glad to go back to Cannes. All her friends are there, with whom she went to school; she says she has no friends here, where the people are "low," and indeed they are.

Your original Christmas box arrived a few days ago. Made myself sick on the contents and am only just recovering. The socks and handkerchiefs are particularly welcome: all articles of clothing have a way of disappearing when you live as I have been doing, first in one place and then in another, with your belongings scattered around in several different places. I gave David his little packet of handkerchiefs with the chocolate cat inside. We amused ourselves here—the nurses, Andersen, and I—by toasting the marshmallows over the coals in the stove.

If the war bids fair to last, I should be glad to see you over here, as you suggest, though I don't like to have you run the danger involved in coming; besides, I couldn't see you for more than ten days, which is what we are supposed to get every four months. Presumably we should get our first furlough in March and another along in July or August. But the truth is, I am beginning to think the war will end soon and am waiting to see what Wilson will have to say to Czernin and Hertling with more anxiety than I have waited for any other diplomatic move since America declared war. I hope that we may be able to buy our discharges over here, when the war is over. In that case, Dave and I, with Alfred[3] or any other friend we could happen to get hold of over here, would take perhaps a month's trip in France and Italy, if possible, and then go home to America.

We are trying to get out another copy of the "Reveille" at the urgent instigation of the Chaplain, and, as soon as I finish this letter, I shall endeavor to produce an editorial, though I don't know what I can say without exposing myself to arrest, imprisonment, and court-martial. The truth is, it seems to me, that we have neither the spirit, the material, nor the public for a really good paper here, but, goodness knows, if anything can be done to make life a little more genial, it ought to be done was well as possible. [. . .]

Yours lovingly, / Edmund

[1]The little Dane: John Andersen (John Andersen Udmark), "one of my closest friends in the unit" (*A Prelude*, p. 211).

[2]Andersen did not fare well in the job market in New York, even with Wilson's help. After the war he lived in Canada. A voracious reader, he later became a writer of "idea books."

[3]Alfred Bellinger, friend of Wilson's adolescent years from Hill School.

Feb. 9, 1918 / France.

Dear Mother:

I am still night orderly and rather enjoying it, in spite of the fact that it is hardly a very soul-satisfying occupation. I am great friends with the nurses on my floor. Every morning at about 4 the two nurses, Andersen, the Danish fire tender, and I have a convivial breakfast of chocolate, toast, jam and eggs; we can poach, fry, or boil the eggs on the little stove that heats the room. I am not sure, however, that, if the night superintendent were to walk in on us, we might not all be reproved because the nurses are not supposed to have any association at all with the enlisted men. It is said that a sergeant who was found visiting a sick nurse is going to have his sergeancy taken away from him. This atmosphere of spying and petty graft rather gets on my nerves sometimes; though nobody has anything on me, the feeling in the Unit can hardly be called one of mutual confidence and good-fellowship. The nurses, especially, seem to hate the officers, perhaps more than they deserve, though, I admit, there is a pretty poor assortment in this hospital. Fortunately, as a night orderly, I don't have to see much of them. The nurses, on the other hand, with whom I have to do are exceedingly attractive and nice. The one whose shift is from 12 o'clock to 9 in the morning is intelligent, also, and she and Andersen and I have long profound discussions during the small hours.

My chief duty is to see that the men are all in bed by 8. I think I was too gentle with them at first and have now adopted a method of "Blood and iron", threatening to report them if they don't behave. When they get word that they are going to be discharged the next morning they usually go out and get drunk and come back late, because they know that they haven't time to be punished for it. I hate to report them and get them into trouble because I know from experience how hard military regulations are and how hopelessly dull the life in a military hospital is; but it is the way things have to be done in the army. Goodness knows that that is not the way any humane person wants to do them.

Of course, you don't see a very cheerful side of the war in hospital work; (I doubt if there is any cheerful side); one of our principal excitements, for example, is one of the insane men—(the worries and hardships of the trenches make quite a number hysterical or mad)—who eludes his guard every now and then and goes wandering all over the building. Part of the time he is sane and a very nice boy, they tell me, but after midnight he begins to hear voices calling him and becomes irrational and speechless. One morning about 2 I went out of the office here into the hall and found the man who has charge of the whole place at night going his rounds with a lantern. He pointed to a rigid figure in a bathrobe which had just glided by us and asked me who that was. I supposed it was simply somebody who had got up to go the bathroom, but as we watched the figure we realized that there was something wrong about it and Backus went up and put his hand on his shoulder. Then the man turned around and we saw that it was the crazy man, who stared at us with the glazed eyes and fixed stare of insanity. Backus, with great presence of mind, told me not to let the nurse know and asked me to help him get the man downstairs. He had come up four flights and clear to the other end of the building from the one where his room was. Backus cajoled him back, while I followed with the lantern. Occasionally he would shy at a shadow or stop short and refuse to go any further. It was lucky that Miss Gano, who was just on the other side of the door all the time, never knew what had happened, because she is very timid and has been afraid of the lunatics all along. [. . .]

The 25 men who were sent to help the Roosevelt Hospital unit came back last night and Christensen, my other Danish friend, brought me a note from Robert Jackson, which was almost as full of anguish as some of the ones I have written. [. . .]

I have lately received your original Christmas box, a razor with blades from Father, a box containing pajamas and socks, a copy of the *Christmas Life*, a pair of socks from Esther, and a huge box of Mirror candy from Aunt Caroline,[1] I suppose; there is no card with it. I have never had so much candy at one time before in my life and fed the nurses and patients for a whole week on it; and finally got sick and had to go to bed about five o'clock one morning. We toasted the marshmallows over the stove. Although candy is an excellent thing, there is no particular scarcity of it over here and, though some of it is more expensive than in America, it is perhaps hardly worth while to send me so much such a long distance. I liked the Dean's box best of all, because we really don't get a great deal of cake and the cake in the box was surprisingly fresh. Also, I have enough socks now and am really well outfitted, though the overcoat has never come. The letter you forwarded was from Tom Shoemaker in China; be is doing YMCA work over there and wants me to tell him how he can get into the hospital service. He is the first person I have heard from in a long time who actually wanted to get in; everybody else wants to get out. I have also heard from Carolyn Wilson,[2] who says that she is on the point of going to Washington to work under the auspices of the President of Vassar upon some publicity commission, whose precise character is not clear. Father's letter has arrived with the exemption board questionnaire in it. We simply turn them in at the Adjutant's office and they attend to them. Remember me with love to Aunt Laura and Aunt Addie,[3] if I don't write to people it is not because I don't think of them or appreciate their letters, but because I have limited time and a great many correspondents. They'll all hear from me in time.

Yours lovingly, / Edmund

[1]Caroline Kimball, née Knox, wife of Wilson's Uncle Reuel, traveled in Europe in family party of 1908.
[2]Carolyn Wilson: a cousin on his father's side.
[3]Aunt Laura: see above. Aunt Addie: Adelaide Kimball, another of Mrs. Wilson's sisters.

Feb. 24, 1918 / France

Dear Mother:

We have just received an enormous mail after several weeks of none; I have had letters from Larry,[1] Morris Belknap, John Bishop (now a Lieutenant of Infantry!), Aunt Laura, Dorothy,[2] the Follow the Boys League, and two from you. I greatly enjoyed your description of the entertainment at Shrewsbury. It had nothing on some of the entertainments which are given here under the auspices the YMCA. At the last one a young artilleryman with a plaintive voice recited the whole of "The Raven," rendering the "Nevermore" in a kind of tenor chant like Hamlet's Father's ghost impersonated by George Stilwell. This made such an impression that the popular slogan everywhere now is: "What did the Raven say?" I have also had a letter from Ninette at Cannes written in courageous but not wholly successful English. She says, "I write in English to make you laugh with my poor capacity." Dave has had letters from his family telling him that Elizabeth's baby died almost immediately after it was born, and he is quite depressed, I'm afraid.

I am still putting in my time at the hospital waiting for the French patients to arrive, doing odd jobs around the place such as coal-carrying, sweeping, making the beds, and washing windows, none of it very exhausting or exacting. [. . .]

In short, I am enjoying life well enough nowadays, but am still pretty anxious to get out, just the same. The German capture of Russia makes the outlook for peace pretty gloomy.

Yours lovingly, / Edmund

[1]Laurence Noyes, friend from Hill School; with Morris Belknap and David Hamilton shared a Greenwich Village apartment with Wilson after the war.

[2]Dorothy Reed Mendenhall, Wilson's much-admired cousin (her grandfather was the brother of Wilson's great-great-grandfather Reuel Kimball). See *Upstate: Records and Recollections of Northern New York* (1969), pp. 59–71.

March 6th, 1918 / France.

Dear Mother:

I have now been permanently assigned to the Parc Hotel, which is in process of being turned into a hospital to be run by Major—late Captain—McGraw. It is the best building we have and will be the smallest hospital with only 500 beds. So far we have done nothing but move out the hotel furniture, move in the hospital beds, and get the place ready for occupancy. I have done so much strong-arm work that I have become capable of carrying mattresses, beds, night tables, rugs, wardrobes, marble top toilet tables, and detached doors up five flights of stairs without turning a hair. The men—Christensen among them—are pleasant to work with and the Sergeant, a private a little while ago, is competent and easy to get on with. Major McGraw, who is giving up his adjutancy to be at the head of this hospital, called us all together this morning and gave us a long lecture on co-operation, etc. He evidently wants to establish friendly relations with us from the start, and I think that in spite of the fact that his nervousness makes him difficult to approach, he really has the right idea in attempting to get into touch with his men and make things as harmonious as possible. [. . .]

Last Sunday, which they gave us as a holiday at the Parc, Dave, John Andersen, Roy Gamble, and I walked out to the little town on the hill where the old church and convent are and then, in spite of violent protestations on my part, because I had a cold, and didn't have much faith in the idea of getting dinner anywhere except here, wandered across the hills in search of food, and when at last we reached a town, found the only café full of French soldiers, and had to get back as best we could in the snow and slush and water that the countryside is just now. Climbing slippery hills and ploughing through fields of soft mud, John Andersen was the only man who had any idea how we ought to go to get home, and finally landed us here too late to take supper in a café (they are forbidden after eight). We bought, however, at a grocery store two bottles of wine, some Swiss cheese, a can of jellied chicken, a can of lobster, a fruit cake, and some bread, to which were added by the Hungarian night cook with whom Roy has a great pull, pin money pickles, marmalade, and preserved peaches, and ate it all in Roy's room with our wet feet on the stove. It reminded me of Sundays at Princeton.

Monday morning I was allotted to the receiving squad and had to get up at half past four to help unload a trainful of patients and carry them upstairs in the Towers hospital. They were the first real French wounded I had had to do with and exhibited among them the results of most of the more famous features of modern warfare: shell wounds, barb wire wounds, trench feet, and gassing, which last, as you probably know, makes the man's face swell up horribly and gives him a severe infection of the throat and eyes. I interpreted most of the time for the lieutenant in charge and was even able to understand and make myself understood in Italian among the Italian patients (victims of the pacifist propaganda which was partially responsible for the Italian defeat who had been transferred after their defection to French regiments at Verdun—a poor-looking lot). [. . .] None of the wounds was dangerous, and I think the men have only been sent here on their way somewhere else. The gassed men and the ones who had wounds in the eyes and other parts of the head were the worst.

The chaplain has stopped censoring the mail now and the other officers apparently take turns doing it: but they issue special envelopes now to be sent for censoring to the Base Censor, and, both because there are officers here whom I don't want reading my mail, and because they are stricter than the chaplain was, I am sending most of my letters now the other way, which may account for some delay in your receiving them. I have had from you several lots of magazines: the Christmas *Harper's,* which I was glad to get on account of Mrs. G[askell]'s story and the thing by Henry James, the theatrical section of the *World,* and any number of Hill School magazines. The *Alumni Weekly* comes regularly, and the Sunday *Times* shows up from time to time. I shall be very glad indeed to get Mrs. G[askell]'s new book of short stories. Please mail me anything you see in the papers or magazines by Mrs. G[askell], Mrs. Wharton, E. A. Robinson (the poet), Bernard Shaw, or Max Beerbohm. I haven't much time now to read anything but papers and magazines at the noon hour, at nights, and on Sunday, and when I do get a chance, I read French books, so although I see by the advertisements that lots of English and American books are appearing that I want to read, there is no point in getting you to send them all the way from America. I have obtained a few English books and magazines through the Paris Branch of Brentano's. If it weren't for these, the *Times,* and the *New Republic* (to which I have subscribed) I'd know little enough about what is going on, because the papers we get here, French and English alike, are mostly single-sheet affairs, badly edited and anything but exhaustive, so that important things are happening all the time which we hear about only indirectly.

Speaking of badly edited papers, I am sending you the second copy of "The Reveille," which again turns out to be dull and entirely different from what I had expected it to be. I wrote the "Editorial" which, as you see, is not printed precisely as I wrote it. The only amusing stuff we had was crowded out because the sheet had to be so small and the results are before you— together with the results of the censorship.—I have heard lately from Dorothy, Aunt Addie, and Aunt Laura, and will answer them all later. I am sorry about your eye, but no doubt you are all right by now.

Yours lovingly, / Edmund.

March 13, 1918 / France

Dear Mother:

Mr. Kemp Smith is now in Paris and has written asking me to meet him, which I want very much to do, although I am chained down as usual and probably the best I can do will be to go as far as the town where Robert Jackson's Unit is in a motor truck. Unless he is going to be in the vicinity, I can hardly ask him to come so far from Paris, and the chances are that I shall never see him. The Assistant Adjutant says he will do what he can for me and last night telephoned the Paris hotel where Kemp is staying, but they said he was out and couldn't use the telephone anyhow because he was a civilian, though he is really in the government service and ought, I think, to be able to telephone or telegraph. We are going to call him up again tonight. (There is such a violent argument raging behind me on politics that I have had to stop writing—)

A day has passed since I began this letter. John Andersen, David, and Roy (in the latter's basement studio) got so stormy over votes for women and other matters that it became impossible to write and I had to turn around and expose their fallacies to them. Just then the Hungarian night cook came in and we put the questions up to him: whether women had as good minds as men, to which he replied—I cannot write his reply—in the negative; and whether politics was as high a human activity as any other. He apologized here and said that he didn't really have brains for anything but whiskey but, if we wanted to know what he thought, why he thought that when one guy got into office the other guy said that the guy who was in office was a robber and called him all kinds of names and said he'd be square if he was there and then when he got in he was a worse robber than the other guy. [. . .]

Last Sunday, David, Roy, and I hired wheels to ride to that city to which David and I bicycled once before, last December. The woman couldn't supply the wheels at the last moment, so Dave and I decided to walk it (14 miles) although Roy scoffed at us, refused to take our challenge, and went to a nearer town to paint a picture. (His pictures, by the way, are excellent. He's done a lot of French peasant houses and street scenes.) We had a wonderful walk, one of the few very pleasant days we have spent since we got here. [. . .]

At five we started back in an open cart. [. . .] On the way, after refusing to give lifts to various parties of French soldiers with women which would have killed the poor old wreck of a horse that pulled us, we picked up a single French soldier. It seemed that he was off on leave from the front and had been walking for two days without much to eat—he said "without eating at all" and it may have been so—on his way to a little town near here where his wife and two little children were. They didn't know he was coming and he would surprise them. He had served for three years as infantryman and his ideas on the war seemed to me to represent pretty well the attitude of the so-called poilu [blank spaces here], the ordinary man who had to leave his home and work to be a soldier. He kept imitating the noise of the guns, which, he said, was terrible and gave him a headache which lasted even then, when they were out of earshot. "You have a nice time back here," he said, "where you can hardly hear them." [. . .] He kept repeating: "Death! Death! Death! two million men! Men that you've never seen! Who never did you any harm! But what to do?" Then he went on to tell us things which, if I should put them in a letter, could certainly expose me to court martial. I have at least the advantage in being a private that I can find out what the privates really think. I asked him whether, if it was only a question of Alsace-Lorraine, he'd be willing to have the war go on. "No," he said, "they were all Boches, anyhow, in Alsace-Lorraine."

And I do think myself, that the [blank spaces here] are handing out a good deal of bunk about Alsace-Lorraine. Even if they aren't quite all boches, the restoration of the provinces should hardly be a sine qua non of Allied policy (which, if I understand the President, it is not). It is only the journalists and politicians who won't stop fighting till Alsace-Lorraine is given back. [. . .] But our friend kept coming back to "Bom! Bom! Bom!" (his imitation of the cannon's pounding). "All day and all night! You don't hear anything but that. Death! Death! Death! You have to kill men that you've never seen! But what can you do?" He was not in any great consternation, having had three years to get used to it, but the continuous beat of the cannon and the continual sight of the dead had apparently got on his brain; and there was something weak about even his sensible "Tant pis!" or "Ce n'est pas d'amusement, ça!" as if something vital in him had been broken.

This is just the way many of the French soldiers have impressed me. They have preserved both gaiety and gentle manners, but after you have talked with them awhile, you see that it is just a little mechanical and that four years of life at the front has destroyed something inside them. I think you may take all this as pretty typical.

Everything I have seen corroborates what Stan Dell[1] told me from his experience; you will almost never find truthful accounts of these things in newspapers, books, or magazines. For one thing, the perfectly well-known fact that, before clearing out on every trench, the soldiers are filled full of a crude and violent form of alcohol (le pinard) was denied by everybody when Jane Addams[2] commented on it, I think, a couple of years ago, and she herself had to suffer a lot of abuse for having calumniated the brave soldiers, etc. etc. You can easily see that this is one of the worst humiliations of the war: to be obliged to do work which you have to be drunk to do properly. If a man comes through this without his having his moral balance and his self-respect vitally hurt he would be an idiot. The wounds inflicted on the enemy are not the only ones. This is not a tract in pacifism but an attempt to adjust any impression you may have gathered from the comic papers of the gay and undaunted poilu "carrying on" through four years of modern warfare. I'll tell you some more about what war does to the soldiers when I get back to

America, where, I earnestly hope, you may not, by that time, be able to see the results for yourself.

In the meantime, we are waxing Major McGraw's floors for him at the Parc—a very tedious and uncomfortable job; but the weather is wonderful and we take long rests looking down at the town from the French windows, which open on little balconies.

By the way, John Peale Bishop[3] has published a book of poems called "Green Fruit" (Sherman, French & Co., Price $ .80), and I wish you would get Brentano's to send copies to Dave, to Mrs. Hamilton, to Aunt Laura, and to Sandy.[4] I think John has "got it" and I want to advertise him. Put the price to the account which includes the storage bills and the other things I owe you for. If there are any of my cards at home you might put them in the copies for Sandy and Mrs. Hamilton.

Yours lovingly, / Edmund.

[1]Stanley Dell, Hill School friend.

[2]Jane Addams (1860–1935): social reformer of Chicago, founder of Hull House. Wilson wrote of her in *The American Earthquake: A Documentary of the Twenties and Thirties* (1958).

[3]John Peale Bishop (1892–1944): Princeton friend, poet, aesthete, and associate on the *Nassau Lit.* Later worked with Wilson on *Vanity Fair* and became Wilson's rival in paying court to Edna St. Vincent Millay.

[4]Sandy: cousin Alexander Kimball, son of Uncle Reuel. Graduated from St. Paul's and Princeton and thereafter had severe mental problems.

January 19, 1918 / France

Dear Father:

I am pretty well discouraged with the hospital business, having just been removed from my job of dental orderly and made night orderly in the same hospital, while the man who previously had the night orderly job has been transferred to the X-ray, a job which, by every right and promise, I should have. Not that there is such a great deal of difference between jobs here. It is chiefly a matter of whether or not you get good doctors to work under. There seems to be a vast amount of petty graft in the assignment of the men to their work.

Do you think that you could do anything to get me transferred into some other branch of the service? Lieutenant Crandall, a friend of Walter Hall's, who is sick in the hospital, tells me that it is possible, through pull, to get an order for transfer from the War Department, and I think this would be safer than broaching the matter to our commanding officer, who, I know, feels himself in need of men and would certainly be unwilling to recommend me simply at my request. The life here is really very sickening and not much better than Detroit; and I am sure that, in most ways, it would be much better for me and that I should be rendering better service if I got a commission in the artillery or the signal corps. It would involve for me the renunciation of everything else until after the war; but I should probably be both happier and more valuable. The chief thing that makes me reluctant is the fact that Mother would worry about me and I, for that reason, about her. The other thing which makes me reluctant is the fact that I had always intended to devote my life to literature and do not want to be easily cheated out of doing so; although, when I see my friends who certainly have as much gift as I for the various lines of work to which they intended to devote themselves, putting it all away in order to make efficient officers in the army and navy, I feel that I probably cannot always be justified in preserving myself for the sake of work which I haven't yet done. Furthermore, I have come to sympathize more completely with America's part in the war. Wilson, I am now convinced, is as much in the right as it is possible for the leader of a nation to be and is shrewd and idealistic enough not to lose any diplomatic opportunity for ending the war on terms less drastic than those which he enumerated in his last message to Congress; and I certainly owe him all the service of a man intelligent enough to understand what the real justice of the President's case is.[1] Also, as the war goes on and the draft comes again and again, I shall find myself in the position of evading it through Hospital work, without even the plea of achieving thereby a part for which I may be better fitted than for that of a regular soldier, and, in the meantime, may fall victim, anyhow, to a special order pressing hospital men of draft age into more active service.

I wish you would give me your advice on this at once, together with your opinions on the international situation, and on the possibility of your getting me transferred from America. I should not be anxious to go back there to train for a commission, which would hardly, I think, be necessary, but, if there were no other way, would be willing to do it. I mention this because I have heard a rumor to the effect that men are being sent back from France to train in America, the camps here being overcrowded. I am very anxious to hear from you, though I have sent you only one letter and a postcard. The single letter I have had from you was evidently written before you received mine. I hate to think of you and Mother alone another winter at Red Bank, though Mother writes me fairly cheerful letters. She gives me good reports of your health, anyhow. One advantage of this night duty (8 to 8) is the fact that you get a lot of time to write letters and I hope now, at last, with this room to myself to write in, to be able to pay off all my arrears of correspondence.

Yours always, / Edmund

[Postscript] I forgot to say that Lieutenant Crandall has written to a friend of his, a former Princeton preceptor now in the Adjutant General's office over here, asking if he can suggest any place where I might fit in and where my qualifications, few as they are, would be of use.

[1]Wilson on Woodrow Wilson and the war: compare a more considered post-armistice statement in *A Prelude,* p. 268: "At GHQ I prepared a statement...."

November 8, 1918 / General Headquarters /
G-2b, Intelligence Section / American E.F., France

Dear Father:

I am very well fixed here now and am only waiting till another interpreter gets out of the hospital to change from this translation work to the department that deals with European politics.

My transfer has been arranged. I spend most of the time now not translating but reading all sorts of books and documents on Poland. They are getting out a report on Poland in the course of a series which is supposed to be designed for the instruction of the Headquarters Staff and the Lieutenant tells me that I shall probably write it, which would be a very welcome piece of work, although rather difficult, because I have never before studied much about the East of Europe. I shall send you copies of these reports, if they will let me.

From the latest news that has come, it looks as if we should have a Republican Congress—a fact which I cannot but regret in view of the fact that Lodge, Taft, and Roosevelt have recently taken it upon themselves to try to discredit Wilson before the world.[1] News on home politics over here is very incomplete, but it seems to me that, under the circumstances, Wilson's appeal for a Democratic Congress was entirely justified. I was very much stirred up by Roosevelt's assertion that the President meant [blank spaces here] Allies and the Republican contention that the League of Nations was an illusion and the fourteen points too vague, though they are the only specific peace terms which four years of war have been able to produce. But now that Wilson's program has been accepted by the Allies, I conclude that Congress doesn't make much difference. One thing I am pretty sure of: all Europe is looking to

America now to get them out of the mess which centuries of Imperialistic politics got them into. And from the "inside dope" which trickles through the Headquarters from the Allied Conferences, it would appear that Wilson is pretty much master of the situation and that not even the "bitter enders" of Europe—let alone the "bitter enders" at home—will ever be able to prevent him from doing what he thinks just. Still, unless something more radical happens in Germany than the recent alleged democratization, there will no doubt be a certain amount of difficulty in admitting Germany to equal membership in such a League of Nations as it seems that the world must have. I should like to hear what you think of all this and if you still support the Republican leaders at this most mischievous hour of their career.

Life is rather pleasant here at Headquarters and consequently everybody always apologizes for being here. I have been entirely free from the kind of nagging that used to drive me crazy in 36.[2] In fact, no one, since I have been here, has given me any orders of any kind, and the officers I know invite me to their messes. I am going tonight to eat with the Lieutenant under whom I soon hope to be, a man named Harding, formerly a journalist and author of a book on China. I have had a very entertaining time with a man I knew a little when I was on the *Sun*.[3] At that time, his real abilities and intelligence were partially paralyzed by alcohol and the New York press, but now that he has had a year of the army he is an exceedingly pleasant companion. Being perfectly free now to speak his mind, he has given me an account of some of the private dealings of the *Sun* which makes me think even worse of it than I did before.

He swears he will never work for a New York paper of that kind again, and I am sure I never want to either, though what I shall do for a living when I get back to America is more than I can tell. It is just possible that this new work I am going to do might lead to something, and I intend to go into it for all it is worth. In any case, I am greatly indebted to you for having got me to Headquarters.[4]

The news that the German delegation has come to receive Marshal Foch's terms[5] just arrived and already an atmosphere has been created like the night before Christmas. By the time you get this letter the War may have ceased forever.

I am glad to hear that you got well quickly at Talcottville. The last letters I have had from either you or Mother were, I think, written from there. I have had none since I have been here, because the mail has to be forwarded and takes forever to arrive.—Please remember me sometime to the people in your office: Miss Parmenteer might see from this letter what an expert typist I have become. I have had to use a typewriter so much lately and have got so accustomed to it that I think I shall use one hereafter for everything.[6]

Yours always, / Edmund

[1]See *A Piece of My Mind: Reflections at Sixty* (1956). Writing of his political conflicts with his father, Wilson mentions the November 1918 Republican Congress and grants Wilson Sr., in spite of his Republican views, flexibility of mind and sound judgment.

[2]Base Hospital 36; Wilson's unit from Detroit went over to France in November 1917 and was assigned to duty there.

[3]*New York Evening Sun;* Wilson was briefly employed rewriting and reporting for the paper from the fall of 1916 to August 1917.

[4]Refers to Wilson's transfer.

[5]The terms that led to the armistice three days later, on November 11.

[6]This resolve faded with the end of the war.

Oct. 9, 1950

Dear Mother: My note is due Nov. 4, and I will attend to it then. I'll also leave till then the question of a further loan, in the hope that I won't have to make one.—*The Case of the Careless Kitten* has not reached Brentano's yet, but I am sending you a dozen of the same writer's books in that series—there ought to be some that you haven't read.[1]

The other book you wanted I think I have already sent you in the package I told you about. Let me know if you find it among them.

Lovingly, / Edmund

[1]It must have been galling to Wilson, author of a famous putdown of detective novels, "Who Cares Who Killed Roger Ackroyd?" to have to supply them by the dozen to Mrs. Wilson Sr.—who never read his own books. More than thirty years later, Wilson is still humoring his mother. He was also, according to Rosalind Wilson, to some extent financially dependent on her. *Near the Magician: A Memoir of My Father, Edmund Wilson* (1989), p. 49.

II. Friends of Youth and Later Years

From his days at Hill School in Pottstown, Pennsylvania, to his old age in Talcottville, New York, Wilson had an enormous capacity for friendship, a gargantuan appetite for personalities, shared interests, and opinions. After the boyhood friendships came a stream of new literary-personal relationships: F. Scott Fitzgerald and John Peale Bishop at Princeton; Edna St. Vincent Millay during his brief stay at *Vanity Fair;* and also in New York, John Dos Passos and Allen Tate. Dos Passos, the radical novelist of the 1920s and '30s and author of the sweeping chronicle *U.S.A.,* was a Harvard man in Wilson's social and literary set in the 1920s, and part of the scene on the Cape; he remained a friend even after he had turned against the left in the late 1930s and become a crusty conservative. In later years, when Dos Passos relocated, Wilson seemed to relish kidding him about his prosperous Virginia lifestyle. Tate, a New Critic, poet, and teacher whose genteel Southern hospitality Wilson enjoyed, was more of an aesthete than Wilson, but neither that nor Tate's conversion to Catholicism, while supplying plenty of material for discussion, caused serious enough friction to break their enduring literary friendship.

Burton Rascoe was a respected newspaperman of the period between the world wars, both as a literary critic and as a columnist. In a famous evocation of the jazz age, *A Bookman's Daybook* (1929), Rascoe records being bitten in the leg by an inebriated Wilson. Other Wilson antics that found their way into the book involved his arrival at Rascoe's doorstep dressed in tails, with Tallulah Bankhead on his arm, ready to "put on a show."

The poet Louise Bogan claimed Wilson as one of her first friends when she came to the city. The letters to her printed here extend through the 1930s and 1940s, even to 1968. Wilson had a particular sympathy with her periodic retreats from the world.

Morton Zabel was edited by Wilson at the *New Republic* and later, as editor of *Poetry,* edited Wilson. The two carried on a correspondence spanning three decades; they shared a number of friends, including Louise Bogan. Lionel Trilling, one of the most brilliant of the New York intellectuals who emerged at the end of the thirties, admired Wilson's writing. Out looking for reviewing work, Trilling met Wilson at the *New Republic* offices as early as 1929. He knew Wilson as an exemplar of the literary life in the Village of the 1920s, having observed the established man of letters at his Bank Street window. Wilson encouraged Trilling with his Matthew Arnold book in the thirties, and even reviewed it favorably (see *From the Uncollected Edmund Wilson*). Trilling was never quite a friend, but wrote of Wilson with great feeling "because he had so personal an effect on me." The letters in this section show Wilson as very open to Trilling's brand of criticism and remarkably unterritorial.

Dawn Powell, the satiric novelist who came to New York in the twenties from the Midwest, met Wilson in 1933. They enjoyed a long friendship that included a daft, joking relationship through the mail. He was Ernest Wigmore, a down-at-heels writer, and she was the Victorian Mrs. Humphrey Ward; later, metamorphosing into a sophisticated French couple, he became Raoul, she Aurore. She said of his 1930s Soviet travels and researches that they would probably result in the establishment of "Bun Wilson Clubs" and that his ashes would be sprinkled over Stalin's borscht. He wrote an influential piece on her called "Dawn Powell: Greenwich Village in the Fifties," in *The Bit Between My Teeth.*

Betty Huling, a staffer at the *New Republic* and well-to-do girl from Larchmont who later fell on hard times, was an old girlfriend from the 1930s, a drinker and a sport to whom Wilson was loyal until her death. Helen Muchnic, Slavic scholar and professor at Smith College, knew Wilson when he lectured for a time at Smith in the early 1940s. Wilson enjoyed being hosted by Helen while on his way from the Cape to Talcottville in later years. She worshipped him, as a writer and as a man, and was disappointed that she was not the fourth Mrs. W.

Cyril Connolly and Isaiah Berlin, two of the most powerful intellectuals in mid-century Britain, were good matches for Wilson in conversation, exchange of knowledge and ideas, and sharing trade practices. Both irritated Wilson with their self-absorption, but each had a quality that touched Wilson's deepest intellectual identity. Connolly, the aesthete, exquisite stylist, concocter of witty send-ups and highly crafted books such as *Enemies of Promise,* appealed to the author of that classic about symbolists and aesthetes, *Axel's Castle.* Berlin, the political thinker and polymath, was obsessed with Russian culture, European ideas, and the history of political reforms, thus becoming a cherished companion for the author of *To the Finland Station.* Never uncritical, Wilson tweaked Connolly about his lack of productivity in a humorous poem in *Night Thoughts.* He also was acerbic in his journals: "He was a queer mixture of lordly courtesy and boorishness and infantilism." Berlin's Oxford donnish style—with its attraction to cliques—was not to Wilson's taste: he preferred Berlin as international scholar and man of the world. Berlin's love and respect for Wilson ("the most unsurrendering intellectual— the most unyielding keeper-up of standards—I have ever met") was matched only by Wilson's for Berlin ("he affected me . . . like nobody else I had known"). This period of friendship reveals many features of Wilson's nature: the restlessness of the writer with numbers of fields to cover, the impatience of the craftsman and independent intellectual with political cant, the painstaking reading and research of the excited scholar.

TO BURTON RASCOE

September 8, 1925

Dear Burton: I am extremely sorry and disgusted about the other night. Whatever the rights or wrongs of the fight may have been, I am sure, from what Seward[1] tells me, that I must have been most obnoxious in the first place. Please tell Hazel[2] that I want to make my apologies to her too.

Yours sincerely, / EW

[1]Seward Collins: owner and editor of the *Bookman* and a mutual friend of Wilson's and Rascoe's—the behavior being apologized for may refer to the incident Rascoe includes in his memoir and, evidently hazy on the details himself, attributes to Matthew Josephson; Wilson is supposed to have bitten Rascoe on the calf.
[2]Hazel: Rascoe's wife.

[Undated, perhaps late 1923]

Dear Burton: Here is the Huysmans[1]—such as it is. By the way, if you should ever have any more novels you could send my friend J. N. Robinson (42 Baker St. Saranac Lake, New York)—unless you don't think he is good enough—he'd be grateful.

I've been having all sorts of troubles, lately. Mary[2] has been in the hospital with pleurisy for going on three weeks, and though she is nearly well now won't be able to come out for some time. I've taken the baby and nurse down to Red Bank.[3]

I was much entertained by the selections from the *Spotlight* about you which you quoted in the *DayBook*.[4] I bet you wrote them yourself. Otherwise, why didn't they ask me to do it?—I thought I had engaged with them to do it from a long while back. I hope things are going as well as can be expected with you and that Bertha [?] is all right. God help us all is what I say.

EW

[1]Joris Karl Huysmans (1848–1907); refers to a review of the *fin de siècle* writer's *Against the Grain* done by Wilson for *Vanity Fair* in June 1923. Huysmans also figures in *Axel's Castle: A Study in the Imaginative Literature of 1870–1930* (1931).

[2]Mary Blair, Wilson's first wife, an actress, from whom he separated in 1925 and was divorced five years later.

[3]Rosalind, their infant daughter, was beginning her childhood sojourns in Red Bank, New Jersey, with Wilson's mother.

[4]The Daybook was a feature in the Sunday edition of the *New York Herald Tribune*, where Rascoe was literary editor. A collection of his pieces appeared in 1929 as *A Bookman's Daybook;* it contains several mentions of Wilson.

August 20, 1929

Dear Burton: I'm sending the Nathan book[1]—I don't believe it will constitute much of a problem, because I don't think it's intended very seriously.

I'm sorry that I've already promised to go back to George Soule's[2] over the weekend and Mary's going down to Red Bank to stay with Rosalind. We want very much to come sometime, however,

As ever, / Bunny Wilson

[1]Rascoe's review of George Jean Nathan's *Monks Are Monks: A Diagnostic Scherzo* was highly unfavorable. It ran in the *New Republic* October 9, 1929.

[2]George Soule: an editor at the *New Republic.*

November 15, 1929

Dear Burton:

[The first sentence of this letter appears in *Letters on Literature and Politics.*] I hope that you weren't hit by the stock market disaster.[1] I haven't heard anything from you, and hope that this is not the reason. I wrote asking whether you would do the Elliot Paul book.[2] I wish you would let me know about it, also the new Oxford dictionary. The James Truslow Adams book[3] you asked for has come in. Do you want me to send it to you?

As ever, / EW

[Postscript] Did you see Mencken on the subject of his disciples deserting him for Paul Elmer More in the Sunday *World*?[4]

[1]The great stock market crash of October 1929, ushering in nearly a decade of economic depression.

[2]Elliot Paul book: probably *The Amazon*, a novel on the 1914–18 war.

[3]*The Adams Family,* about presidents of the same name (no relation).

[4]More, a more conservative critic than H. L. Mencken, was enjoying a vogue.

New Republic letterhead / May 8, 1930

Dear Burton:

Is there any chance of you being able to do those financial books? John Flynn[1] has expressed a willingness to write about them, and I thought that if you couldn't, I would get him to, though I would rather have you.

I am going to get married in Washington, D.C. tomorrow.[2]

As ever, / Bunny W.

[1]John Flynn (1882–1964): another reviewer for the *New Republic* and author of numerous books and articles on money and politics, including *As We Go Marching On.*

[2]Wilson married for the second time, to Margaret Canby, a friend of Hill School buddy Ted Paramore's from California; she died tragically in a fall in 1932.

October 2, 1931 / 7 Lingate Lane / Santa Barbara

Dear Burton: [Portions of this letter appear in *Letters on Literature and Politics.*] I'm terribly sorry you've been having such a bad time. What has been the matter? Ted Paramore simply told me you were in the hospital with an operation.

We've been hoping to go north all summer and counted on seeing you, but due to lack of funds and the complications of having the children have never been able to make it. Now Rosalind and I are going Monday. Margaret is going to stay on with Jimmy[1] a month or so and if you get down here, be sure to look her up; if she isn't at the above address, you can find out through it where she is. Also, if you get to Los Angeles, be sure to look up a young lawyer who writes—did one of these books on Ambrose Bierce[2]—Carey McWilliams, 900 Spring Arcade Building: Trinity 7466. He wants to meet you. I suppose you have seen how Malcolm[3] lays you under contribution in his last installment. I think his stuff is awfully good; I take exception a little to the tone of a mellow old man of letters reviewing indiscretions of his youth from a distance of many decades. Still, I suppose I did something of the same thing in *[I Thought of] Daisy,* and Mumford[4] in his summing up the generation of 1930. I suppose all these premature memoirs on the part of the comparatively young mean that something has really come to an end for them and that they are merely clearing it out of their systems.

I have had a very good time this summer—have ranged around considerably and seen a good many singular happenings.

When are you and Hazel going back East? I don't know whether I'll attempt to live in New York at all this winter—expect to go to Provincetown when I first get back. I've resigned from the *New Republic* as an editor and will get less money but hope to get more writing done.

Give our best love to Hazel. I wish we could have seen you. Hope you will soon be all right. I hadn't known, either, about your father's death—you have certainly had a dose of trouble. Your father's death makes a big psychological difference to you, I think—robs you of something and gives you something new at the same time—at least it did in my case.[5]

As ever, / Bunny W.

[Postscript] The only thing I am writing about Hollywood is about the film that Eisenstein[6] is making in Mexico, instigated and financed by Upton Sinclair,[7] and I wanted to include that in my "Jitters" book.[8] You might find something out from Sam Hoffenstein[9]—Thanks for asking me.

[1]Seven-year-old Jimmy Canby, Margaret's son by an earlier marriage.

[2]Ambrose Bierce (1842–circa 1914): Ohio-born writer of the Civil War era and of tales influenced by Poe. Disappeared in Mexico, having gone to cover Pancho Villa's army.

[3]Malcolm Cowley (1898–1989), writer and editor at the *New Republic;* his reminiscences appeared in *Exile's Return* (1934); later he made important contributions to the careers of Fitzgerald and Faulkner.

[4]Lewis Mumford (1895–1990), writer of books on urban culture whom Wilson admired. Wilson may be thinking of his *American Taste* (1929).

[5]Wilson's father, Edmund Sr., died in 1923.

[6]Sergei Eisenstein (1898–1948), pioneering Russian filmmaker (*Potemkin, Ivan the Terrible,* et al.). Wilson's essay, "Eisenstein in Hollywood," appeared in *The American Jitters: A Year of the Slump* (1932). It deals, in part, with the director's resistance to the studio system and his desire to cast ordinary people.

[7]Upton Sinclair (1878–1968): muckraking journalist of the 1930s known for his exposé of the Chicago meat-packing industry.

[8]*American Jitters,* a later edition of which was called *The American Earthquake.*

[9]Sam Hoffenstein: evidently a contact, perhaps through Paramore, in Hollywood.

January 10, 1940 / Truro Center, Mass

Dear Burton:

Were you editing the *Bookman* in February, 1930, and if so, do you remember anything about a man named Howard Duffield, who wrote an article about Dickens' *Edwin Drood* called "John Jasper: Strangler"? I'm writing something about Dickens[1] and want to discuss the article and would be grateful if you could tell me anything about the author.

How are you? I'm settled up here more or less permanently, I guess. Best wishes to you and Hazel for the New Year.

As ever, / Bunny Wilson

[1]"Dickens: The Two Scrooges," which ran in the *New Republic* in March 1940, was reprinted in *The Wound and the Bow;* it became a celebrated item in the Dickens critical canon and served as a case in point for Wilson's "wound" theory.

January 24, 1940

Dear Burton: I wrote to Sew Collins at Greenwich and got the letter back. If you happen to know where he is, I'd be grateful if you'd address this letter. If you don't, don't bother about it.

Another thing: there is a book coming out in February, published by Modern Age, by an old friend of mine, a man named John A. Udmark.[1] I knew him in the Army, and have been trying since the War to get somebody to publish his books, but always failed because his English was so defective—he is a Dane and entirely self-educated—that nobody wanted to bother with him. Finally, however and without my intervention—he got a bite from Macmillan. They ended by not taking the book, but in the meantime Louis Birk [of Modern Age] has heard about it and is bringing it out. It seems to me about the best of all the outlines of human civilization—it is called "The Road We Have Traveled" and I want to do anything I can to help get it noticed, as people usually don't pay much attention to these paper-bound books. It may not interest you, but I thought I'd mention it, and am having the publishers send you a copy.

As ever, / Bunny Wilson

[Postscript] Don't you think Mencken did quite a fine job on his memoirs?

[1]John A. Udmark: known in the army as John Andersen, "the little Dane" (see section I). Modern Age Books published *The Road We Have Covered.*

Dec. 26, 1953 / Wellfleet, Mass.

Dear Burton: I have been wanting to come to see you, but haven't been in New York except for very brief stays, with a lot of things to attend to. Now we are going to Europe to be gone till about May 1: but eventually I am going to make it. Rolfe Humphries'[1] remark is a mystery to me: I know nothing about the errors in the text of Virgil except what you wrote me, and I haven't seen Rolfe since then—nor do I ever remember, at any time, to have discussed this subject with him.

Love to Hazel and Happy New Year. / Bunny W

[1]Rolfe Humphries (1894–1969): poet, classicist, and critic. Wilson edited him at the *New Republic.*

TO BURTON RASCOE'S WIDOW

April 6, 1957

Dear Hazel: I have been saddened by Burton's death, and I am glad I was able to see him again so recently. You will be lonely now. Will you keep on living in the same place?—He never gets full credit now for all he did in the Twenties and before. In his best days, he was worth a dozen of the so-called New Critics.[1]

We have been living here in Cambridge ever since the middle of January. My boy[2] is a freshman at Harvard and, I am glad to say, doing extremely well. Rosalind works at Houghton Mifflin, and I at the Harvard Library. But otherwise we have been having rather a miserable time—illness and other misfortunes.

It may be a long time before I get to New York, but I want to call you up when I do. Will you be in the same place?

Elena joins me in sympathy.

Love as ever, / Bunny Wilson

[1]New Critics: the essayists and academics of the 1930s, '40s, and '50s—including Cleanth Brooks, John Crowe Ransom, and Allen Tate—who emphasized close reading of literary texts and who have been associated with an ahistorical approach to poems and novels. Wilson was generally cool toward them and smarted when one of their chief outlets, the *Kenyon Review,* rejected one of his essays.

[2]My boy: Reuel, Wilson's son with third wife Mary McCarthy.

TO ALLEN TATE

New Republic letterhead / June 17, 1929

Dear Allen:

Thank you very much for your letter and the review. The latter is excellent, and we shall run it soon.[1]

As for our controversy,[2] you have stated the problem in regard to the past and present admirably. I have those attacks of sour skepticism myself; I believe that they are one of the diseases of age. It is really a pity that we haven't conducted this discussion in print. So far from objecting to your remarks about me in your review, I am only sorry that you didn't name me. I have been thinking of a symposium myself, but of a slightly different kind. If I get any further with the idea, I will communicate with you about it. The weather is suffocatingly hot, and I have been struggling with the proofs of my poems,[3] which I am in no condition to cope with.

I spent the weekend in the country with Raymond and Louise[4] the other day. What with shenanigans of one kind and another Louise nearly fractured her skull, and I sprained my arm, so badly that I had to wear it in a plaster cast. Not only this, but the chair that Arthur Ficke[5] was sitting in collapsed under him with a loud crash. In such a world of cataclysm and uncertainty, what is one to take hold of?

Yours as ever, / Edmund

[1]your review: may have been Tate's "Lost Poets of Georgia," which ran in the *New Republic* July 23, 1930.

[2]our controversy: probably refers to their longstanding difference of opinion over what Tate calls his "anti-positivism" versus Wilson's adherence to aggressively secular scientific humanism. See Tate's "The Hovering Fly" and Wilson's "Marxism and Literature."

[3]*Poets, Farewell!* (1929).

[4]Raymond Holden (1894–1972) and Louise Bogan (1897–1970), both writers, had a stormy relationship, begun while he was married. Their own eventual marriage ended badly.

[5]Arthur Davison Ficke (1883–1945): American poet (*Selected Poems*, 1926).

Oct. 22, 1943 / Wellfleet, Mass.

Dear Allen:

[Portions of this letter, deleted here, appear in *Letters on Literature and Politics*.]

Well, it looks as if my doom[1] were sealed to the *New Yorker* for a year, and I were due to climb back into the important cab for awhile. I doubt whether any good except money will come of it.

[. . .] I have called up John Bishop, and he now tells me that he has decided to take the Washington job.[2] You evidently acted just in the nick of time. He told me that Margaret[3] had to go out to Columbus to attend a stockholders' meeting or something, so important that she had not been able to get anybody to take her vote, at which, I dare say, the question is to come up whether they shall sacrifice their income to patriotism. It would be an ironic but terrible thing if she really became dependent on John now.—But my guess about this may not be correct. [. . .]

[It] was almost like something on the stage, though, my suddenly getting that *New Yorker* offer after lamentations to you over my impoverishment.

As ever, / Edmund

[1] my doom: Wilson had recently agreed to do another stint as book reviewer at the magazine.

[2] John Bishop's Washington job: in November of 1943, at Tate's urging, Bishop was appointed resident fellow in comparative literature at the Library of Congress, but he had a heart attack two weeks later and died within months.

[3] Margaret Bishop: John Bishop's wealthy wife, whose influence over John neither Tate nor Wilson believed a positive one, either for his health or his work. The economic woes Wilson worries about here evidently came to nothing, as the Bishops were to retire to a comfortable estate on Cape Cod where the ailing Bishop lived out the remainder of his life.

New Yorker letterhead / October 24, 1946

Dear Allen:

Here is something else by John that I just found up in the country. It is a parody of Ezra Pound and might go with the other satirical poems.[1]

I'd hoped to be able to see you before I left, but have had so much to do that I'm afraid I can't. I'm leaving for Nevada tomorrow and will be back the middle of December[2] and will hope to see you sometime before Christmas. We're going to spend Christmas in Wellfleet, and I expect to be there all winter. I'll start in the first of the year working on John's prose and ought to have it in time so that both books can come out in the spring.[3]

I am sending you, in your editorial capacity,[4] the MS of a novel by an old army friend of mine named John [Andersen] Udmark. He has published one rather good book. I haven't had a chance to read this yet, but I'd be grateful if you'd try it on your reader and let me know his reaction to it.

I hope you are fermenting and crystallizing. Love to Caroline,[5] who, I understand, thinks I ought to be roasted over a slow fire.

Sincerely, / Edmund Wilson

[1] might go with the other satirical poems: both men were working on posthumous collections of Bishop's work, Tate on the poems and Wilson on the prose; Tate's volume was published by Scribner's in 1948 as *The Collected Poems of John Peale Bishop, edited with a preface and a personal memoir by Allen Tate.*

[2] To facilitate the divorce of Elena Mumm Thornton and her subsequent marriage to Wilson, his fourth.

³*The Collected Essays of John Peale Bishop,* edited by Wilson, was brought out by Scribner's, like the poetry volume, in 1948.

⁴Tate was at the time an editor at Holt.

⁵Caroline Gordon: the first of Tate's three wives, whom he married twice. A Southerner, writer of novels and short stories, she evidently disapproved of Wilson's sour views on Catholicism. She was more sociable when Wilson visited them at their farm in Clarksville, Tennessee (see *The Thirties,* p. 74).

Feb. 15, 1947 / Wellfleet, Mass.

Dear Allen: Will you send me the MS of the poetry and painting essay? I suppose I ought to see what you have done.[1]—I am reading the novel that John wrote during his early years in Europe, and so far I'm inclined to think that he ought to have finished and published it. I think that Scott [Fitzgerald], who is so frantically competitive with him and rather envious of some of his qualities, discouraged him with it for thoroughly bad reasons. It is quite unlike his published fiction but has much more color and wit, more of his earlier self, in it.[2]—I can't throw any light on the dates of these poems. They were probably written after he went abroad, as I think all of these MSS I have here were.[3]

I am very anxious to see you and talk to you about a number of things— but the idea of a "shower" is abhorrent. I've been married too many times and neither Elena nor I wants any fuss made about us.[4]

As ever, / Edmund

[1]to see what you have done: a reference to the fact that both Tate and Wilson were working to bring out posthumous volumes of Bishop's papers.

[2]In the *Collected Essays* volume he edited, Wilson included a portion of this unpublished novel, written in 1926 and titled *The Huntsmen Are Up in America;* Wilson, in his introduction to the volume, again blames Fitzgerald (and a publisher Bishop showed it to) for having scuttled it. In spite of his criticism here Wilson was always a supporter as well as the "literary conscience" of Scott, whom he knew from their Princeton days.

[3]MSS I have here: refers to Wilson's editorial work on the Bishop papers.

[4]a "shower": evidently Caroline Gordon had suggested this, to Wilson, abhorrent way of noting his fourth marriage, to Elena.

TO LOUISE BOGAN

April 9, 1934 / 314 East 53rd St. / New York

[A portion of this letter, retained for clarity, appears in *Letters on Literature and Politics.*]

Dear Louise: I was glad to get your note—sorry to have missed you every time you've been here.—When are you coming back for good? I'm anxious to begin our German course—recently bought a fine set of Heine at a bargain sale at Brentano's in preparation. I think that a certain number of German sessions a week would be an excellent thing for you.—Have you seen these little evanescent poems of Eliot's?[1] Some don't like them, but they seem to me exquisite.—I saw Betty[2] and her new boyfriend last night—I prefer him to Bud and he has more brains, but it's a pity she can't seem to get anything more substantial. I'm hoping to get off to Washington Friday or Saturday for a week—though I may not get off, in which case I'll be having Rosalind here over the weekend and you must let me know if you come in.—Have you read Bill Rollins' novel, *The Shadow Before?*[3] I'll have Cobey Gilman[4] send you a copy, if you haven't.—I've been reading great quantities of history and philosophy of history in preparation for writing a momentous essay on the subject. —I am also very good on Henry James in *The Hound and Horn*, of which I'll have Kirstein send you a copy.[5]

Love, hope to see you very soon. / Edmund

[1]evanescent poems of Eliot: most probably "Five finger exercises" and "Landscapes" of 1934.

[2]Betty Huling, copy editor at the *New Republic* during the 1930s and 1940s. Wilson's affair with her in 1934 was briefly resumed after his separation from Mary McCarthy in 1945.

[3]Wilson had reviewed the novel for the *New Republic.*

[4]Cobey Gilman: a friend of Dawn Powell; he worked at Prentice Hall.

[5]Wilson's essay on the philosophy of history eventually became *To the Finland Station: A Study in the Writing and Acting of History* (1940); his essay on Henry James's *The Turn of the Screw,* entitled "The Ambiguity of Henry James," appeared in the James issue of *Hound and Horn* (7, April–June 1934), edited by Lincoln Kirstein. Revised versions appeared in *The Triple Thinkers* (1938, 1948, and 1959). The essay, with its interpretation of the governess's ghost-sightings as manifestations of Freudian hangups, triggered a great deal of critical discussion.

July 16, 1934 / Provincetown, Mass.

Dear Feine Liebchen: I haven't answered your letter because I haven't been sure what my plans were. Why don't you come down to Provincetown? I brought Rosalind up here yesterday and am leading a very quiet life— completely non-alcoholic. The weather is perfect. So come along, wunderschöne Mädchen,[1] with your Eisenblinken[2] and your Augenfunken,[3] and we can go to the beach in the afternoons and have a go at Heine in the evenings. I think you'll be entertained by Provincetown if you've never seen it.—I've been so pleased to get to a place where life is simple, wholesome, and quiet that I think of staying here through the fall after Rosalind goes back to school.—I have been raking in a few odds and ends of money lately, so am not quite so depressed about this aspect of things as I was. What was my amazement the other day to get a royalty report from Scribners' showing uniformly increased sales of my books—even *I Thought of Daisy*. It just goes to show you that now that the flood of mediocre books has been ebbed, true merit is coming into its own!—Where are you now?—If you're not coming up right away, I am going to send you some of my poetical works.[4]

As ever, Edmund

[1]wunderschöne Mädchen: lovely girl.
[2]Eisenblinken: shining looks.
[3]Augenfunken: glittering eyes.
[4]my poetical works: probably these were included in *Note-books of Night* (1942).

Nov. 16, 1936 / Tuesday

Dear Louise: I like the poem very much. I've written a little piece about this tree-ey spot myself[1]—Which I'll show you when you come out. Paul Rosenfeld[2] has been here and is full of Rilke, about whom he apparently knows a lot. He was much interested to hear that you were working on the subject and said he was going to call you up. Would you like to come out here the Monday of next week? Don't bring liquor on my account, as I have foresworn it for the time being. The Bernard Shaw book will be enough—So get you gone, von Hufel, though with spinach in your beard![3]

Love, / Edmund

[1]tree-ey spot: Trees, the house in which he was then living in Stamford, Connecticut; Wilson later used it as a background setting in *Memoirs of Hecate County* (1946).
[2]Paul Rosenfeld (1890–1946): a critic of music, art, and literature whose death before achieving the full measure of his promise left Wilson much affected. (See letters to Elena Mumm Thornton in section III.)
[3]von Hufel: evidently a jocular reference to previous German sessions.

Feb. 8, 1937 / Trees, R.F.D. 1 / Stamford, Conn.

Dear Louise: It seems that Hatty[1] gave the books to her daughter to take to you. Are you sure they're not downstairs? I'm having her find out about it. I thought she had mailed them.—If you had gotten hold of me instead of having insisted on having Hatty send them, they would never have gone astray.—I am sending *The Dog Beneath the S.*[2]

I don't try to break you down, my dear; I want to keep you up.[3]

I've been doing an awful lot of writing—have stocked the *New Republic* for about three months ahead—and have been preoccupied with other matters. Old Zabel[4] came out here for a night, and I enjoyed him very much. I think that his succeeding to the editorship of *Poetry*[5] and his getting this gloomy-sounding anthology[6] out has bucked him up quite a lot. I talked to Rolfe [Humphries] on the phone one night and he seems to have got into the same rabid state of mind about the Russian trials that the conservative Bostonians got into about the Sacco-Vanzetti case[7].

I read the volume of Louis MacNeice's[8] poems, and it seems to me that he has more talent than any of that group except Auden, and his juices seem to flow more freely than Auden's so that at his best he is really more successful as a lyric poet.—I also liked your poem extremely— even better than before when I read it in *Poetry*.—I asked John Bishop last summer why he didn't do something with his ornithology in his poetry; and now I am afraid that he is going to spend the rest of his life describing Antarctic hoot-owls and flicker-tailed grackles in verse.

I'll be seeing you before long, and I hope you will behave yourself in the meantime.

Love, Edmund

[1]Hatty: Wilson's housekeeper during his period in Connecticut.

[2]*The Dog Beneath the Skin* (1935): one of the three verse dramas that Auden wrote with Christopher Isherwood.

[3]keep you up: like Bogan, Wilson knew what it was to be hospitalized for nerves, a condition with which he was always sympathetic.

[4]Morton Dauwen Zabel (1901–1964): literary critic, a specialist in James, who taught at the University of Chicago.

[5]*Poetry:* distinguished little magazine founded by poet and critic Harriet Monroe; she herself did a 1918 review of Edna Millay's *Renascence* for the magazine.

[6]*Literary Opinion in the United States.*

[7]Sacco-Vanzetti case: when the two anarchists were executed for murder in 1927 a furor arose. Wilson wrote of the case and the trial in *The American Earthquake.*

[8]Louis MacNeice (1907–1963): Anglo-Irish poet, part of the Auden-Isherwood set of the 1930s.

Oct. 10, 1939 / Truro Center, Mass.

Dear Louise: I was glad to hear from you.—We came right up here from the West and hope to stay more or less permanently. We'll be down in New York around Christmas and will hope to see you. We'd like to have you come up here to see us, too—but don't know how we're going to be fixed, due to Polly Boyden's[1] uncertainty as to when she's coming back. We'll talk about it later.—We were moving when Morton [Zabel] was in Cambridge, and by the time we were settled he had to go back, so we missed him. It would be fun if you and he could come up here at the same time sometime. We'll try and keep you from stirring up each other's Ids.

I've just written a long thing about Dickens[2] and am about to try to wind up the Finland Station (now that the Soviets are about to annex Finland).

We are leading a very pleasant outdoor and literary life. Mary[3] sends love and says she wants to see you.

By the way, what has happened to Rolfe [Humphries]? I saw a review by him in the *New Republic.* I'm anxious to know whether his Stalinist faith has survived the recent events. Did you see Hitler's interview with Neville Henderson,[4] in which he said that he didn't want to "turn Germany into a barracks"—that he'd started out "as an artist" and hoped to return to his art? I'm afraid there's a lesson in this for many.

Best love to Maidie.[5]

Love, / Edmund

[1]Polly Boyden: author of a novel and friend of John Dos Passos. Wilson rented her Truro house for the winter of 1939–40.

[2]Dickens: "Dickens: The Two Scrooges," which became part of *The Wound and the Bow* and *To the Finland Station.*

[3]Mary McCarthy (1912–1989): essayist, reviewer for the *Partisan Review;* Wilson married her February 10, 1938, and is credited with turning her toward fiction. *A Charmed Life, The Group,* and other novels were the result.

[4]Sir Neville Henderson: British Ambassador to Germany under Chamberlain. Wilson may be referring to his White Papers, first-hand accounts of Hitler and Nazism, written as reports to Foreign Secretary Lord Halifax. Portions ran in *Atlantic, Time,* and elsewhere in 1939–40.

[5]Maidie: Bogan's daughter.

[Superscript] What with Jarrell's review of Gregory-Zaturenska and your controversy with Ransom, this week's number of *The Nation* is a rich treat for lovers of poetry.[1]

Sept. 24, 1941 / Wellfleet, Mass.

Dear Louise: I'm sorry if I was unduly disagreeable the last time I saw you. I didn't say or didn't mean what Mary tells me you thought I said or meant.—I miss you. The intellectual life up here is really rather poor. There's really no-body now who knows anything about writing except Mary.—A little Austra-lian novelist named Colebrook[2] (who has a book coming out in October) has insisted on borrowing your complete works from me. How she knew about you I don't know.—(What has happened to Morton [Zabel]? He wired us he was seriously ill.—We haven't any cook just now and are about to lose the nurse; but when we're on a better basis, I hope you'll come up for a visit. Let us know if you're in Boston anytime, in any case. —I'm engaged in getting Scribner's my poems and little prose whatnots for a book that the Colt Press are going to bring out. It is going to be a collected volume of those laundry notes that Alfred Kazin says he is eager to read. Did you see his review of my book in *The Herald Tribune*?[3]

And now, Louise, my dear Louise, I'll say farewell with a kiss. Also with love and a squeeze to Maidie.

Edmund W.

[1]Randall Jarrell (1914–1965): poet, critic, and author of *Pictures from an Institution;* he reviewed the Horace Gregory–Marya Zaturenska work, *A History of American Poetry, 1900–1940.* Earlier Bogan had reviewed—unfavorably—John Crowe Ransom's *The New Criticism.* In a letter to the editor Ransom took exception to her objections; Bogan's reply must have amused Wilson: "And may I say that, after having reviewed books for eighteen years, and lived for forty-four, without ever having been called a lady, a four-flusher, a three-flusher, a Southerner, or (implicitly) a fool, Mr. Ransom's calling me all these things made me laugh very much?"

[2]Joan Colebrook, who wrote on Australia for the *New Yorker* and figures as a Wellfleet friend in *The Sixties.*

[3]Kazin made the remark in the course of his laudatory review of *The Wound and the Bow, New York Herald Tribune,* August 31, 1941.

New Yorker letterhead / June 20, 1944

Dear Louise:

I tried to call you up yesterday but couldn't get you. I am just in town until Wednesday. I have read the proof of your Yvor Winters[1] review and think it is very interesting and good. I just want to call your attention to the second sentence of the last paragraph. Don't you think the phrase "always around," without a relative, is a little bit awkward and weak? Wouldn't it be better to say, "that always appears in such quantity," etc., or something of the sort?

How are you? We are working hard at our grisly trade. Rosalind is also coming through as an author and has just sold a story to *Mademoiselle.*

As ever, / Edmund W

[1]Yvor Winters (1900–1968): poet and critic with a classical bent; author of *Primitivism and Decadence.*

March 19, 1952 / c/o de La Roche / 17 E 97, New York

Dear Louise: I was glad to get your card. We are very comfortably ensconced up here and expect to stay till the middle of May. Will you be back before then? If you are, be sure to call us: Atwater 9–8785. After having a more or less awful time last year, we seem to be solvent and happy again. I've just finished a gigantic book of 250,000 words, based on my old articles of the twenties and thirties. I've rewritten them almost to the point of forging my own early works and have added memoirs of people and things. I rather unexpectedly found it fascinating but am not sure how much this was merely due to reliving that period as I went through the stuff. Title: The Shores of Light, from the poetic Latin phrase in luminis oras, which, when you come to read the book, you will see is full of significance.

I was rather disappointed in your poetry book.[1] It sounded as if you were so bored with it that you could hardly remember what all those poets were like, and I thought you had some very odd descriptions of the work of certain people. I finally sent my copy to Morton, but he has never sent me his, and I suppose is adding both of them to his collection of association items.

Good luck with your evangelistic work.[2] Elena sends love,

Edmund

[1]Bogan's critical survey, *Achievement in American Poetry 1900–1950* (1951).
[2]evangelistic work: evidently a reference to the efforts in her volume on behalf of poetry.

July 31, 1968

Dear Louise: I was very glad to get your poems.[1] Last night I had a crisis of gout, and it was only by reading your volume together with a pint of whiskey that I managed to pull myself through. I found several that I didn't remember to have seen before. The old ones seemed as good as they first did.

I was happy about your getting that money from the goddamn government.[2]

Love to Maidie. / Edmund

[1]*Blue Estuaries, Poems 1923–68.*
[2]money from the goddamn government: probably a $10,000 grant from the National Endowment for the Arts, which actually came through in 1969.

TO JOHN DOS PASSOS

Oct. 18, 1932 / Red Bank, N.J.

Dear Dos and Katy:[1] Thank you very much for your letter.—Margaret[2] slipped on a turning staircase coming away from a party in Santa Barbara and fractured her skull—she had been in bed with the flu and had only just gotten up—was probably giddy and uncertain on her feet. One of the last things she did at the party was promise Don Stewart's[3] wife and her sister to give their love to you when she came East.

Thanks for asking me to Provincetown, but I'll have to be around here now. Let me know when you come to New York. I don't know exactly where I'm going to be, but you can find me through the *New Republic*.

As ever, / Bunny

[1]Katherine Smith Dos Passos, Dos Passos's first wife, killed in a grisly car accident September 12, 1947.

[2]Margaret Canby: Wilson's very private and moving recollections of his second wife are to be found in "The Death of Margaret," *The Thirties*, 227–62.

[3]Donald Ogden Stewart (1894–1980): Yale man, contributor to *Vanity Fair;* as a screenwriter his credits include *The Philadelphia Story,* for which he won an Academy Award. In 1933 he was working on *Dinner at Eight.* Always associated with the left, he was blacklisted in 1950.

March 13, 1933 / New York

Dear Dos and Katy: I'm sorry to hear that the old contagion-fighter has at last fallen victim to a germ—hope you are all right by this time.—The inauguration was strange and gloomy—everybody seemed sunk, benumbed. See my account in the *N[ew] R[epublic]*.[1]—I got an unexpected response to my play from your Mr. Aldrich he seemed to think seriously of doing something with it when he is done with his play that opens next week—though I suppose it's very uncertain what anybody will be able to do now. Thanks very much for sending me to him.[2]—I've been feeling pretty sour lately—the depression was all very well till it hit the *New Republic* and the Red Bank First National Bank and Trust Co.[3] And this is always the time of the year in New York when everybody becomes sick and sordid. Hoping you have managed to escape the latter in your wind-washed island home.

EW

[1]Wilson's "Inaugural Parade" on Franklin Delano Roosevelt's inauguration ran in the *New Republic* March 22, 1933.

[2]Dos Passos had tried to assist Wilson in getting a producer for *Beppo and Beth*. The play, a sendup of the leftists and New York sophisticates battered by the Depression, was Wilson's main project in 1932; he hoped to get the Group Theatre to do it, but Lee Strasberg hated it.

[3]According to Rosalind Wilson, the crash of the Red Bank bank had a disastrous effect on the family wealth. Wilson Sr. had left all of his money to his wife, making her "a rich woman. . . . The crash didn't affect her. But Roosevelt's bank holiday laid her out." *Near the Magician*, p. 47.

[Postcard with drawing of a Russian girl in a peaked cap holding a monkey on a string]

July, 1935

[no greeting, but card is addressed to Mrs. John Dos Passos]

A little Komsomol[1] giving her monkey his dialectical materialism.—There is less of this, though, abroad than formerly, according to all accounts. The people are getting cake and candy and a few bright clothes, so that they don't need quite so much of it. The drabness of Moscow is quite appalling to an American, though—they have a new amusement park all in gray which is the [communist] idea of the underworld.—Hope you are well and happy. To be a friend of Dos's here is to be embraced and kissed on both cheeks. As ever, EW

[1]Komsomol: member of communist youth organization.

May 21, 1951 / Red Bank, N.J.

Dear Dos and Betty:[1] We very much enjoyed our sojourn on your acres.—I am back here in Red Bank trying to liquidate my mother's household. Elena has gone back to the Cape.—I hope to get there next week. The state of Israel and the University of Denver have applied to produce *The Little Blue Light*,[2] so it hasn't sunk quite without a trace.—I have nothing of interest to report— this note is merely a tribute to old-time Southern hospitality. It was fine to see the flourishing family, and we were very much impressed by the whole set-up.—Good luck with the marinated beet crop, and don't forget to dash a little hellebore on the second planting of ciatia putiminous. [?][3]

As ever, / EW

[Postscript] Dos might sprinkle his present political views with a suspicion of Paris green to get rid of the parlor Blimpism.[4]

¹Dos Passos's first wife, Katy, was decapitated in an accident in their convertible in 1947. He and Betty married and moved back to his roots in Virginia around 1950.

²Wilson's most successful play, produced in 1951.

³This illegible Latin may be the botanically correct name for a garden plant, or it may be Wilson's jest.

⁴Colonel Blimp began life as a caricature of the insensitive British military man; later he was transformed into the hero of a movie. Here he stands for a pompous and sententious figure.

July 1, 1951 / Wellfleet, Mass.

Dear Dos: Thanks for the enclosures. In return, I am sending you this—Look out! He's got his eye on you as a posthumous prospect. [Enclosure lost.]—Your crack about Acheson[1] is lost on me, as I didn't read those hearings.—In pursuance of any researches into an earlier period, I have been reading Theodore Roosevelt's autobiography and the first installments, just published, of his correspondence, and to my surprise I am quite impressed by him. He looks better at the beginning of his career than at the end as we saw him in our youth. He was a sounder and better equipped character, of course rather simple, than either [Woodrow] Wilson or Franklin D. He early evolved for himself a definite set of ideas and convictions and stuck to them pretty consistently. He had a grasp of history and the contemporary world that none of his successors has had. There are in some of these letters really remarkable observations on America's place in the world (in private he was more realistic,—in these early years, at any rate—less cocksure and less bombastic than he became as a public man). He was always perfectly frank in his imperialism and did not let the people in for wars while pretending to do something else, and his mastery of local politics—unscrupulous though he sometimes was—never gives rise to the unpleasant impression produced by the hypocrisy of Wilson or the prima-donna coquetry of Franklin D. I find it quite exhilarating to read about his adventures in the police department and the New York legislature. He must have worked up, or popularized, the conception of "Americanism" that begins to appear in his writings in the nineties, but he meant something more admirable by it and something that made more sense than the vague implications of the people who used it in a menacing way at the end of the first world war.

We are up to our necks in children at this point, as usual in the summer. I have been enjoying it up here more than I usually do, and am anxious to have Jennie[2] up here (she is still pretty crippled) and sell the Red Bank house. Reuel, instead of being tall as I thought he was going to be is stocky and broad-shouldered like my uncles. He bicycled up here with a friend 125 miles from Newport, making it all in one day when we thought it would take them two or three. Elena sends love to you both,

As ever, EW

[1]Dean Acheson (1893–1971) was Secretary of State and the object of attacks by Senator Joseph McCarthy beginning in 1950; the hearings referred to are doubtless those conducted by Senator Millard Tydings in which Acheson's State Department was exonerated of false charges about communist infiltration. The "crack" was relayed by the increasingly right-wing Dos Passos.

[2]Jennie Corbett: the senior Mrs. Wilson's longtime maid, whose welfare continued to be a matter of concern to Edmund Jr. after his mother's death.

Dec. 23, 1951 / Wellfleet, Mass.

Dear Dos: This is to thank you and Betty on behalf of the whole family for the delicious terrific pickles, which we have been eating with electrical results.—I've just come back from selling my mother's house in Red Bank for about half what it's probably worth,—but I'm glad to get it off my mind. We are going down to be in New York from the first of February on—so be sure to look us up when you come.—It is curious to find Jay in your book[1] going to *Pelléas [et Mélisande]* at the Opéra Comique, which I did too, at that time—it heightened the impression I have been having lately of being plunged back into the past. Harold Ross'[2] death and trying to write a memoir of Edna Millay[3] have added themselves to the other things that have been making me feel dated—also talking to the Wellfleet Literary Club, at their request, about Scott Fitzgerald.[4] I hope to snap out of it later.—You sound unnecessarily depressed about your books. I think you are getting into some sort of new phase that has a kind of poetry the earlier ones didn't.

Best holiday greetings to all of you from everybody here.—Helen[5] had the flu or something . . . but is now emerging.

As ever, / EW

[1]*Chosen Country.*

[2]Harold Ross (1892–1951): founder, in 1925, of the *New Yorker* magazine; he continued as editor until his death.

[3]Edna St. Vincent Millay (1892–1950): an important American poet of the 1920s and '30s, and Wilson's first love. His tribute to her is in *The Shores of Light* (1952).

[4]F. Scott Fitzgerald (1896–1940): their long association culminated with Wilson editing (and, in effect, completing) Fitzgerald's unfinished novel *The Last Tycoon* and his notebooks, as *The Crack-Up*. Together, they contributed substantially to Fitzgerald's literary reputation.

[5]Wilson's and Elena's daughter.

Sept. 8, 1952 / Wellfleet, Mass.

Dear Dos: [A portion of this letter appears in *Letters on Literature and Politics.*] The cartoons arrived, thank you.—You left everything in fine shape here. At my end of the house, I can't detect any trace of your occupancy.—We may be living in New York instead of Princeton, because they seem to have difficulty in finding us a house—I'll let you know when we're settled.

I've been reading the literature of the Civil War—some of which is wonderful. There are a number of books that ought to be classics but aren't because the Civil War has to some extent been a taboo subject. The South wouldn't read the northern books about it, and the North wanted to forget the whole thing. There are some books that Americans ought to read, but that haven't been assigned, in schools and colleges, because they wouldn't go down with the Southerners: Herndon's *Life of Lincoln;* Grant's *Personal Veracity;* H. W. Higginson's *Army Life in a Black Regiment; Uncle Tom's Cabin;* Francis Grierson's *The Valley of Shadows.*

I had a wonderful time in Talcottville, but it was all more or less a headache for Elena. She finally saw a ghost,—which impressed me, because she has no interest in the supernatural and is always bored by ghost stories. It has been calculated that fifty people at least have died in that house.—I have looked up some of the early history of the place.

I have been quite exhilarated by the news. Are you still mourning the non-candidacy of the liberty-loving Taft?

You sounded rather sour about the Hemingway story.[1] I thought it was pretty good, in some ways, an improvement (politically) on his earlier stories— though this story is marred by the personal note of self-regard[?] and self-pity. The way he went on about it in the letters published in *Life,* has, so far, inhibited me from writing him about it. Now one feels that he has already congratulated himself so warmly that there is no point in anyone else's doing it. As ever, EW

[1]*The Old Man and the Sea;* it ran in *Life* September 1, 1952 before coming out as a short novel.

Dear Dos: Congratulations on making the Academy.[1] I suppose that now you will by trying to get Westbrook Pegler[2] in.—Me, I am aiming at Biblical status—am being translated into Hebrew.—We got back a month ago from four months abroad. Israel, in spite of its various worries, seems a good deal more cheerful than Europe. England is relatively comfortable again, and we enjoyed it more than the Continent. The American Seminar at Salzburg, in which I performed for a month, is something very peculiar—I don't believe there has ever been anything quite like it, as an agency for disseminating a national culture, in history before. There are students from all over Europe. The Yugo-Slavs are the most interested and among the most interesting, but can't avail themselves of the scholarships to come to the United States on account of the McCarran Act.[3]—The only people I saw who were really exhilarated were the archeologists in Jordan. Whatever else the period may be, it is the heyday of archeology.—I may be in New York in a couple of weeks. Let me know if you should be going there.—Elena sends love, and we both send love to Betty.

Bunny W

[Postscript] I hope you are not one of those dreadful liberals who are rooting for the downfall of McCarthy.[4]

[1]American Academy of Arts and Letters.

[2]Westbrook Pegler: a famous conservative newspaper columnist of the day.

[3]Wilson is thinking of the 1952 McCarran-Walter Immigration Act under which "foreign undesirables," including Pablo Picasso, were not allowed in the United States.

[4]Sen. Joseph McCarthy (1908–1957), Republican senator from Wisconsin. His 1954 hearings did not uncover a single spy, but did serve to intensify the communist scare that dated back at least as far as the Truman administration. They followed the model set in the 1940s by the House Un-American Activities Committee.

March 17, 1957 / 16 Farrar St. / Cambridge, Mass.

Dear Dos: [A portion of this letter appears in section IV.] I have got awfully fed up with Princeton. Cambridge still has a more serious atmosphere and social nonsense is not so important. Princeton has some things about it that are sickening and I have never been enough involved with Harvard to be worried by what is bad about it. At worst, the students are freer, and have a better chance to mature.

I have only looked at "The Outsider."[1] He is something new for England.

As somebody said to me there, if he had gone to Oxford or Cambridge, he would have talked it all away and never have written a book.

Love to all, / EW

¹*The Outsider,* by Colin Wilson, was a wide-ranging study of alienation in modern literature, including the work of classic figures such as Dostoevsky and figures less familiar in the Anglo-Saxon world such as Barbusse. Although disparaged for its lack of literary style by Dwight Macdonald, the book spoke to Wilson as the author of *Axel's Castle* because of its ambition to bring the news of European experimentalism to a general audience.

[Postcard featuring a drawing of a walrus and the following superscript:] "This is what I am aiming at, but actually I have had to lose weight."

Sept. 14, 1958 / Wellfleet

Dear Dos: I was sorry to miss you, but it is not really necessary to converse with me, because I am writing down in concise form all my opinions on everything, and this will presently come out as a book (reading time ³/₄ hour).

I wish I were not too old, too unathletic, and too unused to rugged living to get the *New Yorker* to send me to the Himalayas to investigate the Abominable Snowman. Have you read the recent book?[1] It sounds like the Dead Sea scrolls of zoology and anthropology.

As ever, / EW

¹*The Abominable Snowman* (1955) by Ralph Izzard.

May 2, 1963 / 12 Hilliard St. / Cambridge

Dear Dos: [Portions of this letter appear in *Letters on Literature and Politics.*] We always mean to come South every spring but never get further than New York. —I have had a belated rapprochement with the Murphies,[1] and on our last trip went out to see them at Sneden's Landing. They lived up to their tradition of gracious living by providing an incredible lunch—for which a special chef had been procured—with the menu à la française, on little porcelain tablets.[. . .]—We have had some hideous winters in Cambridge—aside from Cambridge itself, tax troubles, and various ailments. I have nearly got rid of the latter and the former are pretty well settled, but they have inspired me to write a tract which I hope will be the hottest thing since Tom Paine.[2] The Americans at the present time are being tyrannized over by the Federal Government in a way that ought to give them more cause for complaint than the colonists had against the Crown, but they seem to take it lying down. This is our last winter in Cambridge. We have been hoping to spend next winter in Europe, putting Helen in a school in Switzerland, but I don't know whether we'll have been left enough money by that son of a bitch Uncle Sam.

Yours, / EW

¹Gerald and Sarah Murphy, the couple said to have been Fitzgerald's model for the Divers in *Tender Is the Night;* his mot "living well is the best revenge" summed up an era.

²*The Cold War and the Income Tax: A Protest* (1963); thanks to America's questionable Vietnam involvement Wilson was able to turn his totally unjustifiable anger over delinquent tax charges into a powerful polemic.

[Postcard]

[Undated but probably 1964]

We are spending the winter in Paris at the Hôtel de Castile, 37 rue Cambon. I get a different impression of the city than I have ever had before. The women are no longer so chic, and everything seems more commonplace. The Sunday crowds in Montmartre remind me unexpectedly of Moscow. The young people go crazy about new French singers with bogus American names, who hop around the stage with the tubes of loud speakers that look like garden hoses and make their voices raucous and deafening. The hipsters are called les zozos, and the squares, identified with the older generation, are les croulants et les viceques à la son et lumière. The writers are les zozos Teués. The degrees of excellence are formid, sensers, and bouldame (bouleversant de l'humanité) Helen has just come back for Christmas from her school in Switzerland. She is already quite fluent in French and will no doubt soon be talking this language I want to see the back of.—EW

LETTERS TO MORTON ZABEL

New Republic letterhead / April 14, 1930

Dear Mr. Zabel:

Thank you very much for your review of Babette Deutsch.¹ The only thing I would criticize in it is your statement that the survival of certain qualities in her work "is hardly due to organic consistency." Isn't it true that, even if these qualities are second-rate, their persistence might be as organically consistent as it would if they were first-rate? Or perhaps you haven't said precisely what you mean. Will you think about this when you get the proof?

Yours sincerely, / Edmund Wilson

Nov. 6, 1936 / Trees, R.F.D.1. / Stamford, Conn.

Dear Zabel:

I'm sorry that I've made it a rule not to allow my articles to be reprinted in anthologies. I don't consider that any of them are worth preserving in book-form except the ones that I have worked over and published in books—or that I intend eventually to work over and publish. Especially in the case of the articles which were the original material for *Axel's Castle,* I wouldn't have them reprinted for anything. I didn't even let the *New Republic Anthology* reprint from the *New Republic.*—I'm a great hater of anthologies anyhow and much regret to see you taking what I hope may not be the first false step on the road to Untermeyer.¹ You ought to be writing a book of your own. I've just been reading the copies of *Poetry* you sent me and think you are awfully good on Benet² and Engle³—also, Sandburg.⁴ That's the kind of thing there isn't enough of nowadays when everybody seems so scared.

I'm out here in the woods for the winter. It's a little dark, as Louise [Bogan] says, but has its great advantages, including absolute quiet. I wish you'd come out here for a night when you're on East again. It's very easy to get to: there are trains from the Grand Central every hour, and the fast ones only take fifty minutes. The telephone is Stamford 3-2516. Do let me know if you'd like to come.

I'm very much interested to see what you will do with *Poetry.*⁵

Yours as ever, / Edmund Wilson

¹Louis Untermeyer (1885–1977), enormously popular anthologist who produced *Modern American Poetry* (1919) and *Modern British Poetry* (1920), among other volumes.

²Stephen Vincent Benet (1898–1943), two-time Pulitzer Prize–winning poet and fiction writer. *John Brown's Body* and "The Devil and Daniel Webster" were his most famous works.

³Paul Engle (1908–), poet and educator associated with the celebrated writers' workshops at the University of Iowa. He was a Yale Younger Poet in 1932 with *Worn Earth;* another book of poems, *Break the Heart's Anger,* came out in 1936.

⁴Carl Sandburg (1878–1967), the oft-anthologized Chicago poet and popular biographer of Lincoln.

⁵*Poetry:* the prestigious little magazine of which Zabel had just been named editor upon the sudden death of its founder Harriet Monroe (1860–1936).

July 12, 1937 / Trees, R.F.D.1. / Stamford, Conn.

Dear Morton:

I know that you've been sick, so probably haven't been attending to *Poetry* lately; but I want to make a protest to the proper persons about the treatment of my poems in the July number. I never received any notice of their having been accepted and was never sent any proof. Now I get a copy of *Poetry* with three of them in it, with an idiotic and inappropriate title for the group and meaningless individual titles for two of them. Furthermore, the last line but one of the last poem is misprinted, "Lights enter" instead of "Light enters."

Won't you see that the enclosed correction is printed in the next number of *Poetry*?

I assume that you have been having difficulties around there lately, and am not even clear as to whether you are the editor. I can't find your name or anything by you in this number. I was terribly sorry to hear about your illness and hope that you're on your feet again by now.

I saw Louise [Bogan] after she came back from Ireland: she seemed rather disillusioned about the old sod.

[A portion of this letter appears in *Letters on Literature and Politics* and in section IV.]

As ever, / Edmund W.

[Postcard]

September 29, 1937

Dear Morton:

I've been reading your book with much interest[1]—you're very good on [Archibald] MacLeish. I should have liked to see more of [Van Wyck] Brooks, [Paul Elmer] More, [H. L.] Mencken and Co. and less of [R. P.] Blackmur and Horace Gregory, and I think J[ohn] J[ay] Chapman should have been included. I'll discuss it at length when I see you. Do come to Stamford when you are on again. I'll be back the end of this week—I think it's probably a good thing as far as you're concerned that you won't be editing *Poetry*[2]— believe me, the field of contemporary verse is now too specialized for a critic. I hope you'll be writing more criticism using a larger scope.—Have you read H. James' Bench of Desolation[3]—which seems to me a masterpiece.

As ever, / Edmund W.

¹your book: *Literary Opinion in the United States.*

²Zabel resigned as of the October 1937 issue. George Dillon followed him in the post.

³Henry James's short story "The Bench of Desolation" is in vol. 12 of *The Complete Tales.* Leon Edel says it "belongs to a series of fictions which had their origins in the idea of 'too late.' " It deals with "human waste, mistaken lives, wrong decisions, lost opportunities."

Dec. 3, 1941, / Wellfleet, Mass.

Dear Morton: I was awfully glad to hear from you. I don't think it was entirely the compliments in our direction in which your letter abounds which made it seem one of your most brilliant, instructive, and entertaining. I was sorry to hear you had been so sick, but sometimes a fairly serious illness is just what people need, and you certainly sound as if you were in fine shape now.

I should like to take up each one of your paragraphs and discuss these various matters with you, but if there is any chance of your getting up here during the holidays, I'll wait until I see you. Do try to come. Let us know as far as possible in advance.

Mary has just finished her book[1] and delivered it to Simon and Schuster, who gave her a tremendous ovation and predict that it will be a best-seller— though I imagine that they think of all the books they publish as potential best-sellers.—I've been working on my novel,[2] which I am afraid is going to take me years. I'm also writing in the interstices a series of short stories called *Memoirs of Hecate County* a little in the same vein as the novel, some of which are coming out in the *Atlantic.* I'm curious to see what you'll think of them. This program stretches before me like Gibbon's Rome.[3]—Yes: I'm all washed up with the *New Republic.*[4]

Do come to see us! We've just had to spend two months in Polly Boyden's house while we had a heating system put in here. We are moving back today and preparing for holiday festivities, in which I hope you will share.

As ever, / Edmund W.

¹*The Company She Keeps,* a volume that contains the famous story "The Man in the Brooks Brothers Shirt."

²my novel: a projected work to be titled *The Story of the Three Wishes;* this ambitious undertaking was to survey three phases of Wilson's life: the social intensity of the jazz age, the political commitment of the Depression years, and the retreat to private life on the Cape in the 1940s. The book was never written, although a very different unpublished novel of Wilson's treating the 1920s has appeared as *The Higher Jazz,* edited by Neale Reinitz (1998).

³Edward Gibbon (1737–1794), i.e., his monumental *The History of the Decline and Fall of the Roman Empire.*

⁴The magazine's British backers, the Elmhirsts, and its editorial support for the war had led to an open breach and Wilson's subsequent departure.

Feb. 17, 1942, / Wellfleet, Mass.

Dear Morton: Mary has just been reading and I have been rereading In the Cage¹ and we have been going crazy trying to figure out what the numbers in the telegram mean. The most plausible explanation seems to be that they are the hour, day, and room-number for an assignation—but there seem to be too many numbers for that—and if we are supposed to take seriously what Mrs. Jordan says in the conversation at the end, the Captain and Lady Bradeen, aside from their love affair, had been up to something crooked together.—As a James adept, can't you enlighten us? Does Pelham Edgar, whose book I haven't got, throw any light on the subject?

We were very much disappointed that you couldn't get up while you were East.—We have nothing to report except literary activity. We hope slowly to wear the enemy down along several fronts. Besides Mary and me, Rosalind, now at home on her long winter vacation from Bennington, has been doing signed articles for the *Provincetown Advocate,* and Reuel has just learned his alphabet and is able to distinguish the letters on a typewriter.

As ever, / Edmund W

¹In vol. 10 of *The Complete Tales of Henry James.*

May 12, 1943, / 25 E 86th St., New York

Dear Morton: This is just a note in the confusion of liquidating our affairs here to go back up to the Cape.—I approve of your project for renaming Washington Place and wish I could believe that something will come of it.— The printers made a hideous mess of my anthology¹ (really a history of Am[erican] Lit[erature] in documents) and Doubleday have had to junk two tons of paper. They are printing it again, however, and it is supposed to be out June 4.—I'm glad you're getting along with the Conrad.²—I thought *Little Gidding*³ was better than its two predecessors but not really up to his best— the mystic note, wherever encountered, always gives me a pain in the neck.

As ever, / Edgar Wallace⁴

¹my anthology: *The Shock of Recognition: The Development of Literature in the United States Recorded by the Men Who Made It* (1943).

²See *Letters on Literature and Politics* for more on the quasi-comical story of Zabel's

perpetually deferred study of the Polish-born author of *Lord Jim* and countless other sea sagas, Joseph Conrad.

³*Little Gidding:* the final section of T. S. Eliot's *Four Quartets;* the disdain for the mystical that Wilson displays here is part of his general distaste for Eliot as a social and moral critic. (See his essay on Eliot in *The Bit Between My Teeth.*)

⁴Wilson occasionally engaged in the self-deflating gambit of choosing stuffy or pompous figures as his signature. Another was Edmund MacArthur Wilson. (See letters to Isaiah Berlin in this section.)

Sept. 10, 1943, / Wellfleet, Mass.

Dear Morton: I have written Sylvia Salmi¹ about you. You'd better inquire about prices—she might be more expensive than you're prepared for. I suggested to her, however, that you would be a good number for an exhibition of portraits of men that she is contemplating. We enjoyed your visit a lot. —Mary is going to New York Monday and will be at the Hotel Weston.—I am nearly done with a very long story which is probably the best damn thing I ever wrote—at least, it has given me more satisfaction, so far as I can remember, than anything else.²

As ever, / Edmund W.

¹Sylvia Salmi: a noted photographer who specialized in portraits of writers, including McCarthy in Wellfleet in 1942, Wallace Stevens, and Wilson himself.

²This probably refers to "The Princess With the Golden Hair," the story that forms the longest portion of *Memoirs of Hecate County.*

December 28, 1942 [1943, according to note by Zabel] / Wellfleet, Massachusetts

Dear Morton:

We were awfully glad to hear from you—had been wondering what had become of you.

We are just on the point of moving down to New York, where we're renting Polly Boyden's apartment till the first of April: 230 East 15th Street. Do let us know if you come on. Life is getting very difficult up here, with fuel, gas, and tire rationing, and we have been just overwhelmed by an unprecedented cold snap and blizzard.

Mary went down yesterday, or would send her love and acknowledgement of your special messages.

I am correcting proofs on a vast anthology of 425,000 words.¹ Some of the stuff I have put in it I hadn't reread for years, so that in a sense the book is new to me as I read it in proofs. I am very much impressed by it, and find that certain things are thrown into relief in a way I hadn't expected. If anybody should read it through, as I imagine nobody will, he would really learn a lot of important things about the development of American literature, of which it presents a sort of panorama in terms of the various writers writing about each other.

I am sorry to hear that Pater[2] seems abhorrent to you. In spite of the artificiality of his style, I've always thought he was the most intelligent Englishman of the fin de siècle. How about *Appreciations?* —but I see that you say some of his literary essays are good.

When are you going to finish your Conrad? After reading your letter, I hoped that you had now seen all the national sights, so that there would be nothing left for you to do but to turn to and produce something that the world would not willingly let die.

As ever, / Edmund

[1] *The Shock of Recognition.*
[2] Walter Pater (1839–1894), author of *Marius the Epicurean,* contemporary of Ruskin, and like Ruskin an influence in developing the aesthetic sense of the period.

New Yorker letterhead / September 9, 1947

Dear Morton:

I was glad to hear from you. You must have been having an awfully harrowing time with your sister's illness, but you are fortunate in having her get well: such things do not always clear up.

I was interested to see your Dickens prospectus[1]—I'm glad that you are carrying on the tradition. I've just acquired the excellent old Scribner edition of Dickens that has prefaces by Andrew Lang and, reading these prefaces, I have been struck by the lack of appreciation of the later Dickens that was possible at that time. The popular entertainer in Dickens—the man who could make you laugh or cry—was really the only thing that interested Lang. He thought *David Copperfield* the best Dickens novel and couldn't see anything at all in *Little Dorrit.* The whole development of Dickens' mind and art was lost on him. By the way, you ought to get for your course the edition of *Great Expectations* which has the original ending and a preface by Bernard Shaw. It was published over here, I think, in George Macy's limited editions, but a new cheap edition has just come out of England. The library wrote me about photostating my essay, which I told them to go ahead and do.

I hope you will get to the Cape. Let us know when you are coming and come here—unless the household should be too congested. We have a large and complicated family.

I've just done the page proofs of my European book and have got the volume of John Bishop's prose off to Scribner's, and am about to begin something new. About my articles: I'm going to get together from Doubleday—if I can bear it—a volume of selections from my literary journalism of the last twenty-five years.[2] Glad to hear of your progress with Conrad, who has too long awaited your signal from the grave.

As ever, / Edmund

[Handwritten postscript] The Conrad Portable has come since I wrote this. I haven't had a chance to read it, but I can see how well you've handled it. I should like to do a long article on it, but haven't read enough Conrad.

[1]your Dickens prospectus: Zabel's lifelong interest in Dickens can be seen in his 1927 piece on *Pickwick Papers* in *Commonweal* and in his stream of publications on the novels, notably a famous essay on the structure of *Bleak House* done for the Riverside edition.

[2]Probably *Classics and Commercials* (1950).

New Yorker letterhead / September 30, 1947

Dear Morton:

A tragedy has occurred. I came down last night to New York, full of enthusiasm for your Conrad Portable, with the intention of writing something about it—to find that, through misunderstanding, a note had already been done about it and the magazine was already printed. The Managing Editor here had forgotten that I had spoken about it over the telephone and, due to the fact that my copy had been sent to me direct from the publisher, had found the review copy in the office and given it to the briefer notices man. I am all the more annoyed because he says that the book is one of the weakest in the series when it is actually—as I had been going to say—one of the best, if not the best. The selection and placing of the pieces is excellent—you bring out in an interesting way such unfamiliar short stories as the admirable Prince Roman; and the preface is much the most valuable that I have seen in any of these volumes. (The only faults of this and the commentary are occasional repetitions of facts.) I wanted to say all this in the *New Yorker*. I am much disappointed at not being able to. Another reason for getting out your full-length book—so that I can give it a full-length review!

[F. O.] Matthiessen[1] has just produced a gigantic volume on the Jameses.

I wish he would publish the H.[enry] J[ames] journals instead of exploiting them in this way.

I have just come down from the Cape for ten days or two weeks. Elena is coming Friday. We'll be at the Hotel Carlyle if you should happen to hit New York while we're here.

As ever, / Edmund W

¹F. O. Matthiessen (1902–1950): Harvard professor and writer on American literature— *The Achievement of T. S. Eliot, American Renaissance, Henry James: The Major Phase,* and other books.

Wellfleet, Cape Cod, Mass. / January 31, 1950

Dear Morton:

I was very sorry to hear about your troubles. Louise [Bogan] had told me about your sister's illness. I am glad that you are going to get a vacation. Do get the Conrad out. If you should be coming to New York, be sure to let us know. We are going down there at the end of this week and have rented an apartment for six weeks at 17 East 84 Street—telephone: Butterfield 84312.

We have been up here on the Cape all summer and most of the winter up to now—though I spent several weeks before Christmas in Haiti—am doing some articles about it for a magazine called the *Reporter* that few people have ever heard of. The family are all fine—the children, as they get older, become continually more interesting.

About the Marxism article:¹ I'll be glad to have you use it. I usually get seventy-five or a hundred dollars nowadays, but will knock it down to you for fifty. You ought to have made the publishers pay for the permissions—though I know that this is hard to do.

We are coming back here the middle of March for the boys'² Easter vacation but, if you should come on, we'd be delighted to have you visit us. There's plenty of room now, because we've acquired an annex.

As ever, / Edmund W.

¹Probably "Marxism and Literature."
²Reuel Wilson and Henry Thornton, Edmund's and Elena's sons, respectively, by earlier marriages.

New Yorker letterhead / March 10, 1951

Dear Morton: Thank you for your letter. I am sorry not to have been able to answer it before, but have had to be back and forth a lot between here and

Red Bank, with the negotiations about my play[1] here—it's finally going to be done April 15 by ANTA—and Mother's household and affairs down there. I'll eventually sell the Red Bank house and concentrate on Wellfleet and Talcottville, but in the meantime have to keep it going awhile—partly on account of my mother's old maid, who has been with us ever since she was sixteen and is now in her seventies and doesn't know what to do without my mother, to whom she was a kind of appendage.

About Chicago: I have just made a new arrangement with the *New Yorker* which will enable me to unload on them some of my Americana, and I hope to be able to get along for awhile without otherwise working for a living. In the long run, however, I might sometime come to Chicago and do the Civil War writers. It is really a big subject, which I haven't begun to get up.[2]

I have the Bernard Shaw guide—thank you just the same. It was cute of him to do it as his final flicker.

We'll be here till the middle of April—after that, hope to get off for a trip to the South and then back to Wellfleet early in May. I look forward to seeing your books—please send them to Wellfleet, though. About your going to Europe: I don't know. I suppose it's useless to urge you just to settle down and finish Conrad!—In any case, I hope we'll see you soon. Elena sends love.

As ever, / Edmund W

[1] *The Little Blue Light.*
[2] *Patriotic Gore: Studies in the Literature of the American Civil War* finally came out in 1962.

Wellfleet, Cape Cod / September 22, 1963

Dear Morton:

[. . .] Am reading *Lord Jim* for the first time—a wonderful book.

Don't miss my income tax bombshell[1]—out November 1st, but I'll have a copy sent you.

As ever, / Edmund

[1] *The Cold War and the Income Tax.*

TO LIONEL TRILLING

[Postcard]

July 29, 1937. Trees, R.F.D.1, Stamford, Conn.

Dear Mr. Trilling: Thank you for your letter.—The second statement you quote was made only of Taine. The first one, however, does sound as if it was made about Arnold, too.[1] I stuck him in at the last moment, thinking I ought to mention an Englishman. It's wrong, as you say; and when I get the stuff out in a book, I'll correct it. Yours sincerely,

Edmund Wilson

[1]"The Historical Interpretation of Literature"; the corrected version appeared in later editions of *The Triple Thinkers*.

Jan. 10, 1939 / 233 Stamford Ave. / Stamford, Conn.
Dear Trilling: I just got your *Matthew Arnold*.[1] I read several chapters last night and thought they were awfully interesting; but I have to restrain myself from reading the rest of it immediately, because I've got so much other reading to do. What I'm writing you for is to ask you where you saw Marx's Palmerston pamphlet. I've only been able to get it in French. Is it in a library around here? I couldn't find it in the New York Public Library.

Yours sincerely, / Edmund Wilson

[1]*Matthew Arnold* (1939): Trilling wrote that he was inspired to persevere with his critical biography after Wilson tossed him a word of encouragement in the men's room at the New School for Social Research.

Jan. 16, 1939 / 233 Stamford Ave. / Stamford, Conn.
Dear Trilling: Thank you for your letter. It would be a great kindness if you could get the Palmerston pamphlet out and send it to me. But don't go to any serious trouble about it. I can always come in and read it in the library.

Yours sincerely, / Edmund Wilson

Feb. 7, 1939 / 233 Stamford Ave. / Stamford, Conn.
Dear Trilling: I sent the book back today insured. Thanks very much for your trouble about it. I figure that with the postage and the five cents a day for lateness I owe you about sixty cents.

Yours sincerely, / Edmund Wilson

Sept. 11, 1939 / Provincetown, Mass.
Dear Trilling: Barzun's book[1] has come. I've only had a chance to look into it and thought it was the kind of gracefully generalizing thing that I didn't particularly take to. But if you believe in him, I'll take another try at it.

Yes, I'd be glad if you'd bear me in mind in connection with a teaching job. I guess I got along all right at Chicago, though my performance was full of the ineptitudes of a beginner. Napier Wilt of the English Department offered to recommend me.—We've just come from the West up here, where I'm trying to finish a book before Christmas, by which time we hope to get to New York.

Best regards from Mary and me to both of you.

Yours sincerely, / Edmund Wilson

[Postscript] Congratulations on your assistant professorship—all achievement has its aspects of gloom.

[1] Jacques Barzun (b. 1907), the eminent historian of ideas and a colleague of Trilling's for many years at Columbia; the book was *Of Human Freedom* (1939).

New Republic letterhead / Dec. 4, 1940

Dear Trilling:

Could you be induced to review this long biography of Shelley by Newman Ivey White? If not, do you know of anybody who knows the subject and can write?

Yours sincerely, / Edmund Wilson

New Republic letterhead / Dec. 11, 1940

Dear Trilling:

I am leaving this department the first of January, and I'd like, if possible, to publish the Shelley review before I go.[1] You could have up to 1500 words. Would that be enough?

Yours sincerely, / Edmund Wilson

[1] Trilling's review, "Shelley Plain," appeared in the *New Republic* May 5, 1941.

New Yorker letterhead / September 24, 1945

Dear Trilling:

I am not the Edmund Wilson that Mr. Broughton knew, and I have written him explaining this.

I should like to see you people, and as soon as I can get my house running again,[1] I hope you will come to dinner.

Yours sincerely, / Edmund Wilson

[Postscript] I was very much interested in your review of the Fitzgerald book.[2] You appreciated his real superiorities, which I don't think many even of his admirers do.

[1]Wilson was involved in a stormy breakup of his marriage to third wife Mary McCarthy at the time.
[2]Trilling had a piece on Fitzgerald in the *Nation* on April 25, 1945.

Nov. 1, 1946 / The Minden Inn / Minden, Nevada

Dear Trilling: The Doubleday lawyer has just written me that you appeared at the trial of my book[1] and testified in our behalf. I am really extremely grateful. Such things are a nuisance to do and I don't think that many people would have been willing to go to the trouble and to risk the unpleasant publicity in associating themselves with a writer who had been put in a scandalous light. Thank you so much.

How are you and Diana?[2] I'm sorry not to have seen you in so long. I hope you're writing some more stories.

Sincerely, / Edmund Wilson

[1]The sale of *Memoirs of Hecate County* had been banned on grounds of obscenity: Doubleday appealed. They lost, the book was banned in New York and Doubleday was fined $1,000. A Supreme Court decision split 4–4 when Felix Frankfurter recused himself on the grounds that Wilson was a friend of his, leaving the earlier judgment intact. In spite of a favorable ruling in San Francisco in a new trial, and with a new lawyer, which Wilson won, the book was still considered obscene in New York, Boston, and Los Angeles. (Meyers cites the *New York Times* front-page article of November 7, 1946, pp. 315–16.)
[2]Diana Trilling (1905–1996), a contributor to the *Nation* and author of numerous articles and books, one of which was a memoir of her husband Lionel.

Jan. 15, 1953 / Mansgrove / Princeton, N. J.

Dear Lionel: Not only George Orwell but Eliot has been under the delusion that runcible is not a real word. I suppose you know that a runcible spoon was a three-tined spoon (I think, three) for extracting pickles from jars. I had some correspondence with Eliot about this question, but was unable to move him from his position, based on Lear's[1] having used it curiously as a nonsense word that had nothing to do with the original meaning: runcible cat, runcible bird, etc.—Have you ever gone into Lear aside from his nonsense rhymes? I think he is very attractive, and I do hope some day to write about him.

As ever, / Edmund W

[1]Edward Lear (1812–1888), the English nonsense writer.

Aug. 31, 1953 / Talcottville

Dear Lionel: Going through your *Liberal Imagination,* which Doubleday have just sent me in their reprint edition, I realize that I have never really taken account of your "Art and Neurosis" essay. About *The Wound and the Bow:* I never meant to imply that all art was the result of disease or deformity. Some artists work at their art as steadily and easily as any craftsmen in the less highly developed manual arts, and with as few psychological ups and downs—though I should think that the kind of work that demands intense concentration must always involve severe letdowns. On the other hand, I didn't mean to limit to artists the phenomenon of a wound coexisting with a bow. My collection of essays, like most of my books, was in the nature of variations on a theme—a theme which, for personal reasons (I happen to have seen a good deal of the wound and bow combination),[1] particularly interests me. I recognize, though, the impression that I am generalizing.—Your essay is full of good sense, as you usually are.—I don't think you exactly overdid Scott Fitzgerald[2] as some people seemed to feel. He deserves the "high seriousness" with which you treat him, and I like your essay better than almost anything that has been written about him. The trouble about Scott's case, when one begins talking about Goethe, etc., is that he didn't, in the third-rate Catholic school he went to, get enough of the right kind of education to sustain him in his absolutely first-rate ambitions. He was early bedazzled by the plutocratic society of St. Paul and Chicago and could never quite get over the idea that serious literature did not provide a real, or a sufficient, career. Yet his serious vocation was inescapable: he could never really get away from it to do anything else successfully; and you have to compare him to the great wits and poets that he wanted to emulate, not with the half-baked naturalists or the moderately distinguished popular writers that are so much commoner here.

How are you? Do you and Diana ever get to Cape Cod?—Everybody else does, and I get away in July for this unknown part of New York, where the only other literary man is Walter D. Edmonds.[3]—But in the off-seasons—before the 4th of July and after Labor Day—it is pleasant there and we love to see people.

Best regards, / Edmund Wilson

[1]Wilson may have been thinking of his father, his sensitive and imaginative cousin Sandy, himself, his friends Louise Bogan and Zelda Fitzgerald, and his former wife, Mary McCarthy, to name a few.

[2]"F. Scott Fitzgerald," also in *The Liberal Imagination,* expanded Trilling's introduction to a 1945 reprint of *The Great Gatsby,* incorporating material from his *Nation* piece of the same year.

[3]Author of *Drums along the Mohawk* (1936), and an upstate neighbor of Wilson's with squirearchical habits and tastes.

New Yorker letterhead / Feb. 5, 1955

Dear Trilling: Thank you for telling me about Kadushin.[1]—When I set out to read up Judaism I didn't realize that it is a subject that it is easier to get into than out of. I am still in its toils, but must soon try to cut down on my Hebraic reading and return to the American field.

Your new book arrived just before I left the country.[2] About *Mansfield Park:* I think it is my favorite of [Jane Austen's] novels. When I read it (some forty years ago), it did not seem to me different from the others, nor do I share the objections to it that some people feel. I don't think that Fanny is idealized or presented as a model heroine. Jane Austen is doing a series of portraits of different kinds of women. The girl in *Northanger Abbey* the romantic type; Emma the managing type, etc. Fanny is the mousy type, who devotes herself to people and gets there in the end on account of her dependability. Jane Austen brings out the good qualities by making the London characters rather fast and unreliable. I don't think that Jane Austen regards these latter as complete reprobates: they are part of her artistic scheme. Nor does she think the theatricals scandalous. That is all one episode of comedy, which hangs on the attitude of the heavy father, whom the author treats ironically. You see it all through Fanny's eyes, and the book rather resembles *What Maisie Knew*—which was, I suspect, partly inspired by it.—A certain kind of woman is likely to be annoyed by Fanny, because she thinks that Fanny represents Jane Austen's ideal of feminine character; but J[ane] A[usten] is much more objective and curious—much more like a man, in the kind of interest she takes in life—than the ordinary (even clever and imaginative) woman.

Yours fraternally in whatever it is that you and I are always supposed to represent,

Edmund Wilson

[1]Max Kadushin (b. 1895), *Understanding the Rabbinic Mind.*
[2]*The Opposing Self.*

May 3, 1957 / 16 Farrar Street / Cambridge, Mass.

Dear Lionel:

Bruce Bliven is really incredible. I was first on the staff of the *New Republic* in 1921, when Bruce had nothing to do with it. I threw up the job because

I wanted to go abroad. Afterwards, I was a "Contributing Editor" from November 25, 1925, to November 10, 1926, and after that a full editor till September 9, 1931. During this latter period, I of course attended the weekly editorial meetings. At this time I was not merely "book editor": except for the dramatic criticism, which was written by Stark Young, I ordered all the articles on cultural subjects in the back of the magazine and supplied the middle of the magazine with articles by myself and others. Croly[1] himself at that time directed the political policy—Bruce was managing editor and had very little to say about anything. After Croly's death, I had as much as anybody to do with the general policy and was responsible for giving it its Leftist slant—though the paragraphs and leading articles continued to be written by George Soule and Bruce. I took my name off the masthead in '31, but continued to contribute regularly, traveling around the country partly at the paper's expense doing political and labor reporting. In '33, the Elmhirsts became alarmed at what they thought was my excessive Leftism, and Bruce rejected an article of mine on the Pennsylvania milk strike, though the article had been ordered by him and was politically perfectly innocuous. Later, in '40 and '41, I made an attempt to get rid of Bruce as top editor, which he had been allowed to become, and install George Soule instead (which would have made it possible for me to work there again)—an attempt in which I was heartily backed by everyone connected with the paper, with the exception, of course, of Bruce himself. This is the "ultimatum" of which he speaks. I have told about what happened then in the chapter on war in *A Piece of My Mind.*

There is no need to write you about this but, having recently been given a complete set of the bound files of the *New Republic,* I have been looking it up for my own satisfaction, and may as well give you the benefit of it.

As ever, / Edmund W

[1]Herbert Croly, president and editor of the *New Republic.*

February 28, 1959 / Wellfleet, Mass.
Dear Lionel: I am enclosing a curious example of the way you and I have become inextricably tied together in England. The truth is that I did not care for *Lolita* and haven't even read it all. I have never written a word about it.[1] But the assumption is in England that since you have praised it, I must have too. I had another thing of the same kind in the *Observer,* which seems to have been thrown away. The writer of the Pendennis column said something

like this: "The American intellectuals—i.e., E. Wilson and L. Trilling—are now disgusted with politics." Are we disgusted with politics? Somebody from England who wrote an interview with me,[2] may, I think, have been given this impression, and you, I suppose, got dragged into it. The queerest case of all was a review in one of the English weeklies which began by saying something like, "It looks as if we are going to be obliged to take our ideas about literature from F. R Leavis,[3] Lionel Trilling or Edmund Wilson." The assumption was that the English reader would have to choose between us. I can understand that to choose to be directed by Leavis would necessarily exclude reading anybody else; but I don't see why you and I should be mutually exclusive, especially since we are bracketed so often. I suppose that the important thing is that we have both read Matthew Arnold,[4] so seem to the British something relatively familiar.

Best regards, / Edmund W

[1]For more on Wilson's distaste for the book and his resistance to writing about it, see section VI.

[2]John Wain interviewed Wilson in Talcottville for the *Observer* in 1957; Henry Brandon queried him for the *New Republic* in 1959, the latter "Conversation" reprinted in *From the Uncollected Edmund Wilson.*

[3]F. R. Leavis (1895–1978): English critic; author of *D. H. Lawrence* (1930); editor, with his wife Queenie, of *Scrutiny.* One sharp difference between him and the other two is that, with the exception of Eliot's *Four Quartets,* he was unwilling or unable to appreciate anything written after 1930.

[4]Matthew Arnold (1822–1888): English poet, essayist, and critic whose *Culture and Anarchy* typifies his method of interpreting the practice of criticism as embracing broadly humanist as well as strictly literary concerns—an interpretation emulated by both Wilson and Trilling.

August 25, 1959 / Talcottville

Dear Lionel: I was very glad to get the *Partisan Review* and find out what you had actually said at the Frost banquet.[1] In my opinion, Frost is partly a dreadful old fraud and one of the most relentless self-promoters in the history of American literature. The general acceptance of him as "a symbol of America" —a real old sturdy simple New Englander—has become absolutely revolting. I have always thought—though he bores me—that there was at least a flicker of a poet there, and when I met him for the first time not long ago, I realized he did take literature seriously. (He seemed to me like a clever old elephant, with his thick skin and bright little eyes.) But you have made him sound more interesting than I ever thought he was. I must read the poems you speak of. Certainly the effect of his work is chilling, and whatever is authentic there is not buckwheat pancakes and maple syrup. I am wondering what he said in response to your speech. Is he himself so taken in by the good gray grandpa image that he was as much startled as everybody else? (Carl Sandburg is another old fraud.)

Votre semblable, votre frère,[2] / Edmund W

[1]Trilling's essay has been reprinted in *Robert Frost: A Collection of Critical Essays,* edited by James M. Cox.

[2]A variation on the lines from Baudelaire, famously reworked into Eliot's *Waste Land;* here Wilson seems to use them in the sense of saluting Trilling as his kindred spirit, his brother.

TO DAWN POWELL

[On p. 398 of *Letters on Literature and Politics* there appears under a drawing by Wilson of a wild-haired bespectacled writer (signed J. Sargent) the following note in Wilson's handwriting: "For years Dawn Powell and I carried on a correspondence in which she was supposed to be Mrs. Humphrey Ward and I a seedy literary man named Ernest Wigmore. Later on, we were a sophisticated French pair: Raoul and Aurore." About one such exchange involving a French valentine cum Christmas card Dawn Powell, who has transcribed Wilson's accompanying note, appends this comment: "This handwriting is difficult. Here, very freely, is the substance of the letter:"]

[probably 1963]

Dear Aurore:

I hope I am not too indiscreet in confiding to you that I taught Mme. Anthony almost everything she knows about those intimate mysteries which she describes with such charming nonchalance. As I think you were not eager to permit me to lead you to the end, you obliged me to leave you, so to speak, when only half of the journey had been completed . . .

[on the card a Chevalier-like figure surrounded by hearts says:] Je n'ai pas besoin de grand chose pour te parler d'amour . . . [here the card opens on a disheveled less-Chevalier-like figure waving a shot glass in one hand, carrying a liquor bottle in the other] seulement d'une bonne cuite!

[Postscript in Wilson's handwriting:] Joyeux noël! / Raoul

[Postcard showing a colony of artists at work on their canvases]

Nov. 11, 1937 / Provincetown, Mass.

Spring in Paris—ah, those mad nights and glorious days!

I miss you. Rodolphe

[A jumbo postcard of Monticello]

16 April, 1946 / Charlottesville, Va.

Dear Dawn: I'm visiting Virginian relatives down here. All the Jeffersonian end of it is wonderful, but what has happened to the FFV's [first families of Virginia] is something that has often made me think of you and wish you could go with me to some of the parties in which Southern hospitality has involved me. You don't know what drinking means till you come to some town like this in the South.—They tell me that a Mr. Dos Passos from the North has been here inquiring about buying Monticello and that he has been asking around among the colored population to find out whether there are any who would like to go back to slavery in the service of a kind master.

Esmond Whitmore

February 15, 1948 / Vendome, Boston

Dear Dawn:

We were delighted by your various consignments of curiosa. That combination of sex lecturing with dancing is something of which I hadn't dreamed. I'm going to suggest to the *New Yorker* that they ought to take cognizance of it.

About your book:[1] I had the feeling that I often have with your novels— that you brought it out at a stage when you had merely got the material lined up so that you could see what problems still had to be dealt with. It is full of holes that ought to be filled. Sometime you must give a book six months more and turn out a masterpiece. It is a pity you didn't know Hroswitha.[2] My idea would be that Frederick and Lyle, when they are married, ought to collaborate on a play that would deal with Hroswitha and the men who helped her. The theme of collaboration would enable the play to reflect the relations of Lyle with her former husband. But the piece would be a dreadful flop, and this would seriously trouble Lyle, who would have to find a new collaborator while Frederick reverted to downtown bars. All this would be communicated to the reader in a final conversation between the four old soaks in the bar, when they see Frederick come in alone.

So much of the book is brilliant that the reader is all the more disappointed that certain important aspects of the story are never grappled with at
all. I wish I could have seen it earlier and persuaded you to work at it more.

We are here in the Vendome Hotel waiting for the arrival of the baby.[3]
The place would interest you, because it is mainly inhabited by hundreds of
old ladies, each, Elena, thinks, with an embittered parasite who sits across
from her at every meal.

By a coincidence, we are just about to go over to the Boston Public Library to see the Hungarian scholar[4] who has the theory about Hroswitha and
who is curator of rare books there.

I am trying to picture [John] Dos [Passos] palling around with [J. P.]
Marquand.[5] Be sure to keep me informed of any important developments.

Love, / Wig

[1]*Locusts Have No King.*

[2]Hroswitha: tenth-century German nun, a playwright who wrote lively, humorous
plays.

[3]Helen Miranda, the Wilson's daughter, was born February 19.

[4]Zoltán Horazsti: Wilson's first Hungarian tutor, whose enthusiasm for Hungarian
literature was boundless—see *The Sixties.*

[5]In spite of Dos Passos's political right turn Wilson evidently had trouble envisioning
the author of *U.S.A.* socializing with the author of *The Late George Apley.*

[Undated fragment begins on p. 3]

[probably 1950]

[. . .]

My book of old articles is out.[1] *Time* got a statement on me from Somerset Maugham (who has been over here again presenting to the Library of Congress another one of his apparently innumerable manuscripts of *Of Human
Bondage*). He revenged himself for my criticism[2] with the most scarifying cli-
ché in his armory, saying that *[Memoirs of] Hecate County* was "execrably
bad."

We have been leading such a monotonous life—are both recovering from
colds.—By the way, I am negotiating with a London publisher about bringing
out *Hecate County* in England[3]. It would be a great help to me to have them
pay the advance—I'm standing out for $1000—to somebody over there (as I
did with Gollanz-Henry last summer), because otherwise it takes forever to
collect it. But if I got them to pay it to you, I suppose that you'd have no way
of having me paid over here? My great idea is to get it in time for Christmas.

We are also in considerable penury.—[Hume] Cronyn and the Theater Guild have still not come to terms about my play,[4] though we were on the verge of settling it—or is it always like this in the theater?

Well, we are all rooting for you over here. Don't let those frogs get you down. I'll be interested to see whether you think the English are better or worse than the French. I think you would enjoy Italy. It always seems jolly after France.—Elena sends love and encouragement.

[1]*Classics and Commercials.*

[2]"Somerset Maugham and an Antidote," Wilson's review of Maugham's *Then and Now,* ran in the *New Yorker* in May 1946 and was reprinted in *Classics and Commercials.*

[3]W. H. Allen published the book in England in 1951.

[4]*The Little Blue Light;* it was finally performed by Cronyn and his wife Jessica Tandy in 1950.

Jan. 5, 1952 / Wellfleet, Mass.

Dear Dawn: I had trouble, too, with that part of Dos's book[1]—those ice cream sodas were almost too much for me. But I think it was all a conscious attempt to catch Katy's point of view and impersonate, as it were, her early milieu—it is always the milieux he impersonates, trying to tell the story in language appropriate to the different ones; he is not very good at impersonating his characters. If you have finished the book, you have seen that he has a certain delayed revenge on the bucolic outfit. They really did torment him—as he makes them do in the book—by making up a fantasy that he had been married before and so could not legally marry Katy, and in a lot of other ways.—I hope this answers your question.

I have read Dolby's book on Dickens and quote from it in my definitive essay.[2]

We expect to be in New York by Feb. 1.

Best wishes for the New Year, which I feel /

is going to be a horror, / EW

[1]*Chosen Country* (1951): the novel was conceived as a tribute to Dos Passos's first wife, Katherine.

[2]"The Two Scrooges": in spite of Wilson's light tone the essay did come close to being definitive—Dickens scholar Ada Nisbet has said it began a whole new generation of Dickens studies.

[Postcard of an old synagogue in Safad]

May 21, 1954

Thanks for the *Tribune.*—I'm sorry about Louise [Bogan]. Please tell her I hope she is better. Give her my love.—This old city of Safad is way up in the mountains above Galilee. It is becoming more and more of an art colony, like Taos and Provincetown. In the Middle Ages, the Cabbala was written here.

EW

October 14, 1957 / Wellfleet, Mass.

We have just read your book[1] with enthusiasm. It seems to me more complete and convincing than anything else of yours, and is such a departure from anything else that I was rather astonished by it and dare say I might not have recognized your hand if I hadn't known you had written it.

In aiming at psychological truth rather than satire you have pulled off a masterly performance; the relations between the three women are admirable and never allowed to become melodramatic.

To say the book is much better than TRIO or Mlle. Sagan[2] is not saying very much; but it is as good as the best of these French novels—Françoise Mallet's LE REMPART DES BEGUINES, for example—better than this, in fact, in being more mature. I speak of these French productions, because you are aiming at more or less the same sort of thing. Am much impressed by the French-type purity of style and sense of classical form that you have rather unexpectedly developed. I think you are excellent on both Paris in winter and the Hudson River families. Did you ever read Ronald Firbank's[3] books *Caprice* and *Inclinations* which deal, in a more cockeyed way, with somewhat similar themes?

I've been reading AROUND THE WORLD WITH GENERAL GRANT by an Irish journalist.[4] [. . .] he has a very funny chapter on the Americans in Paris which shows that in the 1870s they were already like what you describe. [. . .]

Edmund Wilson

[1]*A Cage for Lovers.*
[2]*Bonjour Tristesse, Aimez-Vous Brahms?* and others.
[3]Ronald Firbank (1886–1926): novelist with a small cult following, many novelists themselves; *Valmouth* (1919) is perhaps his best-known work.
[4]John Russell Young (1841–1899).

Jan. 26, 1959 / Wellfleet, Mass.

Dear Dawn: Thanks for the Sheilah Graham[1] review and the bulletin from the field in Cuba. Have you seen my S[heilah] G[raham] review in the *N[ew] Y[ork]er*? I saw something of her when she was living with Scott, just after his death, and later on. She is anything but a "pretty hollow shell." She came up to stay with us here when I was working on the MS of *The Last Tycoon*,[2] and I was impressed with her British good sense and her intelligent grasp of what Scott had been doing. She was amusing and very realistic about Hollywood, and I have wondered how she could keep on with that job so long.[3] In those days, she made no effort for glamour and was extremely modest about herself, and, after Scott's death, she made no attempt to exploit her relationship with him. One of the things that particularly impressed me, besides her helpfulness with the MS, was her quietly responsible relationship with Scottie.[4] Later on, when she was married, when Elena and I had lunch with her at the Algonquin,[5] she had somewhat changed her genre in the direction of that picture on the jacket, which does not really look very much like her. She had two children, then divorced her husband. She is very self-sufficient and practical. In Scott's case, she took over somebody who was unreliable in certain ways, and needed support. With a self-reliant husband, she would probably feel uncomfortable. The kind of girl you imagine would never have done for Scott, who was not, I think, easily seduced by sex and who was extremely susceptible to boredom.

Life up here is monotonous, with little prospect of getting away—though Elena hopes to get to New York to see Henry's recent twin girls. I am performing prodigies for the Indians, who have never been given the right kind of publicity before.[6]

Why don't you cash in on the new *Esquire* like everybody else?—Did you see Dorothy Parker on Sheilah Graham?

Love, / Wig

[1]Sheilah Graham: a pretty English girl whose lower-class background and engagement to a titled Englishman provided a model for the girl in *The Last Tycoon; Beloved Infidel,* her account of her affair with F. Scott Fitzgerald, had just been published.
[2]Wilson edited, and wrote an introduction for, the incomplete manuscript of this final novel, which was published posthumously.
[3]She wrote about it in *Confessions of a Hollywood Columnist.*
[4]Scott and Zelda's daughter.
[5]The venerable hotel on 44th Street, site of the legendary Round Table.
[6]Wilson's *Apologies to the Iroquois* chronicles the struggles of the tribe to fend off further erosion of their land under Robert Moses' Power Authority. The book, which first appeared in the *New Yorker,* brought welcome attention to their cause.

March 10, 1961 / 12 Hilliard St. / Cambridge, Mass.
Dear Dawn: We saw [John] Dos [Passos] here—much cheered up by what Houghton Mifflin were doing with his book.[1] I haven't read it yet, but Elena

says that it is much better than his other recent novels.—Nothing of interest to report except that I have developed an occupational disease due to reading dusty and greasy old books about the Civil War.² For the last two winters I have had prolonged attacks of something like hay fever. I finally went to an ear, nose, and throat man, and he diagnosed it. It seems that it is a well-known allergy. They tell me here that there was a librarian who suffered it so badly that he had to give up his job. It makes me feel that I am a martyr to scholarship.—We may get to New York again sometime this month.

Love, / Wig

¹*Midcentury.*
²For *Patriotic Gore.*

[Postcard]

Aug. 20, 1962 / Talcottville

I am furious that you should have gone to [Malcolm] Cowley instead of to me. This I cannot forgive!

Raoul

Hotel Victoria / Via Campania / Roma, March 18, 1964

Dear Dawn:

I hear from Dos [Passos] and Rosalind that you have been sick and in the hospital. Now, Rosalind says, you are out. We hope that you've recovered from whatever it was.

We spent four months in Paris, which is very unpleasant now. The air is bad, the people are drab, and DeGaulle, though entirely out of touch with the people, makes himself everywhere felt as a repressive and oppressive presence. He won't even allow the man who is to run against him in the next election to be heard on TV or radio till two weeks before the election. The cops are everywhere and beat up student demonstrators. And then there is the awful winter weather, which Paris has always had. But we couldn't get away from Paris, because I had had to bring over a whole library to do a long *New Yorker* piece about Canada,¹ and I couldn't travel with it.

Now at last we have come to Rome, which is full of sun and cheerful activity. [A portion of this letter is in section IV.]

Dos did an absurd review of my tax book,² and has sent me something. that is even more absurd. I enclose them for your information. I never should have thought he would be capable (at the age of sixty-seven, I think) of all this pure unadulterated guff. What has happened to your musical?[3] Do write me if you're feeling strong enough. I'll be here till April 10th, then for a month at the Hotel Gellert in Budapest—then back to Wellfleet in May.

Love, / Edmund

[1] This would come out in book form as *O Canada*.
[2] *The Cold War and the Income Tax;* though they had once shared leftist views, Dos Passos had become increasingly conservative and the two wrangled over politics whenever they met, as well as, on occasion, in print.
[3] Powell's adaptation of her novel *The Golden Spur;* she became too weak to complete the project.

TO BETTY HULING

Nov. 15, 1941 / Wellfleet, Mass.
Dear Betty: Thanks for your letter. It looks as if Bruce [Bliven][1] expected the *N[ew] R[epublic]* to fold up. Do you think so? I was asked last summer by *Uncensored* to write them an expose of what had been happening at the *N[ew] R[epublic]*. I declined for the reason, among others, that some of the most important facts I knew came from you and I didn't want to get you in any trouble. If you are going to lose your job anyway, maybe I'll reconsider. Now don't mention this to anybody— that means Otis Ferguson,[2] too. Please be sure to let me know what happens. I'm surprised that you were able to restrain yourself with Bruce. Why, by the way, does he want to get rid of you? Is it a question of cutting down expenses?

As ever, / Bunny W.

[1] Bruce Bliven Sr.: editor of the *New Republic* after the death of Herbert Croly.
[2] Otis Ferguson: the film critic of the *New Republic* in the 1930s.

July 4, 1945 / Hotel de La Ville / Vialistina, Rome
Dear Betty: I was awfully glad to get your long letter and I appreciate very much your paying the bills, etc. Clisby,[1] apparently, has been raising Cain about his rent, and I am having a thousand dollars sent from London to the Red Bank bank. When you get the notice from the bank that this has been received, would you mind calling up Clisby and telling him that he can put through the check I have sent him? I'm coming home early in August. [The

remainder of this paragraph appears in *Letters on Literature and Politics.*] Am going to wind up my work here in Italy, and take two or three weeks in Greece, then go home. Europe, though interesting, is disgusting at present, as the swimming and bicycling season wears on. I think more and more longingly of God's country.

Your question about heart interest came apropos, as what I shouldn't have thought possible at my age, I fell terribly in love in London with a young English girl[2]—twenty-seven and one of the brightest I have ever known and—need I say?—rather neurotic. We talked about getting married and she was trying to join me in Italy. When it looked as if she wouldn't be able to, I flew over to London (which you can do in a night) and spent much of two weeks there. I doubt now whether anything ever comes of it. I suppose, after my experience with Mary,[3] I've been a lunatic to think of getting married to an even younger girl—its like those promoters in New York during the Boom who used to borrow gigantic sums of money to put up gigantic hotels; then, when the enterprise went bankrupt, borrowed even larger sums, which the bankers would lend them in the hope of getting their original losses back, to put up larger and even more unsuccessful hotels. But I suppose that these last years have made me tinder for any real spark and I haven't been so upset since my youth—which I find rather disgusting and embarrassing. I have told no one else about this, so don't mention it even to Rosalind. My story is that I went back to England to arrange about the English publication of my book. I did do this and have got Secker and Warburg to agree to bring it out without changing a word, though Doubleday Doran are now balking. . . . [Several paragraphs, not included here, appear in *Letters on Literature and Politics.*]

There'd be a lot to say about Italy, but I'm not prepared to undertake it in a letter. I hope to be seeing you soon—though you may be away on vacation, I suppose, when I get back in August.

Love as ever, / EW

[Postscript] Postcards [enclosed] show Adam and Eve before and after eating Apple, as portrayed by Italy's late great Buonarotti.

---

[1]Clisby: Wilson's landlord for an apartment he and Mary McCarthy had rented on Henderson Place. Rosalind speaks of the harrowing rent arrears situation in *Near the Magician*, pp. 117–20.

[2]Mamaine Paget; Wilson proposed to her, but she chose to live with, and later married, the novelist Arthur Koestler.

[3]Mary McCarthy, Wilson's third wife, with whom marriage and getting a divorce were equally fraught with difficulty.

Dear Betty: Will you please find out Michael Straight's[1] address and forward this to him yourself?

How are you? I have been having a hell of a time lately. Mother has been very ill and in the hospital at Red Bank—she is now back at home and much better, and I have had to be down there a good deal. At the same time, I have been ill myself, never got over my laryngitis in New York and finally had to have a small operation on one of my vocal chords.

Can't you arrange to come up here and see us this summer? If you can, let us know when.

Love, / Bunny W

[1]Straight, stepson of the *New Republic*'s British patron, Leonard Elmhirst, had become its editor in 1940 and took a strong pro-British line. Wilson's isolationist position led to an open breach; he resigned in December 1940 and never wrote for the magazine again. Many years later Straight would cause a stir with the publication of *After Long Silence,* the story of his career as a Soviet agent.

June 4, 1950

Dear Betty: I am sending you a copy of *The Little Blue Light.* There seems to be a pretty good chance that it will be tried out in Cambridge this summer— at least, the man who runs the little Cambridge theatre has given me some money for an option. I wish you would send me a proof of the *N[ew] R[epublic]* review. Aside from the problem of a job, I don't see why you should grieve at the *New Republic*'s going out of business. There is already nothing left but a greasespot. I'll sound out the *New Yorker* about you, but, so long as Ruth Flint is functioning, I don't think the situation there is particularly hopeful. But I'll keep you in mind, as they say. We're delighted at the prospect that you may come up. Don't hesitate to come during the summer. It would be fun to have you when the children are here. Reuel is here now; Rosalind comes often for weekends; and Henry[1] will be here in ten days or so—he is going to Europe for part of July and August; in the meantime, I'll have to be going back and forth between here and Red Bank, and next time I'll ask you up if I have a chance. Elena sends love.

As ever, / Bunny

[1]Henry Thornton, Elena's son from her first marriage.

July 28, 1950 / Wellfleet, Mass.

Dear Betty: Our general feeling is that we'd love to pay you a visit, but your postcard is rather vague. In the first place, you give no address, so I can only hope this letter reaches you [on Martha's Vineyard]. In the second place, can you arrange for us to stay somewhere because, remembering my other visit, I can't imagine going and coming back all in one day. I should think we'd have to spend at least two nights there—pretty expensive, isn't it? It would be a question of Elena and me and Reuel. My play opens in Cambridge August 14th, so it would have to be sometime before that. If you are really sincere in your invitation, please supply us with more details. Remember that it will take us two hours to get to Woods Hole from here. When do the boats go? I suppose that the weekend of August 4–7 would be the ideal time from our point of view, as Hedwig's daughter can come to stay with her, and she wouldn't be alone in the house with Helen.

Love, / EW

May 27, 1952
Dear Betty: We didn't know about your operation, and would have called you up in the hospital. I'm glad you're feeling so much better—we were worried about you in New York. Why don't you come up here before you go to the Vineyard? We'd love to have you—Elena says to urge you to come. She has been madly conducting the spring housecleaning and reorganizing the furniture so as to absorb the Red Bank stuff, and she fell down the pump-hole in the tool house today, and hurt her knee quite badly.

Otherwise, we are doing well. The children will all be here for Memorial Day. [A portion of this letter is in section IV.]

I am going over to Talcottville the first of the week to get some improvements made, and some new equipment installed then. We are going to spend August there, while the Dos Passoses come to stay here. Now, do try to come to see us. Elena sends lots of love.

As ever affectionately, / EW

Nov. 8, 1953 / Wellfleet, Mass.
Dear Betty: I was interested in the magazine, though I kept looking at it as if it were *Life* and expecting a spot of cheesecake. I'm glad you're enjoying the job. I learn that the *N[ew] R[epublic]* has finally been sold to somebody with no connection with the Elmhirsts.

We have all been rather miserable lately. First I was immobilized with gout (which I'm now over); then Elena, Rosalind, and Helen all came down with this new-type flu. Elena and Helen are still in bed. Otherwise, we are doing well. [The next sentence appears in *Letters on Literature and Politics*.] I am making money out of my paperback editions (have sold four books to the Anchor and Ballantine series), and feel a little, for the first time in my life, as if I were a real success. We are going to Europe at the end of December—I've been asked to do a month (February) at that Salzburg American seminar. After that, if I'm not worn-out, the *New Yorker* will send me to Israel. Back in April, I guess. If I get to town before Christmas, I'll call you—should like to hear about your new magazine.

Love, and from Elena, / Bunny

Jan. 11, 1954 / London

Dear Betty: I wish you would send a copy of your Burgess-Maclean[1] article airmail to Cyril Connolly: Oak Cottage, Elmstead, near Ashford, Kent. He has written on the subject himself and will be interested to see it.

We have been having a very good time here. London seems pleasanter and more normal than I expected it to. Helen feeds the swans in the Serpentine and is clamoring to ride in the park. Elena is seeing her relations, and Poppa is doing a pretty good business with publishers and wittily conversing with English friends.

Love, / EW

[1]The infamous British spies. See letters to Cyril Connolly in this section.

May 24, 1954

Dear Betty: We were glad to hear from you—sorry your magazine has folded up. On our trip we had a good time in London (three weeks), a disastrous week in Paris—we were there during the cold spell and all got sick; a curious month in Salzburg, where I had to lecture at 9 in the morning in a cold baroque castle, coughing and wheezing and blowing my nose; a varied week in Germany in Munich and Frankfurt, partly pleasant, partly depressing. I then set out for Israel, leaving Elena in Germany, where she visited her family[1] and spent some time near where Henry is stationed. It turned out to be somewhat difficult for her— she has been considerably alienated from Germany and was glad, I think, to get away. I went to Rapallo for a couple of days, where Sam Behrman[2] was staying and took us to see Max Beerbohm.[3] Then I sailed from Venice to Israel, where I had a very good time, with a visit of five days to

Jordan. (This sounds, I am afraid, a little like one of Morton Zabel's letters.) You will read about all this in the *New Yorker,* so I won't enlarge upon it. I met the family in Paris, where we had a good week before sailing. [The following two sentences appear in *Letters on Literature and Politics.*] We spent a couple of afternoons with Malraux,[4] who does a good deal to redeem the otherwise rather sorry state of France. I was beginning to have some of my old feeling for Paris and was rather reluctant to leave and come back to the McCarthy atmosphere. Even Israel, with its Arab-Israeli quarrel is idyllic compared to here.

I hope we shall see you before long. Good luck in the meantime. Elena sends love.

EW

[A postscript is in section IV.]

[1] Elena's family founded Mumm champagne and continued to make wine, though the company was confiscated during the war.

[2] S. N. Behrman (1893–1973): Broadway adapter of Marcel Pagnol's novels about Marseilles—which became the 1950s musical *Fanny*—and writer who was working on a profile of Max Beerbohm for the *New Yorker,* later to be a book, *Portrait of Max.*

[3] Max Beerbohm (1872–1956): British caricaturist and wit, author of *Zuleika Dobson.*

[4] André Malraux (1901–1976): author of *Man's Fate;* a celebrated French novelist and writer of whom Wilson wrote often and admiringly.

Dec. 14, 1956

Dear Betty: What has become of you? We went to Europe last July, leaving Helen with friends. Elena came back in August, I in September. [A portion of this letter is in section IV.] I am still doing moderately well—am constantly attacked by the Catholics on account of the D[ead] S[ea] scrolls, and have now had a strong protest from Homo headquarters (Parker Tyler) on account of my chapter on sex in my last book.[1] I'm sending you a copy of this letter, which has something about the *New Republic* crisis of long ago. We are going to live in Boston after Jan. 10, am renting a delightful house. Love from everybody—do write a line.

Edmund

[1] *A Piece of My Mind: Reflections at Sixty* (1950).

Jan. 5, 1957

Dear Betty: We were awfully glad to hear from you. We are moving to Cambridge the 18th to spend the rest of the winter: 16 Farrar St. The *New Republic* people, it seems, have only just found out about the references to them in my book. Michael Straight called up Roger Straus in such a hysterical state that Roger couldn't recognize his voice, and thought somebody was trying to impersonate him. He threatened to sue, and soon after somebody else called up representing himself as a lawyer for Bruce Bliven and the Elmhirst interests. I don't believe, however, that they will do anything except denounce me in the so-called *N[ew] R[epublic]*. The joke is that the magazine had already published a very favorable review by Leon Edel.[1] We are glad you have got a regular job. I tried to get them interested in you, at the *New Yorker* when Ruth Flint died, but evidently nothing came of it.

Love as ever, / EW

[1]The Edel review of Wilson's *A Piece of My Mind* ran December 17, 1956.

Wellfleet letterhead / November 4, 1958

Dear Betty: I've been so long in answering your letter because I've had to take more than a month doing an article about the Pasternak book,[1] which I only finally got off last Saturday. I'm sorry to hear that you've been depressed, but we've been having our low moments, too. I think that the general state of the world makes personal troubles more discouraging. [There follows a paragraph, omitted here, on Wilson's upcoming *Apologies to the Iroquois,* which appears in *Letters on Literature and Politics.*]

We never get to New York anymore. I have to go to Boston to see Reuel (who is doing well at Harvard), work in the Harvard Library, and get my semi-teeth installed. And Elena's old Uncle Walter had a stroke and was out of his mind, and was in an institution there. He has now been sent back to Germany.

[A portion of this letter is in section IV.]

We wish we had a chance to see you. We should love to have you come up here. You can take a plane to Boston, and from Boston it is twenty minutes by plane to Hyannis. (Don't take the other route.)

Elena sends much love—as does your old admirer, / EW

[1]*Doctor Zhivago.*

April 26, 1966 / Wellfleet, Mass.

Dear Betty: I am sending off the proofs[1] to you today. The last three sections of the book will reach you from the *New Yorker,* where they are transferring the corrections from these proofs to the *New Yorker* proofs. In going through them, I have in general only checked on the places—in *Europe Without Baedeker* proper—where I had revised the text of the first edition. Please go through it especially for typos and inconsistencies of usage. When you have finished, call John Peck[2] at Farrar, Straus, and he will come or send someone to get it. And be sure to send me a bill. If you want to ask about anything call me collect: area code 617-349-3746.

Hope you are feeling better. [The following sentences appear in *Letters on Literature and Politics*.] I am feeling rather old myself, and even a pint of Scotch is likely to enfeeble me the next day. But as the Hebrew Bible keeps saying at intervals: Hazayk, hazayk, Venit-hazayk—be strong, be strong, let us make ourselves strong.

Love from us both, / EW

[1]*Europe Without Baedeker: Sketches Among the Ruins of Italy, Greece, and England* (1947). Betty Huling often did freelance editorial jobs for Wilson.
[2]Production manager at Farrar, Straus.

June 1, 1966 / Boonville, RFD 1

Dear Betty: The Straus office is very insistent that they should pay your bill, so make it $150 and send it to me, and I will send it to them. I've been having rather a thin time up here on this visit and am going back to Wellfleet this Friday. I'm getting a big literary award—a medal with five thousand dollars.[1] They're coming up to Utica to present it to me, and immediately afterwards I'm flying back. Rosalind is coming this afternoon to be present for the occasion. I do hope you get a regular job.

Love as ever, / Bunny

[1]The National Medal for Literature.

Talcottville letterhead / Sept. 5, 1968

Dear Betty: Bob Hatch told me you were in the hospital, and I wrote you c/o St. Vincent's. I wonder whether you got the letter because he now tells me that you have moved. I asked you whether there was anything I could do for you—hospital expenses, for example. I am relatively rich now, having had the Aspen Award of $30,000. Don't hesitate to suggest it if you need money. I am sending you Wilfred Sheed's novel *Office Politics*, which will remind you at moments of the *NR*. The big difference is, however, that Sheed was working for the Catholic weekly *Commonweal* and that none of the liberal weeklies could ever have had a Catholic editor, so the whole picture is rather out of focus. But the novel is very amusing.

I have come down with a horrible aliment, shingles—most uncomfortable, and the drugs they give you dope you. Am recovering now, however. I wrote you about the family in my other letter. This morning Elena has gone to the opening fall meeting of what she calls the League of Old Lady Voters.

Get well. I hope to see you when I come to New York later on.

Love as ever, / Bunny

[Betty Huling died in 1969.]

TO HELEN MUCHNIC

May 20, 1946 / Wellfleet, Mass.

Dear Helen: I've enjoyed the Pasternak poems—though I sometimes understand them only dimly. It's the very first feeling of spring, isn't it?—wonderfully conveyed, so far as I can judge.—I'm enclosing a review by Dallia[?] of Schuman's book,[1] which will I hope set you right about this charlatan.

It has been absolute bliss to get back up here and have all my time to myself. This colored man I have brought with me, Annie's son, has turned out to be extraordinary. He can do everything and is getting the house into better shape than it has ever been in, after its period of decline and disrepair under the reign of Rosalind and Jeannie.[2] Am also trying to restore my decaying physique.—Reckie, the dog, is back with me and I feel now that he is my only living link with the existence of my first year in Wellfleet—it is queer to reestablish my relations with him and see him fall back into his old habits. My going away to Europe the spring before last seems to have made a break in my life that I was hardly aware of at the time and, as I have been cleaning out my study here, all the old magazines and bills and remnants of Reuel's toys have seemed connected with some period almost as far away as my school or college days. I alternate between a kind of sad disgust at throwing old cold things away and exhilaration at starting all over again.—I remembered the other night how I used to write you notes in this room that winter in the intervals between lecturing at Smith, and how I used to look forward to seeing you. It meant a lot to me to know you in those years when Mary and I were disintegrating, and it still means a lot to me, dear Helen.

As ever, / Edmund

¹*Soviet Politics at Home and Abroad* by Frederick Lewis Schuman.
²Jeannie Clymer, a longtime friend from Wellfleet with whom Rosalind shared lodgings in several places, including, apparently, the Wellfleet house, for a time.

June 22, 1946 / Wellfleet, Mass.

Dear Helen: I already have [that] Chekhov. Thanks just the same.—I thought the Simonov translation very creditable. Is that a student of yours?

Everything is running well up here. I have a girl who cooks and takes care of Reuel and a man who does everything else. He is the son of my cook in New York last winter and a wonderful fellow: he can do anything—is a carpenter, electrician, plumber, chauffeur and gardener, and does the cooking when the girl is away. The house has never been so clean or looked so well. We have reorganized the whole place.

I am trying to get a divorce from Mary, so that I can marry again as soon as possible, and, though she could settle it easily before she goes abroad at the end of next week, I am afraid that she is going to obstruct it with another fight in court over nothing.

Are you settled in New York now? I'll look you up when I go down in August, if you're there then.

I am horribly bored with my *New Yorker* job, which, together with the house, the household and wrestling with my divorce problems, takes up all my time so that I get no chance to write anything else.

I am enclosing an article by Schuman, which is typical of him.¹ Notice how he pretends to be detached, but asserts that Trotsky is neurotic—something I have never heard suggested before—and implies that the charges against him at the Moscow trials were true.

A Stalinist mosquito is biting my ankle. It is hot, and I think we ought to go swimming.

Love, / Edmund

[Postscript] There were wonderful reviews of my book² in the *New Masses* and *The Daily Worker,* one of them called *Trotskyism: A Self-Portrait,* the other *A Trotskyite in Love.* The *New Masses* characterized me as a "crafty enemy of the working class."

¹"Trotsky versus Stalin" appeared June 8, 1946, in the *Atlantic Monthly.*
²*Memoirs of Hecate County.*

[First page missing—probably 1948]

[. . .]

I'm delighted about your full professorship.—Thanks for the Valentine.

We've been leading an extremely quiet life up here.—Elena working on the house, and I writing. It is a great relief after a year of rocky households, and I am really getting caught up on myself in a literary way.

I hope you will read the Malraux books. I have a very high opinion of him. He must be the most important French novelist since Proust. [A portion of this letter is in section IV.]

I am disappointed in Volodya Nabokov's new novel[1] and for that reason don't think I'll review it. Am curious to see what you will think of it.

Love as ever, / Edmund

[1] *Bend Sinister;* see section VII for the remarkably similar reaction Wilson conveys to V. S. Pritchett regarding *Lolita.* There is more on Nabokov's novels in *A Window on Russia.*

August 4, 1955 / Talcottville

Dear Helen: The 9th would be fine. I don't know much about routes, but your first objective is Utica. Then you travel north to Boonville. When you get to Boonville, just ask anybody to direct you to Talcottville. It is about four miles north on one of the main roads. It is a tiny little village, announced by a sign that says, truthfully, "Talcottville, Slow." My house is on the corner of the only two streets. You can't miss it: it is made of gray stone, with a white porch and balcony.—my telephone is Boonville 418K.

I am looking forward to seeing you.

As ever, / Edmund

TO CYRIL CONNOLLY

Nov. 28, 1946 / The Minden Inn / Minden, Nevada

Dear Connolly: I'm sorry not to be in New York when you arrive. I'm out here in the West and shan't be back till December 18. Couldn't you have dinner with me that night? If you can, meet me at the Princeton Club (Park Ave. and 39th St.) at 7. Drop me a line out here airmail or wire me, so that I'll get it before I leave, the night of the 10th.—Welcome to God's Country! Let me know if I can do anything for you in the way of having you meet people or anything, before I get back.— I'll be delighted to see you. I hope you can get up to Cape Cod to visit me.

Best regards, / Edmund Wilson

Wellfleet letterhead / April 3, 1950

Dear Connolly: I am just about to send my *Horizons*[1] to be bound, but see from your note in the last number, that there is something called *La Littérature Anglaise pendant la Guerre* that I don't seem to have. If you have one, I should be grateful if you would get one of your beautiful assistants to send it to me.—I think it was a good idea to close *Horizon* down. Most magazines go on too long and grow senile, and *Horizon* had just covered its period.—How are you?

Sincerely, / Edmund Wilson

[1]*Horizon:* 1940s magazine of arts and literature; Connolly's brainchild and a great force in the war years.

Aug. 26, 1952 / Talcottville, NY

Dear Cyril: 1) In your review of *Hecate County,* you described the narrator as a "desiccated buffoon."

2) I've always found Thibaudet boring and am surprised at your reading him for pleasure.

3) I've written to Princeton about you. They're beginning a new series of lectures,[1] which involves having each lecturer give six lectures, one a week (on any subject he pleases). He has to stay through the whole semester and, after his own lectures are finished, attend one lecture a week by somebody else. After every lecture, there is supposed to be a "discussion," which probably means that you would be heckled by "New Critics" and Catholic converts. For this you get $5000. They could make it a brilliant affair by getting the right people, but I'm afraid they will ask mostly mediocrities, with whom they will feel more at home.

4) I've also written the *New Yorker* about your Burgess-Maclean supposition.[2] I'm curious to hear your theory about them. [W. H.] Auden thinks that they were simply shot by the English.

I've escaped from Wellfleet—which is now a mad house of vacationers in summer—to a house up here in upstate New York that belonged to my mother's family and that she left me when she died last year. I feel more at home here than anywhere else in the world. I doubt whether anyone can ever really fully understand and appreciate me who has never seen me in the setting of this marvelous landscape in the foothills of the Adirondacks, surrounded by vast pastures of black and white Holstein cattle, occupying a semi-feudal position in a big old stone house (built in 1805) which is the center of a tiny village. Though this country was mostly settled by New Englanders at the end of the 18th century, they completely got away from New England. There is a pleasant lack of interest in religion, and a general atmosphere of freedom. In this little county everybody is amiable and almost everybody comfortable. It is so much an older phase of America than anything I usually see in the East that, when I am away from it, I can hardly believe it is real. Some of my cousins up here look like the people in Rowlandson's drawings, and I get to be like that myself, but I sit here with nothing to annoy or disturb me and think how decadent Wellfleet is—both the vacationers and the native New Englanders. The windows of my bedroom face East, and, in the morning, the views from them, vividly lit, with great trees and fields, a winding river, and blue mountains in the distance, look as if they had been composed as panels. Unfortunately, it is more or less a bore for Elena, who doesn't like living in the country and misses her swimming and Russian friends. There is nothing to do except read and go for drives and walks.—I hope you will visit me here sometime, and I hope you will get over here soon. I'll work on them when I get to Princeton—shall be there from the beginning of October till middle of February. During September we'll be back in Wellfleet.

Best regards as ever, / Edmund Wilson

[1]Set up to honor the late Princeton professor Christian Gauss (1878–1951); Wilson wrote of him in *Shores of Light*.

[2]Guy Burgess and Donald Maclean, two of the so-called Cambridge Spies who fled from Britain in 1951 to the Soviet Union. Connolly wrote about them in *The Missing Diplomats* (1953).

Dec. 6, 1952 / Mansgrove / Princeton, New Jersey
Dear Cyril: There is nothing to do in this Christian Gauss Foundation job except to live here for four and a half months and, during six weeks of that time, give a seminar one evening a week. A seminar consists of sitting at a table with an audience of thirty people and reading or speaking for an hour,

after which a discussion takes place. The only other thing you have to do is attend six seminars by somebody else. The rest of the time you do as you please, and parties are given for you. The last seminar and sometimes the first is followed by a party. I have invited Sonia Orwell[1] down for the one next Thursday, when I give my first performance, so she will be able to give you some idea of what to expect.—I have been plugging you, but they have a list of about seventy names and might not get around to you for years.

I don't remember praising Denton Welch[2] particularly. He wrote well but I think his infantile narcissism prevented him from being very interesting.

As ever, / Edmund W

[1]Sonia Orwell: née Brownell, worked at *Horizon* magazine in the 1940s; married Orwell a few days before he died.
[2]Author of *Brave and Cruel.*

May 30, 1953 / Wellfleet, Mass.
Dear Cyril: I was glad to have more books of yours. I reread you a good deal—I find that it relieves my *Angst* when I wake up in the middle of the night—and there is not half enough of you. I have come to the conclusion that *The Rock Pool* and "Where Engels Fears to Tread"[1] are about your best things, and I hope you are making progress with the literary detective story that Sonia told me about. I was delighted by the way in which at the end of *The Diplomats,* you meander in, resolving Burgess and Maclean into one of the indefinable and faintly aromatic elements of the charm of the Riviera.

2) In my next miscellaneous book, I want to have a group of pieces on the sex maniacs: [the Marquis de] Sade, Genet,[2] and Swinburne. I couldn't think of a general title till I remembered your word Pornocrats. Did you invent this? If so, I ought to acknowledge it. I would dedicate this section to you if I didn't think it might give rise to misunderstandings. That you mightn't like.

3) About elegiacs: I am particularly fond of this meter[3] and have been trying to do an equivalent in English. Here is a specimen[4] in which I have tried to produce the effect of the balance of the self-contained classical couplet by having criss-cross rhymes in each unit—on the accented syllables before the caesuras and at the ends of the lines. I haven't kept to the classical rule of not admitting spondees—or rather, in English, two-syllable feet—to the first two feet of the second half of the pentameter, but nobody, so far as I know, has ever observed this rule in English. But it turns out to be very difficult to

handle this meter in English at all, and it has not been attempted often. The trouble is that the natural rhythm of traditional English verse is always throwing the movement forward into couplets: it is especially hard to rein oneself in for the pause in the middle of the pentameter. This movement always ran away with Swinburne when he tried to write elegiacs. For some reason— probably because there was no traditional German rhythm and they could simply apply themselves to imitating the classics— Goethe and Schiller were able to turn out any number of German elegies of perfect correctitude.

As ever / Edmund W

[1]"Where Engels Fears to Tread": Connolly parody of one Christian de Clavering's progress from 1920s aestheticism to 1930s Marxist activism. Printed in *The Condemned Playground.*

[2]Jean Genet (1910–1986), French dramatist (*The Balcony, The Maids*) and author of *The Thief's Journal* and *Our Lady of the Flowers,* among other books.

[3]See "Note on the Elegiac Meter," reprinted in *Night Thoughts* (1961).

[4]specimen: which cannot be included; it has evidently been lost.

[undated fragment, probably from late 1953]

See especially on p. 13. You use titivate for titillate on p. 672 of your *Short Novels.* Other errors: it was Bergotte not Swann, who thought about Vermeer's Yellow,[1] and *Lord Jim* is hardly a short novel—150,000 words. Otherwise, as usual, you touch nothing you don't adorn. Very illuminating on *Between the Acts.*[2]

We are coming to London on Jan. 5 to stay two or three weeks. Do call us at the Basil St. Hotel and come to dinner or something.

EW

[1]In Proust's *A la Recherche du Temps Perdu.*

[2]*Between the Acts*: novel by Virginia Woolf.

Basil Street Hotel letterhead, London / Jan. 27, 1954

Dear Cyril: Here is the article. I can't write about Santayana, because I know nothing about his philosophy.[1] In connection with Doubleday, I meant to warn you that they now have one of these gigantic New York contracts, by which they try to induce you to sign away all your rights, tie you up for your next book, etc. You must slice away about a third of it—which Epstein[2] will expect you to do, though he cannot suggest it himself. I hope you will do some good business with them.—Do try to find out about Petronius.[3] Mario

Praz[4] would probably know.—We were sorry not to have seen more of you and Barbara.[5] Tell Barbara from me that she is a beautiful girl and does much to redeem the London literary world from the blight of homosexuality.—I hope that you will both soon be coming to the States.

As ever, / Edmund W.

[1]Nevertheless, there is an account of Wilson's visit to Santayana in Rome in *Europe Without Baedeker.*

[2]Jason Epstein: editor, at the time, at Doubleday, later editor in chief of Random House; a great Wilson champion, who instituted Anchor paperback editions of Wilson's books.

[3]Petronius Arbiter: Connolly's favorite author, whose *Satyricon* he used to read (undetected) in chapel at Eton.

[4]Mario Praz (1896–1982): author of *The Romantic Agony* and professor at University of Rome. Wilson praises him in *The Bit Between My Teeth* and elsewhere.

[5]Barbara (Skelton) Connolly, Cyril's elegant, temperamental wife; once a model for Schiaparelli.

Talcottville letterhead / July 2, 1956

Dear Cyril: We are coming to England the 26th, shall be at the Basil St. Hotel for a week or ten days. Will you be in or around London then? I am hoping to see something of you. Let me know where I can reach you. I don't know whether you are still at your old address.

As ever, / Edmund W

[Page 1 missing—starts on page 2]

[Probably 1956]

We have had a distinct feeling that your spirit was with us during Lys's visit.[1] She has been dreaming about you, and I have been finding it hard to get up in the mornings and have sometimes been a prey to inexplicable fits of melancholy.

We have all been reading Angus Wilson's novel[2]—which seems to me extremely good. I was surprised at his operating so successfully on so relatively large a scale. It seems to me that he and Stephen Potter[3] are the most brilliant portrayers of certain aspects of contemporary England. I hope that you will come over here— as Lys says you may—and get away from all that for awhile.

I am glad you are writing about Flaubert. Have you seen the new complete edition of the very amusing *Dictionnaire des Idées Reçues?* There has also appeared lately a volume with the early drafts of *Madame Bovary.* It is curious to see that some of the most wonderful passages are originally written in the most inept way—he seems to have begun by getting everything wrong. I think that what happened was that he first assembled the details that he wanted to use, then worked at the style later, as if it were something completely separate.

Edmund W.

[1]Lys Lubbock worked for *Horizon* and lived with Connolly during the 1940s.
[2]Angus Wilson (1913–1991): author of *Anglo-Saxon Attitudes.*
[3]Stephen Potter (1900–1969): author of *One-Upmanship.*

TO ISAIAH BERLIN

June 5, 1949 / Wellfleet, Mass

Dear Berlin: I'm sorry you've been ill. I called up the night you left to find out whether you'd arrived safely, but you evidently weren't at home. You were a great success up here. The Russians[1] say that you are even better in Russian than in English.—Your unique understanding of the Russian and British mentalities has led me to take up with Washington an idea which has occurred to me since your visit. It is proposed (though the project is still secret) to set up, a little later in the present administration, a department of Colonial Culture, of which—this is all confidential, of course—I am likely to be the head. I feel that you could render indispensable services in connection with this department. (The problem of your British citizenship would by that time not present serious difficulties.) Your immediate job would be to supervise the translation of my own books and those of a few other American writers into Russian and into the archaic dialect of American still spoken in the British Isles. But we should hope that you would extend the work in the directions of other potentialities of the cultural and anthropo-sociological fields which suggest a fruitful amplification of certain trends being stressed in the current activities of our ethno-educational agencies.[2] (You would of course have the benefit of the advice of an adequate staff of trained anthropologists, sociologists, ethnologists, and psychologists to help you with aspects of the work with which you might not be at home.) One of the methods employed, for example, will be a gradual familiarization of the English with a selected set of basic Russian idioms through the airborne dissemination of verses in the English folk-form known as the limerick. I enclose examples below.[3] They represent the first attempts of our folk-verse propaganda department, and you may be able to make fruitful suggestions for handling this problem better. Do not suppose, however, that the discrepancies represented by the rhymes with the current pronunciations of foreign languages is due to the inadvertence of our limerick-men. It is congruent with our policy of standardization of national pronunciations using American as the norm.

I hope that you will not delay long in letting us know your reaction to this, as we are anxious to implement our program well in advance of any emergency that might eventuate and which we do not want to catch us unprepared. Let me point out that, should you be tempted to hesitate, you should take into consideration that our government will be in a position, once our position of ascendancy is established, to conscript socially useful flairs and skills.

Yours sincerely, / Edmund MacArthur Wilson

[1]There was a considerable Russian community in Wellfleet, presided over by the Chavchavadzes, distant relatives of the Romanovs. See *The Fifties* (1986) and other Wilson journals.

[2]Wilson is sending up the sort of international agency engaging in propaganda activity during the Marshall Plan era of which the Voice of America might be an example.

[3]Wilson attached two pages of the multilingual limericks, which we omit here for reasons of space.

Wellfleet letterhead / Dec. 27, 1951

Dear Isaiah: We expect to be in Boston the 5th, 6th, and 7th, and shall hope to see you. I'll call you up when we get there. Best season's greetings in the meantime.—You never need to apologize to me for talking too much. The usual complaint against me is that I don't let anybody else talk, and I think you've listened patiently to some fairly long lectures.

As ever, / Edmund W

Feb. 5, 1952

Dear Isaiah: I don't know whether you will be much surprised, after our conversation of the other evening, by the announcement I am going to make—I am afraid that you will not be sympathetic with the step I have decided upon, for it was plain when we talked, that you believed yourself definitely to have closed your mind on certain subjects in which you must have seen that, in spite of my sometimes satirical approach to them, I took a real and deep interest. But I know that you, too, have thought anxiously about man's mysterious role in the universe and his attempts at moral self-justification. These problems, in my opinion, must always be beyond our grasp; but we have always at hand—disregarded so often and too much disregarded by me—an inexhaustible source of spiritual strength that, even without our fully understanding, can always renew our faith in life, which can make us see the inevitability of the otherwise sickening and discouraging spectacle of human folly and crime and which can reconcile us—by its inextinguishable but completely irrational hope—to the deficiencies and deceits of reason. I have wanted you to be among the first to know what I am going to do, and I am sure that you will believe that, though the final resolution came to me in what I can only call a moment of inspired impulse, I have been led by a compelling logic, long silently at work in my mind. It is a comfort to me to know that you will not be tempted to associate mine with such cases as those of Greene and Waugh[1] when I tell you that I have made up my mind to join the National Wildlife Association. I have always been fascinated by the lower animals, and the contemplation of their habits has upon me, as I was telling you the other night, a distinctly fortifying effect. I do not think that any American species should be allowed to become extinct.

Another announcement I want to make is that we are going to New York the 13th to stay the rest of the winter: c/o Mme. De la Roche, 17 E 97—telephone Atwater 9-8785. Do come to see us.

As ever, / Edmund W

[1]Graham Greene (1904–1991) and Evelyn Waugh (1903–1966), famous literary converts to Catholicism. Greene's *The Power and the Glory* and Waugh's *Brideshead Revisited* are often viewed as "Catholic novels."

Nov. 23, 1955

Dear Isaiah: We are delighted to hear about your getting married. Also, that you will be in New York. Do come one night for dinner with us—how about the 29th or the 30th? We'll probably be coming down a few days after Christmas, and I may be there at some time before—in which case I'll call you up.

As ever, / Edmund

Wellfleet, Cape Cod, Mass. / March 18, 1956

Dear Isaiah: I forgot to say that, when you go to Israel, I think it might be worth while for you to look up David Flusser.[1] You will find a description of him at the beginning of Chapter V of my Scrolls book. He is a wide-ranging scholar, a brilliant fellow, and an incomparable zydak [tzaddik? A righteous or good person]. Address Alkalay St., Beth Matossian, Jerusalem. He tells me that he has just been married and has been appointed to a chair in the Hebrew University. He writes me letters in Latin, which he says is his best language for communicating with non-Czechs. I'll tell him to look out for you when I write him again.

As ever, / Edmund

[1]The polymath Wilson profiled in *The Scrolls from the Dead Sea* (1955). His enthusiasm and intensity fascinated Wilson.

Hotel Lotti letterhead, Paris / Sept. 11, 1956

Dear Isaiah: I am sailing the day after tomorrow— earlier than I originally intended—and am extremely sorry to miss seeing you. Elena had to leave three weeks ago, and I ought to get back, too, to attend to my devoirs de père de famille: Reuel enters Harvard next week.

One of my present pleasures in Europe has been giving moral support to the two freethinking scrolls scholars, John Allegro[1] and Dupont-Sommer.[2] The Catholics are now much alarmed and are going after them and me.[3]

I hope we shall see you soon in the States.

Please remember me to your wife.

As ever, / Edmund W

[1]John Marco (Johnny) Allegro, controversial scholar whose views on the Dead Sea scrolls were regarded in some quarters as fanciful.

[2]André Dupont-Sommer, Semitic language scholar at the Sorbonne, praised in *The Scrolls from the Dead Sea* for his daring in advancing the idea of Essenism as the precursor of Christianity.

[3]Wilson was in the habit of making digs at Catholic scholars, perhaps because the *Hecate County* censorship campaign involved some Catholics; this did not, however, prevent him from being friends with Martin D'Arcy, S.J.

Wellfleet letterhead / December 12, 1956

Dear Isaiah: We were delighted to hear from [Stephen] Spender that you were married, and congratulate you enthusiastically.

Thanks very much for the Proust, with its richly rabbinical inscription. I noted with especial appreciation the use of the Hithpael.[1]

What I couldn't remember the other night: people named Shapiro are supposed to have come originally from the town of Speyer. The curious explanation of Rapaport is to be found in the old Jewish Encyclopedia.

We hope to see you in the summer. Please remember us to your wife.

As ever, / Edmund

[1]Hithpael: Hebrew word to denote something done with strength, i.e., hithnashem— to breathe deeply.

Talcottville letterhead / August 11, 1957

Dear Isaiah: I was glad to hear from you—thank you for the [Wilson renders this title in cyrillic: it is Turgenev's "Pozhar na More"—"Fire at Sea"] piece.[1] Yes, of course he must have had this incident on his conscience and wanted, before he died, to put himself in a better light. I agree with you in general about Turgenev and have given a different picture of him from, so far as I know, any by a Western writer— shall send you my article when it is out.[2] The Russians, in their different ways, also have their stereotyped ideas about Turgenev. There is an accepted idea, for example, that ["Pesn' Torzhestvuyuschei Lyudei"—"Song of the Triumphant People"] is no good—with which I don't agree; and no one seems to pay attention to his constantly recurring theme of the implacable Evil Force,[3] which figures in this story. What do you make of the strange story ["Chasi"—"The Hours"]? Elena thinks it contains an element of social fable—which didn't occur to me when I first read it.

When your letter came, I had just been thinking about you—in the following connection. I have been working on a grandiose project of having the little square panes of this old house engraved, here and there, with verses by distinguished poets. The windows of the third floor are devoted to high conceptions and elemental forces. I have a passage from Aeschylus' *Prometheus* confronting, in the room that faces it, a passage from Léger's *Vents*.[4] The effect of these decorations—inscribed with a diamond-point pencil—is sometimes very fine. They are invisible part of the time, but may be suddenly brought out by effects of light; and I sometimes look up from my work-table to see the [Greek words translatable as "God is air and swift-winged breezes,"] etc. apparently engraved on a cloud. It has occurred to me that this Aeschylus passage ought to be balanced by a suitable verse from Isaiah, which I should like to get you to write, signing it simply [in Hebrew letters, Isaiah] which would stand for both the transcriber and the author. We hope to get to London in February, and I shall bring the diamond pencil and a pane of glass in the hope of getting you to do this.

We are pleased about your professorship and your knighthood.[5] Elena sends love. Please remember us both to your wife.

As ever, / Edmund

[Postscript] I became extremely fond of Ivan Sergeyevich[6]—read him all through the course of a couple of winters and came to regard him as a friend and companion.

[1]Berlin translated "Fire at Sea"; it appears in a volume of Turgenev short stories titled *First Love,* published by Viking in 1983. In 1972 Viking also brought out Berlin's *Fathers and Children: Turgenev and the Liberal Predicament*—the underlying subject to which the Berlin-Wilson correspondence on Turgenev is addressed.

[2]Ivan Sergeyevich Turgenev (1818–1883): Wilson's essay, "Turgenev and the Life-Giving Drop," appeared in the *New Yorker* October 15, 1957; it is reprinted in *A Window on Russia* (1972).

[3]Evil Force: "a constant factor in Russian life, an ever-recurring phenomenon of history: the bad master whom one cannot resist, Ivan the terrible, Peter the Great, Stalin."

[4]*Vents* [Winds]: poem by Alexis Saint-Léger (1887–1975) who wrote as St. John Perse and received the 1960 Nobel Prize for literature. Wilson knew him as a friend of the Biddles on the Cape.

[5]In 1957 Berlin was named Professor of Social and Political Theory at Oxford and was granted a knighthood.

[6]Wilson is referring to Turgenev, using a familiar form of the author's name in the Russian fashion.

Wellfleet letterhead / Dec. 14, 1957

Dear Isaiah: Someone has told me that you are the person who arranged to have the Pasternak novel [*Doctor Zhivago*] translated. I was wondering whether there was any chance of my getting hold of the Russian original. The English translation, I understand, is being made in England from the same text as the Italian one, already out. And who is the translator—do you know?

Merry Christmas and [Hebrew script for Shanah toubrah—Happy New Year] / From Edmund and Elena / To you both

May 16, 1958 / Wellfleet, Mass

Dear Isaiah: I was much pleased with the little Dead Sea jar—though I thought at first that the package might contain a bomb from the Arabs.—About Turgenev: the rumor had reached me that you were for some reason annoyed with me in this connection. I couldn't make out what had happened, and I don't understand your note. I have never written a word about ["Pozhar na More"—"Fire at Sea"]. As a result of my *NewYorker* article,[1] Farrar, Straus got Magarshack to translate the ["Literaturnie Vospominanie"—"Literary Recollections"] and have bought it out with my essay in its unabridged form. I had nothing to do with the translation, haven't even read it. Having read the ["Pozhar"] in Russian, I haven't examined either his or your translation. Did he plagiarize you or what? If he did, please let me know: the publishers ought to know about it. I didn't mention the ["Pozhar"] in my essay because it wasn't relevant to my line of interest. I recommended to Farrar, Straus that they include your note on it from the *London Magazine*, but I suppose that, since it was Magarshack's book, they thought he ought to be allowed to explain it himself— I am sending you a copy of the Farrar, Straus book and having the *New Yorker* send you an article of mine on another subject.

I still haven't read the Pasternak novel, but the publishers here have promised to send me the Russian text. [. . .]

As ever, / Edmund

[1]my *New Yorker* article: Wilson's article on Turgenev.

Talcottville letterhead / June 8, 1958

Dear Isaiah: I was glad to have the Turgenev mystery cleared up, but I don't think you understand what happened. As a result of my *New Yorker* article, Roger Straus decided to get the memoirs translated and, without consulting me, arranged to have Magarshack do it. The ["Pozhar"] is of course part of the memoirs. Some of the chapters were sold by Straus to various magazines— but I didn't know till I got your letter that ["Pozhar"] had appeared in the *Reporter,* so couldn't imagine what you were worried about. I had nothing to do with the translation and haven't even read it—I agree with your opinion of Magarshack.

I don't know when we shall get to Europe. It is a question of money and how soon I get done with the Civil War, which I can't take travelling with me.

The Pasternak original is at last supposed to be on its way to me, and I am looking forward to it.[1]—There are many things I should like to discuss with you but all too long for a letter: Harry Levin,[2] the nationalist movement of the Iroquois Indians (which has been largely kept out of the news but which I am preparing to write about), the role of the U.S. in the world (which I more and more disapprove of), the problems of translating Turgenev (with special reference to the passage about the cat in ["Pervaya Lyubov"—"First

Love"] and the similar one in ["Veshnie Vodi"—"Torrents of Spring"].)
These will have to wait till I see you.

As ever, / Edmund

[1]Presumably Wilson had yet to read *Zhivago;* his review would appear in the November 15, 1958, *New Yorker.*

[2]Harry Levin (1912–1993): Harvard professor, literary critic and, evidently, from remarks in the journals, a difficult, hypercritical man. Wilson suggested the following solution to Levin's insulting manner: "Stop it, stop it. Down, Pongo, down!" He and Elena were, however, on cordial terms with Levin and his wife in Cambridge.

Wellfleet letterhead / December 29, 1958

Dear Isaiah:

Thank you for your letter. I am not necessarily modest about my own performances, but I really don't think my Zhivago article was as good as you say. I had the advantage of having read the Russian and of having Elena, who is extremely good on all these Russian subjects, so I was closer to the book than the other reviewers. But aside from this, the article appeared in rather an unsatisfactory state. I am used to having plenty of time and any number of proofs for my *New Yorker* stuff, but in this case—due to Pasternak's being in the news—I had to get the review out in a hurry and revise it over the phone, with the result that there are passages garbled or not very well expressed. There are also a number of things that I ought to have said but didn't, either on account of lack of time or because I hadn't yet discovered them. The water imagery connected with Larisa, for example, is really very important. Water is the fluid element and associated with life. Storms and thaws play a great role all through the book. In the calendar of the Orthodox Church, St. Larisa's name is supposed to mean ["morskaya ptitsa, chaika"—"sea bird, seagull"]. St. George has, it seems, in the temples to Poseidon along the Lebanese coast, been confused with Perseus, and his dragon with the sea monster slain by Perseus. A mythological Larisa was the bride of Poseidon. (Actually, this is a kind of thing that bores me, but there is a good deal of it in Zhivago, and Pasternak manages to make it alive, as he does everything else.) My biographical data, also, were vague—thank you for helping me fill them in. Eventually I'll revise and improve the article.[1]

The various adventures of the Russian text—both in Europe and over here—are surrounded with rumor and mystery. I have heard a good deal about them, but the stories are so inconsistent that I have found it as hard to make out what has been happening as the truth about the real or false Anastasya.[2] At the time I had the photostats of the Russian text, I used to get nocturnal GPU[3]-type calls from an old Trotskyist now employed by the University of Michigan Press trying to make me give it up to them so that they could check by it a version that they had and that they wanted to bring out. They and Pantheon, who will import Feltrinelli's edition, have now agreed to divide the American market, one taking the West, the other the East. The mutilation of the text of the English translation in the Pantheon office in New York—to which, I have now learned, some of the things I complained of were due—is also rather mysterious. Max Hayward,[4] whom I have recently seen, was very upset about the whole thing. But even the English edition is unsatisfactory—they were told, it seems, that they had only three months for it. I sympathized with young Hayward, who is simply, I think, inexperienced in dealing with publishers; but somewhat less with Miss or Mrs. Harari, who has written me a letter of what seem to me rather stupid excuses for her omissions and mistranslations.

[Wilson appends two words in closing: in Hebrew the word "l'chaim"—"to live" and below it the Russian the word Zhivago which has as its root the infinitive "zhit", meaning "to live."]

Edmund

[1]Refers to the second article in *The Bit Between My Teeth,* "Legend and Symbol in Doctor Zhivago."

[2]Anastasya: legendary Romanov who was thought possibly to have escaped the execution in 1918, subject of a 1950s movie and much speculation, laid to rest by recent DNA testing.

[3]GPU: the Soviet Secret Police, founded in 1922.

[4]Max Hayward: a colleague of Berlin's at Oxford; at one time a flatmate of T. S. Eliot's whom he edited at Faber and Faber.

Wellfleet letterhead / February 17, 1959

Dear Isaiah: I read your lecture with interest and moral approval, but I didn't want to review it for the reason that it is really a philosophical paper and ought to be dealt with by someone who is expert at this kind of thing. I am now in a state of mind in which I tend to approach all these social phenomena from a more or less zoological point of view, and if I were going to discuss your way of dealing with them, I should have to formulate a counter-approach, which I'm not at the moment prepared to do—though I'm going to try to make my ideas clear in my book on the American Civil War.

You are very good on the principle of forcing people to take what it is thought they would want if they knew enough to want it and (p. 43) on the desire for recognition which is not literal equality or freedom.[1] I don't remember to have seen either of these points really brought out in this way before. Suggested corrections: of for or four lines from the bottom of 20; and (p. 23) it was not Cephalus himself but Sophocles quoted by Cephalus who made the remarks you quote. If you are reading *Zhivago* again, you will notice that it has a strong element of *Finnegans Wake*. The death and resurrection theme is in the first lines of the book. See Luke 24.5 of the Russian New Testament. [Russian words for "Why seek ye the living among the dead?"] The sign that keeps recurring: [Russian words for Moreau and Vetchinkin, Seeders. Threshers.] is a cryptogram that contains a key. Notice that it appears when the road branches: [Russian words for Vetchina, ham, and Vetchinka, hamlet] etc. I am writing something about all this, which I'll send you.[2] About Hannah Arendt: I haven't read her. This is the treatise-type kind of book which I never read.[3]

As ever, / Edmund

[1]Refers to Berlin's *Four Essays on Liberty;* Berlin's doctrine of negative liberty (i.e., freedom of individual choice) was meant as a challenge to social planning and other liberal measures that could lead to tyranny.
[2]"Legend and Symbol in Doctor Zhivago" appeared in the *Nation* April 25, 1959; it is reprinted in *The Bit Between My Teeth*.
[3]Evidently refers to Arendt's *Origins of Totalitarianism*.

12 Hilliard Street / Cambridge, 38 Massachusetts / February 17, 1960 Dear Isaiah: Don't worry about the Pasternak letter. Let us, by all means, blame it on Harry Levin. I can get another copy from Kurt Wolff, to whom it was written and who sent it to me.

The trouble about Oxford for me is that I doubt whether I shall ever have anything to offer there. I do expect eventually to get out a little book of Russian essays; but I have made no systematic study of Russian literature and do not expect to make any. I merely write on scattered topics from time to time.

You ought to get out a volume of essays and include the Moses Hess,[1] which hangs together with your other recent writings.

As ever, / Edmund

[1]Berlin's piece about the nineteenth-century author whose *Paul and Jerusalem* is important to Zionism.

12 Hilliard Street / Cambridge, 38 Massachusetts / March 3, 1960

Dear Isaiah: It would be pleasant to go to Oxford, and I am grateful to you for suggesting it, but I really have nothing to give them and don't want to work up a year of lectures, which would be a waste of time for me. I think that lectures are a bore anyway, both to give and to listen to.[1] I have a schedule of projects that I hope to accomplish—if God spares me—by the time I am seventy, and it can none of it be adapted for lectures. After seventy, I should go on to publish my scrappy book of Russian studies[2] (which would not make a set of lectures) and edit my personal journal from 1914 up to date, which can hardly be published during my lifetime, let alone read aloud at Oxford.[3]

We do, however, hope to get to Europe after one more winter in Cambridge.

As ever, / Edmund

[1]Wilson's blunt remarks about academic lecturing, his anxieties about filling time in the classroom and his general lack of enthusiasm for teaching, at Oxford or anywhere, are evident throughout his letters and journals. He did, however, agree to read from his own work on occasion.

[2]*A Window on Russia* was published posthumously; the essays deal, as is usual with Wilson, with figures who interested him at the time.

[3]Wilson's "journal" became the five posthumously published journals of the '20s, '30s, '40s, '50s, and '60s.

Wellfleet, Cape Cod, / Mass. Sept. 5, 1961

Dear Isaiah:

I was awfully glad to hear from you and to know that you were back in Cambridge. We expect to be in Boston sometime before Christmas and shall look you up then, but in the meantime couldn't you come up here for a weekend (or during the week) sometime in October?

I agree about the epilogue to *War and Peace,* which is a very important part of the book— also, about the fox-hedgehog theory of Tolstoy— though I don't quite see Plato and Dostoevsky assigned to the hedgehog category.[1]

I borrowed [Stephen] Spender's book[2] for a night from the *New Yorker* office and read all the parts about other people, skipping most of the parts about himself.—I didn't think he was particularly good on his friends. I may have done the book an injustice by reading it in this way.

I have become quite fond of Berlioz's hunt,[3] which I was playing the other day.

I won't go on at length, as I hope to see you soon. Do let us know whether you can come in October.

As ever, / Edmund Wilson

[1]In his small and densely packed essay on Tolstoy, Berlin makes a famous distinction between unitary, centripetal thinkers with an all-embracing system (hedgehogs) and intuitive, centrifugal thinkers with darting, quicksilver minds (foxes).

[2]Stephen Spender's *World within World* chronicled his life among the intellectuals.

[3]Hector Berlioz's opera *Les Troyens* contains a section called Royal Hunt and Storm, during which Dido and Aeneus take refuge in a cave.

Nov. 23, 1966 / Wellfleet, Mass

Dear Isaiah and Aline: Elena says you have some idea of going to Boston in December. We are going to be there from the 8th on and are celebrating our 20th wedding anniversary on the 10th. We'd be delighted to have you come to dinner with us on the occasion.—I was interested in the interview with Isaiah in the *Sunday Times*—I suppose that it has some bearing on his ideas for the new college.[1]

Best regards, / Edmund

[1]Presumably, Wolfson College, Oxford.

III. Marriages

These letters register the unease and bitterness as well as the intellectual attraction and strange erotic excitement of one of the most inharmonious marriages in American literary history. McCarthy and Wilson met in 1937 when she was at *Partisan Review* and the magazine was entertaining Wilson in the hope of getting a contribution. Their literary connection soon moved to dining and drinking, weekends and sex. McCarthy says she married the distinguished middle-aged critic—no Adonis, with his jowls, paunch, and set ways—in 1938 out of guilt at having slept with him while on a visit to his Connecticut rented house "Trees." From the early days of their marriage Wilson encouraged her to write fiction—and eventually was comparing her to Stendhal. Their life together was spent at Trees and Shippan Point in Connecticut, at Truro Center and Wellfleet on the Cape, and in various Manhattan rentals and temporary residences, including the last at Henderson Place. In the summer of 1939 McCarthy took their infant son Reuel (born December 25, 1938) to Chicago where Wilson was teaching at the university; readers of the letters will note that she and the baby soon departed for the Northwest to visit her grandmother. The marriage ended in 1944 when McCarthy left him a "pincushion" note in the apartment at Henderson Place and went to live in the Stanhope Hotel with Reuel, agreeing from the start to give Wilson full visitation rights. The Wilson/McCarthy affidavits contain fairly unoriginal charges. Each maintained that the other was a spouse beater. McCarthy focused on his alcoholism and random violence; Wilson cited her demented fits of temper and destructiveness. In later years they said good things about each other's work, no surprise to those who understand the strong literary bonds between these two keenly observant social critics.

Jan. 2, 1937 / Red Bank, New Jersey
Dear Mary: I'm writing this in pencil because I can't write with the kind of pens they have down here. I've been having a pretty sour time since I saw you—no need to describe it in detail. Holidays are usually a poisonous period with any family. Yesterday I went up to New York and paid New Years calls on Peggy Bacon,[1] Dawn Powell, and Louise Bogan. I came down in the subway from 169th St., where Louise lives, thinking there was a half-past one train to Red Bank from the Penn Station, to find that the next train left at 3:34 on the Jersey Central from Jersey City. So had to wait in the Jersey City Station

and had a horrible trip, arriving here at 5 in the morning. In general, I've started the New Year as badly as possible.

I've missed you. I hope everything was all right. I'm enclosing your thing about the telephone, which you left. I'll be in New York with my daughter[2] this week—she leaves 3:40 Thursday afternoon. Would there be any chance of your being able to be free during the latter part of that afternoon or that night? I'll call you up at the office[3] Tuesday or Wednesday.

Best love***** / Edmund

[1]Peggy Bacon: caricaturist, printmaker, and writer of children's books, evaluated by Wilson in *The Shores of Light.*
[2]my daughter: Rosalind, daughter by Mary Blair.
[3]office: at the *Partisan Review.*

Dec. 1, 1937

Dear Mary: I'm delighted you're coming out[1] Monday. Have been thinking about you a lot. Nothing exciting has happened to me since your departure. I have written an article on Edith Wharton[2]—went for a ride this afternoon. The Hoellerings[3] are coming to dinner tonight and have just called up to say that Margaret Marshall[4] is arriving to spend the night with them, so she will be here, too. I don't expect to hold her on my lap, though. As for Byron, he has been written about a lot lately, and I don't think his reputation is low. I've got a certain amount of stuff here on him that might be helpful to you, if you decide to go through with him. He's very interesting. I've got a book on his political career—which didn't really amount to much in England.

We must finish "Eastward, Ho" sometime.

Fred Dupee[5] has just written me saying the *Partisan Review* is going to use my Stalin poem, but I have become convinced that it is a bad idea myself.

Drop me a line, my dear.

Love, / Edmund

[1]coming out: to Trees, the house Wilson was renting in Stamford, Connecticut.
[2]"Justice to Edith Wharton"; written originally for the *New Republic,* it was reprinted in *The Wound and the Bow.*
[3]Hoellerings: nearby neighbors in Connecticut; he was Franz Hoellering, longtime editor of *Berliner Zeitung,* author of a novel of postwar Europe, writer for *The Nation.*
[4]Margaret Marshall: writer for the *Nation,* editor, friend of Mary McCarthy and Wilson.
[5]Fred Dupee: a *Partisan Review* editor.

January 18, 1938 / Tuesday

Dear Mary: I was awfully glad to get your letter this morning. Today has been bright and quite beautiful with the snow: but Hatty's[1] lips seem to be getting worse, if anything, and I am going over to the hospital with her to get them looked at. I am writing a lot of inconsequential articles in order to pay my bills, and spending my evenings with the Owl and the Pussycat (Marx and Engels). I wish you were here to enjoy the snow with me. I've been sleeping horribly all week. Look forward to seeing you Saturday. I've written to Ben,[2] but haven't heard from him. Well my dear, be good and take care of yourself—I don't think you do take care of yourself enough.

Love as ever, with *** (though you say they mean comparatively little to you) / Edmund

[1]Hatty: Wilson's servant at that period.
[2]Probably Ben Stolberg, a leftist friend of both of them. Wilson mentions him in *The Thirties.*

Wednesday Jan. 19, 1938

Dear Mary: Hatty is really in a very bad way, so that I'm not going to have Ben come Friday. I'll go to New York that day. Did you say you had to do something that night? If not, we might do something together. Drop me a line that I'll get Friday morning. Hatty sits in a chair like a general and trains the children to cook the meals, wait on table, etc. They are very cute. If Friday night's impossible for you, let's meet fairly early Saturday morning. Today is a marvelous day. A girl[1] whom I haven't seen much of for years is coming out to see me. She is the original of Daisy in my work of that name—though only in the sense in which a model poses for an artist: the story is not true. I am writing innumerable lousy little articles.[2]

Love as ever, / Edmund

[1]a girl: identified by Jeffrey Meyers as Florence O'Neill, friend of Ted Paramore, Wilson's Hill School chum.
[2]lousy little articles: reference to some of the fine short pieces in the latter part of *The Shores of Light*—i.e., "Give the Beat Again," on Edna St. Vincent Millay.

January 26, 1938 / Wednesday night

Dear Mary: I've just gotten back from Boston and was glad to find your letters. I intended to write you on my trip, but was involved in such a social round—as people constantly came to see me in my rooms—that I didn't get much chance. I had a highly entertaining time—too many things to tell about in a letter. I saw Harry Levin, Matthiessen, Laughlin[1] and a lot of other people—will tell you about them when I see you. I had dinner with the Frank-furters.[2] Felix thinks that the CIO is raising a hue and cry about the Stalinists to divert attention from their other troubles and put the blame for recent unsuccess on a "foreign element," as they have been in the habit of doing in the past. I think that this may be true, in which case Ben has probably been partly used by somebody. There must be other elements in the situation which he hasn't been aware of.

This afternoon I stayed over in Boston to go to a matinee of Thornton Wilder's new play.[3] It has its defects, but I was so moved by it—perhaps partly for accidental reasons—that the impression hasn't even yet worn off. The last act seems to me one of the most terrific things I have ever seen on the stage. I've always claimed that since Wilder has become popular, he's been very much underrated by the highbrows. I'm curious to see what you will think of it. It's done in something the same way as "The Cradle Will Rock" but in every other respect is at the opposite pole from Comrade Blitzstein.[4]

I had an awfully good time down here with Ben. I find that people you know in New York always seem much better in the country. Saturday night we had a long conversation, in which we both surpassed ourselves.

I've missed you and thought about you all the time—have thought constantly how I wanted to tell you things, talk over people with you, etc. Night before last I had a dream about you, which was so delightful and went on so long that two professors with whom I was supposed to be having lunch at one had to come to rout me out of bed.

How about this Saturday? Maybe we can get in to Walt Disney by this time?

The *Partisan Review* hasn't come yet.

> Good night, my dear, It was so nice to find your letters, /
> Love, Edmund

My lecture was chiefly attended by young undergraduate intellectuals in spectacles from Harvard and Radcliffe and very old people from Cambridge with earphones.

Franz[5] came over again last night, and we had another profound conversation about politics and the relations between the sexes. We were leaping around the packing cases like a couple of antelopes.

[1]Laughlin: probably Henry Laughlin, president of Houghton Mifflin publishing company, whose offices were in Boston.

[2]the Frankfurters: he was Felix Frankfurter, the distinguished American jurist.

[3]*Our Town*—Wilson championed it in *The Shores of Light*.

[4]Marc Blitzstein (1905–1964), author of the book, lyrics, and music for *The Cradle Will Rock*. Wilson evidently felt Blitzstein had injected too much communist ideology in the show.

[5]Franz: an unidentified friend, possibly Hoellering.

Friday Stamford / June 17, 1938

Dear Mary: I have been trying to persuade Rado[1] to take you himself this summer, thinking that we could get a place out here where he is going to spend his vacation. He has just let me know definitely that he thinks it would be inadvisable, because his vacation will last only a few weeks and part of that time he will be going away on trips. In the fall, he says, he is completely booked up, so that he couldn't go on with the treatment. He is coming out to the Erkeguns[2] this weekend, and Franz had hopes to persuade him; but he sounds as if it were out of the question. He says that you must have the same analyst from beginning to end of your treatment and that he is trying to get you somebody first-rate.

I think, however, that it might be better, in any case, if I can possibly afford it, to be around here rather than down in New Jersey and am going to look at some houses today. You could commute to New York part of the time, stay in New York some nights of the week. I don't want our life to get disassociated; and things would be easier here than in New Jersey. Tell me tomorrow how you feel about Stamford for the summer. In the meantime, I'll try to rustle around and find a house; but I haven't got many days. We could always find something else for the fall if what we moved into now didn't work out.

About the pregnancy question, I have thought it all over again and I can't come to any other conclusion but that you mustn't go through with a child at this time. It's a disappointment because we'd counted on having one but, after all, we can always have one; and in the meantime it will land you in a situation that you are really unprepared for. You want it very much when you are feeling good about things; but you are still in a generally stirred-up condition and I think you are somewhat confused about this as about other things. You oughtn't to be let in for relationships and responsibilities which you're not ready for at the present time and which might ruin your relationship with me as well as interfere with your psychoanalysis. The psychoanalysis is the main thing and there's no question that it will go better if you get the pregnancy over. There are also the practical difficulties: with the baby you would be badly tied down and the expenses of baby and psychoanalysis, too, would certainly be more than we could afford. I think, too, that you and I will get along better with this question out of the way: you won't find your situation with me closing down over you in so oppressive a way as I'm afraid you have been feeling it during the last month or so.—Rado told me on the phone today that this question must be settled at once before he could do anything for you.

So get the thing over and then you can come out to Stamford and you can start a gay summer life between New York and the psychoanalysis and your loving husband. I felt much better after our talk yesterday. We are going to be happy in spite of the psychoanalysis, etc. I don't think we've made such a false start, and I love you as ever, my dear, and I miss you and want you back with me terribly for as much of it as you can stand.

Edmund

[1]Rado: Sandor Rado, Hungarian psychoanalyst.
[2]Erkeguns: neighbors on the Cape.

Thursday June 23, 1938

Dear Mary: Here are a number of items which might interest you: the *New International* with Trotsky's article, the *New Republic*, a card from Louise Bogan, a note from Nancy Macdonald[1] with the checks. I'll send you the *Partisan Review* as soon as I can get a copy.

I called up Mr. Moe[2] this morning and he told me that the members of his committee had been away attending commencement exercises, but that he would be able to let me know in a few days.

I went alone last night to a new Russian film called *The Country Wife*, of which Dwight Macdonald[3] should certainly take cognizance. It tries to take the curse off some of the present tendencies by caricaturing them: comic characters who bring charges of sabotage and conspiracy, etc. A pretty thoroughly poor picture. I'm going down to Stamford this afternoon and will write you from there special [delivery?] so that you will get it sometime tomorrow.

I miss you, dear. I hate to go back there and be there without you. I think I'll get all the stuff moved down to Pt. Pleasant the first of next week.

I called up the doctor this noon, and he told me you were in good shape.

I'll see you Saturday—am on to the doctor at 2. Take things easy in the meantime.

All my love, dear, / Edmund

This is the kind of pen that ruins my handwriting.

[1]Nancy Macdonald: married to Dwight Macdonald; helped edit *Partisan Review* from home.

[2]Mr. Moe: Henry Allen Moe, director of the Guggenheim Foundation.

[3]Dwight Macdonald (1906–1982): writer of the left, essayist and critic, part of the *Partisan Review* crowd; later wrote book reviews for the *New Yorker* and movie reviews for *Esquire*.

University of Chicago letterhead / July 31, 1939

Dear Mary: I've been in a partial state of decline since you left—my throat got worse, I had strange pains in my arm and side, and I took to my bed with a slight fever. I've just been to the doctor: he says I've got a lingering bronchitis combined with muscular strain due to bicycling with Gerry Allard[1] and his boy and Rosalind yesterday morning. He gave me some medicine and I'm now on the mend.

As a result of this, I haven't been doing very much except the—very pleasant—bike ride and taking Rosalind and the Evanses to the circus. [The last two sentences are also in section IV.] I was feeling low—let down by your not being there, as well as ill—and little Mrs. E rather depressed me. She is in such a shaken state that she was made very uncomfortable by the freaks and sat through most of the performance with her fingers in her ears so that she wouldn't hear the shots and explosions. She told me they had had a tragedy at home: Malcolm, the rat, had eaten Venus, one of the canaries, and they had had to chloroform him. She kept talking about cruelty to animals all evening, and quoted with approval the statement of somebody to the effect that Christianity had nothing to say about two subjects of great importance: sex and kindness to animals. I can't see that they have been doing much to further the second of these, with their habit of letting the fox visit the hen roost.—The circus has been hit much harder by the strike than the publicity would lead you to believe. In fact, it must have been cleaned out: there wasn't a single act that I remembered seeing before. Everything was new, and some of the acts were good: but the trapeze-performers were flopping all over the place. The show culminated in all three of the trapeze teams missing at the same moment. The triple somersault was never successfully performed even in two tries. I guess everyone walked out except the gorilla. The gorilla, however, lived up to my expectations: he really is enormous: four or five times as large as the ones we saw at the zoo, and very formidable looking, though when we saw him, he was languidly lying on his back with his legs up in the air and toying with a bit of rope.—I thought about you all the time and wished you were there. [A portion of this letter is in section IV.]

I miss you, and think that part of my decline has been due to trauma caused by your departure.—I hope you arrived without too much wear and tear. Write me when you get this, dear.

Edmund

[Postscript deleted]

[1]Gerry Allard: a communist, a labor activist in Chicago, and a Wilson friend.

August 6, 1939 / Morton Zabel's House

Dearest Mary: I was glad to get your letter and telegram and know you'd arrived all right. Sorry to hear about your trials on the train. Everything has been very quiet at the apartment, and I have had no gaiety up to this weekend.—The heat has been pretty bad, but it's cooler now.

Saturday we took Henrietta and her little boy and Jeanne to the zoo.[1] Jeanne was ravished by everything and took innumerable pictures of the animals, including a closeup of one of the giraffes who stuck his head over the barrier. Henri's little boy behaved just as badly as she. Evans had warned me that he would and [he] spent most of the time howling and bawling because he couldn't go back and have another ride on the merry-go-round. He is bright and attractive, though. His father handles him better than his mother. We went to dinner at the Hollands' afterwards, and I put in a formidable session with Hubert [?] and his father, who reminded me of some of the types in Dickens. Hubert has just had a salary cut and was grouchy. He is all for the Soviet Union now on account of what he thinks England might get out of it, and is inclined to think Krivitzky[2] must be a fake (you ought to be here to read K's last article in the current *Post*). We all drank a great deal of whiskey, wine, and port and ended up in an altercation about England which might have been acrimonious under less convivial circumstances. In the enthusiasm of the moment, I invited them all to dinner next Friday (including the old man) and now am somewhat appalled as to what I am going to do with them when they come. I asked the old man if he had seen anything of the O'Neills in Bermuda, explaining that O'N was a playwright. He said, "Did he write a book then? Some chap wrote a book there."

We came in late in the evening to Morton's. He lives on the lakefront just before you get to Evanston. Their place is quite bright and attractive, but rather crowded for sleeping space—there is only one bedroom and people have to flop on the couches—so I don't know whether we'll stay over tomorrow night. We go swimming, I write letters, while Morton composes gigantic epistles to Louise [Bogan], and [. . .] regales me with University scandal. The apartment is all silk-shaded lamps, carefully chosen prints of the masters, little china animals, and the most exclusively belle-lettristic library I have ever seen: social criticism, politics, and history completely barred out and with several sets each of favorite writers like Walter Pater and Henry James—he always seems to be buying new ones. Photographs of Morton and his sister as children dolled up in fancy white clothes like little angels. The sister and mother sleep together in the bedroom, and Morton sleeps in the living room on the couch. I don't wonder he gets neurotic at such close quarters. I can't imagine how they arrange it when he's sick. He sends you his regards. [Deleted portion appears in section IV.]

Write me often. I'm combining what I think ought to be some fruitful plans for the fall. I don't think I'll stay here for more than a week after my courses are over—will meet you in the East. Will let you know about it definitely soon. I hope you're enjoying yourself

Best love, my dear / Edmund

[1]Henrietta, one of the Fort sisters. She and her sister Louise were old friends from Boston and the Cape. See *The Fifties,* pp. 279–81.

[2]Walter G. Krivitsky (nom de guerre of Samuel Ginsberg), top Soviet espionage agent in Western Europe; he became the first KGB defector in 1939, exposed Russian purges in the *Saturday Evening Post,* and was reviled by Malcolm Cowley and others. He was murdered by a Stalinist agent in a Washington, D.C., hotel room in 1941.

University of Chicago Department of English letterhead / Aug. 19, 1939
Dear Mary: I've moved my departure ahead by combining my two examinations on one day and cutting out my visit to Dorothy Mendenhall. I'm going to leave here Thursday night and arrive P[rovince]town Saturday. This will give me more time to find a place to live in the event of your having to leave before the end of August. I've been terribly bored and exasperated here lately and can't wait to pull out.

I've done nothing of any interest to report lately—have had all kinds of things to attend to winding up my courses. Last night I underwent another academic outing. [. . .] It wasn't quite so bad as the other experience, but to a less degree had the same depressing effect on me. This and having the Allards to dinner Wednesday and [several Chicago faculty] come in afterwards have been my only social activities.

The Idiot of Dickens has had her paper approved by Wilt and myself and is now radiant. The next to last session I had with her she said she felt as if she were going crazy herself.

I was glad to get the snapshot, which is quite beautiful. I can't buy you a fur coat now, because I am completely cleaned out and will have to borrow money to get away. I still have Dr. Frank, the moving and storage bill, and gas and electric bill at Stamford to pay. But if you can pick one out and get them to set it aside for you, I'll try to get it for you at Christmas. When you write me after you get this letter, send it to General Delivery, Provincetown. [A portion of this letter appears in section IV.]

I'm writing this in haste to let you know when I'm leaving, as I've a million things to do.

Will soon be seeing you, dearest. / Edmund

August 19, 1939

Dear Mary: By all means stay till the 7th. But be sure you make connections on that Hyannis train. You know how tricky the Cape Cod timetable is.

You are not saving anything on the fur coat, as I shouldn't have been able to buy it now in any case. You have very strange ideas of economy. I am down to my last dollar—though I hadn't realized how literally till I received your announcement that you had cashed all the checks I gave you. You promised me you would let me know about each one. I'm having difficulties over my own ticket: I find that in order to go by way of Pittsburgh I have to buy a new one all the way, sending the other in to be redeemed. I'm having a hard time raising enough money to get us back to the East and pay Jeanne for her last month—to say nothing of the bills. The storage people—from whom you neglected to inquire the cost of packing and moving labor—have sent me a bill of nearly a hundred dollars.

I believe I told you, in writing you yesterday, that I was arriving in Provincetown Saturday when I should have said Sunday. I may take another day at this end since you're not coming on right away, so that I shouldn't get there till Monday.

I don't suppose the enclosed is of any importance, but am forwarding it
[A portion of this letter is in section IV.]

No news.

Love, / Edmund

Aug. 26, 1939. / Chicago.
Dearest Mary: I have stayed over here an extra day; am leaving for Pittsburgh
tonight; and expect to arrive in Provincetown Tuesday. I am enclosing a
check, though I haven't got a thing in the bank at the present time. I'll try to
get something deposited Monday; will wire you from P'town about it; so
don't cash check till you hear from me. I'm glad I'll be seeing you soon; have
been missing you dreadfully; didn't know how much you meant in my life till
you left. Also, little friend. One night I dreamt that you were back and he was
able to talk.

I felt awfully let down and nervous when I'd finished my courses, as I
always do when I finish things. I went up to Madison and spent the night with
my Cousin Dorothy Mendenhall, whom I was immensely curious to see. She
turned out to be wonderful. It is a pity we didn't go up together. She is very
handsome, very intelligent and an excellent talker—keeps a marvelous house
with marvelous meals—the most attractive house I have seen for ages—I wish
we had one like it: big and rambling and all the downstairs rooms with doors
that open on to gardens, sloping lawns, moonlight in the trees. After three
months of Chicago and this apartment, it was almost intoxicating to smell
such things again. I had long conversations with her on politics, academic
affairs, Gertrude Stein, [W. H.] Auden and Co., marriage and child rearing,
and the family—about whom she is more illuminating than anybody except
myself. She was educated in Germany and when she got back and was supposed to come out, she ran away from home and went to Johns Hopkins to
study medicine. The family was so ashamed of her that, when she was at
medical school, they would say she had gone socially for the winter. Later she
discovered a pathological cell, which was named after her. She belongs a little
to the Gertrude Stein category; but is even more regal. She is always worrying
for fear the women aren't leading their own lives. She detests Phil Lafollette,[1]
and is of the opinion that the old man's wife was the only one of the family
who ever amounted to anything. She is wonderful on the subject of Merwin
Hart,[2] who, she says, has really "convinced himself that black is white and
white is black."

I came back this morning and have been liquidating all my affairs here. Jeanne has decided to stay on in Chicago, as her creditors are after her in Connecticut and she is afraid that they will put her in jail. She is off for a holiday now in Wisconsin with some of her friends.

The day of my last class, I had a little spree with Mrs. Evans, Henri, and Lady Esther.[3] Lady Esther is an ash-blonde, who sort of gets herself up like Barbara Hutton.[4] She is very pretty and chic and rather nice. All went well, till Mrs. Evans, seeing her daughter off in the Union Station, found a stray kitten and decided she would have to take it right home and give it some milk—which meant that we had to go to her house. Whenever she went out of the room, we had to pledge ourselves to see that the kitten didn't eat the canary birds, which were flying at large around the room. We also had to look to it that they didn't send their liquid droppings down on us. My impression is that under the pretense, or rather under the conviction, that she is being kind to these animals, she is really encouraging them to prey on one another.

I think I went over pretty well with my students, who paid me little tributes when it was all over.

Best love, my dear, / Edmund

[1]Philip LaFollette: Progressive governor of Wisconsin who, in the mid-1930s, helped secure the passage of influential pro-labor legislation.

[2]Merwin Hart: evidently a relative of both of them who held extremely prejudiced views; see letters to Elena Mumm Thornton in this section.

[3]Perhaps an acquaintance nicknamed after a line of beauty products then featured in *Vogue,* or, conceivably, the eponymous Lady Esther herself. In *The Fifties* Wilson prefers Marianne Moore as a friend for Henri (Henrietta).

[4]Barbara Hutton: the much-married heiress, numbering among her exes Cary Grant.

Sept. 13, 1941 / Wellfleet, Mass.

Dear Mary: Here is some money and your mail. I'm trying to get Scribner's to advance me a hundred dollars for the book,[1] so I hope that will be all right.

I had a mildly pleasant evening last night with the Mannings[2] and Nina Ch.[3] It seems that Bones was founded by a Taft.[4] David has been giving Helen a rush, and Nina thinks it would be a great thing.—She has invited me with Peggy Day[5] to dinner at her house tonight.—Aside from this, no excitements, except a session with Charlie Walker,[6] in which he talked about his writing and I gave him a lot of advice, and a visit to Tim[7] from two teachers of the Shipley School, who inordinately admire my writings. Reuel is fine, and we have had a lot of fun together. I've been devoting more time to the house—

cleaning things up and getting them in order, hanging pictures, etc., and he has been helping me.—Carl Gross[8] has been taking pretty vigorous action on the furnace, but finds that some of the parts will have to be replaced, to the tune of $40 or $50—The weather has been marvelous—I wish we could have had a picnic yesterday.

When you come back, I think you ought to make use of these last days, while Edna[9] is with us, to get as far as possible toward finishing your book. You don't need to worry about my lunch and breakfast. Just get what you want for yourself, and I'll get along as I've been doing lately. If we haven't got a cook, we can go out to dinner part of the time: Edna gets along perfectly well by herself. In any case, you won't need to worry about the household till the afternoon. You must make up your mind not to let other things get between you and your writing: otherwise you won't do either your writing or the household to your satisfaction.

I miss you, dear. I've been counting on this part of the year. I was in rather a bad state of mind myself when I came back from Bennington, and probably made your situation worse. I'm feeling very cheerful now and am yearning for you.

All my love, / Edmund

[1]the book: Wilson edited Fitzgerald's *The Last Tycoon;* the fees eventually went to Scottie Fitzgerald.

[2]Mannings: friends on the Cape.

[3]Nina Chavchavadze and David, Russian friends at Wellfleet. Nina gave Wilson some lessons in speaking Russian; David, her son, commented wittily on Wilson's clumsy pronunciation. The Helen referred to is evidently one of the girls of summer.

[4]Bones: Skull and Bones, a senior secret society at Yale University. William Howard Taft's father Alphonso founded it and it was thereafter a club for the elite, including members of the Bush, Bundy, and Pillsbury families.

[5]Peggy Day: from the family of the author of *Life with Father,* Clarence Day.

[6]Charlie [sometimes Charley] Walker: a friend from Wilson's army days, Yale graduate and professor there; neighbor at Wellfleet.

[7]Tim: an unidentified Wellfleet friend.

[8]Carl Gross: local handiman.

[9]Edna: the hired help of the moment.

July 13, 1944 / Wellfleet, Mass.

Dear Mary: I have decided that there is no point in my going down and am wiring you. I'll expect you up here Sunday.—I make this suggestion: come back up here for the rest of the summer on a purely friendly basis. I promise you that I will not drink anything all summer. I think it is hard on Reuel to wreck the family in the middle of the summer like this. It would be easier for you and me to set up separate establishments in the autumn when he will be going to school. If you could get a cook in New York, the household itself would be easy. (Miss Forbes, by the way, however, seems to expect her vacation soon.)

I feel terribly badly about this, and I know that it was my fault that things got into such a mess. In spite of everything, I thought we were pretty well off in the earlier part of the summer. It is always true that Rosalind upsets the balance of the family when she comes; and the heat, the Geismars,[1] and my own bad habits did the rest. But it may be that you and I are psychologically impossible for one another anyway. I had already got discouraged about everything before I left New York in the spring; but I have never wanted things to be as bad as that because I have really loved you more than any other woman and have felt closer to you than to any other human being. I think, though, that it is true that, as lovers, you and I scare and antagonize each other in a way that has been getting disastrous lately (though sometimes I have been happier and more exalted with you than I have ever been with anybody). And when you make me feel that you don't want me, all my fear of not being loved, which I have carried all my life from my childhood, comes out in the form of resentment.

I know that the difference in our ages is a real difficulty between us. I prevent you from doing things that are no longer to my taste but that are perfectly natural for you to want to do; and you don't sympathize with the miseries—like the death of old friends, bad habits and diseases of one's own, and a certain inevitable disillusion with the world that has to be struggled against—that hit you when you get on in your forties.

I want you to know, too, that I know that you have made an effort to keep house for Reuel and me, and to be good to Rosalind, and that we all appreciate it. You have been wonderful except when you turn the whole thing into a kind of masochism that is calculated to make other people as uncomfortable as you are. There is no question, though, that you have been very much better this last year. There have been long stretches when you seemed to me to handle things better and to be a great deal happier than at any time since we have been married—isn't that true?—and I am sorry that I have sometimes been demoralized myself and let you down when you were doing your best. We have been leading a quiet life. Rosalind and I have both done a lot of writing. I am struggling with the rather uncomfortable job of writing something about Dos's book.[2]—We went over to P[rovince]town Monday with the Geismars and found the town full of exhilarated friends who were celebrating the christening of a magnificent new fishing boat which Jack Hall has had built for himself and which he is going to operate with a Portuguese crew. Matsons, Bubs Hackett, Joan Colebrook, Harl Cook,[3] the Portuguese crew and many others were all on board drinking various kinds of liquor. The boat was moored at the end of one of the docks. We had dinner, on the Geismars, at the Flagship and paid the Dos Passoses a call. Afterwards, when we got back here, Rosalind had to call up Nick[4] in Canada, so I went to the Holiday House with them and had a long and rather interesting talk with Max [Geismar]. You are mistaken in thinking he is a stooge of mine: we seem now not to agree on much. He has his own ideas and is very tenacious about them. They gave us back the gas coupon when we went to Provincetown; but afterwards, Rosalind tells me, just before they were going, Ann [Geismar] tried to get it back—but Max wouldn't let her. Other days, Gull Pond and the ocean.

Come up and stay here and let us make a modus vivendi for the next two months. It wouldn't work out in the long run; but we could make other arrangements in the autumn. I'm entering a period of sobriety and work (have even initiated a diet) which may be tiresome for you; but I will do my best to be considerate and not nag you. In the meantime, I want your company, which, aside from other considerations, I prefer to anybody else's. [Marginal note: I shall have to go to New York sometime and you can, too.] We all miss you terribly, my dear.

Love, Edmund

[Postscript] Please answer this letter or wire me where and when I could call you in the afternoon.

[1]Geismars: Maxwell Geismar and his wife Ann; he a literary critic and author of *Writers in Arms*. Wilson helped Geismar publish his book in England.

[2]Dos's book: *Number One*, a novel.

[3]Matsons (et al.): part of the fluid and numerous social life typical of a seashore community in summer. They will not figure in notes hereafter unless warranted.

[4]Nick: evidently a special friend of Rosalind's at the time.

Aug. 6, 1944. / Wellfleet, Mass.

Dear Mary:

[A portion of this letter is in section IV.]

Sandor and Peter came over Friday and had a picnic with the Gutmans at the Gull Pond beach. He invited me to come but Miss Forbes didn't give me the message till too late. I went over and saw them in the afternoon. Sandor said he was terribly sorry about everything having gone wrong the day you had gone over to see him and I think had come over here—hiring a taxi—particularly to see you. Later the Nabokovs and I went into P'town, called on the D[os] P[assos]'s and had dinner at the Bonnie Doone restaurant—not especially exciting. Volodya made a few unsuccessful attempts [indecipherable words.] I ran into Betty Spencer, Katie Schmidt and her husband, and I have invited them over to have dinner with the Nabokovs and me at the Holiday House tonight—I am rather dreading having to deal with Irvin's infantile disease of Stalinism.

The problem of providing a chaperon for Miss F[orbes] has proved a considerable nuisance. Adelaide never turned up, Ruth Berrio let me down late at night, and I finally had to resort to going over and spending the night with the Solows.

The next day I got the Nabokovs, with the demoralizing results I had anticipated. Charlie was supposed to arrive last night, but when he finally came it turned out that Adelaide was coming, too, so that it was impossible for him to stay here, and I had to get Vladimir up out of a sound sleep to come over here with Vera. Tonight and for the rest of the time I am going to arrange to have Miss F. herself go over to the Walkers to sleep, which she says she is willing to do. She is capable, kindly, and well-intentioned, but she is really of a formidable stupidity. Sandor went to a lot of trouble to get Karen Gutman to deliver a telephone message here, inviting us to his picnic, and Miss F. never let me know about it nor know that he called for me at noon. She was under the impression that I would not want to be disturbed—and has done other things of the kind. She means to be helpful, though.

I was relieved to discover after I had frantically started writing a *New Yorker* article that I had a week more of vacation than I had figured, so am returning to my other work tomorrow.

Volodya[1] tells me to send you his love. We all miss you. The Nabokovs have gone back to the Billingsgate. Reuel is playing the phonograph. I have been cleaning up my study. (It is Sunday morning.)—Nina and her friend think that Vera is like a very highclass Russian governess and find her rather heavy going. It has suggested to me a theory that Volodya has reverted to some governess-relationship of childhood. Vera's ideas of breakfast and mine are, however, exactly the same, and we have reduced the eating of the morning meal to an astonishing minimum of work. The Nabokovs contributed bologna this morning.

I hope you have been getting a lot done. All my love, my dear.

Edmund

[1]Volodya: the familiar form of Vladimir Nabokov, author of *Lolita;* he and his wife Vera became friends of Wilson's early in their stay in America. Their correspondence, as edited by Simon Karlinsky, was made into a script for a staged reading by Terry Quinn under the title *Dear Bunny, Dear Volodya.* It has several times been presented in New York; Dmitri Nabokov has taken the part of his father; William F. Buckley Jr. has read Wilson.

Jan. 17, 1945

Dear Mary: I have just had a letter from Reese[1] and have talked to him on the phone. I don't want to sign a separation agreement now for reasons that I have already explained, and I don't see that you have anything to gain by it except the satisfaction of feeling that you have somehow scored off me. Later on, we can separate, or divorce, if you want to. I will sign a paper, if you like, agreeing to do this when I get back. In the meantime, do relax. I wish you would go to Kardiner[2]—not because I want him to talk you into any different course of conduct, but because I think you really need it. I talked to him on the phone some days ago and he told me that he was still holding a place for you, but I don't suppose he will hold it indefinitely. I think he thought you might change your mind, and I think you probably ought to call him up and let him know if you're sure of not going. Let me pay the bills for awhile and count it against the money for storing and cleaning your coat, which I wasn't able to pay at the time. I am going to be all right for money. I just had lunch with Shawn[3] and they are prepared to take an article on Europe from me every other week while I am away and will pay me a thousand dollars for three thousand words. He thinks they can advance me a couple of thousand. I'll be making more money than I was last year.

Please think all this over while I'm away these next few days.—I always miss you so much when you're on bad terms with me, and I'd like to see something of you under more cheerful conditions before I go. I may be back from Red Bank Saturday—Sunday at latest. I left checks on my table upstairs.

Love, / Edmund

[1]Reese: the attorney who handled Wilson's and Mary MacCarthy's separation and divorce.

[2]Kardiner: evidently an analyst or therapist Wilson wished McCarthy to consult.

[3]William Shawn, a fact editor, later Harold Ross's successor as editor of the *New Yorker.* Wilson was about to embark on the travels that resulted in *Europe Without Baedeker,* first as a series of articles for the *New Yorker,* then as a book.

March 21, 1946

Dear Mary: I am still very seriously strapped with no relief in sight. Harold Ross[1] has shut down on my European articles, because they are now so far out of date, so that I'll have to sell them, if at all, to other magazines which will pay me much less money; and I have just had a bill from my lawyers for over a thousand dollars. [Remainder of this letter is in section IV.]

[1]Harold Ross (1892–1951): founder of the *New Yorker* in 1925, and its editor until his death.

New Yorker letterhead / April 5, 1946

Dear Mary: My book is making money and I will send you whatever back installments I have missed. I know that I skipped one week, but I'm not sure that I didn't send you $50 instead of $60 one week. Please let me know. I am going to Virginia next Thursday for about a week. Will expect Reuel the 21st or 22nd. I have circus tickets for the 23rd. That girl who worked for you wants to take on the whole household, doing cooking and everything. Do you think she is capable of it? I am going to have one other servant anyway. When does Reuel get out of school this spring? Please write me so that I will get it before Thursday.

EW

[Letters to Elena begin, April 11, 1946]

New Yorker letterhead / October 25, 1946

Dear Mary:

I am enclosing a check for the two months last summer during which, at your suggestion, I did not pay you maintenance. I want you to try to get a more comfortable apartment than the one you are in. [A portion of this letter is in section IV.]

Your spices and things are in the cartons in my office. Miss Patricia Farrell or Miss Terry will let you in if you want to come and get them. I am afraid it is too late to do anything about the rug which you left at Henderson Place. Buy another one.

Sincerely, / Edmund

Jan. 24, 1949 / Wellfleet, Mass

Dear Mary: [A portion of this letter is in section IV.] Mother has turned over to me two war bonds which she bought in Reuel's name (worth $50 apiece), and I will send them to you as soon as I can find them. She seems to be worried about that miniature of me as a child, which she doesn't want to get out of the family. You have it, haven't you? You might give it to me sometime, and I'll give it back to her—I don't suppose you care about keeping it.

Cyril Connolly has written me that he is pleased with your story.[1]

Sincerely, / Edmund

[1]"The Oasis."

March 8, 1949 / C/o Eitingon / Hillcrest Park, / Stamford, Conn
Dear Mary: This is only half of what I owe you, but more is coming.—I suppose you know that a real Mr. and Mrs. Joseph Loucheim[1] have turned up, who are making trouble about your story. If you don't, Miss Steloff at The Gotham Book Mart[2] can tell you about it.

Edmund

[1]Mr. and Mrs. Joseph Loucheim: characters in the Mary McCarthy story "The Oasis," a tale of intellectuals experimenting with rural life.
[2]Wilson long treated the shop as his personal bookstore and bore great affection for its owner, Frances Steloff. One of few instances on record of his asking anyone's forgiveness is in a letter to her dated May 31, 1943: "Dear Miss Steloff: Mary tells me that one of her checks that you cashed has come back. I am very much embarrassed, as you must think by this time that we come to the Gotham Book Mart for the purpose of cashing bad checks. Here is one that I know is good. Please forgive me. Yours sincerely, Edmund Wilson"

Jan. 22, 1961 / 12 Hilliard St. / Cambridge, Mass
Dear Mary: [A portion of this letter is in section IV]

We have been having a quiet time this winter, since I don't have a job with the University. I suppose you have heard about the great immigration from Harvard to Washington. Arthur Schlesinger[1] has been asked to be "assistant to the President" in The White House and has accepted for a year and a half. He doesn't seem to know exactly what he is supposed to do.

Barbara Deming[2] has gone in for non-violent resistance to nuclear warfare—has just come back from Europe where you may have seen her. Angus Wilson has been here and did a very good lecture which received the greatest ovation I have heard anybody get since Oppenheimer.[3]—I don't quite know why, except that he covered a great deal of ground—contemporary English fiction—quickly and rather amusingly and gave the students the impression that he was on the level.

I am now getting near the end of my book on the literature of the Civil War, which may not be my most brilliant book, but is certainly my longest.—I hope your own projects are progressing.

As ever,

[1]Arthur Schlesinger Jr. (b. 1917): Harvard historian who became a trusted advisor in the Kennedy administration.

[2]Barbara Deming: activist, feminist, and neighbor at Wellfleet.

[3]J. Robert Oppenheimer, physicist on the Manhattan project, who came under a cloud as an alleged conveyor of atomic secrets to the Soviets.

April 14, 1961 / 12 Hilliard / Cambridge 38, Mass

Dear Mary: [A portion of this letter is in section IV.]

I am nearly at the end of my Civil War book—have been suffering, along with my other complaint, from an allergy caused by the dust from old books. I had never heard of this before, but it seems that one of the librarians here had to resign on account of it, and some of the people who do research have to wear gauze masks. We have been getting rather oppressed with Cambridge and go away as much as possible—have just for the first time in years had a week of gaiety in New York. (My ballpoint won't write on this paper.) We miss the [Robert "Cal"] Lowells and the [Arthur] Schlesingers here. Cal has been in the hospital, but more briefly than usual, and he and Elizabeth [Hardwick] are living separately. My most recent enthusiasm is [Mike] Nichols and [Elaine] May, whose acquaintance I have made. They are extremely interesting young people—he immensely intelligent, she something of a genius, and seem to me to have possibilities much beyond what they are doing at present. I agree with you and Reuel about *Hiroshima Mon Amour,* but haven't found anybody except Sylvia Marlowe[1] who is not enthusiastic about it.

Barbara Deming is deep in the peace movement and has partially carried Mary[2] with her. Mary's painting remarkably improves. I think that losing her mother has made her more mature and self-confident.

My compliments to your husband.[3] Keep in touch with me from time to time and let me know where you are. I've been invited to go to Russia and should like to take the family there in the fall—should really like, it it's possible, to spend the winter in Europe—since I shan't need to be near a library or to be dragging books around in cartons once my book is finished. All best wishes.

As ever, Edmund

[1]Sylvia Marlowe: concert harpsichordist.

[2]Mary: Mary Meigs, Barbara Deming's companion, a painter and writer who charmed Wilson in his later years and was a source of romantic fantasies.

[3]James West, the last of McCarthy's four, a diplomat posted in Paris.

July 7, 1962 / Wellfleet

Dear Mary: [A portion of this letter is in section IV]

About *Pale Fire:* your article[1] was the only one I have seen which really grapples with the book. The other reviewers didn't even know what was supposed to be taking place. But I don't see how you can possibly think it is one of the great works of art of our time. I thought that—although the idea of the commentator's substituting himself for the poet is amusing in itself—the book as a whole was rather silly. I was irritated and bored by all his little tricks, and did not bother to try to figure everything out as you did. I believe that in some cases you attached to details a significance that he [Nabokov] did not intend. *Patriotic Gore* has had the honor of being denounced in editorials by *Life* and *American Heritage*. Dan Aaron[2] had written for the latter a long appreciative article, but the editors—who include Bruce Catton[3]—decided that if they were to publish it, they would be taking the bread out of their own mouths.

I am staying on here longer than usual this summer, but going up to Talcottville at the end of this month.

As ever, / Edmund

[1]your article: "A Bolt from the Blue" appeared first in the *New Republic;* it is reprinted in *The Writing on the Wall.*

[2]Daniel Aaron (b. 1912): professor, chronicler of progressive authors in *Writers on the Left;* he acted as co-editor with Elena Wilson on *Letters on Literature and Politics.*

[3]Bruce Catton (b. 1899): Pulitzer prize–winning Civil War historian.

August 2, 1965 / Wellfleet

Dear Mary: [A portion of this letter is in section IV.]

Did you see my review of Nabokov's Pushkin in the *New York Review of Books*?[1] He is furious, and we are now engaged in a polemic. This is the first time for years that I have been at Wellfleet this time of year—on account of all the family converging—and so far I am rather enjoying it.

Have you read Christiane Rochefort's[2] *Les Stances à Sophie*? I have become a great fan of hers. The book has been actually well translated—which

I shouldn't have thought possible. To my surprise, she has just sent me, with a touching *dedicace,* her translation of a book by that literary Beatle, John Lennon. Janet[3] must have told her I admired her. Have you ever met her in Paris?

What are you doing nowadays? (Thanks for the card from Trier.) The only news about you I hear is of your presiding at literary congresses. We spent the whole academic year at the Center for Advanced Studies at Wesleyan—a profitable but dreary experience. The people we saw most of in the second semester were Jean Stafford[4] and Father D'Arcy,[5] the Jesuit priest, who is extremely literary and very amusing. We have now returned to Wellfleet more or less for good—our old routine of staying here through New Year's, then having a couple of months in New York.

Let me hear from you.

Love, / Edmund

[1]The beginning of the famous literary war of the titans between Wilson and Nabokov, Wilson's scathing review appeared first in *The New York Review of Books* July 15, 1965, and was reprinted in *A Window on Russia* (1972).

[2]Christiane de Rochefort: wrote sexually explicit books about French working-class people, as he notes in his letters of the same period to Clelia Carroll (see section V). Wilson admired her boldness and lack of bourgeois sentimentality.

[3]Janet Flanner, literary journalist who, under the nom de plume Genet, wrote the Letter from Paris which appeared periodically in the *New Yorker* for many years.

[4]Jean Stafford (1915–1979): novelist, short story writer, and critic. As a young woman she was married to Robert Lowell, and later wed A. J. Liebling.

[5]Father D'Arcy: friend of a number of literary people. Wilson wrote in *The Sixties* of a great ceremony honoring him and sent the manuscript to Clelia Carroll.

Sept. 1, 1965 / Wellfleet

Dear Mary: [A portion of this letter is in Section IV]

I can only find one copy—which I need—of the Nabokov polemics,[1] but I'll send you one later.

The end-of-the-season cocktail parties are now in full swing. We had sworn we were not going to any, but have been twice trapped by being told that it was just a few people. When we arrived, there were many cars, and it turned out to be the regular Wellfleet mopping-up operation.—Mary [Meigs] and Barbara [Deming] and their little French-Canadian protégée (the novelist Marie-Claire Blais),[2] have been away in Maine and I miss them. They now have a strange ménage à trois, with a black Lesbian dog that tries to bite all the men, picked out, with unerring instincts, at the Animal Rescue place.

With time, I have got to be very close friends with Mary. Her painting has had a most extraordinary development. For the first time, she has been going in for figures and has painted unexpectedly startling portraits of Marie-Claire and her family.

Walkers, Chavchavadzes, and Jenckses aged a little but just the same.[3] Remember me to Sonia [Orwell] and Isaiah [Berlin].

As ever, / Edmund

[1]polemics: Nabokov's counterblast in the Pushkin dustup ran in *Encounter*.
[2]Marie-Claire Blais: French Canadian writer; Wilson wrote about her in *O Canada: An American's Notes on Canadian Culture* (1965).
[3]All members of the Wilson social circle on the Cape.

Wellfleet, Cape Cod / April 15, 1967

Dear Mary: I am going to be in Paris at the Hôtel de Castille, from May 24 to 29, on my way back from Israel and Jordan, where I am going to bring my scrolls book up to date. Won't you call me up there?—I'm not sure of your number.

I thought your Vietnam article[1] was excellent—the only thing I have read that gave me an idea of what it was actually like.

Love, / Edmund Wilson

[1]Came out as a book titled simply *Vietnam.*

Wellfleet letterhead / June 10th, 1971

Dear Mary: Thanks for the plug at Nice.[1] The money is very welcome.

[A portion of this letter is in section IV.] I had a bad fall on a trip to New York and injured my back. I am more or less helpless but enjoying my idleness.

As ever, Edmund

[1]plug at Nice: thanks to the recommendation of McCarthy and James Baldwin, who were on the committee, Wilson was awarded the Golden Eagle; it brought him $5,500.

TO ELENA MUMM THORNTON

A charming cosmopolitan woman who was married to a Canadian business-man, James Thornton ("Jimmy"), when Wilson met her, Elena was a member of the champagne Mumm family and traveled to Johannisburg [Germany] after World War II to visit relatives and to see to her interests in the concern. She met Wilson on the Cape in the early forties when she was a paying guest at Nina Chavchavadze's. She worked for *Town and Country* as an editor and became friendly with Wilson after a section of his *Memoirs of Hecate County* was published in the magazine. After she became his fourth wife in 1946, they lived in Wilson's Wellfleet home, purchased with a bank loan in 1941. Elena loved the social scene on the Cape and detested the rural isolation of Wilson's beloved Talcottville.

New Yorker letterhead / April 11, 1946

Dear Elena: I came to the office here full of joy—everybody seemed so pleasant, all the women good-looking—and have been only slightly dampened by having lunch with an English publisher. Am now about to take the train.—I think about you all the time. Even that sordid old house seems cheerful.—I think that Mrs. Lehovich and Denika[1] have supplied a kind of needed touch without which nothing of the kind is ever complete.—I've just received a check from Doubleday which isn't as much as I'd expected but something.— Drop me a line soon.

All my love, / Edmund /

(that's what you ought to call me)

[1] Mrs. Lehovich and Denika: figures in the ballet world in whose house Wilson and Elena had enjoyed an assignation.

April 13, 1946 / Charlottesville, Va.

Dear Elena: I came down here with my cousin Susan in a remarkably comfortable and uncrowded train. Susan is my only surviving close Wilson relation, and, though she is not particularly interesting, I am fond of her and like to be with her, because, through our relationship, we have something in common that I don't have with anyone else. Years ago she pulled herself away from the Virginia side of her family and the more or less decaying community down here and got herself a job in New York, where—being a predestined spinster—she has become something of an authority on occupational therapy for the insane and spends most of her time translating Anglo-Saxon poetry.—We got in late Thursday night. I have a room in a tourist house here, with a big old bed, and I lay in it and wished you were there beside me. I went to sleep thinking about you and woke up thinking about you in the morning.

I had to devote most of the next day to calling on and going around with Susan's relations, who rather bored and exasperated me by their Southern combination of wooliness and slackness with unshakable self-complacency. The old lady who is head of the family is still indignant over Theodore Roosevelt's having asked a Negro to lunch at the White House, and has always disapproved of the New Deal because it has made the Negroes lazy by encouraging them to go on relief. They gave a cocktail party for Susan and me yesterday afternoon, and at first I was deeply depressed by the array of university professors and unidentified elderly relatives, but the food and drinks were awfully good and by the time all the guests had gone and I was left with the family, I was feeling much more genial and beginning to like them. Everybody had had a great many old-fashioneds and they began to tell me what they really thought of my book,[1] which I had been hoping they had not read. I decided that the old lady was quite admirable. She is eighty and has had one breast removed, from cancer, but still manages to preside over the family and keep it in order and hold it together, as I don't believe any of her children could do. They belong to a quite different world. In the evening, Venable Minor, her son, took me over to the University, which is really one of the things best worth seeing in this country. It had impressed me as a child when I used to visit here and when the Minors lived on the "Lawn," and it was mainly to see it again that I came down. It seems to me more extraordinary and beautiful than ever. It was designed by Jefferson, you know, and it must be the best piece of architecture in America. I won't go on about it, because I don't want to bore you with a travelogue, but I wish I could bring you here sometime. At night the great "Rotunda" and colonnaded quadrangle imposes itself as a realized Jeffersonian dream of liberal learning and classical republicanism, and I was enchanted to go into Poe's old room and into the house (part of the original central design), with Empiresque sphinx-ornamented cornices and a portico of Corinthian columns, where I had used to go in my childhood. Nothing I have seen in this country has moved me so much for years (I suppose the old-fashions had contributed to this).

Forgive all this if it doesn't interest you, but I think about you all the time and want to communicate with you and don't know you well enough yet to know exactly how to talk to you in a letter!—I have got to the point now where I keep thinking that other women resemble you and, when someone new comes into a room, that it is going to be you.

It is marvelous spring down here. There is still quite a lot of snow on the Blue Ridge, but dogwood, Judas-tree, and tulips are out all over, and the whole landscape is taking on varied and delicate shades of green.—I am getting depressed as I write because you are not with me. I am going to write in my note-book some more descriptions of you so that I can never lose the images of how you looked at certain times.

All my love, / Edmund

[1]*Memoirs of Hecate County.*

April 20, 1946

Dear Elena: Mary called up Saturday afternoon to say that Reuel was ill and might have measles, though no spots had come out yet. If he shouldn't come to town, perhaps we could have lunch Tuesday.—I went to bed early and slept off my drinks, then woke up about midnight, very restless and longing for you terrifically. It was such a wonderful afternoon.—I'll call you Monday.

All my love, / Edmund

April 24, 1946

Dear Elena: Could you come up for lunch at 12 Friday? If this isn't a good idea for that day, let's have lunch at the Weylin or somewhere anyway. Reuel is going out that day with Rosalind. I am taking him down to his grandmother's late that afternoon. Will call you up tomorrow.

I'm pretty well exhausted with the complications of life. I get no exercise, do no solid work, worry about everything and can't sleep at night. I was cheered up by getting your note this morning.—Have just taken Reuel to the new Disney film,[1] which is not very much good. Like so many other things in America, Disney has been developed beyond a point—went so far and then slipped back.

Don't hesitate to destroy my letters—you embarrass me by behaving as if they were valuable manuscripts.

All my love, / Edmund

[1]*Song of the South.*

May 14, 1946 / Wellfleet, Mass.

Dear Elena: Just after I'd mailed that letter, the boy at the *New Yorker* gave me your message from Saturday. I wish I had had it in time.—I arrived here late Sunday night, and it seemed to me that I've enjoyed few things so much in my life as waking up the next morning in the beautiful May weather and finding myself in this house with all my own things around me. The great thing about it up here is that—because of the lack of smoke and the sand, I suppose—there is never any dust, and when you come back to a house that has not been lived in for six months, everything looks perfectly clean. Two ceilings have been taken down, and everything is in awful shape, but I'm not so much appalled as I was last autumn. Gus has been doing a very good job cleaning, and I've got three men coming up from Dennisport to work on the place and clear the garden—I hope to get all this attended to properly for the first time since I've had the house. I still have serious problems of carpentering and plumbing, but when these have been taken care of, the place will be inhabitable again, and it will only be necessary to install you and the peacocks.

I saw Nina yesterday afternoon and told her that I wanted to marry you. She thought it was an excellent idea and surprised me by telling me that she had been wishing from some time back that it could happen and had even mentioned it to Mrs. Lehovich. [. . .] I think of you all the time and hope I am not becoming unreal to you by absence. My joy at getting up here is all based on the idea that I shall have you here with me. I wish you could come up during June. Perhaps you can arrange a weekend.—Write me about developments.

All my love, / Edmund

May 18, 1946 / Wellfleet, Mass.

Dear Elena: I definitely think that you ought to tell Jimmy[1] before he goes and get the whole question of a divorce settled. If he agrees, we can get married before the summer is over. It seems to me unfair to let him go off without knowing what the situation is, and, at our end, it leaves a messy state of things. I would like to have it understood by people when you come up here that you and I are going to get married.—But if you do break the news to Jimmy, how will you live the rest of the time, before he goes? I suppose that this problem can be solved. In any case, I think you ought to have it out with him now.

Nina came in to see me last night on her way home from a party. She is already making plans for our wedding. I am going to her house for dinner with Polly Boyden tonight.

Gus, the colored man, is so wonderful that I am beginning to be afraid he won't last—that he's a genie and will go back into his bottle. He does laundry, mends the furniture and is getting ready to plant a garden.—The girl who took care of Reuel last summer and who wants to work for me came to see me this morning and she also made a very good impression. She is twenty, rather cute-looking in a gawky New England way, and apparently rather curious-minded: she is studying "home economics" in Boston and wants to take over the whole household here. Doesn't mind sleeping next to Gus on the third floor. She is coming to me at the end of the first week in June.

I continue to be intoxicated by my freedom. I eat whenever I feel like it, playing the phonograph and walking around. We are still living on the roast turkey we brought with us. Cleaned out my study last night—it was like burying a whole period of my life that is dead.—My health has improved: it nearly killed me to bicycle into Wellfleet the first day I was here, but now I do it with relative ease. [. . .]

When I am not elated, I find myself in a vacuum caused by my not having you with me. I want you very very much, my dear. Do take some action about it. If you want me to do anything, let me know. I could come down at any time. The idea of your situation makes me more and more uncomfortable.

All my love, / Edmund

[Postscript] Thanks for checking on the whoring locale in Rome.[2]

[1]James Thornton, a Canadian from a once-wealthy family (his father founded the Canadian Pacific Railroad); he was Elena's husband at the time Wilson met and courted her.

[2]Presumably for a piece he was writing, by utilizing her resources as an assistant editor at *Town and Country*.

May 20, 1946

Dear Elena: I just got your letter of the 18th and will call you when I go into town to mail it.—I don't understand your point about Mary. She is going to Reno to divorce me as soon as she gets done teaching at Bard College. I have just written to ask her precisely when this will be.

Progress is going along here at a great rate. The house has never seemed to me so pleasant. I brought the dog back the other day. Our reunion was very emotional, as he is an extremely emotional dog, and it made me sad to find him very dirty and all covered with ticks and with an unhappy and sullen look on his face. I think that he has been brutalized living with those people. He was delighted to get home again and has fallen into all his old habits. It touched me because it reminded me of the days when he was a young dog and Reuel was a little boy. I went for a walk with him in the woods yesterday.

Saturday night I had dinner at Nina's with the Sharps and Polly Boyden—the usual local gossip and admiration for some small improvements that Nina is having made on her house. Harl Cook, it seems, has just married Carol.—I had dinner with the Dos Passoses in Provincetown last night.

I am depressed to find that *Hecate County* has sunk out of the best-seller list, just at the moment, apparently, when the big new printing is being distributed, and I am afraid that the supply of prurient-minded readers is rapidly running out, and that I am not going to be able to buy all the new things I had hoped.

I wouldn't worry about St. Paul's if Henry[1] is entered there. There are some very good things about it and, when he gets to college, there will be some advantage in his having gone there. The principal alternative to that kind of school seems nowadays to be Exeter and Andover, and I think that they're much too hard-boiled for him.

I have just read, for purposes of review, a long new novel by Somerset Maugham[2] and have got to apply myself to writing something about it.

It is wonderful here today—the weather has taken a turn for the warmer. Shad bush and beach-plum bushes are out with their white blossoms all over. My white lilacs are just coming out, but the purple and Persian ones are way behind.—If you come, we might try swimming on Gull Pond, where I met you first. I haven't the heart to go there by myself.

I worry about you. I'm sure you know how to handle things, but I don't think you ought to let Jimmy go without getting things settled.

All my love, / Edmund

[1] Henry Thornton, Elena's son.
[2] *Then and Now;* Wilson's piece ran as "Somerset Maugham and an Antidote" in the June 8, 1946, *New Yorker* and was reprinted in *Classics and Commercials.*

July 31, 1946

Dearest Elena: I got the impression on the telephone that things weren't going terribly well. I knew that you would have to struggle, but don't let it get you down. It's very important, I think, to change your living arrangements after you get back from the Berkshires. Otherwise, you'll just be having endless wrangles.—I hope to get to New York next week—perhaps before the end of the week. I had forgotten, when I proposed coming down this weekend, that you were going to the [Berkshire] music festival.

Yesterday the Dos Passoses and Nina came in, in the afternoon, and we had a lively conversation. The Dos Passoses are coming here to dinner tonight to eat an enormous turkey cooked by Polly, and I am going to invite the Groszes. Did I tell you about my seeing George Grosz last evening at Phyllis's? He told me he liked *Hecate County,* and it pleased me because I used to admire so much the drawings he did in Germany just after the war, and there is a macabre-satiric element in my book that has something in common with them.

I learned only almost a week after it happened that my old friend Paul Rosenfeld,[1] the music critic, had died. He was one of my literary friends whom I had kept through all the years from the early twenties, and it made me very sad. I had seen him just before I came up here. He is the fourth of my close friends who of recent years has died in middle age, with work unfinished and leaving the impression that they had never completely fulfilled themselves. You think that people are just on the point of producing their best work, and then suddenly they are dead and it appears that their work has been done. It has always been characteristic of writers and artists in America that they have not put through their careers. They tend to die prematurely, to go to pieces with drink, or to sell out to the popular market. It has been harder in this country than in others to swim against the current: people either give out and expire or allow themselves to be carried in the other direction. We used to talk about this in the twenties at the time of the big literary revival, and assume that our generation was different from the rest, so that now it is dismaying to find the same thing happening to many people. Paul Rosenfeld, who had flourished in the days of such highbrow magazines as *The Dial* and *The Seven Arts,* wasn't able to sell his stuff in the era of Henry Luce[2]—though he was certainly one of the most brilliant and best-equipped American writers in his line—and I think it was partly discouragement that caused him to die as he did.

I hate being separated from you. Everything seems temporary and incomplete, and I am haunted by images of you that, when you are not with me, get to seem like the images of a dream that I am afraid will never be realized. It excites and enchants me but makes me very restless to think that, only a few days ago, I had you with me in the room above my study here, and was able to see you looking so beautiful at Gull Pond and in Minor's woods.

Don't let yourself get depressed by the present situation. I'll be with you soon in New York. [A portion of this letter is in section IV.]

[. . .] We have gone on having beautiful days. I feel that you and I have never been able to spend the whole of one of these days—in the sense of getting out of it all that it is worth—the way it might be spent.

Good-bye, my dear / Edmund

[1]Memorialized in Wilson's "Paul Rosenfeld: The Three Phases," in *The American Earthquake.*

[2]Henry Luce (1898–1967): founder of the phenomenally successful middle-brow magazines *Life, Time, Fortune,* and *Sports Illustrated.* See section VII also.

July 31, 1946

Dearest Elena: I am writing this just after talking to you on the phone. It would be absurd for you to put off a decision till Thanksgiving. How could you live with Jimmy and be having a love affair with me at the same time? Or if you agreed not to see me, how could you give Jimmy a fair trial if you still cared anything about me? [marginal note: If, on the other hand, you spent the time seeing me and put off a decision about me, I'd be going crazy and you'd be under a continual strain, with the decision still ahead.] It would also be absurd for me to have a talk with Jimmy. If you are going to put it through, you ought to do it right away. You know that I want you more than anything, and you must decide whether you want me enough.—When you come back from the Berkshires, if Jimmy doesn't leave the apartment, you ought to go somewhere else. I don't see how this can prejudice your position very seriously, since you will not be deserting Henry. If you really want to marry me, there is nothing, in the long run, that Jimmy can do to prevent it. The worst that could happen would be that you would have to live by yourself without being divorced till Jimmy became convinced. He would not have anything against you that would make it possible for him to take Henry away from you. I know from my own experience that it is a great mistake for the parties to keep on seeing one another and arguing and hashing over the past. You ought to serve an ultimatum at the end of this week and then not discuss it any more except by phone or letter.

I am trying to get tickets for the Berkshire festival next Friday. My idea would be to motor down from here and have you meet me there. When you are there, please find out how we could handle it—at about what time of day the opera will be and whether we could get a train away afterwards. If we couldn't get a train, we could always take a taxi to some other place and spend the night there—that is, if you are free to stay away from town.

I want you in the most terrific way. I suppose the looming difficulties make it stronger. I must see you this coming week, and if I can't get tickets for the opera, will come to town anyway.

All my love, / Edmund

July 31, 1946

Dearest Elena: This is the third letter I have written you since morning, but I have had such a passion for you all day and my phone conversation made me anxious.—What I want to say to you is that you've been compromising for years with the problem of being married to Jimmy, and that you oughtn't to go on making compromises even for only a few months unless you want to go on that way for the rest of your life. I couldn't bear to have you on those terms, and you have told me that you thought you would shrivel up (though I don't think that is really what would happen) if you went back to the old situation.

I've heard from the *New Yorker* that they had no trouble in getting me seats for *Peter Grimes* the 6th, and I'm going to get them to change it for the 9th.

All my love as ever, / Edmund

Aug. 14, 1946 / Wellfleet, Mass

Dearest Elena: I was glad to get your letter and the message that Nina just brought me this morning:—I've been somewhat ill the last few days—not seriously: I've just had a cold and been rather out of sorts. The couple are supposed to come this afternoon or tomorrow. I've been getting our breakfast and supper (canned peppers, canned turkey à la king, peanut butter sandwiches), and going to the Ship's Bell for lunch. A man was supposed to be coming to stay here tonight and draw me, but I got in touch with him and put him off. Dos Passoses have asked me to dinner tonight. I'm going to try to make it.

My English publisher has sent me a piteous plea to change the text of my book, because they cannot find a printer who will set it up, but I am remaining adamant.[1]—It is raining and dreary today.—Reuel's clothes arrived yesterday. They are fine, and he is delighted with them—looks a lot better.—This is not an exciting letter, but my life is in rather a low key. After lunch, Charley Jencks[2] is coming to play with Reuel and I am going to go to bed and read

George Crabbe. In the evenings I've been reading Reuel *Uncle Tom's Cabin.*
I've never read it before myself, and am surprised to find how good it is.[3]

All my love, my dear. / Edmund

[1]*Memoirs of Hecate County;* for more on the difficulties involved see section VI.
[2]Son of Gardner and Ruth Jencks, friends of Wilson on the Cape.
[3]Years later Wilson was to take much the same attitude in his chapter on Harriet Bee-
cher Stowe in *Patriotic Gore* (1962). Wilson's reassessment was an early entry in the modern
resurgence of the novel after a period of utter neglect.

Aug. 17, 1946 / Wellfleet

Dearest Elena: I've really been in a state of suspended animation ever since I
left you. I'm functioning fairly actively now, but still have no voice and can't
taste or smell.—I hope that the new couple will last till the end of September,
but it is more or less the same story as Chris and the Dehazes:[1] the girl has
worked mostly in shops and knows very little about cooking and nothing
about serving meals. Neither of them has any idea of time and they never do
anything when I tell them to.

Peggy Bacon came to dinner last night. She brought Reuel a pastel set
from Provincetown and showed him how to use it. He did a ship, a house,
and a dog that were not so terribly bad and was so interested that I have
arranged with her to come and give him some lessons. He is getting bored
with the Jenckses, who continually invite him over. I think that I will take him
and Charlie Jencks and the Macdonald boy[2] to see *Anna and the King of Siam*
in Orleans next Monday afternoon.

I won't keep telling you how much I miss you—but it's wrong for us to
be separated like this at this time. It means I live with a phantom of you.

All my love, / Edmund

[1]Evidently hired help that didn't work out.
[2]Probably the elder of Dwight Macdonald's two sons, Michael.

August 18, 1946

Dearest Elena: I have nothing at all exciting to report, but am feeling a lot
better.—I don't have any more *New Yorker* work to do for awhile and am
getting back to my book.[1]—Joyce and Bill seem to be working out all right:
they are at least pleasant and cheerful instead of sulky and morose like the
DeHazes. [A portion of this letter appears in section IV.]

[. . .] Bill has found out how to get more hot water, but it involves having the radiator on, and the weather in the last few days has become extremely hot for here.—Bambi has to be tied up on the porch because he has a Scotch terrier girl friend in Wellfleet.—This is the spiffy deep-summer season when the pace always becomes accelerated. So far, I have kept well out of it. Having this prolonged cold, which has been lodged in nose, throat, and ear, has made me feel that I was sealed up from the world.

I am now hoping that it will be only a few days before you will be coming up. I wish you would visit me here—I don't how it could do any harm unless the situation is very bad. But do whatever you think best.

All my love, / Edmund

[1] *Europe Without Baedeker.*

August 20, 1946 / Wellfleet

Dearest Elena: My party went off pretty well, at least painlessly, last night. I asked a few other people at the last moment that I had to do something about, and now don't have to do anything else about anybody. The surprise of the evening was a beautiful married daughter that the McAllisters brought (McAllister is the federal judge from Michigan): she has long yellowish blond hair startlingly combined with eyes that are not merely brown but absolutely black. Unfortunately, though she has been to Bryn Mawr, her conversation is not up to her looks, and when I spoke of her strange coloring, she said, "Yes: it's one of the mysteries of heredity." It was only a little later that I realized that she was the same type as the golden-haired woman in my book[1]—and that I had been complimenting her on her appearance in the same way (though not of course so romantically) as the man in the story. It turned out that she had read the book, because she mentioned one of the other stories. It was curious because the incidents in the story were mainly made up, and I had never known a real woman who had precisely that color combination.[2]—[Some of the local residents] have begun to bore me, and I don't think I shall see much more of them. Nina looked very well in a gray and white striped blouse—not so chunky as she has sometimes looked lately.

Joyce did a fairly creditable job on the dinner, though that, too, involved some surprises. She really wants to do things properly and worries about not cooking and serving right—I have to be reassuring and consoling her all the time. This is a relief after the complete indifference of the DeHazes. She is a typical Harlem darky, but more amiable than most of them are—rather pretty. She does her hair while cooking over the gas stove and sings continually while she works—all the current colored torch songs. The man is all right, too. He was a gunner in a bombing plane in the Pacific.

Come up on Labor Day if you'd rather—though couldn't you do both? Joyce and Bill want to save up their days off to go down to New York over that weekend, but this, from one point of view, would probably be just as well.—I'm longing for you terribly, my dear—wish I could talk to you instead of just writing these letters.[3] Reuel goes swimming every morning with Chuckie Walker and the rest, so I haven't been to Gull Pond or the beaches once since I got back from the Berkshires. He and I have been having a good time, though, together. One of my most remarkable achievements lately has been reading *Uncle Tom's Cabin* aloud to him and impersonating all the various characters with their various dialects—something you really have to do— while stopped up and choked with my cold—which sometimes ends in convulsions of strangulation.

I have learned more in the last ten days about the housekeeper's point of view than I ever did from just looking on. I believe I could become not bad at it, but it really is a full-time job. My mistake at the beginning of the summer was that I did nothing about it at all.

I was very glad to get your letter yesterday, which really did sound as if you were getting things straightened out.

All my love, / Edmund

[1]Section in *Memoirs of Hecate County* called "The Princess With the Golden Hair"— the section that called obscenity charges down on the book and got it banned in various places.

[2]There was, nevertheless, one Elizabeth Waugh, a married woman who ran a needle shop in Provincetown with whom Wilson carried on a mostly one-sided affair (she wrote most of the letters); this correspondence has now been published under the title *The Princess With the Golden Hair*, a reference to the fact that Wilson did use her as a partial model for Imogen.

[3]Telephone calls were problematic because Elena was still sharing an apartment with her husband, Jimmy, and had no private phone at her offices at *Town and Country*.

Sept. 7, 1946 / Wellfleet

Dearest Elena: There is nothing new to report up here. Reuel goes with Charlie Walker in the mornings and Rosalind takes him swimming or to the movies in the afternoon, so that I now have all day to myself for reading and writing—with the result that I don't take any exercise and am getting so that I don't sleep. Otherwise, it is wonderful to be able to be uninterruptedly literary.

I have had a feeler from Hollywood about selling *Hecate County* to the movies, but I know the man who is working on it and he is extremely unreliable—I can't imagine he will get anywhere with it.—The Henderson Place people have written me that they won't let the house under any circumstances after the first of October.—I was astonished, a couple of days ago, to get a letter from Edna Millay, whom I haven't seen for more than fifteen years and who was answering a letter written her about John Bishop's death two years ago. She said that she had been in the hospital with a dreadful nervous breakdown, and the letter sounded rather convalescent and queer. The queerest thing—which, however, I found rather reassuring—was that she said she mainly blamed the breakdown on the violence she had done her conscience by writing bad poetry for propaganda purposes during the war.

I haven't seen Nina lately, but am going there to dinner tonight. She was furious with the Redmans because they had drunk up part of her liquor as well as their own and taken away two half-finished bottles.—Night before last, we all had dinner very pleasantly at the Jenckses—Ruth's sister and a past boy-friend were there. We left at 9—I go to bed and read nowadays at the same time Reuel retires.—Joan Colebrook came in last night to bring back some books. She tells me that she is going to Reno in a couple of weeks.

Why don't you take Henry to *Caesar and Cleopatra*? I should think it would be a good thing for him to see. I can go by myself or take somebody else.

Don't bother to send out Mary [McCarthy]'s proof—I have been rather avoiding her writings. Reuel has just had some postcards from her: she says that she has bought her passage back.

By the way, you shouldn't use enervating in the sense of the French enervant, as you did in your last letter or the other day at the station, when you said that your suitcase that popped open was "enervating." To enervate in English means to make you feel languid and nothing else, as when we say that a climate is enervating. Enerver in French means something like exasperate—just the opposite idea.

I'm enclosing a clipping about a plane crash. Do not go West in this way. I did it once, and I can tell you that crossing those mountains is dangerous. They have frightful accidents all the time.

I will be in New York week after next, and I hope that we can get all our plans definitely settled then.

All my love, my dear, / Edmund

Sept. 9, 1946 / Wellfleet

Dearest Elena: The Tudors came in with Nina after dinner last night. I liked them very much but I think that Mary talks too much, or at least too steadily, and, when she is not being funny, gets a little boring. I hadn't realized, though, when I saw her before, how very pretty she was.—She is a typical Pittsburgh girl—I guessed from her accent and mannerisms that she came from there—and reminds me of Rosalind's mother and her mother's sisters.—I have invited them to come here again tonight—the Jenckses are coming to dinner to eat a turkey.

Saturday night I had dinner at Nina's with the Chermaevs[1] and that couple that Nina knows of which the man is a cancer researcher—she gives him Russian lessons. It was pleasant: the cancer researcher talked lucidly about his subject, and after dinner I became involved with the Chermaevs in one of those arguments about the Soviet Union which I am becoming extremely tired of, but which, once started, seem to have to run their course. This one did not become acrimonious, as is sometimes the case. I didn't think Chermaev so bad—though he is certainly a queer product. Did you read George du Maurier's novel *Trilby*? He looks like a composite picture made from the illustrations of the various male characters—with the Polish Jewish hypnotist Svengali amalgamated with the well-groomed young Britishers. It is his wife rather than he who is the intransigent Stalinist, sharp and grim, though she let him and me do most of the talking, while she was no doubt despising me as a Trotskyite.

I have an absolutely first-rate contractor from Chatham who is going to go to work on the house here this week. I am first going to get all the essential things done—of which there are a good many: window-frames, screens, roofs, ceilings, foundations, etc., and have two new rooms put in where the attic now is, before trying to do anything about the barn and my study. The barn is really collapsing, it seems, so that an almost completely new building will have to be put up. I hope that you will be able to get up here to help decide how the upstairs will be done.

I'm afraid that you've been having a pretty trying time. Mary Tudor thinks that you have been wearing yourself out. I hope that the next week or two will see the main problem settled.—Later this morning, I'll call you up.

All my love, my dear, / Edmund

[1]Chermaevs: part of the large Russian colony around the Chavchavadzes.

Sept. 10, 1946 / Wellfleet

Dearest Elena: A great boredom suddenly descended on me today, due to not being able to see you. When I called you this morning and said that it wouldn't be a week before Henry would be going to school, I thought it was Wednesday, but then realized it was only Tuesday and that it really would be a week.

I told you about last evening on the phone. I let Rosalind invite people in because she enjoys it so much, but am not going to have any more people this week.—We have spent most of the afternoon in a rather aimless but not unpleasant drive.—Tried to call on a cousin of mine who had written me that she was at Orleans, but didn't find them home and did a lot of shopping in Orleans.—Reckie [the family dog] ran away during the party last night to visit a girl-friend in Truro, and we had to go and get him back.

Nina brought us the bad news that Gull Pond has all been sold for lots.— Dos is just back from New York, where he seems to have had a dreadful time being baited by a couple of Stalinists on an Author-Meets-Critic broadcast.— Joyce and Bill seem to want to stay here longer than the 1st. Bill, who is extremely stupid, would like to go back to the Army, in which he says he spent eight years; but Joyce won't let him, and he confided to Rosalind that she had something on him which she could ruin him by revealing, so that he had to do what she wanted. They are all right, but rather depress me. I hear them having long angry arguments after they go to bed at night.—I have just bought the complete works of Wedekind and Schnitzler,[1] and hope to read them this winter with your help.—We've acquired a DDT bomb that slays the mosquitoes all right but leaves a very stifling unnatural smell in the air that suggests atomic extinction and almost makes you wish that you were back battling man to man in the more human old-fashioned way.

Mary has written Reuel that she is coming back this month and has her passage.

This is a dreary enough letter and written, besides, in a thick kind of ink that I can't seem to write decently with, the better kind having given out. I've been feeling rather let-down today. I am sure that you, at your end, must have been having a wretched time. Shall call you up in the morning. Good night.

All my love, / Edmund

[1]Wilson always credited Elena with being very helpful to him when reading works in German. Wedekind and Schnitzler are perhaps best known for adaptations of their work: two Wedekind plays were adapted by Alban Berg for his opera *Lulu;* Schnitzler wrote the work on which the French film *La Ronde* is based.

Sept. 24, 1946 / Wellfleet, Mass.

Dearest Elena: I'm very sorry that I kept you out so long the other night—I'm afraid it made you worse. I do hope your jaw is better today. Don't try to do too much about the office.

A cable has just come from Mary, but it has been so garbled by the idiotic Western Union man here that it is impossible to tell when she is arriving—the 30th perhaps, but I'm getting him to check. She says "Apartment prospects"—which doesn't sound very reassuring.

The Dos Passoses came in last night while I was talking to you on the phone. They are leaving for Virginia tomorrow and I may not see them again before I go West, so we asked them to dinner.—Dos says that Idaho is full of beautiful scenery. [A portion of this letter is in section IV.]

Joyce and Bill had a violent quarrel while I was away. I'm going to let them go the first of October. They are so undependable and behave so queerly that we'll be rather relieved not to have them here.

It seems that V[ladimir] Nabokov has been approached by the State Department with a view to getting him to do Russian broadcasts. I hope it works out, as I understand that it is pretty well paid—though it is difficult to imagine him repressing his tendency to perverse humor that has sometimes gotten him into trouble.

George Brett, the head of Macmillan, has just written me, in all innocence, apparently, asking me to send them a statement championing *Forever Amber,*[1] which is being prosecuted in Massachusetts.—I found a letter here, by the way, about translating *H[ecate] C[ounty]* into German.

I have been thinking about Jackson's book,[2] and, though it seemed to me when I was reading it that he had rather nobly chosen a subject which would make his story impossible for the movies, I have now come to the conclusion that, with a very little change, *The Fall of Valor* would be all right for Hollywood. A middle-aged professor, disqualified to serve in the war, and patriotically unhappy about this, becomes devoted, in a hero-worshipping way, to a brave and attractive young soldier. This causes him to neglect his wife, who does not understand his feeling of frustration and leaves him. But in the end things are set right again by the letter slipped under the door.

I'm sending a check, which I'm sure you'll need, if you have to get your reservations, etc. You'll have your dentist to pay, and I think you ought to make your lawyer send you a bill. I've always insisted on this, no matter how well I knew the lawyers or how willing they said they were to do things for me for nothing.

I worry about your poor darling face and am afraid you will try to work when you are feeling sick.—I wish you were with me: it is so much pleasanter than that old haunted house in New York. It is beautiful up here: the weather soft and dry, the fields full of golden-rod, purple asters, and pink swamp mallows.

All my love, my dear / Edmund

[1]*Forever Amber:* a best-selling bodice-ripper purporting to be historical; the book's trashy sex and melodrama revolted film director Otto Preminger, who forced himself to finish the project, a 1947 picture with Linda Darnell.
[2]Charles Jackson, author of *The Lost Weekend.*

Oct. 4, 1946 / Wellfleet

Dearest Elena: I am back here. It is a beautiful day. If you were here, we would take our lunch and go swimming in one of the ponds.—I miss Reuel.—Joyce and Bill left at 6 o'clock this morning, and Rosalind and I are feeling rather relieved. The top floor, where they lived, is all smoked up with a queer smell, and I am certain that Bill smoked reefers. He got more and more lackadaisical and made less and less sense. They had a violent quarrel while I was away— the immediate result, it appears, of a fight between Reckie and Bambi.—I got Bill to paint the floor of the bedroom above my study, which looks a little less like an attic now.

I had a pleasant time in Cambridge with the people there. Took the Nabokovs to dinner at the hotel and afterwards went to the [Harry] Levins. Vera is wonderful with Volodya: she writes all his lectures, types his manuscripts, and handles all his publishing arrangements. She also echoes all his opinions— something which would end by making me rather uncomfortable but which seems to suit Nabokov perfectly. She won't let her fourteen-year-old son read *Tom Sawyer,* because she thinks it is an immoral book that teaches bad behavior and suggests to little boys the idea of taking an interest in little girls too young.—I went to see them yesterday afternoon, and we had the inevitable conversation about Tolstoy and Dostoevsky, the latter of whom they loathe.

I am enclosing a check—which you will need. Get a compartment in the train, if you can.—Also some clippings, which please keep till I come down. Cary McWilliams is the man that I told you I called up in Los Angeles.—I think I'll leave here Wednesday, so shall be seeing you, I hope, Wednesday night. Rosalind is having friends come to visit her here the rest of this month. And after that Nina may come to live here.

The wonderful contractor from Chatham has of course done nothing about the house. I am going to try to get somebody from Wellfleet to do something about the garden now.

I'm hoping that we're over the worst of our difficulties. I already feel more cheerful and relaxed—and am beginning to realize how worried and bad-tempered I've been more or less all the time since I got back from Europe a year ago.—It will be wonderful to get away together.

All my love, my dear, / Edmund

Dec. 10, 1947 / on train from Boston to Chicago

Dearest Elena: I tried to phone you from the station in Boston, but it was 1:30 and I suppose you had gone to town.—I came down on the bus and train with Betty Spencer and had quite a good time with her, as I haven't seen her alone, and had hardly seen her at all, for something like ten years. Her Portuguese husband's mother has just died and her house has been filled with the family mourning in their Portuguese way and arranging masses for the old lady's soul, with the young people constantly playing the radio. She had finally had a crise de nerfs, but is irremediably saddled for the time with a sister who had always lived with the mother and to whom she had been persuaded to say that she could "always have a home" with her and Ernest. She was on her way to New York to try to induce a rich Wall St. uncle to help her out with money. The whole situation is fantastic: I found that she knew almost nothing about what had happened to her old friends, and I spent a good deal of the journey putting her up to date. I asked her whether she couldn't come to see us, and she at first said positively: "No: Ernest's grammar is too bad and his manners are too bad,"—but it seems that he sometimes goes without her to spend the night at Orleans at the house of a judge he works for, and she intimated that she might come without him. I told her I would call her up after Christmas. I have always liked her in spite of her queerness. She says that she is happy with Ernest, that her life at last has reality "on a peasant level," and that the great advantage of her not going around socially is that she doesn't have to go to Truro drinking parties.

I wired the *New Yorker* in the station, and you ought to hear from them tomorrow.—I was touched by the Turanos' letter[1]—will send them a postcard or something from Zuñi.[2]—I have fortunately got a lower berth—have just had dinner and am about to retire with Swinburne or Ben Jonson and John Collier on the Indians.[3]—I think about you all the time. We were running the gauntlet of the photographers at this time last year.—I have been happier with you than I should have thought I could possibly be with anybody before I knew you. I'm sorry that we've had such difficulties about money, which I didn't expect when we were married.—Take good care of yourself, my dear.

All my love, / Edmund

[1]Tony and Ann Turano, a Greek American couple in whose Reno house Edmund and Elena had married. Wilson writes warmly of them in *The Fifties.*

[2]"A Reporter in New Mexico: Shálako" appeared in the *New Yorker* April 19, 1949; it was later included in *Red, Blond, Black and Olive. Studies in Four Civilizations: Zuñi, Haiti, Soviet Russia, Israel* (1956).

[3]Wilson's nighttime reading bore the following fruits, respectively: a long essay on Swinburne in the *New Yorker*, reprinted in *The Bit Between My Teeth*; "Morose Ben Jonson," included in later editions of *The Triple Thinkers*; and *Apologies to the Iroquois.*

July 30, 1948 / Lenox, Mass.

Dearest love: We had a smooth trip down yesterday, but for me a rather disagreeable one, as I was done up from the day before and my tooth ached all the way. After Mary had taken Reuel, I went to bed, worn out and depressed and with my tooth still making me miserable. There was a student concert I should have liked to hear, but I didn't feel up to going over. I went out about 9 to get a sandwich at that merry little restaurant where we used to go last summer. Then I shaved, had a bath, took a double dose of anacin and went to sleep. It was hot here yesterday, but is cooler this morning, and I waked up feeling fine, with the toothache gone. Have just had a not bad breakfast here. I feel relaxed and ready to do things.

I'm sorry I was disagreeable the other night. I continually have it on my mind that I am not giving Reuel the right kind of attention. You have been wonderful with everybody, and I know that it has been a strain for you.—That last day was pretty overpowering—though I had good conversations with Clurman[1] and Dos. Clurman stimulated me about my play, made me feel there was some chance of getting it done.—I hope to do a lot of work on it this fall. Dos drank enormous shots of whiskey and got himself into very good spirits. After a day that he said had been getting him down, with the funeral and packing up in the home.[2] He had just seen a Portuguese cousin from Madeira, a lace manufacturer, whom he had never met before and who told him about the Portuguese end of the family. It seems that the name was initially Dos Passos di Christo (steps of Christ), and that the family crest is a crown of thorns and three nails. He said that he had been feeling very sorry for himself, but that this amused him and made him feel better. Susan had asked him to look out for Topie,[3] and he had told him he would help him through college.—Of course Susan may have left him something.—Susan's dismal funeral, with everybody sniffling in that room while odd fragments of the conventional service were read, depressed me with the thought of how little there was left of the original idealism and enthusiasm of the old Provincetown group. I approve of her idea of having her ashes scattered at Truro, and think seriously of having mine, if possible, scattered between the Spectacle Ponds, where they might lie among the roots of the little wild orchids. This would be less of a nuisance than throwing them out to sea.[4]

Mrs. Kilgas has given us a gigantic room which runs almost the whole length of the bottom floor, the bathroom facilities are admirable, and there is certainly enough space, but it has the disadvantage—though this does not worry me seriously—that you can hear everything that is going on among Mrs. Kilgas and her guests. The furniture is extraordinary: there are Empire chairs and sofa, which might please Mario Praz,[5] but are impracticable for any purposes of mine, electric light fixtures of carved gilded wood with the bulbs encased in crystal beads, and a dainty boudoir screen of embroidery, gilt, and mirrors. On the table is a small set of Shakespeare.

I miss you and am already counting the days till you come. I looked over for you this morning to the other bed and was startled not to find you.—You need a vacation from the family. The little girl and Miss Carter[6] will do all right without you. There are two concerts today, and I shall go to both. I feel full of life and ideas after being so at bottom yesterday.

All my love, dearest / Edmund

[1]Harold Clurman, theater director and critic, founder of New York's Group Theatre in 1931, and director of Odets, Williams, and others.

[2]Dos Passos was still suffering over the death of his wife Katy in a grisly accident.

[3]Topie: Sirius Proestopoulos, one of the Greek community on the Cape, friend of Rosalind's—see section IV. Susan Glaspell, a writer who, with her husband George Cram Cook, founded the Provincetown Players in 1915, was Topie's aunt by marriage.

August 1, 1948 / Lenox

Dearest Elena: I missed you acutely at the concert last night, with an empty seat beside me. The music was not terribly interesting: a new symphony by Walter Piston[1] (which, however, getting there late, I had to listen to from outside), an early violin concerto by Prokofiev, and Brahms's first symphony. My tooth was making me uncomfortable, as it has been doing a good part of the time, and, if it isn't better tomorrow, I'm going to the dentist here. I saw our friend the little violinist Cherkovsky[2] and asked him to dinner Monday night.—I am going to give my extra tickets to the next two concerts to Mr. and Mrs. Kilgas, with whom I am now on excellent terms. They have had this house, it seems, only three years. It was built in 1788 by the revolutionary General Patterson, who is commemorated by the monument opposite.

I ran into Lewis Perry yesterday, the former headmaster of Exeter, who is now president of the Friends of the Berkshire Festival, the money-raising organization. He gave me some advice about schools. He is staying at the Monument House.—I am puzzled about Nicolas'[3] behavior yesterday. I called to him as he was going out the door. He turned, shook hands with me, said, "Hello, Edmund," and was off like a shot without another word. I think he must have been with some important person, who was getting too far ahead of him.

Yesterday afternoon I saw the students do operatic scenes. The pretty girl that we liked is not here anymore—or did not appear; and Goldovsky[4] has another prima donna whom I didn't care for so much. He still insists on announcing every number with his bad jokes and his comic accent. Tonight they are doing a new opera by a contemporary Russian composer, based on Gogol's comedy *Marriage*.

This afternoon I fear that I am going to take a lot of punishment in the shape of an immense Mahler symphony that fills almost the whole program. Milhaud[5] was to have conducted a symphony of his own, but that has fallen through, and they are substituting a symphony of Haydn.—I read Koussevitsky's[6] little piece in the *Atlantic* and thought it quite admirable and noble.

I have decided to try to avoid another of these dreary funerals by writing, while I am here, something to be read when my ashes are scattered at Spectacle Pond. The directions will be, *Mit durchaus eructam und feierlichen Ausdruck* and it will rise at the end to a lyric passage: *Sehr feierlich, aber schlecht— Choralmassin*[7]

It seemed to me that Dos had picked himself up and recovered his old enthusiasm and appetite. He seemed excited about studying Portuguese and going to Portuguese countries—felt that he had been occupied with the Spanish at the expense of his own Portuguese tradition.

There are two crouching white iron dogs at the antique store down the street which I want to buy for the terrace.

I think about you constantly, my dear, and can't wait to have you here.

All my love, / Edmund

[1]Walter Piston (1874–1976): orchestral composer who employed a neoclassical style mixed with jazz idioms; he worked with Serge Koussevitsky and the Boston Symphony Orchestra.

[2]Evidently a member of the string section of the Boston Symphony Orchestra.

[3]Nicolas Nabokov (1903–1978): composer, musicologist, memoirist. It was at his suggestion that his cousin Vladimir wrote to Wilson in August 1940.

[4]Boris Goldovsky (1908–2001): known to the millions of opera listeners as the intermission voice of opera background notes on Texaco's Metropolitan Opera broadcasts from this period.

[5]Darius Milhaud (1892–1974): French composer whose music was influenced by Brazilian melodies; served as Paul Claudel's secretary in Rio de Janeiro when the diplomat was assigned there.

[6]Serge Koussevitsky (1874–1951): conductor of the Boston Symphony Orchestra and founder of the Berkshire Music Festival. Wilson was at the festival to write a piece for the *New Yorker*, "Koussevitsky at Tanglewood."

[7]A loose translation might be: "To be played with fiery intensity throughout—very passionate, yet restrained—for full chorus."

Aug. 2, 1948 / Lenox

Dearest Elena: After I called you last night, I went to the end of the alley with the grape arbor and lay down for a rest in the grass outside the hedge. When I went over to the theatre later, I ran into Nicolas, who explained to me that he had been unable to stop to speak to me the other day because he was with the Koussevitskys, and murmured something about somebody catching a train. Then he groped around for a few moments, a little at a loss, till he remembered that I could perhaps help him at the *New Yorker* with an article he is writing on Stravinsky—which he said he wanted me to read. He then had some obvious moments of hesitation as to whether he and I could sit together, as he was staying with Koussevitsky and wanted to sit in the roped-off official seats, but finally invited me to join him, and everything was all right when it turned out that I knew the Perrys and Mrs. Hirshman (the sister of Joyce's friend, Paul Leon, whom we met last summer). Before the people arrived, however, he opened up on Tanglewood, about which his feelings are very hostile. He seems to dislike the combination of music with nature, and was very funny about the raising of musicians like crops or cattle. He says that the concert halls are just like cowsheds and that they milk the contrabasses in the morning. He thinks that Koussevitsky plays too much the role of Führer, and that Copland, Lehrman, and Piston are now "power boys," who control all the music schools. He doesn't like the mass turn-outs for the Sunday concerts. I can't make out whether there is something in what he says or whether it is simply that, though he is staying with Koussevitsky and though K. has asked him to write something more for the Boston Symphony, he feels rather out of sorts here. After the concert, we had something to eat in that little place in Lenox, and he told me a lot that was interesting about what he hears from Russia. He said that he had been in Moscow twice and convinced me that it was true. He is here for the Voice of America.

Mme. Milhaud, an attractive little French woman, told us that one of Copland's pupils had been confused by the appearance of Milhaud, when Haydn had been announced on the program, and had said that the symphony he had just listened to had given him an entirely different conception of Haydn.—Old Grechaninov, eighty-four, was there bowing and beaming. He has produced in his old age an incredibly dreary opera on Gogol's [Russian word for Marriage], of which the students did one act. This morning he has been sitting on the wrought-iron bench between the two white iron dogs in front of the antique store on main street, as if he felt he were a public figure.

I don't think Nicholas likes America at all. I get the impression that his ideal for the arts is not merely that they should be practiced by an elite, but that they should also be enjoyed only by an elite. He gave me a description of what he says is now the formula for an American symphony, which, according to him, Piston's new one precisely fits. The 2nd movement is always an old Kentucky folk-song, with a little lemon squeezed on it; the 4th a very simple fugue. He says that Koussevitsky, though he is giving up the Boston Symphony, will come to be a more conspicuous national figure, as he will be travelling all over the country as a guest conductor.

I went to the dentist this morning, and he told me that my teeth were in such a mess that it would take weeks to straighten me out and perhaps land me in bed. He says that they have not had proper attention, and that the attempts to build up my "bite" have had the result of putting the other teeth under a strain and that this, not the wisdom tooth, has been the cause of my toothaches. I am rather disillusioned with Tingly, but don't know what to do. This morning my tooth is all right, so perhaps I can let it go till I get back to Boston.

This morning I have had a letter inviting me to sit on the stage during the proceedings on Tuesday. Archie MacLeish[1] is going to preside and Ted Weeks[2] perhaps going to speak, but I suppose that I ought to accept. The whole thing, I think, will be very amusing. I wish that you were going to be here, and I count the days till you are coming.

All my love, / Edmund

Love to the children.

[1]Archibald MacLeish (1892–1982): poet, author of "Ars Poetica"; Wilson kidded him in a famous parody, "The Omelet of A. MacLeish," a take-off of "The Hamlet of A. MacLeish" (1928).

[2]Edward Weeks: editor at *Atlantic* and, according to Rosalind (p. 223), "my father's *bête noir*"—Wilson took against him for holding a Nabokov manuscript too long.

September 22, 1948 / Wellfleet

Dearest Elena: You must have been feeling the vibrations that I have been sending out toward you lately. I was glad to get your cable and know that you had arrived all right. We are all fine.

Waldo [Frank][1] came over Monday afternoon and we had one of our animated conversations. He cannot resist with me the same impulse that used to annoy Sherwood Anderson: the moment I spoke of wanting to go to Haiti, he suggested that it would be wonderful if we go there at the same time and that if I would just let him know when I was leaving he would fly over from Caracas and join me. He is about to go to Puerto Rico to lecture. This reminds me that I saw Brownie L'Engle[2] at the Seldeses[3] and she said to me that I must come over soon for a "musical evening." She has been working on her guitar and found it one of the "most absorbing" things she had ever been interested in.

Bob Bensen has written me that the New Mexico University Press is very eager to have my Zuñi piece, so I am going to fix it up for them today. I haven't yet finished my poem and may try to put off for another week the *New Yorker* article about Faulkner.

The Franks gave a farewell party yesterday afternoon to which Nina took Rosalind and me. I drank nothing but a little punch, but have signs of gout this morning. I hope to forestall any worse development.

Reuel seems to be having a very good time and is reluctant now, I think, to go back to New York. He and Charley alternate between one another's houses. I give him a little poetry in the morning and read to him, as usual, at night: Poe and Sherlock Holmes. Last night we all played Parcheesi. Miss Carter won. [A portion of this letter is in section IV.]

My hands have been stained violet from putting Gentian (not Jennilou's) violet on the dogs. Reckie has developed a strange sentimentality—as Rosalind calls it—continually moaning to us—which may mean that he misses you.

I suppose that you are by this time on your way to Switzerland or about to start. I love you, dear, and yearn for you terribly, but shall have to put a brake on it still for another four weeks.

Edmund

[1] Waldo Frank (1887–1967): a friend from the 1920s, critic and novelist; "at his best, he touches tragedy and, at his worst, embraces melodrama." See *The Shores of Light*.

[2] William L'Engle and his wife Lucy ("Brownie"), friends from Provincetown, were watercolorists and frequent companions of Wilson (see *The Thirties*).

[3] Gilbert Seldes (1893–1970) and his wife, neighbors on the Cape; he wrote *The Seven Lively Arts* and Wilson wrote of him in *The Shores of Light*.

September 24, 1948 / Wellfleet

Dearest Elena: Your cable from Zurich came this morning. Jack Phillips has been here worried for fear he would delay too long about accepting the offer of his other prospects, so I will tell him to go ahead. It would be an extravagance for us anyway.

I had an attack of the gout yesterday, which came on in the night and kept me awake and made it difficult for me to get around, but today it has completely disappeared. I realize now that I got it from eating candy. That must have been the trouble after I had been in the Berkshires and this recent attack must have been brought on by Rosalind's birthday candy.

Everything else has been fine. Rosalind has been handling things a good deal better than usual, and Mrs. Kerr seems to be all right. We have bought a new Parcheesi set and have been playing long games of Parcheesi in the evenings. I have been reading Faulkner's hair-raising novels, which are usually better than that bear story we plowed through when we were in Nevada.

I have been languishing for you this week. When you are not here to keep up my morale I lie awake in bed at night worrying about Reuel and Rosalind. On clear days, the house is really pleasant at this time of year, but on muggy days it seems shabby and sloppy, as if the summer had pretty well wrecked it. I think that we must try to get away more. Today is the first really somber autumn day we have had.

Sasha came in the other afternoon, looking haggard, dishevelled, and distraught and had a session which seemed to last hours with Rosalind. I asked what she had said today and Rosalind explained, "Well, I think she's very much in love with Jack, but she's also in love with Paul Shavalov and Harl Cook." I am having the Chavchavadzes come in this afternoon, to see whether I can do anything for Paul.

I am taking Reuel down Saturday to stay over Sunday with Mother. I hope his mother will be back Monday, but I have not heard a word from her.

We have been eating the tomatoes out of the garden.

These letters of mine are not very exciting. I am wondering whether there is any chance of getting one from you before I leave tomorrow morning.

I have been writing this letter before and during breakfast. When Rosalind brought the tray in, I suggested that she and Reuel might pick a few of the apples that are ripening on the tree just behind the house and she told me that they had many more urgent tasks. Just now I went out to get more coffee and found them both playing Parcheesi at the dining-room table. Miss Carter has a headache this morning from playing too much last night.

I hope that things have been going well and that the family situation is not too trying.

All my love, dearest / Edmund

September 24, 1948 / Wellfleet

Dearest love: I found your letter at the post-office just now when I went to mail my letter out to you. It has cheered me up. I didn't know that you were traveling second class, as I hadn't grasped how much the price of passages had risen. I'm afraid you had rather a dreary trip. I didn't send the notes. Maybe Walter did.[1]

We're getting Reuel packed up to go. He and Charley are discussing outside whether to make a farewell trip to Gull Pond. I have given them the stamps on your envelope, which they were very much excited about.

This is just to send you my love. I won't try to tell you how I miss you—

more than I ever remember to have missed anybody else—as it will be more than four weeks before I see you again.

Today is the first really dark day of fall, with the wind beginning to howl and everything with that tarnished October look. [A portion of this letter is in section IV.]

All my love, dearest, / Edmund

[1] Elena's younger brother, Walter Mumm.

Sept. 29, 1948 / New York

Dearest Elena:

I brought Reuel up to town yesterday morning and bought him a lot of clothes at Rogers Peet. After lunch, I called up Mary, who exaltedly explained that she was engaged in typing the last seven pages of her manuscript, but would send Bowden[1] down to get Reuel. When Bowden arrived he announced, with the air of someone who was privileged to communicate a matter of great public interest, that Mary had just finished a short novel of a hundred and one pages.

In the evening I had Marcelin[2] to dinner at the club. Though a mulatto, he is pretty dark and absolutely African in appearance, with intense and piercing black eyes. After dinner, we went down to Dawn [Powell]'s, where we found Cobie Gilman. The whole evening was so strange that when I woke up this morning, it seemed to me almost that I had dreamed it. In the first place, Marcelin himself involved me, as we talked, in an atmosphere completely different from anything I had ever tried to adapt myself to before. He has hardly been out of Haiti. He spent only a year in France in his office, and this is his first trip to the United States. It seemed to me that his life was not merely incomplete but tortured. He says that the position of the mulattos among the blacks in Haiti is like that of the Jews in a community that discriminates against them. He has decided that he cannot live there, and has come to the U.S., leaving his wife in Haiti in the hope of making himself a place here in some official capacity as a promoter of cultural relations. The half-brother with whom he has been writing these novels is "très courageux," lives with the peasants and is a very *détraqué* alcoholic who has just come out of a sanitarium. I had guessed rightly in supposing that Philippe did almost all the writing, while the other man supplied the voodoo lore and first-hand knowledge of peasant life. The new novel deals with a different milieu and I gathered that Philippe was better satisfied with it. He discussed very intelligently the weaknesses of the others. He himself drinks quietly and steadily, having always to have a bottle of rum at his elbow. He deplored the effect on some of the other Haitian writers—such as the author of that *Gouverneurs de la Roses* that I was reading—of their Communist politics; but later in the evening began to talk with bitterness of the French and American "bourgeoisie." He made me feel again the validity of the genuine non-Stalinist social-revolutionary point of view. There is really, I suppose, no place for such a man in any part of our world as it is constituted. As a mulatto, he is up against the color-line, crossing either the whites or the blacks, and as a writer and social critic, he is out of place in a country whose whole life is an exploitation by both blacks and whites of a primitive and impoverished peasantry. I liked him and enjoyed his combination of Negro slyness with French irony, but the whole thing disconcerted me, and I couldn't understand all he said—his French is very peculiar. I had asked the *New Yorker* about sending me to Haiti, but it seems they have promised to send Liebling.[3] Marcelin asked me whether I would like to have the government ask me there as an official guest. Due to there being other people around, I didn't get a chance to talk to him as I should like to do, and I should like to have him to dinner when you come back. You will be able to understand him better than I do. He gave me the manuscript of a book of poems, which are strange and seem rather remarkable—quite unlike anything I know in French poetry.

At Dawn's, he suggested taking us to the apartment of a friend, who had made some recording of voodoo chants. We went to Morton St., and found ourselves in deepest Greenwich Village, and I didn't know it existed anymore. I'll have to break off at this point, as I've got to catch the 6 o' clock train.— Henriguez is going to meet me at Providence. I'll write you the rest of my adventures from Wellfleet. Rosalind says that everything is fine.

All my love, / Edmund

[1]Bowden Broadwater, Mary McCarthy's third husband: a Harvard graduate, one-time fact checker for the *New Yorker*, editor, writer.

[2]Philippe Thoby-Marcelin, (Phito) Haitian writer who collaborated with his half brother Pierre; the two were visitors with Wilson upstate.

[3]A. J. Liebling (1904–1963): longtime *New Yorker* writer, and author of *The Wayward Bus*.

Sept. 30, 1948 / Wellfleet

Dearest Elena, [A portion of this letter is in section IV.]

At the end of my last installment, you saw me mounting the steps in Morton St. to the apartment of Marcelin's friend. She turned out to be a Russian

(Jewish, I think) girl, quite pretty, who had been to Haiti on a Guggenheim, doing research on the native folk dances. There was also a young Chinaman there, with whom I gathered she was living. The apartment was fantastically furnished, but very neat and clean. There was a collection of seashells on shelves, a black canary in a very large cage, named after Guy de [?], the voodoo god of death, whom the owner had made her patron divinity, and a lot of Haitian drums. Two objects which I remarked on under the impression that they came from Haiti turned out to be a Victorian mirror and a Chinese kite. The girl had recorded Haitian chants and drums in wire by means of an apparatus of which I had never heard, and played them while she did the dances with little fat soft white bare feet and a modified rotation of the rump. The chanting was quite beautiful, but got to be rather monotonous—with this recording on wire, you never get to the end of a record. When she finally turned it off, the Chinaman went into action with Chinese "boxing dances," which are a kind of physical culture involving a fresh variety of movements, each of which flows into the next in a peculiar and rather graceful way. The girl said he was teaching her this—every movement had a metaphysical significance. It was all mixed up with rum and attempts to talk French with Marcelin, who seemed to become less audible in proportion as what he was saying was more serious. It was such a Greenwich Village evening as I haven't had for years, and I enjoyed it, but was too tired fully to do it justice. Marcelin interested me very much—I want to have a more satisfactory talk with him, but he distresses me—he is tubercular and obviously rather frail. He says that New York is too much for him.

The next day I had lunch with Elder.[1] He told me that they had announced to him two weeks ago at Doubleday that they were no longer interested in anything but books that were certain to have big sales and that he was to devote himself exclusively to going after this kind of book and to drop his former activities as scout for the more serious kind of talent. He said frankly that I "had no future with Doubleday"—he had just talked to his superior about me—and he advised me to find other publishers for the two books for which I have contracts with them—a conclusion I had already reached. He said that the publisher regarded television as a worse menace to them than even radio, since people would simply sit around watching it in the evenings instead of reading books. [A portion of this letter is in section IV.]

Margaret de Silver[2] is driving up here for the weekend and probably bringing Dawn [Powell]—They will stay in Provincetown or at the Holiday House.

I am afraid that you have been having a harrowing time seeing your relations over there. Don't worry about the money if it doesn't materialize. I figure that I have now passed half of the time that you were to be away. Let me know when the boat is supposed to arrive. Since Rosalind will be up here, I can come down for several days. I should like to have you spend two or three nights in New York before coming back up here. You and I have had so little chance lately to do anything together. I have a feeling that the next two and a half weeks will pass a little more quickly for me. I have rather looked forward to this time up here, which will give me more leisure than I have had. Shall go back to my poem tomorrow.

All my love, / Edmund

[1]Donald Elder, an editor at Doubleday.
[2]Wealthy patron of the arts and Dawn Powell's close friend; Wilson rented her house in Connecticut.

October 2, 1948 / Wellfleet, Mass

Dearest Elena: [A portion of this letter appears in section IV]

Lloyd Rose has been here yesterday and today. He has put up the barn door, so that it is solid across the doorway with a smaller door that opens in it and is fixing the windows and roof so that it will not rain in on the ping pong table. He has also mended the corridor where it leaks and I am going to get him to put up a bookcase there and attend to some other things.—Mr. Johnson also turned up yesterday. He has had weeks of "hospitalization" and described to me his complaints. He promised to come today and start in on the carrot weed if the weather was all right, but, though it is beautiful and very warm, he has of course not put in an appearance.

I wrote all evening last night, for the first time, I think in years. I can't get used to not having Reuel here to read to and see into bed. The Seldeses have asked me over for drinks this afternoon and I shall go if can get Larrue to take me. I have had nothing from you since Monday and am hoping for a letter today.

All my love, / Edmund

October 4, 1948

Dearest Elena:

I have not had a letter from you since Monday, so I have just called Johannisburg. I have a feeling that you ran into difficulties in Zurich, but don't worry about it if you did.

[A portion of this letter appears in section IV.] The Seldeses gave a small farewell party last Saturday and as it was the first time in months that I had been to such a thing without any responsibility about getting back, I threw myself into the spirit of it more than usual. I had long conversations with Lorna about the Bishop and with Phyllis about Haiti and an argument about Peggy Bacon and others with George Biddle who is both opinionated and stupid and, like all mediocre critics, runs all the better artists down.

Phyllis invited the Seldeses and me to dinner so we went over there. I paid a call on Polly and found her in one of her periodical moments of crisis and momentous decision. Archie is having an affair with Emmy Swan and they are going to move into Polly's house, while Polly goes to visit her mother in Chicago. She says that she has plans about Chicago of the most serious kind, which she will not divulge and that she may never return from there, though on the other hand she may be back in two weeks. Tut and Jordan have sold out their interest in the restaurant to their partners. Phyllis's daughter is being psychoanalyzed in New York and her husband from whom she is now divorced, has suddenly arrived at Phyllis's with their child, and seems to be paying a prolonged visit—Yesterday afternoon Polly turned up over here, presenting us with a jar of grape jelly and asking to borrow some novels of Henry Fuller[1] about whom I had been talking to her the night before. I read her my verses and played her some records and finally went back to Truro with her to call on the Givens again. We found the usual melange of the four generations of Phyllis's and Polly's families. Then Polly drove me home and came here for dinner. After dinner, she became absorbed in a series of chess games with Rosalind that went on so long that, after arranging books in a little bookcase that Lloyd Rose had built in the hall, I took Faulkner and went to bed before they had finished. Polly is lonely and depressed and told Rosalind that the other day she had decided to commit suicide, but that, just afterwards, Archie had beaten her at croquet and that she had decided to wait to do it until after she should have beaten him.

The peaches are ripe now and—rather to my surprise—turn out to be delicious. Mr. Johnson has not been seen since the first day he presented himself and told me he was coming next morning.

I hope that you are not having too much trouble. Whatever happens, you will soon be back with us. Let me know whether the boat is supposed to arrive Tuesday or Wednesday. The money got to the bank.—Thank you.

All my love, / Edmund

[1]Henry Fuller (1857–1929): a Chicago novelist; Wilson wrote about him in *The Devil and Canon Barham: Ten Essays on Poets, Novelists and Monsters* (1973).

June 21, 1949 / New York

Dearest Elena: It is horribly hot down here, but I have spent an air-cooled evening. I succeeded in getting a seat to *South Pacific*[1]—in the last rows of the top balcony, but rented opera glasses and managed to see the show pretty well. I thoroughly enjoyed it and was in tears during the last scenes, as I was afraid Ezio Pinza had been killed and would never see Mary Martin again. I had an early dinner at the Blue Ribbon and in between spent three quarters of an hour watching a revolting stage show at the Roxy. Now I am back at the [Princeton] club. The perspiration is pouring onto the table as I write and I am going up to bed.—I have missed you and thought about you my dear.

Edmund

[1]The Rodgers and Hammerstein musical that brought the famous operatic bass-baritone Ezio Pinza to the Broadway stage, starring opposite Mary Martin, beloved musical comedy star since the 1930s.

June 22, 1949

Dearest love: The weather is still terrible, but I have succeeded in accomplishing quite a lot—went to the library in the morning and did some shopping, had lunch with Betty Huling, did some more shopping, and have just had a very satisfactory interview with [Roger] Straus. I think I have solved the problem about my book of literary articles. He is trying to sell Penguin Books the idea of bringing out *I Thought of Daisy*, but I can't exactly see it in that series.—Betty sends you her love. My story about the Russian schoolboy slightly put her pro-Soviet back up. She says, however, that she has it from somebody who knew [Alger] Hiss that he and [Whitaker] Chambers were on intimate terms.—Farrar, Straus want my book[1] by the end of August, so that they can publish it in January or February. Straus, thinking I should like to see an old neighbor, summoned Carol Cook from a back room to see me. I had forgotten she worked there.—This is not very interesting and they only have the kind of pen here that I can't write with—but I wanted to send you a message, even though it means bringing in Charley Bean. I hope that everything is going well. I miss you and look forward to getting back Saturday.

All my love, / Edmund

[1]*Classics and Commercials.*

Dearest Elena: I rather enjoyed the trip yesterday—sitting in a comfortable little compartment in all those well-fitting new clothes. The train was so clean and modern that even you wouldn't have minded it. It was stimulating after Wellfleet to see the industrial efficiency of Philadelphia and Wilmington for the first time in years.—I went through quite a lot of my Haitian literature. The report on the Unesco mission there—which the *Reporter* wants me to check on and write about[1]—shows that the "capitalist" countries are being driven to at least make some gestures in the direction of meeting socialism halfway. It is curious to read about these attempts to encourage rural cooperatives and popular education in Haiti and then read Bellyards' book about the American occupation, in which it appears that we did everything possible to prevent them from having schools. I had my usual depression at night, but woke up early to see the dazzling golden light on the green palms and little pine trees strung with Florida moss. I have never been in Florida before and was fascinated by the pageant of bird-life that goes past the window: snowy egrets, several kinds of beige and bluish heron, and other darker long-winged birds that I take to be buzzards—all looking as if they had flown right out of Audubon—he must have gone crazy when he came here. There are some smaller birds that fly in flocks with quick wing-beats, and it gives an almost musical pleasure to see the contrasts of tempo between these and the slower rhythms of the longer-winged birds. They all fly close to the train and not far above the endless pale swamps and plain. It is wonderful to see an egret alighting and folding its wings from the flying position with deliberate dignity and grace.

Miami is not so attractive—it is, in fact, of an unimaginable awfulness—much like other American seaside resorts but on an unprecedented scale: acres of cheap white shops, mountain-ranges of white hotels. After lunch, I had a taxi drive over to Miami Beach. It goes on for miles—thousands of hotels and houses and monotonous lines of palms. I can't imagine how people live here nor why so many of them come: it all seems a great insipid vacuum—less amusing than Southern California, because there is no touch of fantasy about anything.—I turned back after a few miles and visited the aquarium in town here—then bought a white suit made of some new Dupont product call "sharkskin."

—Now it is after five, and I am going to take a rest and a bath and get to bed early, as I'll have to get up before 7 in the morning—the plane leaves at 9.

I have thought constantly about you and the little girl and missed you—I felt pangs at parting from you, and it seems wrong to me to be here without you.—I hope to be able to get myself set up and do some writing of my own in Haiti before I start in on article-writing.—I don't know whether you went up to Wellfleet today. Do write me every other day or so.

I love you always, / Edmund

[1]"UNESCO at Marbiel" ran in the *Reporter* May 23, 1950; another section, "Haiti: Landscape and Morale," appeared June 6, 1950; and both were reprinted in *Red, Blond, Black and Olive.*

Letters from the 1950s

April 11, 1950 / Red Bank

Dearest Elena: Mother's blood pressure has come down to 180, and her appetite has been reviving, but the doctor doesn't think she will live long and she seems to think herself that she is going to die, as she has given orders as to which undertaker to get and that she does not want to be sent to a funeral parlor. She is conscious and makes sense, though she does not talk much.—I am having Rosalind go back this afternoon—am giving her this letter to mail, so you may get it by noon tomorrow. She has been very nice and helpful down here. If she hadn't known what to do, I shouldn't have been able to get mother into the Red Bank hospital. The doctor at the head of it does not like mother's doctor, but his wife is an old friend of ours, and he arranged to postpone one of his operations so that mother could have a room. [A portion of this letter is in section IV.]—Jennie[1] is a complete wreck and spends a good deal of the time in bed. She had an awful ordeal before we came, alone in the house with mother at night and not able to sleep because she had to listen for her. Gerda has come back and gets meals, but is not in very good shape either. Rosalind and I went out to dinner last night to give them both a vacation. When we got back here, Margaret Rullman[2] came in—the wife of the surgeon at the hospital. She was a childhood friend of mine—very nice and mildly artistic, paints—tiles and trays. She went to school with Mrs. Biddle,[3] who was talking to me about her last summer. I had not seen her in years and was just thinking how pleasant it was to find a faintly intelligent person down here when she began going on about Palestine in a way that indicated plainly that she had swallowed some anti-Semitic propaganda. The worst of it was that it sounded like the brand that my cousin Merwin Hart has been putting out. I think I will ask her and her husband to dinner, though.

I miss you and do not like being away from you so long, but I shall have to stay here till we know what is going to happen to mother. There is still a possibility that she might recover enough to come back to the house with a nurse.

William is here to get this letter and take it to Rosalind, who has gone to the hospital just before taking the train.

Good-bye, my dearest love—I'll call you up tonight.

Edmund

[1] Jennie Corbett, Mrs. Wilson Sr.'s longtime servant.

[2] Margaret Rullman: *née* Edmunds, a friend of Wilson's from his early Red Bank years. See section VIII.

[3] Katherine Biddle, a poet; she and her husband Francis (U.S. Attorney General in the 1940s) were friends of the Wilsons on Cape Cod.

April 12, 1950 / Red Bank

Dear Elena: Mother is definitely better. Her blood pressure is down to normal, her appetite has revived and the pain in her head has become only intermittent. She was quite all right when I went in this morning and asked to have the paper—though she very soon got tired and wanted to rest. At the end of the week, if she continues to improve, we will move her back here with a nurse.—Jennie must have had an awful time—she does not want to go to see Mother in the hospital (has only been once), saying that she thinks it is a good thing for them to be separated for awhile.

I have today begun organizing my life, so that I can get some writing done—same schedule as I had at home and same diet. I don't seem to have gotten any results on the diet so far, though, as I have just bought bathroom scales and discovered that I weigh a little over 200. I haven't been keeping to it, though, during the last few days.—The *New Yorker* is sending me some books, which I'll write about and make a little money.—My reading matter lately has been getting me down. When I thought about it the other day, I realized that, in every book I had read for weeks, the people were either homosexual or in jail or both: Wilde's prison letter and a book about him and Douglas, the two books by conscientious objectors, Genet's *Notre-Dame des Fleurs*,[1] the nasty memoir of L. P. Smith[2] by his disappointed protégé, and *The Big Con*—about professional criminals who have to work hard to keep out of jail. In comparison with all this, Chekhov seems cheerful and normal.—I am quite impressed, though, by the Genet book—it is better than *Journal de Voleur*—a novel which he wrote in jail and in which he included an account of his jail experience while he was living it. [. . .]

I have seen more of Red Bank during the last few days than any time for years. When I went to buy the scales just now, I found the old hardware store that used to be below my father's offices turned into a department store that took up the whole block. The proprietor greeted me and told me that Father had been planning to buy the block just before he died and to install him (Mr. Kislin) there, and that he (Mr. K.) had only just succeeded in buying it. He explained that he had left Father's offices exactly as they were and took me upstairs to see them. He had not, however, preserved them with quite the piety his tone implied, as they were filled with the stock of his store, but he reminded me of what each room had been used for, with a certain pride in having acquired them.—Said that Father was the best friend he ever had.— Rosalind told me a curious story about the Rullmans, the surgeon at the hospital and his wife. Many years ago the doctor was made the victim of a confidence game—an attractive woman came to him for treatment, seduced him and got him to write her compromising letters, then she and the two men she worked with—they travelled around and made a living at this—proceeded to try to blackmail him. Margaret found out what had happened, was terribly upset and thought she would leave her husband. She came to Mother and told her the story, and Mother advised her to go away and allow the crisis to cool—she gave Margaret the money to go to Europe and when she returned, she went back to her husband.—I hadn't realized till I read *The Big Con* what an important element in American life confidence games are. Now I find them quite often in the papers—there was one on the front page of *The Herald Tribune* the other day.—By the way, did you see in last Sunday's *Times* the astonishing disclaimer on the editorial page of some casual remarks about the Catholics in Phillip Toynbee's review of Lionel Trilling's book?[3] It is worth looking up if you didn't notice it.

I stopped writing to have lunch and afterwards had a talk with Jennie. She is really on the verge of a complete nervous breakdown and wants to get away from the house and go to visit her niece, who lives in the next town along the river. I told her to go ahead, but she then began to worry because there would be nobody to take care of the house. I think it will be impossible, even with a nurse for Mother, for Gerda and Jennie to take care of her when she comes back to the house. I ought really to engage someone else and have her here when Mother comes.

Do write me.—And there is one thing that I wish you would do at your leisure. On my table or somewhere in my study, you will find the manuscript of Phito's poems. Please make copies, with a couple of carbons, of the ones that I have marked with a cross or a carat in the upper right-hand corner—I think that is how I have marked them. I want to send them to *Botteghe Oscure.* Just keep them till I get back.

I miss you terribly, dearest love.

Edmund

[1] Jean Genet (1910–1986), French dramatist of *The Balcony* and *The Maids;* author of the two books Wilson mentions here—*Our Lady of the Flowers* and *The Thief's Journal.*

[2] Logan Pearsall Smith (1865–1946), Pennsylvania-born essayist who lived in England and wrote witty *belle lettres;* the book Wilson has been reading is *Recollections of Logan Pearsall Smith* by Robert Gathorne-Hardy.

[3] *The Liberal Imagination.*

April 16, 1950 / Red Bank

Dearest love:

I think that things are clearing up here a little. We may bring Mother out of the hospital Wednesday, with either a trained or a practical nurse. It is very hard to make her accept the fact that she has to have a nurse and she is perfectly merciless with Jennie, keeps complaining that she doesn't come to see her and can't understand what bad shape she is in. Jennie said today, when Rosalind called her, that she had had some sleep and was feeling better, but her niece was on the point of calling a doctor to her yesterday. We are sending her to [her Dr.] Lovett for a check-up tomorrow. Mother says she suffers from boredom. Almost the only thing that she is able to enjoy is eating and she has been ordering breast of chicken, fried sweetbread,—peach tart and orange jelly from home. She now takes an interest in the flowers sent her, and when she doesn't like them has them sent back to the florist and exchanged for something she likes better. But I don't think that she can completely recover. The truth is she has had a slight stroke—one corner of her mouth is contracted.

[A portion of this letter appears in section IV.] I have just had another proof from the *Reporter,* restoring my original text. The editing is sloppy, the proof-reading is sloppy, and the printing is incredible for its badness. I have sent the enclosed telegram to the *Saturday Review* though I had meant to keep out of that controversy![1] Please put it on my desk. I may want to check up on it later.

Rosalind has to go to New York Wednesday to do some work at the New York Houghton Mifflin office.—If Mother seems to be all right here, with somebody to look after her, I might get up to Wellfleet at the end of the week.

I am longing very much to see you. My throat isn't quite all right yet, but otherwise I am healthy again.

goodbye, dearest love. / Edmund

[1]The November 11 *Saturday Review of Literature* had featured an article on Edna St. Vincent Millay by John Ciardi; in the December issue the Letter to the Editor column printed a letter from an E. W. Paramore (Ted Paramore was E. E.) pronouncing himself "angry and disappointed" at the magazine "for printing such a petty and malicious requiem." At this late date it seems unlikely more would be printed, and no telegram was found, but Wilson mounted an eloquent counter-requiem for her in *The Shores of Light.*

March 15, 1954 / Rapallo

Dearest dearest love: I had a very easy trip and made perfect connections at Milan and Genoa. My symptoms have mostly disappeared—though my eye is still sore and watery. I am feeling much better. Rapallo is a delightful town, a much better place than I expected, and entirely free from the squalor of the Italian cities further south. It is warm and the sea is beautiful. There are orange and lemon trees full of fruit. I wish all the time that you were with me and should like to bring you here sometime. This hotel is first class and my room looks out on the water. Unexpectedly, I found Sam Behrman here; he had been to London working on a film and had just come back again. We had an exhilarating and luxurious dinner, which he insisted on paying for. Today I did tons of writing in the morning and afternoon (skipped lunch) till three when I set out with Sam for Max Beerbohm's. It has made me feel happy and normal to be writing something again. I think that one trouble with me lately has been that I have had no chance to write. Today has been an absolute joy. I always like coming to Italy from other countries of Europe. The only thing that has depressed me has been you not being here—you would love it—and the idea that you are struggling with Johannisburg. [A portion of this letter appears in *Letters on Literature and Politics.*]

On the way back, I left the car in the town and walked back up here to the hotel. This—a walk of fifteen minutes—Sam thought was absolutely fantastic. I'd made him take a tiny walk after dinner last night and he bitterly complained and protested, said he had not done anything of the kind in thirty years.

Dearest love, I long for you and the little girl. I hope that Henry's visit has cheered you up. You have been with me all the time and I am already looking forward to seeing you in Paris. Do be sure to write me at length about everything that happens.

All my love, Edmund

Hotel Royal Danieli letterhead, Venice / March 17, 1954

Dearest love:

I just got here (9 at night) and found your wire. I hope you will be comfortable and get a rest. I am perfectly all right now—even my eye has almost cleared up.

I stayed in and wrote all day again yesterday. The weather at Rapallo was beautiful. [A portion of this letter appears in *Letters on Literature and Politics*.]

I left Sam complaining bitterly about the movie script he was working on. I don't quite understand how he manages always to be so rich. He always lives in luxury hotels and has specially engaged cars dragging him around and waiting for him. I almost killed him by making him take a little walk and, last night, bringing him for dinner to a very second-rate restaurant. He insisted on paying for most of the dinners and taxis. He is rather a good thing for me because he makes me feel, in comparison, like such a robust and energetic person. He really improves my morale and health.

It was queer to get in here—at Venice—tonight and go to the hotel in a gondola. It reminded me of arriving with Esther and Sandy [Kimball] back in 1908, in the same way, at night and how excited we were about it, and it made me sad to think that all of the family are dead, except Sandy in the asylum. The second time I came here, in 1921, I was alone and rather uneasily dodging a more or less insane man in the hotel who rode over to the Lido with me one day and engaged me in a mad conversation. It is curious to see the place at this time of year, with natives in black coats drifting quietly through the streets or standing idle in the Piazza San Marco. There is a kind of Sunday atmosphere that does not seem characteristic of Venice. The Danieli has put up a new annex that is much like a Statler hotel, and that is where I find myself, instead of in the old Palazzo, which I liked. I should enjoy it all, though, if you and Helen were here. It must be the oddest city in Europe. I don't see how they built it with primitive methods.

I didn't mention above that Frau Jungmann[1] cheered me up by saying that my head resembled that of Michelangelo's portrait of the Prophet David on the ceiling of the Sistine Chapel—I must look this up. I had been feeling, with my diseased eye, that I must look like the Marquis de Sade's *vieille citrouille confite en jus de* [illegible].

I miss you two darling ladies.—I am buying Helen a little necklace with Venetian-glass birds on it. I have definitely decided to get back from Israel in time to sail April 27, so when you know the money is in the bank, you can go ahead and get the passages. Have written Roger Straus and Mason.[2]

Write me in detail about your adventures. Did I leave a lot of my ties in Frankfurt? I find I don't have them with me.

The boat sails at 2. I have so far been surprised at the efficiency of everything in Italy. Trains are always on time—I haven't yet had a hitch.

I'll write you on the boat and mail it when I arrive.

All my love, / Edmund

[1]The German woman who took care of Max Beerbohm in Rapallo.
[2]Harding Mason: *New Yorker* office manager at that period.

Adriatica Venezia letterhead / March 21, 1954

Dearest love:

This trip has really done me good. I feel perfectly normal again. Have had nothing to drink on the boat.

When I found out we were going to be several hours in Athens, I wired my old friend Eva Siphraios,[1] and she met me at the boat, with her 18-year-old daughter. It was evident that she was now a very important person. She was the first person to come on board, accompanied by a uniformed official, who held his hat in his hand all the time that he was with her and sped me through the formalities of going ashore. She is not so pretty as she was; her little black eyes are still cute, but the lower part of her face has hardened, and she seemed to me much more like a conventional European woman. Her husband is in the government, occupying the queer-sounding post of "Minister to the Prime Minister." She makes official trips with him—especially to Yugoslavia—and goes to official dinners, one of which she had that night, so that I wasn't able to dine with her. She had a car and a chauffeur and drove me to a restaurant in Athens, where she had chocolate and I had whiskey. One of the first things she told me was that she had had a baby two years ago. This surprised me—her other two children being twenty and eighteen—and I asked her if she had the same husband, to which she answered, "The same husband and the same mother-in-law," and added with a sly smile, "I have become motherly." I wondered whether the baby was the husband's—I thought he was about twice her age. The mother-in-law lives in the house with them and has always been a great source of annoyance to her. She is the kind of rather stuffy French-speaking Greek that Rouvier's mother's family evidently are.

Her daughter, who she says is exceptionally bright, spent three months in America last year and wants to go to Barnard. The boy is studying at

Princeton. [. . .] She was kind enough to say later, in some other conversation, that she liked Americans because they were so straightforward, you always knew where you were with them.

I took her back to her apartment at 7 and on the street outside met a terribly pretty little girl, a friend of her daughter's, who turned out to have gone to school at Dobbs.

She thanked me for what she called my "pack of Christmas carols"[2] and I told her to have her daughter look us up if she came to college in the states. She is spectacled and quite plain, does not resemble her mother.

I have done a lot of writing on the boat—a detailed account of our trip. At the rate I am chronicling it, it will be the most completely reported episode in my entire life.[3] It is a great relief to pour myself out. It seems to me that rhythms of work become vital to one's life and that breaking them up may have bad effects. I think that one thing that has been wrong with me lately has been not being able to get into my writing rhythm, which is my most satisfactory kind of functioning. At Salzburg, I found that it was even a relief to write a few letters. With you, your vital rhythm is in your functioning in connection with the Wellfleet place and one reason you don't like Talcottville is that it breaks that rhythm up.

I miss you and Helen constantly and sometimes it seems to me I'm crazy, when I have such a wonderful family, ever voluntarily to be separated from them.

The sea has been getting a little rougher today: we arrive at Cyprus at 6 in the morning and do not leave until 6 p.m.

All my love, dearest, / Edmund

[1]Along with Mamaine Paget, Clelia Carroll, et al., another of Wilson's platonic loves.
[2]A reference to Wilson's habit of sending little printed Christmas poems as Christmas cards.
[3]Certain portions of his trip were in Wilson's articles for the *New Yorker;* ultimately most of the Middle East portion found its way into *Scrolls from the Dead Sea* (1955), and, when one adds the journals of *The Fifties* and the letters in this and other volumes of Wilson letters, his point seems well taken.

Talcottville letterhead / June 31, 1957

Dearest love:

We drove to Lowville after I called you up, and then went on to Cape Vincent. We had a drink at the Carleton Hotel and then started back. I had dinner on the way at Constableville. Then sat on the front porch here and discussed what bad had happened to many old friends, some of whom nobody knew anything about. I am becoming old and *grincheaux* and give horrible accounts of everybody that equal the malignancy of any Oxford don. Now the ladies have gone to bed at 9:30. Margaret [de Silver] says that her visit has been having a relaxing effect on her. She has been ill and, Dawn [Powell] tells me, has been going through the trying experience of having [her daughter] Ann on a visit home with two attendants. Dawn says that she was so unstrung that she (Dawn) had worried about her making the trip, but that it has done her good to get away.

I told you about Walter Edmond's new wife. The effect on him has been electrifying. I think you will like her. She is handsome and, though quiet like an Englishwoman, somehow gives more life and ease to everything over there. Walter, who used to say that he had never read anything, even got to the point of telling her that he thought he would take up books. I forbore to say that I was afraid it was too late.

I went to see Mrs. Burnham and found her alone and on her back in bed. She had had a second fall walking around the house before she was well. We talked about the troubles of the Loomises[1] and Dorothy Mendenhall's fall, and she said to me with a sweet humorous smile, "Well, Edmund, it looks as if all our good times together"—when she didn't go on, I asked her what she meant. "Why, it looks as if all our good times together were spoiled."

I had some very good days of concentration, and little eating and no drinking before Dawn and Margaret came and shall revert to this regime when they leave. Dawn, to my surprise, has mastered enough French to read *Histoire d'O*[2] and has taken it to bed with her.

I have just found another checkbook with checks amounting to $356.77.—The last, for $127.92, the last check for the Cambridge Telephone. Now a bill for Choate, Hall, and Stewart has just arrived for $155.50.

The Edmondses and Mrs. Burnham have eagerly inquired when you are coming.—On my way to the Edmonds, I stopped off with George to see the herd of Brown Swiss that the Munns now have on the Speyers' farm. I get the impression that buying this herd has been a move on the part of the parents to keep the boys in Talcottville. George says that he wants to go South and when Lou came to clean here—which she does very well—just before my guest arrived, I thought that she was rather exacerbated, and she also had a black eye, which embarrassed her. I imagine she has flare-ups of Southern Temper and is trying to get George away.

This has been a humid and drowsy day, but it is cool in this house.

Good night, my dear. I have been longing for you lately terribly.

Edmund

¹Like the Sharps in the letters that follow, these friends and family figure in *Upstate*.
²The classic of French erotica.

Letters from the 1960s

July 14, 1960

Dearest Love: This has been a very quick week, but I have accomplished a good deal. Have seen nobody but the Sharps. The grandchildren left Dorothy weak and she was slightly ill but is now recovering. I took a walk in Whetstone Gulf one day with Malcolm. I had never seen the part that is interesting: an enormous canyon of pale gray rock, with a little stream at the bottom.—I have seen Huldah Loomis only once, when she brought me strawberries. Mrs. Burnham has been reduced to selling her herd. She could hardly bear it, and didn't want to be there when they came to take them away. Thea also brought me some strawberries one evening. I have had dinner with the Crostens once. Last Sunday I took three little girls to the new Disney film, *The Snow Goose:* Kay Hutchins, Clara Crofoot and another girl whose name I don't know. Old Reber did some painting for me and other odd jobs. Since he is now over eighty, I thought he was working too long one day and he didn't come back the next. He had had a spell of dizziness and collapsed and says he can't paint any more. Mrs. Hutchins is still taking care of me. Her salesman activities, which she evidently loves, do not interfere seriously. She has given the house a sensational cleaning and even scrubbed the chest of Dorothy Mendenhall so that it is now as white as snow. The other night she produced a wonderful dessert which she had discovered in a cookbook—something called Ambrosia which was made of sliced orange, shredded coconut and whipped cream. (Thank God for all the dainties you sent me—I have been eating my way through them.) Beverly I haven't seen at all—she is going to bring her husband around some evening. Do think up a wedding present for her.

Reuel writes me as follows: "I hear from my mother, who is in Warsaw about to take a trip to Normandy with her 'promesso sposo,' and Bowden,¹ who has taken an apartment in Venice with Gregory Corso, the beat generation poet."

When Mary [Meigs] and Barbara [Deming] were here they would spend their mornings at Dry Sugar River playing their flutes and Mary would make sketches. She has a special interest in cows, due to the fact that her father was an expert in cattle diseases and she made some sketches of them. She was so much interested in the landscape, certain features of which she says she is going to introduce into paintings of hers which are really based on the countryside in France. She even admired that awful tumbledown yellow house just beside where the Sharps live.

Did I leave Cora the Cobra in Wellfleet? I thought I had brought it with me. Did you send the pyjamas and the books to Pemberthy? I am enclosing my polemic with Moses[2]—leave it on my desk, also Burke's bill—pay it out of my account.

My non-formal garden is quite beautiful now. Clara Crofoot tried to clean it up so that I could get it replanted but it was too much for her—she could only do a corner so it has simply been growing wild, and is now filled with some high growing small daisy-like flower; among which show hollyhocks, pink, red and lemon, black-eyed Susans, some kind of yellow daisy which must have been among the things I planted, sweet Williams and those sprays of wild purple bells. It reminded me of the work of some nineteenth century painter, but I can't remember who. I planted the cleaned out corner in scarlet runner beans and go out every day to see if they have sprouted. For some reason, the gooseberries have made a great comeback—I haven't seen them so abundant since my mother's time.

I talked to Dawn [Powell] on the phone. Joe[3] is still sick in the hospital but hasn't been operated on. They are treating his cancer with x-rays, with apparently good results. Dawn goes everyday to see him, but thinks she might fly up here at some point.

A curious thing happened while I was writing this letter. I had invited the Indian school superintendent at West Leyden to come to see me at three. A little before three, an Indian appeared at the door. I thought he didn't look like a school superintendent, but welcomed him warmly. He turned out to be a tree surgeon from Watertown. He is a Micmac, originally from Canada. He is now sawing down the little dead tree in front of the house, across the road, and is going to take down a dead branch from out of the trees on the lawn. The other trees that are dying I am going to let alone till they are further gone. Since the last sentence, Lincoln White, the school superintendent, arrived. I told him that the tree surgeon was a Micmac, and he said he had supposed he was, that one could tell from his appearance that he was not an Iroquois. White is a Mohawk with French blood married to a Mohawk wife. He is a graduate of Cornell with a Master's degree. His father was an hereditary chief, and he himself is one excellent type of the top level of Iroquois. I liked him very much and had a long conversation with him. He says that growing up on the St. Regis reservation with its lack of internal solidarity which the Seneca reservations have, he had to brace himself against the contempt for Indians on the part of the surrounding white world. Now he is finding difficulty in making his three boys realize they are Indians and what it means to be an Indian. All they know about Indians is the nonsense they see on TV. Though he himself is, as he says, pretty well "acculturated," he follows everything that goes on in the Iroquois world and told me interesting things that I didn't know. He says that there is considerable rivalry between the U.S. and Canadian steel workers and that the ones on our side of the line resented the fact that the book gave so much attention to the Canadian ones. He is going to ask me to dinner and has offered to take me on a trip to some of the Canadian reservations which I haven't seen. He says he likes it in this part of the world because being an Indian doesn't make any difference to people one way or the other.

I have read the other Swinburne novel,[4] which is something of an unrecognized masterpiece. You must finish it.

Now Malcolm has just come in to say that Dorothy is in bed with a fever.

I have been writing this letter off and on almost all afternoon and it has made me feel closer to you. Why do we have to have these crises every summer? It is an awful waste of energy and upsets you when you ought to be resting.

All my love, Edmund

[1]'promesso sposo,' [intended husband] and Bowden: McCarthy's husband-to-be number 4, James West, and Bowden Broadwater, number 3.
[2]Robert Moses had sent a news clipping about Mad Bear Anderson, an activist Indian battling Moses' Power Authority, being found drunk and fined $100. Wilson wrote back saying that he supposed with all the guff Mad Bear had had to put up with in his contest with the Authority it was worth $100 to get drunk and ease a little what must be his monumental frustration.
[3]Joe Gousha, Dawn Powell's husband.
[4]the other Swinburne novel: probably *Lesbia Brandon*.

August 5, 1960

Dearest Elena:

I tried to get you again at 4:30. Now Bill is here, and it is hard to talk on the phone. We can't let things go on like this till the autumn, so you must come up and talk to me without recriminations. You know, I don't even know what the story is about Sheila.[1] You seemed to accept her at first, then suddenly got rabid. What happened? I didn't want to ask you before. I left on account of the state you were in.

Love as ever, / Edmund

[1] hired help?

June 29, 1961 / Talcottville

Dearest Love:

The Straus office says that they will get a check for $700 to you—made out in your name—right away.

I have got myself rested and dealcoholized from New York and have been leading a very comfortable life. Fred Reber, 85, has been here repainting the doors and putting new screws on them. Marcie—tell Helen—just rode up to the door on her new horse named Star. I think riding has improved her figure. Two elms are entirely dead and will, I suppose, have to be taken down. I have spent some time today and yesterday cutting away the plant life from the front porch—which I found overgrowing everything—and planting petunias and geraniums. You will be surprised at how shipshape everything has become under Mrs. Hutchins' care—the house no longer even has that musty smell. I found here four huge volumes of Calvin and a consignment of whisky from my friend in Bogota, New Jersey;[1] also a translation into Japanese of *Hecate County*, with a strange enigmatic cover.

The Costas[2] have come back from Europe and Loren has had a heart attack, so nobody has seen him. Beverly had a nervous breakdown during the winter but is now back in the store, and I thought seemed less nervous and more subdued than usual. Lou left George last autumn—lived in Boonville for a while, then went South to her father, then came back to the laundry again. George had taken up with another woman, but in the meantime, on one of his long Western trips, he fell asleep while driving; the truck went off the road and overturned, he was seriously hurt and put in a hospital. As a result of this, he lost his job and now seems to be out of work. You know that Mrs. Burnham is dead. She continued to live in her house till she was on the very point of death, when they removed her to a nursing home. Albert Gribel is still functioning and takes me to Boonville every day.

I am enclosing a letter from Reuel—put it in the top left hand drawer of my desk. Please send me the little colloquial Hungarian book on the big table in the inner study and the Hungarian reviews of my plays from the folder marked *Five Plays* in the second drawer of the high filing cabinet. The Hungarian woman[3] who works in the drugstore is going to help me translate them.

The very disappointing thing is that the Sharps[4] are not coming back. Dorothy sprained her ankle and fell and broke her hip and ever since has been in a wheelchair or on crutches. The Loomises[5] pointed out to her that she will be better off here where she won't have to leave the ground floor instead of struggling with the three flights at her place in Chicago, and they hope she will come on in July.

I hope that you are resting and relaxing. Let me know what Dr. Burke says about the hormone situation.

All my love, / Edmund

[1]Jacob Landau, Wilson's correspondent on matters of Hebrew; see section VII.

[2]the Costas: Richard and Jo, upstate friends; he wrote a memoir of Wilson, *Our Neighbor in Talcottville*—see section VIII.

[3]Hungarian woman: Mary Pcolar, the last of Wilson's romantic ideal women—see section VIII.

[4]the Sharps: Malcolm, a professor at the University of Chicago law school, and his wife Dorothy, a distant cousin of Wilson's.

[5]The Loomises: three Talcottville sisters who later sold their house, just down the road from the old stone house, to Rosalind for a token sum, dubbing it Villa Rosalinda.

June 27, 1961 / Talcottville

Dearest Elena:

I got back here last night; it is a relief after the heat of New York. It turned out when I went back to the doctor, that I had already lost 4 lb.s and that my blood pressure had gone down. My gout, the second day I was there, flared up on my left side, so that I couldn't use my left hand and had to limp with my left foot. This wore off, but then my right calf and right groin got sore again and it is still rather hard for me to get around, but I am taking my gout medicine and dieting. It is true that Metrecal is a stain on the nerves, because the stomach is used to working and is frustrated by not having anything to work on, but I supplement it with celery and raw carrots and have larger breakfasts and dinners—no alcohol. I lived in the Algonquin as if it was a sanitorium and did not too much mind the heat, because I would only leave my air-conditioned room to hobble across the street to the air-conditioned *New Yorker* office, where I wrote my Introduction and the George Kennan article[1] (both part of the same operation).

I made no engagement with anybody except to call up Dawn [Powell] late every afternoon and arrange to have dinner together. We had dinner together for four nights running in the same restaurant, 68 5th Ave. very quietly. Dawn is very comfortable in times of strain or indisposition. She told me all the gossip [who is courting whom] .Then we would go to some off-Broadway Greenwich Village shows. We saw *Leave it to Jane,* an old [Jerome] Kern and [P. G.] Wodehouse musical revived from 1917; Genet's *The Balcony,* which is quite terrific on the stage; Dylan Thomas' *Under Milk Wood* and *The Premise,* a kind of Nichols and May show put on by the same Chicago group with which they were originally associated—but very inferior. The girl of the troop imitates Elaine abjectly. I can't get over how much better these off-Broadway shows—all "theater-in-the-round" productions—are than the uptown ones. The Genet and the Dylan Thomas were extremely well acted and directed (by Quintero). At the restaurant we saw [a married writer friend]'s New York girl, a tall rather buxom blond. Dawn had been telling me how beautiful she was, but I didn't find her particularly attractive.—The first night I arrived I went to a Peter Sellers picture with Barbara Epstein;[2] Tuesday I had lunch with Clelia[3] and Jason.[4] That evening Clelia and her husband, the Epsteins, and I all had dinner at 68, and went to *The Premise* together and afterward sat around at the Algonquin. Clelia's husband, a lawyer, is quite nice and Dawn thought he was fantastically handsome. He is one of those old-fashioned Americans, conventional but rather attractive, with an old family place and a dowager mother in the background. Clelia had had a dream the night before that I was giving a party at Carroll Hall (the family place), a perfectly marvelous party at which they were only hovering on the fringes, and she was studying how I made things to go so well and even took notes on the subject. I suppose that this was based on my Looking-Glass receptions at the Algonquin. Her husband, the same night, had dreamed that he was about to marry Barbara—I suppose because both Barbara and Clelia were pregnant—but it wasn't that he wanted to be related to Jason.

In spite of my ailments, my trip to New York was very successful. For once I did almost everything I intended to do. Everything went well with publishers: *Night Thoughts* coming out in November, Civil War book in April.

Now about taxes: from the first of August, we shall have to keep accounts of everything, and you must put down all your expenses (from Aug. 1) before you come on here, because hereafter it will be to our advantage to charge everything we spend against living expenses. This will set free your own money to be used however you please. I am enclosing a letter from Pemberthy.[5] They seized the trust company money because I delayed signing and returning that document that they sent me in which I acknowledged the debt; but my understanding is that they will later release it. Please return the Pemberthy letter.—The enclosure in the other envelope was addressed before I left but I failed to mail it. I am sending the movie contract to Sidman for him to check.

Give my love to the Thorntons. I want the little girls to have the other Russian baba which is sitting on the window sill in my study. It is on a more multiple scale than the other one. The tiniest one has been lost.

Mary Pcolar would like to have a cat and I am going to try to find other people who would like one, so that you can bring some on over when you come. Mary has been a godsend. She now shops for me and drives me to Utica. This morning she has been retyping, for the third time, a part of my Introduction. It is rather a ticklish matter and I am afraid that when it reaches Oxford they will utter shrill shrieks.

All my love, / Edmund

[1]"Unscrupulous Communists and Embattled Democrats" ran in the *New Yorker,* September 9, 1961, and was reprinted in *Bit Between My Teeth.* It is about draft protests, and, like his introduction to *Patriotic Gore,* a strong antiwar statement.

[2]Barbara Epstein: a founder of the *New York Review of Books,* at this period wife of Jason.

[3]Clelia Carroll, known to Wilson as producer of The Looking-Glass Library, a series of children's books for which he was a consultant—see headnote to section V.

[4]Jason Epstein, editor of Random House, and a great Wilson promoter—he saw to it most Wilson titles were kept in print in his Anchor series.

[5]Pemberthy: the lawyer involved in straightening out Wilson's tax difficulties.

July 8, 1961 / Talcottville

Dearest Elena:

Here is something important that I forgot. In one of the early volumes of the collected Lincoln facing the big table in my small study, you will find the rest of the Lincoln-Douglas debates. They took place in 1858. Look for the year on the back of the volume. Then look inside the back cover and see if I have a page reference to Douglas' imperialism. If not, look through the debates and see if I have marked it in the margin. If I have, please copy it, with the date, and send it to me. If I haven't, you will have to send me the volume. I need the passage for my introduction.

The conference with the tax people has been shifted to Thursday. I am going to dinner at the Glyn Morrises[1] tonight—the first time I have dined out since I have been here this summer. Mary Pcolar and her family are going to visit relatives near Boston so she won't be able to come until next Friday. She is getting to read my writing and is genially capable, besides amusing me with Hungarian lessons. Louise Bogan is supposed to be coming on Thursday, so I will pick her up after the taxes.

I am glad that Helen is having a good time.

All my love, / Edmund

[1]the Glyn Morrises: important figures in Wilson's Talcottville support system; see headnote to section VIII.

August 4, 1962 / Talcottville

Dearest love:

Our trip went off very well, though we didn't get to Cummington until almost 7. I couldn't make out as a Turk the man who wanted to see me at Cambridge, then discovered that he was another of those young Scandinavians, a Swede, who for some reason had been substituted for the Turk. Reuel ran into a friend, which delayed our departure, and when we arrived at Cummington, we found the Sigaburgs, the Linscotts, Newton Arvin and Helen and Dorothy all assembled on the porch.[1] The evening was very pleasant, with the usual champagne and those light fish [. . .] that Helen's so good at making— Also a dish of whipped avocado. Their house is now most attractive. Dorothy is building a real old-world brick wall. The Sigabergs had come up from the Tanglewood festival. Sonya kept pouring Roman's champagne into her own glass. Reuel helped Helen with dinner and talked fluent Russian with her and the Sigabergs. The Nabokovs, they told me, spent two weeks in New York and are now back in Europe. Newton Arvin seems to be blooming; it is as if the public scandal had relieved him of his shyness and self-consciousness,[2] and he has finished a book on Longfellow. He says he can't believe in the reality of the characters in Baldwin's novel.[3] Everybody regretted your absence.

We got up so late the next morning that I called off the lunch with [a neighbor]—shall see him next week. Reuel, as you know by this time, has decided he will be better off in Boston—which I am glad of since he can come to the Cape. In Cambridge, I bought *Commentary* to read Warren's review of *P[atriotic] G[ore]* which pleases me more than anything else that has been written about it, because he gets deeper into the book.[4]

I had written to the Sharps inviting them to have dinner with us, but Dorothy is not yet up to going out, and they had supper at home while we went to Constableville. We there found the Edmonds dining, and they have asked me to dinner Sunday. ([Other Talcottville neighbors] have called me up and are coming in this afternoon). Malcolm came here and we had a long talk after Dorothy had gone to bed. I was awfully glad to see him. I went over there yesterday afternoon and found them as usual on the back lawn. Dorothy was practicing walking without crutches. A little of it tires her out. She and I had a conversation, which, as she said, couldn't have been more "injurious"—all about our ailments and miseries. She says that her being crippled has had "a psychological effect" on her and that she doesn't enjoy life much nowadays, hates everything [. . .] there are a radio and a dog now in that wretched house next door (from which the sagging porch has now been stripped) and these get on her nerves. They have just had her daughter and her family with them, and I suppose they had worn her out. Malcolm is constantly attentive to her.

The house here looks better than ever. The [local handymen] have cleaned the walls, and Mrs. H. has got out a number of things and polished them up that I didn't know were here: brass candlesticks and silver napkin-rings, and in the kitchen an iron wall-bracket for flowers. Beverly had rather a hard time with her baby and has to wear a girdle for her back.

The day after our arrival, I was in a state of collapse, but am in good shape today and looking forward to weeks of work. The weather has been wonderful. I haven't seen Mary Pcolar yet. She has people visiting them for the weekend, but is coming over to take me to town sometime in the afternoon.

I have had a letter from [André] Malraux, giving me the information about the government-subsidized publishing in France, which proves to be surprisingly extensive.[5] He sends his "homage" to you. Everybody asks about you and Helen. I have been thinking about your beautiful eyes,—I miss seeing them around. Write me a letter with all the gossip.

All my love, / Edmund

Am depositing the $1,000, but it always takes a little time for them to send it to the other bank.

[1]Wilson often broke his trips between the Cape (or, in this case, Cambridge) and Talcottville at the home of Helen Muchnic and her companion Dorothy. He met Helen, a Russian specialist, while teaching at Smith. Newton Arvin was also a Smith professor. The Sigabergs he knew from the Cape, the Linscotts from New York.

²Newton Arvin had lost his position at Smith as a result of a scandal in which his alleged homosexual activities figured; Wilson came strongly to his defense—see section VII.

³James Baldwin (1924–1987), author of *The Fire Next Time* and *Another Country*, the novel in question, among other works; considered a significant voice of African American protest writing and openly gay fictional themes.

⁴Robert Penn Warren's review appeared in *Commentary*, August 1962.

⁵Wilson was sounding out Malraux about the *Pléiade* (the inexpensive, standard editions of French literary classics); he was agitating for a similar arrangement in the U.S. His efforts were later credited with being largely responsible for the creation of the Library of America.

August 7, 1962

Dearest Love: Pemberthy thinks that the best thing to do is for him and me to go again to Syracuse. His office has just called me up, evidently so that he could tell me about an appointment, but then it turned out that Pemberthy himself had—characteristically—already left the office, so I suppose I shan't know till tomorrow.

I am going to dinner with the Costas tomorrow night and with the Morrises the following one. I had a livelier time than usual with the Edmondses. He is doing a novel on the early days of Canada, and we discussed Parkman[1] at length. They are about to go to Iran, where Walter's son is now living. Walter was quite animated and jovial. Yesterday the Gausses took the Sharps to visit that Russian monastery, so I didn't see them, as usual, in the afternoon, but I am going over today. The Marcelins are descending on Saturday. I am going to take them to [Noel Coward's] *Blithe Spirit*, which is being done by that theater group.

Mary Pcolar is now working with this group. She attends to the make-up and, to some extent, the costumes. She seems much happier than she was. She approves of the new drugstore where she is working in Rome, [N.Y.] which she says, unlike Kramer's, is well organized, and they have given her full control of the cosmetics department. With that and the play this week, she hasn't been able to do much for me, but she came over and typed some letters last night, bringing me a big glass jar of Hungarian stew and a box of arboratums for the things on the porch.

I have been reading two books that have depressed me: Oscar Wilde's letters and Henry Miller's *Tropic of Capricorn*. Wilde's last years were dreadful: he was poor and ill and had to worry all the time about money. His wife cut off a small allowance when he went to live again with Douglas and wouldn't let him see his children. He was despairing and almost entirely dependent on the help of his pederast friends and after the *Ballad of Reading Gaol,* could not get himself to write any more. The Miller book is more interesting than his others, because it tells more about himself—his German family and his youth in Brooklyn, which was frustrating and very sordid. He came to hate America and had no other idea about it except that he would like to see everybody and everything he knew destroyed. I think I must go back to Parkman.

I long for you a great deal, darling, and think about your beautiful tanned legs and your rose-colored bathing suit. Write me about Reuel and other things. Love to Helen—I just heard the hoofs of a horse which is ridden by one of her friends.

All my love, / Edmund

[1] Francis Parkman (1823–1893): historian of the American frontier and Canada; author of *Montcalm and Wolfe.*

Princeton Club letterhead / July 21, 1963

Dearest Elena: I felt rather empty after you left. My arm was so sore that I left the *New Yorker* office in the middle of the afternoon. Applying for my passport in the hot weather had also got me down. We shouldn't have left that air-conditioning on—it was sleeping next to it that put a crimp in my arm. I found that it was perfectly easy to turn it off and open the window. I called Dawn, hoping to have dinner with her, but Jo-Jo[1] was home for the weekend, so I haven't been able to see her. I went to *Oliver* alone and enjoyed it, but I wished I had been able to take Helen. It is a very good show—especially for children: Dickens's melodrama is just the thing for this kind of musical.

Yesterday I had a bowl of oatmeal in the Algonquin lobby—no service in the club over the weekend and the Algonquin dining room was closed—and spent the afternoon revising my pamphlet.[2] I think it is a pretty good piece of work, but I wish I could strike somewhere a more affirmative note. Roger says he can probably get it into type by the end of this week, so I'll soon be sending you a copy and am anxious to hear what you think. I had dinner with Lili Darvas.[3] I had invited her here but discovered that the dining room was closed, and the Algonquin, too, so we went to a small but excellent French restaurant in her Hungarian part of town, 79th Street, and 2nd Ave. She is terribly nice and interesting to talk to—she is an educated woman who knew Schnitzler and Hofmannsthal,[4] and has none of the airs of an actress. Much less fatiguing than my other Hungarians, and not much of a Hungarian patriot. It is hard for her nowadays to get a job, and she says she doesn't really care much about acting any more. She is an expert Hungarian cook; and does catering like our friend at Sneden's Landing. She has an attractive little apartment, with two toy poodles. She thinks you are very beautiful. She didn't like Lillian's play[5] and says that Lillian wouldn't let her put any human feeling into the old grandmother: she wanted all the characters to be stupid.

I went home early and got a good sleep, and this morning my arm was all right. I put off my departure to this afternoon, and am writing this in the lounge while waiting for 2 o'clock. This has been a satisfactory visit, and I have got more accomplished than I sometimes do.

All my love, / Edmund

[1]Jo-Jo: Dawn Powell's neurologically damaged son.
[2]Probably *The Cold War and the Income Tax.*
[3]Lili Darvas: Hungarian-born star of stage and screen, Ferenc Molnár's third wife; won praise for a 1971 film, *Love.*
[4]Hugo von Hofmannsthal (1874–1929): Austrian poet, dramatist, essayist, opera librettist.
[5]Lillian Hellman's *Toys in the Attic.*

Sept. 11, 1963 / Wellfleet

Dear Elena: [A portion of this letter appears in section IV.]

I am going to start in on my Canadian piece. I saw Marie-Claire[1] several times, took her to the movies twice. She explains to me what I don't understand. I haven't heard a word about her personal affairs; she has always talked to me very intelligently about literature and Canada. Of course, she is very much impressed by you and hopes she can consider you "une amie."

I am surprised at the voracity with which she reads—she knows all about Emily Dickinson and Virginia Woolf. We went to two movies together. I also saw part of *Cleopatra,* which is badly acted, badly directed, badly written, stupid and vulgar throughout.

I had dinner last night with the Chevchavadzes. They have acquired a cute and lively little pug dog, to which they are much attached. Nina has had a rather alarming nosebleed, after which she found that alcohol was repulsive to her, and now she doesn't drink at all!

Barbara [Deming] drove me up here from Boston. She had just come up from Washington, where she had been given the for her rather taxing job of screening the recruits for the peace march. She was confronted by such problems as whether one should make it a principle to exclude marijuana-smokers and drunks—but sometimes one found that they were serious. I made her a little angry by saying that the Negroes all over the world had not shown very much ability in the direction of organizing or governing.

It is beautiful up here now and would be pleasant now that the demons are mostly gone. I miss you terribly. If I have to stay a long time, you might come back, and then we could go to Europe later, before Christmas. [A portion of this letter is in section IV.]

Mary [Meigs] is going to take me to town. Before then, I'll call up the hospital and let you know what they say. I've got a woman—Caroline Tibbetts, who says she once did some cleaning here—to get me breakfast, etc. She is coming in this afternoon. [Marginal note: She has been here, and this is all settled. She is getting me supper tonight.]

Where did you put the George Grosz catalogs? Where is the thing you put over Button's[2] chair? He is here with me, and Betsy has brought on his food. How do you turn on the furnace? It is beginning to get cooler.

Please call up Simmons at W. H. Allen[3] and explain the situation and thank him for making the hotel reservation. If you have time, why don't you call up the [Stephen] Spenders?

All my love, / Edmund

[Postscript]—Page proofs of *Protest* [*The Cold War and the Income Tax*] have just arrived.

[1]Marie-Claire Blais: French Canadian writer mentioned in *O Canada;* protégée of Mary Meigs and Barbara Deming.
[2]The family cat.
[3]One of his English publishers; see section VII.

May 1, 1967 / Jerusalem

Dearest Elena: I enjoyed the trip over. They overwhelm you with food and drinks—the dinner, with a French menu, goes on for hours and then, while you are still watching the moon rise on one side, the sky turns red on the other. But you pay when you get to Europe with the ravages of not having slept enough. Darina met me at the airport with a huge embrace across the barrier. She talked without stopping all the way to the hotel and I could already see that she was in very bad way. She fusses about things all the time in a neurotic way I don't remember noticing before. The Victoria was just the same; same men at the desks, same fat doorman. It made me feel a little desolate at first to be waiting in that lobby without you and the girls, when Darina was invariably late for appointments.

The first day she brought to her lunch with us that priest from India who showed us those rooms in the Vatican and who seems to be her closest friend in Rome. I think he is intellectually rather remarkable and a good man, but all Indians irritate me slightly. Darina, however, has become very much involved with India, and talks about going to live in Delhi.

I slept in the afternoon and had dinner very late with the Silones[1] at the excellent little restaurant just around the corner from the hotel where we had dinner with them once, and much bad French was talked.

[The following sentence appears in *Letters on Literature and Politics:* The next day I hired a car and went out to Bomarzo with Darina.] She talked all the time—something like six hours in all: the story of her life and her bad relations with Silone, whom she always refers to as "S"—she says that she has never been able to call him by his first name. She says that you have heard this—that they have never had "conjugal relations," that she does not feel that she is really his wife, that they never go out together and never entertain, that he breaks off all her friendships with other people and turns against all his own friends, and that she is trying to think how to leave him. She described her early love life at length—she says it was for a long time inhibited by Irish Catholic puritanism. When we stopped for lunch on the way back, I discovered that the driver knew English and I warned Darina about it but it restrained her very little. At Bomarzo, I had to shut her up in order to pay attention to what I was seeing. [A portion of this letter deleted here appears in *Letters on Literature and Politics.*]

It was a beautiful day and the countryside was lovely, but somewhat obscured by the worries of Darina, who is afraid that she may go "round the bend."

When we got back, I made a short call on Silone, then went on to the hotel, where I had dinner with Paolo Milano.[2] He says that it is not true that the Silones have never had conjugal relations, that their relations are undoubtedly unsatisfactory, but that Darina has a variety of explanations of why they are. He confirmed me in the suspicion I had clearly had that her stories about her life are partly imaginary. He says that she is a fearful liar, but at the same time "an honest and brave woman." He thinks that she and Silone have been very bad for one another and are destroying one another.

I gather that everyone in Rome knows about [a prominent Irish Catholic writer] and his affair with the wife of the Time-Life representative. Darina also knows his family in Dublin.

The trip here in the Jordan plane was longer than it was supposed to be because the airport at Jerusalem is being reconstructed for jet planes, and the flights don't go any further than Amman. They never even opened my baggage in the customs, and I brought on here without difficulty a large bottle of black label Johnny Walker Scotch, a present from Darina, which I found when I arrived at the hotel. I was driven to Jerusalem in a bus and did not get here till nine. The director and his wife were in bed, but got up and made me some supper. They are young people and seem very nice. He is at Princeton and teaches ancient Eastern history. I think they suffer somewhat from boredom; they complain that at the cocktail parties they always meet the same people and they say that the thing that keeps them going intellectually is the *New York Review of Books*. But I like staying at the school. It is absolutely clean and very comfortable, with big rooms that have—what hotels don't have— bookcases and big tables to work at. It is completely quiet at night, actually not a sound of any kind. There is a big iron gate in front and a patio with flowers in back. In the daytime, you hear from remote streets wailing Arab cries and songs. I skipped the seven o'clock breakfast this morning and have so far done nothing but study a little Arabic in bed and write this letter to you. Shall now go down to 12:30 lunch.

All my love, / Edmund.

[Postscript] There was a holiday radio program on the bus. The only things I could understand were references to America, accompanied by repetitions of "CIA" which were followed by bursts of laughter.

[1]Ignazio Silone (1900–1978) and his wife Darina, he the left-wing writer, author of *Bread and Wine.*

[2]Paolo Milano: an academic and visitor upstate in the 1960s.

King David Hotel letterhead / Jerusalem / May 11, 1967

Dearest Love: I was very glad to find two of your letters when I got here yesterday morning—and another one came in the afternoon. [A portion of this letter appears in *Letters on Literature and Politics*.]

I have been feeling very well. I think that this bright dry climate is good for me. Even my scrofulous condition has disappeared. There is very little drinking. Pearlman last night offered me nothing but beer, though there was a well equipped bar. Plenty to eat of a Jewish or Middle Eastern kind. With breakfast and lunch you get two kinds of cheese.

I miss you. It is getting more difficult for me to go off on these trips alone. Write me often. Since I'll be flying at 8:45 the morning of the 24th, I suppose I'll be spending in Tel-Aviv the nights of the 22nd and 23rd, so try to be sure letters reach me here before that. Find out how much I still owe that Boonville bank and pay the whole amount.

All my love, / Edmund

[some Hebrew words] I'm practicing Hebrew script.

May 20, 1967

Dearest Elena: [The next two sentences appear in *Letters on Literature and Politics:* I hope you are not worrying about the news. Nobody that I have seen takes this "crisis" seriously.]

Since my last letter, I have been writing in my journal without any carbon paper, and instead of writing it all out again at length, I'll read it to you when I get back. [A portion of this letter appears in *Letters on Literature and Politics.*] . . .

I have had a lunch at the University and dinners with [Moshe] Pearlman and the Grodjenskys. Tonight an English Jew who teaches English at the University and whom I knew when I was here before is coming to dinner with me. The food in the hotel is in its way almost as dreary as in Jordan. The kosher observances produce depressing results: no toast on the Sabbath—which today is—and no eggs except hard-boiled ones from the day before, because no cooking can be done. One misses bacon for breakfast. You invariably get cottage cheese and another kind of cheese. The coffee is no good.—But I enjoy myself here as I did before. I am in much better condition than I was at home. I'm sorry that you have been having such bad weather. It is bright and delightful here. I have seen the Chagall windows, which are gorgeous.

You don't say anything about work on my study.

I am leaving Wednesday morning for Paris. I hope you will write me a letter there—have sent postcards to Helen and the little girls.[1]

[Hebrew words] This means <u>blessings I love you.</u>

---

[1]Perhaps Elena's granddaughters, children of her son Henry Thornton.

IV. Wilson and His Children

This section consists of letters to the Wilson children as well as passages about them excerpted from letters to others. No ideal parent (drink, overwork, and old-time aloofness were always factors in his paternal relationship), Wilson nevertheless was acutely aware of his children's need for fun and guidance, kind words and attentive interest. His famous Punch and Judy shows and magic tricks—not to mention all the reading aloud, movies, plays, and assorted treats—were part of his steady attempt to amuse and educate. There was, however, always an undertone of impatience about getting on in the world, doing well in studies and later at work. Rosalind (1923–2000), child of actress Mary Blair, essentially was raised by Wilson's mother in Red Bank after the couple divorced in 1929. She was educated at Bennington College, worked in editing and publishing, and wrote her own version of life with father, *Near the Magician* (1989). Talcottville was a congenial place for her: she lived near Wilson and was with him when he died in the Old Stone House in 1972. Reuel (b. 1938), the son of Mary McCarthy, lived principally with his mother, although he spent extended periods with Wilson at Wellfleet. He enjoyed the swimming on the Cape and the companionship of local boys. Although his father found him difficult, they got along well enough for tutoring in poetry and companionable pursuits like games and listening to music. Reuel attended St. Bernard's in Manhattan for a time and graduated from Harvard. He was influenced by Wilson to the extent that he became a scholar of Slavic languages. Helen Miranda (b. 1948), child of Elena Mumm, attended school in Switzerland, studied at Barnard College, and eventually became a prominent painter of landscapes.

Rosalind

TO MARY BLAIR

Sept. 19, 1936 / 571 Commercial St. / Provincetown, Mass. Dear Mary: We are leaving here next Wednesday. Betty Huling's sister is coming up to drive us down. We will stop over in Boston and Rosalind will go to the oculist Thursday morning, and I hope I'll get her down to Red Bank Thursday night.—Her eyes seem to be much better than they were. Certainly they look much better and do not turn out unless she gets tired.—In general, she has improved enormously during this last year: people who come here remark on how well she behaves. And her observations on the people she meets are quite penetrating. I have had a very good time with her—really, the best summer we have ever spent up here.—Her grandmother is making so much fuss now about bringing her back to have some new dresses made for her by the dressmaker that I guess I'll have to take her down there. Christmas I'll bring her to Pittsburgh. [. . .]

Rosalind has gone over to play ping pong at the tennis club with Ann de Silver,[1] who is staying with us while her mother stays with the Dos Passoses, and Jeannie Clymer.[2] She loves all the visitors and guests: great excitement for her! When I asked her the other day whether she wanted to go over to the Walkers' with me, she said, "Yes: I like to see how people live." [. . .]

Best love, / Bunny

[1]Ann de Silver: the daughter of Margaret de Silver; see letters to Elena Mumm Thornton in section III.

[2]Jeanne Clymer: Rosalind's best friend during the Wellfleet years and long afterward.

TO MORTON ZABEL

July 12, 1937 / Trees, R.F.D. 1 / Stamford, Conn.

Dear Morton:

[. . .] Have just brought my daughter out here for the summer and am settling down to a lot of work—along with other things, I've got to give her some tutoring, as it turns out that the schools she has been sent to have failed to teach her even to distinguish the parts of speech. Her English teacher told me that they didn't cover nouns, verbs, etc. in her course, but had been specializing that term in the gerundive, which I didn't know existed in English. [. . .]

TO MARY MCCARTHY

University of Chicago letterhead / July 31, 1939

Dear Mary:

[. . .] I haven't been doing very much except the—very pleasant—bike-ride [with Gerry Allard and his boy and Rosalind yesterday morning] and taking Rosalind and the Evanses to the circus.

August 6, 1939 / Morton [Zabel]'s House

Dearest Mary: Everything has been very quiet at the apartment, and I have had no gaiety up to this weekend. Rosalind spent the afternoon and had dinner in town one day with Jeanne—found it something of a trial, as she said Jeanne would go into the department stores and spend hours talking to the sales girls, flattering them grossly and trying to make friends with them. [. . .]

I miss you terribly: it seems queer and uncomfortable to be living again as I was before we were married and I tend to be depressed. I worry, thinking that I am not giving Rosalind the kind of life she ought to have. [. . .]

University of Chicago letterhead / Aug. 19, 1939

Dear Mary:

[. . .]—I'll be glad to write to your grandmother when you drop a line to Rosalind. You haven't even said good-bye to her. [. . .]

TO MORTON ZABEL

February 17, 1942 / Wellfleet, Mass.

Dear Morton:

[. . .] Rosalind, now at home on her long winter vacation from Bennington, has been doing signed articles for the *Provincetown Advocate*. [. . .]

TO MARY MCCARTHY

Jan. 14, 1945

Dear Mary:

[. . .] My salary from the *New Yorker* is about $135 a week—This will be put at your and Rosalind's disposal. [. . .]

[. . .] You never answered my question about the Goya picture. [. . .]— Also, is it true as Rosalind thinks that Mrs. Berno stole the car last winter? I want to know for my future dealings with her.

TO ELENA WILSON

Sept. 24, 1946 / Wellfleet, Mass.

Dearest Elena:

[. . .] Rosalind, during my absence, has had a great rapprochement with Bill Jencks, Edward's son by his first wife. She has been down visiting him in Cambridge, and is showing more interest in him than I have known her to do with anybody for years. He is at Harvard studying to be a psychiatrist. [. . .]

TO HELEN MUCHNIC

[undated but could be 1948]

Rosalind has a very serious beau, who wants to marry her, and I think she is taking him more seriously than she has taken any boy for years. "Jig" Cook, George Cram Cook, who got up the Provincetown Players, lived in Greece in his last years, and his children were educated there. His daughter married a Greek poet, and their son,[1] who has been all through the war in the Greek army, has come over here to go to Harvard and has been staying in Provincetown with Cook's second wife and widow, Susan Glaspell. I don't know whether she will marry him—he is four years younger than she—but, as I say, she shows a lot more interest in him than I have known her to do in anyone else lately. He is studious, serious-minded and, like all Greeks, full of Greek politics. I have a very good opinion of him, but view with a certain amount of alarm the possibility of an alliance with the Cook family [. . .]—Rosalind is away just now or would send love.

[1]Sirius Proestopoulos, known as Topie.

TO ELENA WILSON

Sept. 30, 1948 / Wellfleet

Dearest Elena:

[. . .] I got away on the 6 o'clock train, leaving some of my business unfinished because Rosalind was to go to Boston in the morning. When I arrived about one with Henriguez, I found her obviously upset. She said that she had just had a quarrel with Topie on the phone and that she wasn't going to Boston to work on the *Globe* after all; she didn't want to be near Topie and have things go along on the old basis, and she hated newspaper work and living in Cambridge anyway—had had a horrible time last winter. I made my usual scene, roaring like a bull, and she declared she was going to her grandmother's. Today I have had another talk with her, and she wept and I was on the verge of weeping and now it has been decided that she will go on living here until you come back, and then get a room in Providence or somewhere and work on her writing. She says that she has written several stories, and is depressed because they have been rejected. She has promised to show me some of her work tonight. I am worried about her. I don't believe that she and Topie will really marry. In the meantime, she told me today, they have not been having a love affair, and the situation is getting on both their nerves. I wish she would find someone else. [. . .]

Let me know when the boat is supposed to arrive. Since Rosalind will be up here, I can come down for several days. [. . .]

October 2, 1948 / Wellfleet, Mass

Dearest Elena:

I have been trying during the last two days to go to the mat with the problem of Rosalind . . . have had two almost sleepless nights and have had a long talk with her every day. She has shown me a number of the things she has written. The manuscripts are so badly typed that they are enough to discourage any editor, and some of them were unfinished and stopped in the middle so that they made no sense. She may write something someday, but the truth is that she hasn't worked at her writing any more seriously than at anything else, and I don't believe for a moment in her project of taking a room somewhere, living on $50 a month that her grandmother gives her and devoting herself to literary activity. She will simply pay her grandmother a long visit, pay Jeannie a long visit and eventually land back here. But I have decided that if she is going to go and try to carry out her program, she might as well start right away and the present plan is she is to leave in a day or two—then she will of course go to her grandmother's. I have told her that I don't want her back here again until Christmas. She has lately become one the retainers at George Chavchevadze's court and has spent a good deal of time fishing and spending the evenings with him. He has just gone off to Vermont for the purpose of seeing the leaves there change color, and wanted to take her along, leaving Lorenzo to cook for me! (One day they caught thirty pickerel in a very small pond nearby.) She and Topie are now in a position to marry, as far as the legalities go, but he says he doesn't want to because he is living on money borrowed from Dos and I don't think she really does either or she would try to earn a little money.—I feel that I have to face the fact that she is incapable of making anything of her life; her attitude towards her writing, her relations with men and her relations with her family are equally unrealistic. I don't know how she is going to do anything with her good qualities because she apparently doesn't really want to. All her stubbornness and force of character are exerted in a negative way in the direction of <u>not</u> doing things and making it possible for her to slump along. I am depressed because I was so fond of her as a child when I spent all my summers alone with her and she was such an attractive little girl.

October 4, 1948

Dearest Elena:

[. . .] I have changed my mind about Rosalind again and am having her stay here until you come back. Since she doesn't want to take a job, she might as well be here as anywhere else at present. We are getting along all right— though I count the weeks till you will be back, almost they way I did when I was in quarantine in Odessa—[. . .]

Yesterday [. . .] Polly [Boyden] drove me home and came here for dinner. After dinner, she became absorbed in a series of chess games with Rosalind. [. . .]

Rosalind has been handling things better than usual and is now trying to make some grape jelly in accordance with Polly's instructions. [. . .]

April 11, 1950

Dearest Elena:

[. . .] I am astonished to see how Rosalind has matured just since she has been at Houghton Mifflin. She is full of ideas and has quite a grasp of publishing problems. I have had a very good time talking to her—and am sorry to have her go.

TO BETTY HULING

June 4, 1950

Dear Betty:

We're delighted at the prospect that you may come up. Don't hesitate to come during the summer. It would be fun to have you when the children are here. [. . .] Rosalind comes often for weekends. [. . .]

TO ELENA WILSON

April 16, 1950 / Red Bank

Dearest love:

[. . .] I have been having a good time with Rosalind and we have had many conversations and may take a long walk this afternoon. I have been telling her in installments about the Wilsons, Kimballs, Bakers, etc., about whom I find she knows very little. We have let all the servants go, and as a result the water-heater went out, and Gerda had to be summoned back to start it. While we were in the cellar, Rosalind and Gerda told me about a great brown sewer rat that once came to live there alone. Mother and Gerda were trying to catch or poison it, but Jennie had become attached to it and was secretly protecting it and feeding it at night. At last, mother called in an exterminator.

[. . .] Rosalind has to go to New York Wednesday to do some work at the New York Houghton Mifflin office.

TO BETTY HULING

Nov. 8, 1953 / Wellfleet, Mass.

Dear Betty:

—We have all been rather miserable lately. First I was immobilized with gout (which I'm now over); then Elena, Rosalind and Helen all came down with this new-type flu. Elena and Helen are still in bed. Otherwise, we are doing well. [. . .]

TO HAZEL [WIDOW OF BURTON RASCOE]

April 6, 1957 / Cambridge, Mass

Dear Hazel:

[. . .] We have been living here in Cambridge ever since the middle of January. [. . .] Rosalind works at Houghton Mifflin, and I at the Harvard Library. But otherwise we have been having rather a miserable time—illness and other misfortunes. [. . .]

TO BETTY HULING

Wellfleet letterhead / November 4, 1958

Dear Betty:

[. . .] I don't think that Rosalind has made up her mind what she is going to do with her year off and her grandmother's money. She told people that she was first going to go to pieces for six weeks. [. . .]

TO ELENA WILSON

Sept. 11, 1963 / Wellfleet

Dear Elena: Rosalind is still in Mass. General. She has been clearing up, but not as fast as they hoped.[1] But I was very much encouraged on Monday when she asked me about the cats, told me what to do about the car and gave me the names of friends that she wants to have come to see her. She still had delusions, though. The man that she talks about marrying is not the Russian, but a young man named Jacques de Spaelbach, who works at Houghton Mifflin. When I asked her whether he had asked her to marry him, she said, "Not person to person," but she thinks that he has been courting her over the radio. That was what she was talking about when I went to her apartment that night. She imagines that Steve Fassett has wired it so that Jacques can communicate with her. Paul Chavchavadze tells me that that twirp she thought was going to marry her before denied that he had ever asked her, so that may have been a delusion, too. She has confidence in Dr. Schwarz, and if she has to continue to stay in a hospital, will go to Mass. Memorial, to which he is attached. He turns out to be a former student of Mrs. Zetzel's, and he and she keep in touch about Rosalind.

I had lunch on Sunday with the Zetzels, and we discussed Rosalind's case. [. . .]

Rosalind is beginning to remember a little what happened to her and she is losing some of her misconceptions. She told me she thought at first that the doctors were all actors made up as doctors, and now she says as a joke that the young doctor in charge of her case gives the impression of Ed O'Connor[2] impersonating a psychiatrist—and I find him a little boring myself. This breakdown has evidently been coming for quite awhile. Paul Brooks[3] says that her work was deteriorating, that she was behaving rather irresponsibly. He made it clear that they would have to let her go. This is going to make the problem worse. If she really clears up completely, I should like to have her come up here while I am here. [. . .]

[1]Rosalind suffered a serious nervous breakdown, accompanied by delusional episodes.
[2]Edwin O'Connor: friend from the Cape and Boston novelist (*The Last Hurrah*) with whom Wilson wrote alternate chapters of "Baldini."
[3]Rosalind's superior at Houghton Mifflin.

TO DAWN POWELL

Hotel Victoria / Via Campania / Roma, March 18, 1964

Dear Dawn:

[. . .] Rosalind and Helen are joining us this week—it is Helen's spring vacation from school. I was pleased with Rosalind's story[1]—I didn't know she could write so well. [. . .]

Love, / Edmund

[1]Rosalind had won the *Mademoiselle* short story contest (*Near the Magician*, p. 112), but that was in 1944, and Wilson had expressed serious doubts in the interim.

TO MARY McCARTHY

Aug. 17, 1965 / Wellfleet

Dear Mary: [. . .] I'm in no position to do very much for them [Reuel and family] until after this year. Rosalind is still dependent on me—I've described my tax difficulties in my other letter. [. . .]

TO GLYN MORRIS

Wellfleet letterhead / Oct. 26, 1966

Dear Glyn: My daughter Rosalind is going to try the experiment of going up next Monday and staying in the stone house alone. I'm afraid that she will get lonely, though some friends are coming up later—and I'd be extremely grateful, if you're not too busy, if you would call her up and drop in on her. [. . .]

TO CLELIA CARROLL

Aug. 1, 1967 / Talcottville

Dear Clelia:

[. . .] Elena is still in Wellfleet with her son and his family and a Russian cousin is joining her later. I am here with my older daughter.[1] She has had some pretty bad years lately and I am hoping she will get to know and like this place and will spend a certain amount of time in it. Nobody else in the family enjoys it here, and I don't like to sell it. It is probably unsaleable anyhow. This is a place no one wants to live. In my own case, though I used to be capable of spending part of the summer alone in order to get something written and though it still seems wonderful at first to get away to this freedom and quiet from the traffic and visitors of Wellfleet, it gets more difficult to live here. [. . .]

[1]Older daughter: This is the way Wilson has habitually referred to Rosalind when writing to Clelia Carroll, who met him in 1958. In an earlier reference to her under this rubric (December 22, 1965), he has told Carroll that, in a dream, "I had left my house to my elder daughter, but I don't know what she would do with it." He did, in fact, leave the house to Rosalind, who preferred to live in a house down the road, sold to her for a token sum by old Talcottville friends, the Loomis sisters. They called it the Villa Rosalinda. She tells us in *Near the Magician* (243) that when her father came up she and he led separate lives, dining together once a week or so.

Sept. 22, 1967 / Wellfleet, Mass.

Dear Clelia:

[. . .] Rosalind has been happy at Talcottville, is still there. That has been a success. [. . .]

Jan. 7, 1968 / Wellfleet

Dear Rosalind: This book about the wolves is marvelous—one of the best animal books I have ever read. I'm so glad you gave it to me.

We have recovered from the holidays and are functioning normally again.
Come up and see us soon.

Love, / Father

TO CLELIA CARROLL

July 1, 1968 / Talcottville

Dear Clelia:

[. . .] I am still here in Talcottville—on account of the proposed new road and
other things, I am more involved here than I usually am. My older daughter
is with us . . .

[Rosalind Wilson died October 30, 2000, in Talcottville.]

Reuel

TO MARY MCCARTHY

University of Chicago letterhead / July 31, 1939

Dear Mary:

[. . .] I hope you got the baby's harness straightened out. I keep thinking of
how cute he looked on his hands and knees in the upper-berth, looking out
with his bright little eyes, with attentive though bewildered interest.—I miss
him and think it is he every time I hear a baby cry. [. . .]

August 6, 1939 / Morton's House

Dearest Mary: [. . .] I think a lot about the little boy and miss him. [. . .]

University of Chicago letterhead / Aug. 19, 1939

Dear Mary: —I've been terribly bored and exasperated here lately and can't
wait to pull out. [. . .] Will I be glad to see the Atlantic?—not to mention you
and the little boy. [. . .]

February 17, 1942

Dear Morton:

[. . .] Reuel has just learned his alphabet and is able to distinguish the letters on a typewriter. [. . .]

TO MARY MCCARTHY

Aug. 6, 1944 / Wellfleet, Mass.

Dear Mary: Everything is OK here. Thursday afternoon Reuel and I went over to Truro with Nina and her friend, and Reuel stayed to supper with Ebbie. The next day they brought Ebbie over here in the morning and he spent two whole days with Reuel—spent the night in the room on the third floor and left after supper yesterday. He and Reuel and Charlie Rose turned on the sprinkler and took showers and Miss Forbes gave them a picnic under the apple-tree.

Jan. 14, 1945

Dear Mary: [. . . A separation agreement] would involve making arrangements about Reuel's custody which I don't want to discuss now, because we can't know how we shall be living when I get back. At that time, we can make whatever arrangements seem proper. I have no intention of trying to make you live with me if you don't want to or of trying to keep you from having Reuel. [. . .]

New Yorker letterhead / Sept. 26, 1945

Dear Mary: St. Bernard's School has just called me up very much upset because the school at Bard had written them for information about Reuel. They had him entered at St. Bernard's, said you never notified them that he was not coming back. They are furious because they say they have held a place for him, refusing a lot of people who wanted to get their children in, and they would really probably be within their rights if they tried to hold me for a term's tuition. I am afraid that it may prejudice my chances of getting him back into the school. Is this your way of proving that you're a responsible person? [. . .]

New Yorker letterhead / Nov. 13, 1945
Dear Mary: Let me know when you will bring Reuel in and how long he will stay. I'll arrange to have someone at the house when he arrives. [. . .] There are also some rubbers belonging to you and Reuel in the chest that used to be in the dining-room and is now in the little room off the kitchen.

You never answered my question about the Goya picture nor told me whether you ever did anything to notify St. Bernard's about Reuel's not coming back. I want to know about this matter, as I shall have to give them some kind of explanation. [. . .]

New Yorker letterhead / Dec. 18, 1945
Dear Mary: Here is the agreement. I've just been through it, and I'm afraid I'll have to insist on having the final decision about Reuel's education. I don't, however, expect that we'll have any disagreement. If you want to stay at Bard another year, I don't mind your sending him to school there. I suppose that your decision depends partly on whether or not they ask you to come back and that you may not know about this till spring; but it is desirable to know as soon as possible whether he is going to be in New York, because it may be difficult to get him back in St. Bernard's. Once there, he ought to stay there. If it's feasible to give him a year or two in Europe, that will mean another shift. Most St. Bernard's boys seem to go to Groton or Exeter, and he may want to go where his friends are going. I shouldn't mind Exeter, though I am not enthusiastic about it in spite of the fact that so many of my family went there. I'll inquire into the matter and we can talk about it. It is a great advantage for a boy to have other boys he knows when he goes away to boarding school, and afterwards to college. When it comes time for him to go to college, Reuel can have something to say about it himself, but in the meantime you must not, as you sometimes tend to do, put it up to Reuel where he wants to be sent: what school or whether he wants to go abroad. Of course his feelings ought to be considered; but the decisions have to be made for him. This also applies to the periods which be spends with you or me.

I hope you will do something about this agreement right away. Here is some money if you want to call up your lawyer or make a trip to New York. If you should have to spend more, let me know.

About Christmas: You can bring him here Christmas afternoon or evening, if you don't think his party and other festivities will have been too much for him. If you think he will be too tired, you can bring him the next morning. Please wire me when you get this that you have received it and exactly when we ought to expect you.

Sincerely, / Edmund

March 21, 1946

Dear Mary:

Will you let me know how I can get in touch with the girl who took care of Reuel last summer? What was she like, and how much did she do?

I want to have Reuel through the whole week of the 21st—am getting circus tickets for the 22nd. You will remember that you took him away from the house in the middle of February a year ago without even letting me know where he was; that when I got back from Europe, he was with me for only a few days before you took him away to Red Hook, when it was impossible for me to see him except during vacations; and that, when his vacations came, there has always been some very good reason why you could not let him be with me. I have seen almost nothing of him for more than a year, and his grandmother has hardly seen him at all. I know how much satisfaction this kind of thing gives you, and that you are always able to find excellent reasons for the unpleasant things that you do, and I know that I must be prepared to settle down to a lifetime of unpleasantness with you wherever Reuel is concerned. But I want to remind you that I am also in a position to make things difficult and uncomfortable for you, and that it is not a good thing for Reuel to be made an object of continual hostilities between us. In view of the fact that you have spent the whole of the last year with him, you have no right whatever to demand to keep him through half of his Easter vacation.

EW

New Yorker letterhead / April 5, 1946

Dear Mary: —Will expect Reuel the 21st or 22nd. I have circus tickets for the 23rd. That girl who worked for you wants to take on the whole household, doing cooking and everything. Do you think she is capable of it? I am going to have one other servant anyway. When does Reuel get out of school this spring? Please write me so that I will get it before Thursday.

EW

April 30, 1946

Dear Mary: You can put this check through the end of this week.

I'm perfectly willing to have you keep Reuel out there another year, if you want to. I've done nothing about St. Bernard's as I was waiting to hear from you.

Let me know exactly when you want Reuel to come to me. I am going to Wellfleet the beginning of next week, but coming back to town again during May. I will arrange the time so as to take Reuel with me when I go up again.—If you have no use for the washing machine this summer, I want to get it back from Adelaide, as I shall need it.

EW

[Superscript] Please wire me how long you are staying and whether divorce is OK. Also, let me know exactly what you did about St. Bernard's, and when you are coming back and when school opens in the fall.

June 19, 1946, / Wellfleet

Dear Mary:

I received the enclosed letter from Phyllis. [The letter complains of Reul's bad behavior.] I think that she exaggerates the situation absurdly and have written her a strong reply. But it was true that when Reuel first got up here, he wouldn't obey anybody and said and did very mean things to people. Both Gus and Chris have complained to me bitterly, and Chris says she won't stay if he keeps it up. I punished him, and he has lately been better, but I want you to talk to him when you are here.

Sincerely, / Edmund

TO ELENA WILSON

July 31, 1946

Dearest Elena:

[. . .] Reuel has missed you and the boys. I have rather enjoyed the days that he and I have spent alone in the house here. He is getting old enough to be a real companion and now knows how to amuse himself reading and play-ing the phonograph. . . .

Aug. 17, 1946 / Wellfleet

Dearest Elena:

[. . .] Peggy Bacon came to dinner last night. She brought Reuel a pastel set from Provincetown and showed him how to use it. He did a ship, a house, and a dog that were not so terribly bad and was so interested that I have arranged with her to come and give him some lessons. He is getting bored with the Jenckses, who continually invite him over. I think that I will take him and Charlie Jencks and the Macdonald boy[1] to see *Anna and the King of Siam* in Orleans next Monday afternoon. [. . .]

[1] Probably the elder of Dwight and Nancy Macdonald's two sons, Michael.

August 18, 1946

Dearest Elena:

[. . .] —Peggy Bacon is, I hope, coming late this morning to give Reuel a pastel lesson and stay to lunch. He and I spent a good deal of yesterday after-noon and evening playing checkers and Chinese checkers and reading *Uncle Tom's Cabin,* and I went on playing Chinese checkers in my sleep all through last night, with interludes of springing up and banging at mosquitoes with an old copy of *Life.*

Reuel and I have a good time together, and I really enjoy being here alone with him. I have begged off from almost all invitations to dinner, and, in the case of a large party at the Worthington's, said I would go and then didn't go.—Tonight, though, I am going to the Dos Passoses for dinner. [. . .]

TO MARY MCCARTHY

Feb 5, 1947 / Wellfleet, Mass.

Dear Mary:

[. . .] I am worried about Reuel's illness. You <u>must</u> find a decent place to live. You cannot keep him there another year. [. . .]

July 1, 1947 / Wellfleet, Mass.

Dear Mary: The Jenckses say they cannot go to Vermont and Charlie has just gone to camp for a month. I think, besides, that it is perhaps not a good thing for Reuel to go back and forth between us at this age too much. It is hard enough for him as it is—he complained to Elena that entirely different things were expected of him in the two households. He is always disobedient and does a lot of showing off when he first comes to us in the summer. We took him to Boston (where he had all his dentistry done) the week before last, and he got so out of hand that I told him he couldn't use his new bow and arrows until he had been good a week. Unfortunately, I had to go away the next day, and I gather he raised Cain—that was when he wanted to talk to you. When I got back, however, he was perfectly all right and has been so ever since. He is mad about monopoly and chess, and goes to a swimming class in the afternoons which he loves. His swimming has improved remarkably. He is amiable and good again, as he was after the first few weeks last summer.

The clothes and bicycle came. The bicycle is much too big for him—it is even bigger than mine; but he can still get along on the old one. [. . .]

New Yorker letterhead / [Before December 8, 1947] / Sunday

Dear Mary:

[. . .] I have just been over the financial situation. [. . .] I get only $91 now, will have to pay Reuel's school bill, and owe the bank $2000. I will, however, raise money to outfit Reuel if any more is needed. [. . .]

[. . .] I'm now getting tickets for the Wednesday matinee of *Command Decision* the day before Christmas to take Reuel [. . .]

I went to St. Bernard's and talked to Mr. Jenkins and Reuel's new master. I gather he is getting along all right. I shall go to see them again later. [. . .]

Vendome letterhead, Boston / March 10, 1948

Dear Mary:

[. . .] We want Reuel to come up on the 20th because Henry will have to bring him, and Henry's vacation ends the 26th. Henry is in New York now and I will arrange to have him meet you at the Grand Central. I will call you up about it next week.

Please tell Reuel that Elena was delighted to get his letter and that the little girl is named Helen Miranda. [. . .]

Vendome letterhead, Boston / March 17, 1948

Dear Mary:

[. . .] I don't think it is such a good idea for Reuel to go to Europe with you this summer. Conditions in those countries are awful, and you might get caught in a crisis. You will have enough trouble doing things yourself on such a brief trip. [. . .]

August 25, 1948 / Wellfleet

Dear Mary: Reuel's lessons so far have amounted to nothing more than learning a few stanzas of poetry and identifying the rhymes and the beat of the verse. I had him learn some Omar Khayam because he is very much steamed up about Persia and demanded to read some Persian poetry. He mastered everything with an ease that astonished me up to the time when he began having difficulty in identifying the accented syllables. Now he seems to have mastered that too. I'm afraid he has been resorting to the technique of playing one parent off against the other. This seems to be inevitable in these situations, but ought to be discouraged.—About the BB gun: he is a little young yet to be shooting it off around here, where there is a baby and a lot of animals and people, and where I am trying to work in a room that is open on three sides. But he can shoot it out back with Henry.

Reuel's school seems to open on Tuesday the 28th. I was planning to take him down the Wednesday or Thursday of the week before. Will you be back in New York then?

Sincerely, / Edmund

TO ELENA

New Yorker letterhead / Sept. 29, 1948

Dearest Elena:

I brought Reuel up to town yesterday morning and bought him a lot of clothes at Rogers Peet. [. . .]

Sept. 30, 1948 / Wellfleet

Dearest Elena,

[. . .] Reuel's visit to Red Bank worked out better than I expected. Mother was less nervous than she had been before. Reuel is old enough to handle himself better. He had a good time, and she seemed to like having him there—had his hair cut and bought him some clothes the day that I went to New York.

TO MARY MCCARTHY

Jan. 24, 1949 / Wellfleet, Mass
Dear Mary: This check [a check for $120 attached] takes it through Feb. 7. Mother has turned over to me two war bonds which she bought in Reuel's name (worth $50 apiece), and I will send them to you as soon as I can find them. [. . .]

TO REUEL WILSON WITH NOTES BY REUEL WILSON

Port au Prince, Haiti, / December 5, 1949
Dear Reuel: This is a hand–painted native picture of a man beating a Haitian drum. These drums are used for voodoo ceremonies but also at ordinary dances and for entertainment in bars. I sometimes hear them going all night.

I made a hair-raising trip the other day to a place called Jacmel on the south coast.[1] Going there by plane was easy and took only twenty minutes, but to get back we had to charter a public bus called La Sainte Famille (The Holy Family) and spent most of the night navigating a road that crosses a river, by actual count, eighty times. The rivers here are always overflowing and changing their course, so that it is hardly worthwhile building bridges—they are likely to be left high and dry. The result is that such traffic as there is has to plough right through the rivers, and in this case the riverbed is sometimes identical to the road, so that you are driving upstream like a steamboat. The river is extremely strong, and you have to stop every so often to hammer stones out of the tires. Between bouts with the river, you go up along the mountains, with precipices yawning at your elbow. It makes you appreciate American roads to go to a country that has literally no decent ones.

Before my trip to Jacmel, I made another trip, driving, to Cap-Haïtien on the north coast. You get a good idea up there of what the life of the planters was like before the slaves and mulattoes revolted at the end of the 18th century, drove the whites out and set up their own government. The slave-owners had enormous estates, of which there is sometimes nothing left now but the gates opening onto a wilderness. I climbed on horseback to the great citadel that the Negro King Christophe built on the top of a mountain but which he was never able to finish. When he was old and ill and facing a revolt he shot himself with a golden bullet which he had been saving for such emergency. It is a ride of two hours through a forest of mahogany, bamboo, coconut, coffeebean, cocoa-bean, breadfruit, mango, calabash, citronella, and a lot of other things. This may suggest a fruit salad, but actually it is all green.

I hope you are doing better at school. I am looking forward to seeing you at Christmas. It will be nice to be all together back in Wellfleet. Elena writes that great progress is being made with the house for you and Henry and that the big house is being painted.—I have bought one of the mahogany heads of the Haitian patriots like the one the Givens have—though I don't know precisely what I am going to do with it.

Affectionately, / Father

[1] EW visited a UNESCO literacy project at Marbiel, near Jacmel.

TO MORTON ZABEL

Wellfleet, Mass. / January 31, 1950

Dear Morton:

[. . .] The family are all fine—the children, as they get older, become continually more interesting. [. . .]

TO BETTY HULING

June 4, 1950 / Wellfleet, Mass.

Dear Betty:

We're delighted at the prospect that you may come up. Don't hesitate to come during the summer. It would be fun to have you when the children are here. Reuel is here now. [. . .]

July 28, 1950 / Wellfleet, Mass.

Dear Betty: Our general feeling is that we'd love to pay you a visit, but your postcard is rather vague. In the first place, you give no address, so I can only hope this letter reaches you.[1] In the second place, can you arrange for us to stay somewhere because, remembering my other visit, I can't imagine going and coming back all in one day. I should think we'd have to spend at least two nights there—pretty expensive, isn't it? It would be a question of Elena and me and Reuel. [. . .]

[1]Huling is on Martha's Vineyard where it is customary for summer residents to pick up their mail at the local post office.

TO REUEL WILSON WITH NOTES BY REUEL WILSON

Mansgrove, Princeton, N.J. / February 24, 1953

Dear Reuel:

Your recent report is not bad, but Mr. Ashburn has written on it that it represents only a "moderate effort" and that you ought to be doing better.

We have recovered from all our illnesses, though Helen only went back to school today. She had flu on top of chickenpox. Henry has been with us for several days, and Rosalind was here over Washington's birthday. Henry has been drafted and goes off to Washington tonight. He will be sent somewhere to camp for four months of basic training. He tells me to send you his best. Elena is depressed about having him go, but I think he is rather relieved at having the problem settled.

We played a big game of anagrams when Rosalind was here, and Rosalind beat us with many long and impregnable words.

We are all going to New York Friday. We are going to take Helen and Hedwig to the Walt Disney *Peter Pan* in the afternoon, and then Elena and I are going to the Stravinsky opera in the evening.

We look forward to your vacation in the middle of March and hope to get off then for a trip to Washington. We were glad to hear you were out of the infirmary. When you get this, drop me a line and let me know how you are doing. This is the dull season everywhere, and there is usually not much to report except work and occasional diseases. I have bought a small phonograph to brighten things up a little. Elena sends best love.

Affectionately, / Father

Talcottville / July 24, 1953

Dear Reuel: I am glad to hear that you are enjoying yourself [in Wellfleet]. I was sorry to leave you and miss you up here. Everybody asks about you and is disappointed you didn't come this summer. The house looks wonderful now. All the outside part has been painted; blinds and porches restored, etc.

We went to a barn-dance the other night. It was terrific; the barn was enormous, and they had a three-piece band and an announcer with a loud speaker. The boys moving the girls around so violently that Helen Augur came out of one of the square dances quite dizzy. There is an interlude in one of the dances during which any boy or girl on any part of the floor can approach any other girl or boy and swing them. There is also a moment in this dance when you have to kiss your partner. Perhaps you know all about this. By 11 o'clock when we left, the thing was really formidable. At the end of each dance, the boys all stamp, and, in the square dances, there are moments when they mark the beat by stamping.—There are also the "Polish hops," which I think of attending some Saturday night to see them do Polish dances.

Drop me a line when you get this. Have you heard from your mother lately? She hasn't answered my last letter, but I assume she will be in Wellfleet by this time.

Love, / Father

London, Basil St. Hotel, Knightsbridge, / Jan. 19, 1954

Dear Reuel: We have been having a very good time in London and have often wished you were with us. Henry has been here on a week's furlough, just went back to Germany this morning. He wanted to go to Cambridge for a year on the G.I. Bill of Rights after he got out of the army, and went up there to find out about it, but discovered that there was too much Greek and Latin required. He then looked into London University and thinks he can make it there. Elena's sister Olili is staying with us here. Last night we went to the Elizabethan dining room, with wainscoting and a floor strewn with rushes. The tables are lighted with candles, and while you eat a girl in costume sings old songs and plays the virginals, an ancient kind of piano. You drink mead, a kind of wine made of honey and apples, and the dinner consists of sixteenth century dishes carefully reconstructed from ancient receipts. I am enclosing a copy of the menu. You eat on wooden trenchers and are given no spoons for the soup, but have to drink it out of large bowls. After dinner, what is left on the plates is scraped into an enormous "alms-dish." And you are told that it is to be fed to the poor, but actually, I believe, it is simply fed to pigs. The queer food made Elena ill, though I think it was mainly a psychological reaction to tackling unfamiliar dishes in an atmosphere of semi-darkness where you could not see exactly what you were eating. Certain of the courses were rather heavy going for everybody.

Helen has been riding in Hyde Park almost every day. She has jodhpurs and is learning to post. I have taken her to two Christmas "pantomimes," one on ice, a magic show, and Mme. Tussaud's waxworks.

Your mother writes that you want a dinner jacket. I'll try to send you enough for this, along with your other expenses, when you are starting your vacation. . . .* By February 4 we'll be in Salzburg, where I hope to find a letter from you. . . . We have missed you very much. I hope you're getting along all right.—Elena sends love.

Love, / Father

[Postscript] In Paris we can be reached c/o American Express.

* These dots in the texts of the letters mark deletions.

American Seminar, Salzburg, Austria, Feb. 11, 1954 [hand-written on two postcards]

Dear Reuel: Why don't you write? We haven't heard a word from you.— This card shows the old Salzburg castle. We are living in a more recent one built by a sporting archbishop. The other card shows the pool where he used to have his horses watered. Note the murals of the horses.—We all got sick in Paris, where it was unexpectedly cold, and even now we haven't quite recovered. This is a very queer life here, living in a rococo palace, full of cupids and decorations that look like Viennese pastry, eating rather bad meager food and associating with students from all over Europe, including Jugo-Slavia, to whom we lecture on American literature. I can't make out what, if anything, they get out of it . . . [Here I omit short messages from Elena and Helen, transcribed by EW and RW.]

—Be sure to write us.

Love, Father

That summer EW sent me another double-postcard missive from the stone house.

[hand-written on the backs of two postcards: one depicts "Logging on the Moose River near Boonville, N.Y., "the other "Main Street in Winter, Boonville, N.Y."]

July 18, 1954, Talcottville, N.Y.

Dear Reuel: I hope you are enjoying yourself, I look forward to your coming up here. I'm afraid you'll have to stay a month, but we'll break it up with a trip to Canada—I brought back here from New York two Persian kittens for Helen and Elena—a male and a female—extremely lively: they dart around all over the house and crawl up the back of my neck when I am working.—There are more barn-dances than ever this year. I think you may want to investigate them, though the crowd is not so high-toned as at the Chequesset Club [The sailing and golfing club in Wellfleet].—They are not playing any more baseball at the diamond back of the house. All those boys seem to be grown up and working at jobs—the house has been greatly improved—Bring up a few of your records—*Dreimaedalhaus,* if it still survives, as I have a phonograph.

Affectionately, / Father

[Postscript] Love to your mother and Bowden.

[EW, Elena, Helen, Hedwig, Bambi, and the above mentioned Persian cats, Light Ginger and Dark Ginger, spent a portion of the winter of 1955 in New York City at 26 East 81st Street. Helen entered the Nightingale-Banford School. In one of her letters Elena describes the apartment as "very large, rather dirty and the bedrooms are gloomy." She also reports that "Bambi has his usual *succès fou* with old ladies in the park . . .]

TO RICHARD KNOWLES

May 28, 1954

Dear Mr. Knowles:

Thank you very much for your letter. I was already grateful to you for your kindness to Reuel at St. George's, about which he had told me. He has been doing well at Brooks. He is quite grown-up now—has to shave and smokes a pipe. I find, by the way, since studying Hebrew, that his name has really three syllables instead of two. It is one of the names of Moses's father-in-law and means either "friend of God" or "Shepherd of God"—an old family name.

I am afraid I shall never get to Armenian. I've already got to the age at which it becomes more difficult to remember vocabulary.

Thank you for inviting us to look you up in Newport. I hope we may sometime be able to.

Yours sincerely, / Edmund Wilson

TO BETTY HULING

Dec. 14, 1956

Dear Betty:

[. . .] Reuel is in Harvard and doing well, but constantly gets himself bunged up wrestling. [. . .]

TO JOHN DOS PASSOS

March 17, 1957 16 Farrar St. / Cambridge, Mass.

Dear Dos: About Harvard: Harry Levin said to me lately that it "no longer belonged to the Ivy League," that the policy was to make it into a big whole-sale dispensary of education, and that the danger of this, from his point of view, was that the other students would not get the opportunities they ought to have. Since I have been here, I have come to see what he means. I find, for example, that Reuel is involved with his prep school friends in feuds with what they call the "hoods"—short for hoodlums—students from high schools, etc., who behave in a lowdown way that was very unusual in the days of our youth. These battles between Harvard students on different levels re-semble the old town vs. gown quarrels. The college is crowded, the classes are sometimes gigantic, and the professors do not get much chance to give indi-vidual attention to their students. What you say about Pusey and his entou-rage would fit in with my general impression. Pusey, I gather, is not much liked by most of my friends on the faculty.—Reuel, however, has been doing well and enjoying himself, and I am not sorry I sent him here. [. . .]

Love to all, / EW

TO HAZEL [WIDOW OF BURTON] RASCOE

Cambridge, Mass. / April 6, 1957

Dear Hazel:

[. . .] We have been living here in Cambridge ever since the middle of January. My boy is a freshman at Harvard and, I am glad to say, doing ex-tremely well. [. . .]

TO BETTY HULING

Wellfleet letterhead / November 4, 1958

Dear Betty:

[. . .] I have to go to Boston to see Reuel (who is doing well at Harvard).
[. . .]

TO MARY MCCARTHY

Jan. 22, 1961 / 12 Hilliard St. / Cambridge 38, Mass

Dear Mary: I can't tell from Reuel's last letter where he is now—he seemed to
be uncertain whether he would get his visa for Poland renewed. Please forward the enclosed letter to him and drop me a line about him. [. . .]

April 14, 1961 / 12 Hilliard / Cambridge 38, Mass

Dear Mary: [. . .] We have just heard from Reuel. I have written him that I
think it would be a good idea for him to try for a job with the State Department. He didn't tell me about the *Harper's* article.

I agree with you and Reuel about *Hiroshima Mon Amour,* but I haven't
found anybody except Sylvia Marlowe who is not enthusiastic about it. [. . .]

July 7, 1962 / Wellfleet

Dear Mary: Reuel is staying with friends and has given me as his address simply Department of Slavic [Languages], U of C., Berkeley. He is coming on
here July 20—perhaps sooner, if I can induce him to. [. . .]

TO MARGARET RULLMAN

Wellfleet, Mass. / January 1, 1962

Dear Margaret: [. . .] My boy Reuel is out in Berkeley getting a master's degree
in Slavic languages. He spent a year in Poland on a scholarship. Did you see

his article in the October *Harper's* on education in Poland?—with considerable attention to the nightspots frequented by the students? He lately had a bad accident. I can't visualize exactly what happened, but he says that, on the way to a party with a friend, feeling a little high, he tried to jump into a Japanese garden and fell eight feet. He broke his jaw. The friend took him to a hospital, where he was operated on. He had to lose a tooth and his jaw was wired for weeks.

Love as ever, / Edmund

TO MARY MCCARTHY

Hotel Victoria letterhead, Rome / March 14, 1964

Dear Mary: Reuel has just written that he needs money for dentists and other things. I am sending him a hundred, but he evidently needs more. Will you send him something? [. . .]

Aug. 17, 1965 / Wellfleet

Dear Mary: You may not have had my letter, sent to Paris. Reuel tells me that he thinks you are at Spezia. He has just found a place to live outside Madison: 1902 Parmenter St., Middleton, Wisconsin. He will have a teaching job—four hours a week—for which they will pay him only $200 a month. He of course cannot live on this, and in the meantime his place is unfurnished, and they will have to be buying things. I'm in no position to do very much for them until after this year. [. . .] Can't you continue to send Reuel an allowance? He says he has heard nothing from you lately, and he is worried about this.

Sept. 1, 1965 / Wellfleet

Dear Mary: I was glad to get your letter. Reuel has just called me up. They have taken a new place: 7612 University Ave., Middleton, Wis. He is down to $90. I have sent him $20, but have only a few hundred in the bank myself. Do send him something to tide him over.—It's true that he's awfully vague about his engagements. He was very shortsighted to use up all that money on their trip to Spain & Portugal, and then arrive here with practically no money.—It isn't true that I never wrote him last winter. On the contrary, Elena and I were in constant correspondence with him. There may have been a gap when he hadn't heard for some time. [. . .]

September 24, 1966

[Handwritten postscript] Dear Mary: I wonder if you have seen this book[1] and approved it in its present form. If you haven't seen it, I think you should. The author is evidently an idiot. [. . .]

[1]Doris Grumbach's biography of Mary McCarthy, *The Company She Kept;* it contains unflattering references to both Wilson and Reuel.

[Handwritten superscript by Mary McCarthy dated 10/12/82: "has read the Grumbach book"]

Oct. 3, 1966 / Wellfleet

Dear Mary: I was relieved to know that you had not ok'd that book and that you were going to do something about it. I think it is very dangerous to let people make tape-recordings. Some years ago I let Henry Brandon tape-record an interview with me and he was perfectly decent about it—I checked and rewrote the whole thing; but I have never allowed it since. [. . .]

About Reuel: he wrote me that at the advice of some professor, he had shifted to Comp. Lit. because this would enable him to get his Ph.D without linguistics, which he hates. They have lately been on a vacation in Florida and write, in their postcards, that they have been having a very good time. We haven't seen Reuel for more than a year, but hope they will come on for Christmas. I don't think, by the way, that stupid woman ought to be allowed to characterize him as "a student of sorts"—which sounds disparaging. [. . .]

TO CLELIA CARROLL

June 17, 1967 / Wellfleet

Dear Clelia:

[. . .] My son Reuel and his wife have just been here. She has a baby under way. Helen [. . .] is now studying Russian at summer school. Reuel's teaching it at Chicago summer school. I suppose that Elena and I are responsible for all these languages—though we have put no special pressure on them. [. . .]

Sept. 22, 1967 / Wellfleet, Mass.

Dear Clelia:

[. . .] My son Reuel's wife is going to have a baby, so I'll be for the first time a grandfather. [. . .]

Helen

TO MARY MCCARTHY

March 10, 1948

Dear Mary:

[. . .] Please tell Reuel that Elena was delighted to get his letter and that the little girl is named Helen Miranda.[1] [. . .]

[1]Helen Miranda Wilson: daughter born to Edmund and Elena February 19, 1948.

TO ELENA WILSON

September 22, 1948 / Wellfleet, Mass.

Dearest Elena:

The baby has been perfect—very cheerful and good. She is giving her little yips of boredom in the middle room now, and I will go in to see her when I finish this.

Sept. 30, 1948 / Wellfleet

Dearest Elena,

Helen is fine. She is cutting a tooth in her lower jaw. I went in this morning and found her sitting up in her pen, which she had accomplished by herself. I think she would crawl if encouraged and given a free field on the floor. Her eyelashes are long and rather dark while her hair remains completely blond. [. . .]

October 2, 1948 / Wellfleet, Mass

Dearest Elena:

I have been trying during the last two days to go to the mat with the problem of Rosalind . . . Helen on the other hand has been making great advances and is now able to crawl quite quickly. I bring her in here and put her on the yellow rug from the front room, which has been cleaned. Yesterday she got hold of a magazine and tried to eat it and pulled the metal rod out of one of my filing cases. [. . .]

October 4, 1948 / Wellfleet, Mass.

Dearest Elena:

[. . .] The baby comes in to see me every afternoon and I let her do some crawling on a rug on the floor. She will go after a magazine if I put it on the other end or come over to see me if I sit down on the floor. She has developed a little interrogative noise—described by Miss Carter in the enclosed letter—and is very curious about everything. She sits up now by herself and makes efforts to hold on to things, which are evidently attempts to get up on her feet. Her hair is a lot longer than when you left and I should say completely flaxen. [. . .]

Nov. 26, 1949

Dearest Elena:

[. . .] I have thought constantly about you and the little girl and missed you. [. . .]

TO BETTY HULING

July 28, 1950 / Wellfleet, Mass.

Dear Betty: Our general feeling is that we'd love to pay you a visit. [. . .] It would be a question of Elena and me and Reuel. [. . .] I suppose that the weekend of August 4–7 would be the ideal time from our point of view, as Hedwig's daughter can come to stay with her, and she wouldn't be alone in the house with Helen. [. . .]

May 27, 1952

Dear Betty:

[. . .] Otherwise, we are doing well. The children will all be here for Memorial Day. Helen is maturing rapidly. I have been looking up the birds we see in a book and reading to her the descriptions, which are in an old-fashioned and rather flowing style. Someone gave her a little insect book and the other day she chased a white butterfly with every evidence of a collector's enthusiasm and then went to look it up in the book. She found a picture that she thought resembled it, and then pretended to read out the description: "This beautiful little white butterfly flies through the air with the greatest of ease." That night, after she had gone to bed, her mother found her trying to look up a fly that had been annoying her. [. . .]

Nov. 8, 1953 / Wellfleet, Mass.

Dear Betty:

[. . .]—We have all been rather miserable lately. First I was immobilized with gout (which I'm now over); then Elena, Rosalind, and Helen all came down with this new-type flu. Elena and Helen are still in bed. Otherwise, we are doing well. [. . .]

[Postcript to a letter from Europe]

May 24, 1954

Helen wrote one of her friends: "When I get back, I'll tell you about my good days and bad days on land and on sea." In another letter, she described in great detail the process of making wine at her uncle's place in Johannisburg, and ended, "And the last thing is, you drink it."

Dec. 14, 1956

Dear Betty:

[. . .] —We went to Europe last July, leaving Helen with friends. Elena came back in August, I in September. [. . .] Helen just had to have her appendix out, but is now doing splendidly. As soon as she came to from the ether, she rang for the nurse and asked for a television set. On her way to the operating room, she had seen a sign that said that TV sets were available. [. . .]

Dear Betty:

[. . .] Helen is tall and vigorous. [. . .]

TO MARY MCCARTHY

April 14, 1961 / 12 Hilliard / Cambridge, Mass

Dear Mary:

[. . .] We are going up to Wellfleet today for the ten days of Helen's vacation—with our hound dog, two adult cats and four one-week-old [kittens]. [. . .]

TO MARGARET RULLMAN

Wellfleet, Mass. / January 1, 1962

Dear Margaret: [. . .] We have come to Wellfleet for the holidays—back to Cambridge when Helen starts school on the 10th. She is now a tall good-looking girl who wears her mother's clothes. [. . .]

TO ELENA WILSON

September 11, 1963 / Wellfleet, Mass.

Dear Elena:

Tell Helen how sorry I am that I've seen her so little lately. [. . .]

TO CLELIA CARROLL

Oct. 23, 1963 / Basil St. Hotel / London

Dear Clelia:

We are going to Paris on Saturday, because Helen will be there on an excursion from her school, and we want her to stay with us. [. . .]

TO MARY MCCARTHY

Hotel Victoria letterhead, Rome / March 14, 1964

Dear Mary: Reuel has just written that he needs money for dentists and other things. I am sending him a hundred, but he evidently needs more. Will you send him something? Rosalind is coming here next week, and also Helen for her vacation, so my expenses will be pretty heavy. [. . .]

TO CLELIA CARROLL

June 3, 1965 / Talcottville

Dear Clelia:

[. . .] I awakened from a dream in which I thought I was talking to Elena here and telling her that I wanted Helen to come up for a while this summer because I didn't want her completely to lose touch with the place (she has not been here for two or three summers). [. . .]

TO MARY MCCARTHY

Aug. 17, 1965 / Wellfleet

Dear Mary:

[. . .] Wellfleet this year is less overrun than usual, but we have had quantities of family converging on us. It is so long since I have been here, however, at this time of year that I find I am rather enjoying it. [. . .]

TO CLELIA CARROLL

Sept. 21, 1966 / Wellfleet, Mass.

Dear Clelia:

[. . .] Elena is taking Helen down to Barnard tomorrow. [. . .]

Nov. 28, 1966 / Wellfleet, Mass.

Dear Clelia:

[. . .] Helen was here, followed by several beaux who seem to me more or less creeps, though Elena says I don't do them justice and am merely put off by their clothes and their ways of wearing their hair.

June 17, 1967 / Wellfleet, Mass.

Dear Clelia:

[. . .] Helen thinks she's not going on at Barnard but is going to get a job. I'm hoping she'll eventually go back. She is now studying Russian at summer school. Reuel's teaching it at Chicago summer school. I suppose that Elena and I are responsible for all these languages—though we have put no special pressure on them. [. . .]

Sept. 22, 1967 / Wellfleet, Mass.

Dear Clelia:

[. . .] Helen did well with her Russian this summer, and now thinks she's looking for a job in New York. Her interest in Russian has been stimulated, we think, by her having a Russian boyfriend. We haven't seen him yet, though his sister has been up here with us and we liked her. They are related to the Nabokovs, whom we know, and he sounds rather more promising than some of her other admirers. [. . .]

Nov. 30, 1967 / Wellfleet, Mass.

Dear Clelia:

[. . .] Helen is back with us till after Christmas. A crisis in her Russian family occurred while we were in New York. The boy had been in the Greek Orthodox seminary, presumably preparing to be a priest, and Helen was working for the monks at the synod; then the boy, to the consternation of his pious and conservative family, suddenly abandoned the seminary and decided he would enroll in the Peace Corps and came home, so Helen, who had been living with them, couldn't stay any longer in his room. I think that, anyway, they regarded her as a subversive influence. [. . .] Helen spends her time here riding and sleeping. She thinks she is going back to college after the holidays. [. . .]

January 10, 1968 / Wellfleet, Mass.

Dear Clelia:

[. . .] Helen is at loose ends, doesn't know what she wants to do. She worries and irritates me. How are your daughters? Helen gave me a pup for Christmas—evidently a mixture of boxer and we don't know what. He is full of beans and quite a nuisance—eats my books and the ornaments off the Christmas tree. [. . .]

[Postcard of Cape Cod Canal and Sagamore Bridge from Wellfleet, Mass., July 14, 1970]

Any chance of your being up in this part of the world this summer? I am leading a double life between here and Talcottville—writing a book about the latter, to which I am returning in August, and trying to do justice to my family here: four grandchildren, with their parents, our daughter Helen with a friend who is acting as my secretary, two Siamese cats, one semi-Persian cat, and a dog; but one of the Siamese cats has disappeared. All around us roars the holiday traffic of the midsummer Cape. [. . .]

Talcottville letterhead / Sept. 2, 1970

Dear Clelia:

[. . .] Helen is in Maine at art school. [. . .]

Wellfleet letterhead / Dec 14, 1970

Dear Clelia:

[. . .] Our daughter [Helen] has a serious admirer, a young sculptor, who is the grandson of an old New England friend of mine, and we are rather reassured about her. [. . .]

V. Clelia Carroll:
An Epistolary Romance

Wilson met Clelia Carroll in 1958 when they worked on Jason Epstein's Looking Glass Library, a children's book series at Anchor Doubleday. Clelia was the editor, and Wilson, along with W. H. Auden and Phyllis McGinley, was a consultant. A strong attraction soon developed, at least on Wilson's part. Clelia was from an old and distinguished Maryland family and was married to Philip Carroll of Carrollton, Maryland, a descendent of a signer of the Declaration of Independence. She had a curious appeal for Wilson, reminding him of a young woman of his own generation come to life as a vibrant, beautiful presence at midcentury. He began an extended epistolary flirtation, showering her with compliments, sharing confidences and gossip and dreams, and making her into yet another impossible love. Clelia—like Mary McCarthy and the lesbian Mary Meigs—was deeply appealing to a man who loved cultivated beauties of his own class. The "Carroll affair" seems heavily one-sided, and yet Wilson's determination to tell Clelia so much at such length makes the correspondence a notable document.

February, 1962

Dear Clelia:

This is a premature Valentine.—I was very glad to hear about your boy.[1] I suppose you are back in the office.—I expect to be down to New York in March.

Edmund

(Illustration enclosed: Valentine with the following rhyme:)

A Valentine
Just For You
There's a cabinet particulier in my heart
JUST FOR YOU
Filled with many memories and warm wishes
For your happiness,
I hope you'll always keep a corner
in the Algonquin
JUST FOR ME!

[1]Clelia's son Philip Delafield Carroll, who was born December 29, 1961.

February or March, 1962

Dear Clelia:

I now have this different kind of pad, which enables me to write longer letters. (Our letters will eventually be known as "the yellow-pad correspondence" and will eventually bring as much as £5 at Sotheby's.) These moths, or, as he called them, bats from Tutankhamen's tomb, were made by an old man for a shop opposite the British Museum that sells Punch and Judy figures and magic supplies. I bought some when I was last in London, and lately got an English friend[1] who lives in New York to buy me some more on her trips to England. [Three cloth moths were enclosed with this letter.] The first time she went, she was told that the man who made them was 91; I hastened to order some more, and the next time she went over, she found that he had just died, but had left six dozen, which she bought up for herself and me; four for me and two for herself. This gives us a certain feeling of affluence. They are useful in certain kinds of emergencies. I am planning to use mine to send to people who write me disagreeable letters. I am enclosing one for your boy.

Our life has been of a monotony which would be incredible for anybody but another writer, but it provides me with excellent conditions for working on something like the Dead Sea scrolls. I spend most of my life in the late B.C. and early A.D. centuries. Yesterday I was rudely recalled to the present. A Sunday lunch party, already fairly high, came on to have drinks with us. I hadn't expected them and was concentrating, trying to get something finished. They were the Chavchavadzes, our Russian-Georgian friends and Peggy (*Life with Father*) Day.[2] Peggy and Elena differed violently about Vietnam; then everybody discussed translations of the Bible, about which I have had to learn something. I tried to tell them the answers to their questions, but nobody paid attention: they were all in the shouting stage. I talked to them about Old Church Slavonic, which the scrolls have also got me into, and Nina Chavchavadze, who had studied the Slavonic Bible in her youth, began reading aloud my Slavonic text of the Book of the Secrets of Enoch, Peggy having now returned to her enthusiasm for Vietnam and denunciation of Fulbright and the "intellectuals" for tearing the country apart. The effect on my nerves was shattering, and I was very bad-tempered at dinner. Encounters like this up here are rare, but all the more violent because life is so boring. The Chavchavadzes and I are in most cordial correspondence with Svetlana.[3] They are very eager to know her—Nina is a Romanov, daughter of one of the grand dukes, and he is a member of what I take to have been one of the great families of Georgia (Svetlana being a very patriotic Georgian) and I arranged it through George Cannon. It was conveyed to her that both their fathers had been shot by the Bolsheviks. I had a letter from her about my article, and she now says she is coming up to meet us all. The whole thing amuses me enormously, but Elena is afraid that Svetlana will take a cottage up here for the summer, and that we shall be getting command invitations alternately from her and from

Nina. Nina herself is afraid that we shall be surrounded by what she calls "the Okhrana" by which she means the FBI. They are afraid she will seduce Paul and me, though we are both rather old for that.

I don't approve of your learning Spanish. I have a prejudice against Spain—except Goya—and have never learned to read the language, though I love Italian and Italy. I expect we'll get away from here at the end of March, and spend a few days in New York, and get at least as far as Charlottesville.

Your most affectionate, humble servant, / Horace Walpole[4]

[1]Probably Penelope Gilliatt.
[2]Peggy Day: one of the family depicted in Clarence Day's famous play.
[3]Svetlana Alliluyeva (b. 1925): Stalin's daughter and also, in her book about him, one of his severest critics.
[4]Of a piece with his Edgar Wallace and MacArthur signatures.

Oct. 23, 1963 / Basil St. Hotel / London

Dear Clelia:

I am so glad you wrote to me on a yellow pad because that is my favorite medium: all my books are first written on them.

We have been having a very good time here, giving ourselves up completely to a life of pleasure. London seems so calm and restful after life in the U.S. I flew from Boston in five hours—you have hardly finished dinner when you see the dawn—and everything seemed rather unreal for several days; my sense of time was upset. There were moments when I thought I was back in the London of 1908, when I went to Maskelyne's Temple of Mystery in Regent Street, and this has led me to visit magicians' shows and shops; then, going to the Hyde Park Hotel, I thought I was in war correspondent's uniform again and limping painfully down the steps with gout—that was 1945, and it seemed to me chronologically all wrong that I should then have been so badly crippled and now almost never suffer from gout at all; then the Basil Street Hotel—now very run down and about to be demolished—reminded me of earlier visits with Elena and Helen when our relations and friends, now aging, used to come to see us here, and I was capable of more conviviality. For awhile, it was disconcerting; and Elena, who had just come from seeing her family in January, said that she, too, had been put back into the past and didn't know what age she was. But we are now straightened out and have readapted ourselves to the present. I made a point, however, of going out to see Angus Wilson because he lives in the country in Suffolk near a town that my mother's family came from. This was rather spooky (on a dark day). They came over in 1634, and it was strange to see the little church in which they must have worshipped, with the family name figuring on plaques in the wall. It made me a little uncomfortable—I felt that, after three centuries, I had become alienated from that past and could never make contact with it. [. . .]

We are going to Paris on Saturday. [A portion of this letter appears in section IV.] After that, we'll probably go to Rome and spend the winter there. Elena was depressed by Switzerland, going back there after many years.

Our Paris address is Hôtel de Castille, rue Cambon, but I don't expect we'll spend more than two weeks there.

I hope that your being in Carrollton will dispel from Philip's dreams those undesirable people that used to get into his house. Last spring, before going to Talcottville, I dreamt that I was back there and went up to my bedroom and found a lot of horrible things clustered in the corner and on the wall: living organisms like lizards or slugs, of a kind that I sometimes dream of, that always have the form of something else, sometimes of human faces. I knocked down a red one with my cane and began cutting it up. I realized with disgust that I should have to get rid of them all. The next night but one, I dreamed again that I was back and found workmen—though I had not sent for them—doing repairs on the bottom floor. They took me up the stairs to a part of the house that I had not known was here—a bedroom and sitting room full of beautiful old furniture and well-bound books, better than most of the things that are actually there. I was delighted. I suppose those two dreams show a certain ambivalence of attitude.

I don't know what you mean about Jason [Epstein]. I hadn't heard about any financial trouble. The last two issues of the *[New York] Review [of Books]* have just reached us, and I think that they are making a good thing of it.—I don't know what you mean by your "social cowardice." I've always thought you quite independent.

Love, / Edmund

Wellfleet, Mass. / June 11, 1964

Dear Clelia:

I suppose you're in Maryland now—and more or less for good—We came back from almost eight months in Europe—four winter months in Paris, which is awful now. I ended with a month in Hungary—new to me and extremely interesting. I am going next week to upstate New York to settle down for the summer (Boonville RED I, Oneida Co.) and very glad not to have to bother any more with hotels, waiters, taxis, airports, foreign languages and foreign currencies.—I find that, on account of my income tax pamphlet, my getting a "freedom" medal is being denounced in Congress and exploited in Republican campaign literature—along with the award to Oppenheimer and the Bobby Baker scandal[1]—by some of the critics of Johnson. Remember me to Philip.

Edmund W.

[Illustration enclosed: postcard, Budapest]

[1]J. Robert Oppenheimer was the physicist who led the Manhattan Project; he was later accused of passing atomic secrets and denied clearance. Robert G. (Bobby) Baker, secretary to the Senate majority leader and long associated with Lyndon Johnson in the Senate, was forced to resign his post when a civil suit named him in connection with kickbacks in the defense department. He later faced charges of income tax evasion and spent time in prison. Wilson was apparently amused to find himself in their company.

August 23, 1964 / Talcottville

Dear Clelia:

I was very glad to get your letter, and I've had it here on my writing table all summer, rereading it from time to time. I haven't written because, though I got a lot of writing accomplished, as I always do up here, I've been depressed and for the first time felt out of tune with this place. The John Birchers have invaded Talcottville, and also the youthful delinquents. One of my neighbors had a poster on his house: "Save the Republic. Impeach Earl Warren!" The delinquents have been less of a nuisance since one of them ran into a cow on his motorcycle, killed the cow and landed himself in the hospital; but my bad dreams were almost realized when one night I found three boys getting drunk on beer on my porch. I was here alone for six weeks in the end part of the summer, seeing almost no one but my Hungarian secretary, who has had so many other things to do that she wasn't able to give me much time. She has her personal problems, her boss in the drug store having fallen in love with her. The husband of the woman who keeps house for me suddenly died of a cerebral hemorrhage, and she has been too prostrated to work. My older daughter [Rosalind] came on for two weeks in August, and my cousins are staying in the other family house, and now Elena is here. We are going back to Wellfleet this week. From the end of September, my address will be 131 Mt. Vernon St., Middletown, Conn.—I've got one of those sinecure appointments at Wesleyan University there.

I've been working all summer on Canada—*New Yorker* article or a small book—which has become rather interesting for the first time in history. I went up there for ten days, and it caused me to go back and forth between the French and the English and hear what they said about one another. You wouldn't believe they could live side by side with so much animosity and so little communication. The English up to recently have absolutely refused to learn French, and I found it rather gratifying to be in a place where people were grateful to have me speak French, instead of, as in France itself, being annoyed by the kind of French I spoke. But French Canada is a gloomy and frustrated and terribly ingrown little world. Its literature is almost suicidal, and the young people, as you probably know, have been putting bombs in English mail-boxes.

If we ever get to Washington, we'll let you know, but I don't see any prospect of it. Perhaps we may coincide in New York. I'm going down in September for the first time in over a year—shall be staying, I suppose, at the Princeton Club.

This letter, I know, sounds doleful, but I'm not really as low as it sounds. Do write me from time to time.

Love, / Edmund

June 3, 1965 / Talcottville

Dear Clelia:

I was uncertain of your address and my valentine must have gone astray. It's a pity because it was handsome and enormous.
[Valentine]
You're All Woman! And That's the Best Kind!!!
(This is the best I can do.—My invention, though not my affection, is flagging.)

It is delightful up here now. Elena and I are relaxing from Middletown and cleaning up and repairing our respective places. The morning your letter came, I had just awakened from a dream. [A portion of this letter appears in section IV.] I was interrupted by someone at the door, and it turned out to be four reporters, who wanted to ask me about a newspaper story that said that my property had been illegally "taken" in the first place. I said that it had been in the family since the eighteenth century, but they said that, according to the story, the title was very dubious. I hope that Philip in his nightmares has not gone as far as this.

When I am living alone here like this, my habits are rather peculiar. I never have anything for supper but canned pork and beans and canned corned beef hash; but I offset this by caviar for lunch. This is almost my whole diet. It does get a little monotonous.—I'll have to go back to Wellfleet after the 4th of July. Helen is going to France at the end of the month to study at the University of Tours, and Reuel is coming back from Europe, and though I usually avoid August in Wellfleet, I want to be around when they are there.

I don't know who the Gerald is by whose death you say Brendan [Gill] has been affected.[1] But I agree that he seems rather down. What depresses me about him is that I feel he has lost his ambition and is merely marking time at his job and struggling with his innumerable family.

I always think of you in the Algonquin lounge. I suppose you know— Brendan must have told you—that the turmoil in the *New Yorker* office is the result of silly *Herald Tribune* articles.[2] I think that Shawn made a mistake in raising a howl and trying to stop them. They should have been simply ignored.—I understand that my book about Canada has aroused the fury of the English Canadians. I have been fiercely attacked in a Toronto paper by a young Englishman who accuses me of "ignorance" but has only been in the country three years. It is written very much in the vein of those *Herald Tribune* articles, which seems now to be a recognized genre. I always enjoy annoying people.

My Hungarian superwoman[3] is still able to console my solitude. Having long ago tamed her husband, she has now got her boss muzzled, and if he doesn't want to give her time off, says, "Well, now that I've trained those girls, you really don't need me any more." With all her other occupations, she took night courses for almost two years at Utica College, but finally broke down from overwork. Having no nieces, I've become a sort of uncle to her.

Write me sometime—in spite of the fact that we hardly know each other well enough to correspond—there are always things in your letters that I don't understand—such as your reference to Brendan's Gerald[4]—someday I hope we may meet and you will explain that to me.

Love, / Edmund

[1]Brendan Gill: (1914–1998): *New Yorker* writer, biographer of the magazine (*Here at the New Yorker*), and Wilson's fellow consultant on the Looking Glass Library.

[2]Tom Wolfe's mischievous and—to some of the *New Yorker* staff—offensive articles (which ran in June of 1965), touched on the magazine, Shawn (its editor), and what Wolfe termed its "mausoleum"-like qualities.

[3]Mary Pcolar: see section VIII.

[4]Gerald, Brendan Gill's son-in-law, died of cancer.

Dear Clelia:

"All these months and not a word." I sent you a large valentine, which you coldly ignored. We have just escaped from Middletown, Conn., where I was a "fellow" at The Center for Advanced Studies—everything paid for and you are paid for being there. Otherwise, it is a dismal place. Brendan came up at one point and took me on a personally guided tour of old Hartford.

I'm on my way to Talcottville, New York (Boonville RED 1, Oneida Co.) where I suppose I'll find some of the horrors I dream about. But it will be a great satisfaction to be living in my own house again. I am too old to be successfully transplanted.

Love, / Edmund

June 29, 1965 / Talcottville

Dear Clelia:

I have been writing about the new French novelist Christiane Rochefort, and it seems to me that you ought to read her. You probably haven't read *Les Stances à Sophie,* and I am having a copy sent you. The title has to be explained, because the heroine is not called Sophie. Les Stances à Sophie, it seems, is an indecent *chanson de corps de garde*—I have not heard it but I gather that the novel is a woman's extremely rough reply to a rough song about a woman. This and her other books are, in any case, the only things I have read that really tell about Paris as it is today and as foreigners do not like to imagine it. The only things I know that are like them are Dawn Powell's novels, but these are even a great deal tougher.

I've had a good five weeks up here this year—last summer was rather depressing. Have had a lot done to the place—an old stone barn reconstructed and a collapsing wooden one pulled down. But I'll be glad when Elena and Helen come tomorrow. We're going back to Wellfleet the 9th—No: we're not going, thank God, to have another year at Wesleyan. We're returning to our old routine, abandoned for now six years, of staying in Wellfleet till after New Year's, then going to New York or Europe. I hope we'll coincide sometime.

Love, / Edmund

[Postscript] Let me know how you like *Sophie.*

Jan. 14, 1966 / Wellfleet, Mass.

Dear Clelia: [Portions of this letter appear in *Letters on Literature and Politics*.]

I have already acquired *Tosca*[1] and have played it twice. I think you must have seen it when you were very young and being carried away by the melodrama—of rather an old-fashioned kind: "Ha, ha, my proud beauty—your lover shall pay for this!" But there is a good theatrical moment at the end of the Second Act, when Tosca has just killed Scarpia and says,

E morto! Or gli perdono! [He's dead! Now I forgive him!]
E avanti a lui tremava tutta Roma! [This is the man before whom all Rome trembled!]

I have a recording in which Callas sings Tosca, and she seems to lower her register most effectively for this.

How are you getting along with the Ring? It is really much more interesting, I find, to listen attentively to an act or two at a time on the phonograph than to hear it in the opera house. I never thought seriously before about the meaning of *Götterdämmerung*. The *Siegfried* is a strange conception. (Siegfried tells his life many too many times. As Bernard Shaw says, he is telling it again when they kill him.)

I have never read *The Hobbit*[2] but Helen, when she was younger, read it or had it read to her innumerable times, so it must be a good children's story. I can't imagine it in an English course, though.

We have been madly reading Balzac—another valuable resource for spending winter in the country. I don't suppose you have enough time on your hands for this, but if you should ever want to, let me make you some recommendations. You have undoubtedly at some point in your education had to read *Père Goriot* or *Eugénie Grandet*. I read these early, and they rather put me off him, and I have only lately been getting interested in him. Some of them are immensely amusing.

I don't know whether you see the *New York Review* so am enclosing a copy of this play—with Ted Gorey's[3] illustrations.

My line about Truman Capote is that he wants to be the feminine Elsa Maxwell.[4]

We expect to be in New York for a week or two at the beginning of February. Do let me know if you will be there.

As ever, / Edmund

[1] *Tosca:* the Puccini opera. Set in revolutionary Italy, it features love, patriotism, torture, murder, betrayal, etc.

[2] *The Hobbit:* prefatory novel of J.R.R. Tolkien's *Lord of the Rings*—Wilson skewered it as grossly overpraised in "Oo, Those Awful Orcs!" included in *Bit Between My Teeth.*

[3]Edward Gorey (1925–2000): writer and illustrator of the light-hearted macabre, one of whose earliest boosters was Wilson. In addition to his illustrations for Wilson's play *The Duke of Palermo*, Gorey also illustrated a poem of Wilson's, "The Rats of Rutland Grange," which ran in *Esquire* and was later published by The Gotham Book Mart. See section VI.

[4]Elsa Maxwell: hostess of the international set, a strikingly vulgar and unattractive woman, yet the darling of her followers.

February 24, 1966 / Wellfleet, Mass.

Dear Clelia:

Your book,[1] I'm sorry to say, has never reached me. It has never been received at the *New Yorker*. You don't suppose it was sent to the New Yorker Hotel by mistake, as sometimes happens?

I enjoyed seeing your mother and father. I've always thought about you that you were like a girl of my generation who had somehow turned up in a later one, and I found that your parents were much like the parents of my friends of my own generation. Your father seems to have the old-fashioned idea that the unemployed could always find work if they wanted it.

Elena and I both came back from New York; I strained a ligament in my leg getting in and out of the two-seater Provincetown plane that doesn't have any real steps. This brought on my gout, and I was immobilized. I have recovered now, but Elena has never recovered from the thing that she caught weeks ago in New York and which is thought to be the "Asian flu" that is desolating the West Coast.

I suppose that Philip knows that a Tolkien club is in existence. Auden addressed it the other day. I'm sorry that I can't send Philip a message in elvish.

I don't know much about the younger painters either. I hope you don't have to bother with pop art and all that.

Love, / Edmund

[1]Evidently a book on which Clelia Carroll served as editor.

March 12, 1966 / Wellfleet, Mass.

Dear Clelia:

Your book about dreams just came. I had read about it but hadn't seen it, and I am very glad to have it. I have so far only looked at the pictures, which are fascinating. I see that he gives some attention to dreams of flying.

About gout: I don't think I believe the theory that it necessarily implies superior brains. There is a gouty physical type—stocky and rather florid—which my mother's family and which I have perfectly represented, and the disease is supposed to be hereditary. My grandfather and my mother had it badly—not that they weren't bright, but the one of my uncles who had it worst was very much less bright than his brother.

We have been leading a very comfortable but very monotonous life. I get up, have breakfast and read, then do a little work, eat a light lunch while I read the morning's mail: about 3 we go for a little walk in the woods or along the shore, collect the afternoon mail, the paper and some whisky for the evening. I do some homework on German, then read Goethe aloud to Elena—who turns out to be wonderful as an interpreter of *Faust* in connection with its social and historical background. In between, I play solitaire and drink: but I have exhausted the games I know, having won them so many times, and am anxious to learn something new. I go to bed with an Elizabethan play in connection with something I am writing.[1]—Today we have decided to break up this routine by asking in the few available friends who are here. I hope the excitement doesn't give me a coronary.

The clipping is for Philip. I don't understand it, but no doubt he will.

Thanks very much for the book.

Love, / Edmund

[1] *The Duke of Palermo.*

September 14, 1966 / Wellfleet, Mass.

Dear Clelia:

I'm very sorry to hear about Philip's accident. Does he know that they are now making better Gilbert and Sullivan records, with more attention to the music? There is an excellent one of *Trial by Jury* with selections from *Utopia Limited*.

We are going to Martha's Vineyard on Friday. I have done an autobiographical volume, compounded of old diaries and new reminiscences, and I am going to show a cousin there the part about her family. I am apprehensive about this. Another cousin is coming here today, and I'll have to show her the part about her family—which is also a delicate matter. She has an aunt who is capable of suing me.

I don't know anything about Ted Gorey[1] except that he sent me one of his many recent books. (I had a curious dream, by the way, about you one night.)

I haven't been in New York since last winter, but I expect to go in October, to deliver this book when it is typed.

Love, / Edmund

[1]Without really knowing each other the two formed a mutual admiration society. Wilson was an early supporter of Gorey's and Gorey dedicated his 1963 *West Wing* to Wilson. The book referred to here is probably *Gilded Bat.*

Sept. 21, 1966 / Wellfleet, Mass.

Dear Clelia:

The clerihew is an irregular four-line verse invented by Edward Clerihew Bentley, the author of a well-known detective story called *Trent's Last Case.* Two of the best known are:

> *Sir Christopher Wren*
> *Said, "I am going to dine with some men.*
> *"If anybody calls*
> *"Say I am designing St. Paul's."*

> *George the Third*
> *Ought never to have occurred.*
> *One can only wonder*
> *At so grotesque a blunder.*

A lot of other people have written them, too. Auden has several in one of his books:

> *Mallarmé*
> *Had too much to say.*
> *He couldn't quite*
> *Leave the paper white.*

The record of *Trial by Jury* is London 455–1 155. A semi-amateur in Washington has been doing the less-known Gilbert and Sullivan operas. Here is the information about it—you don't need to send it back. I have the *Utopia Limited,* which is perhaps worthwhile if you haven't heard it, but not well recorded and rather pale.

When I wrote you, I had forgotten exactly about my dream, but I have now looked it up in my journal and shall try to tell you about it when I see you again.

Our three days on Martha's Vineyard were a great success. I saw my old friends Lillian Hellman,[1] Max Eastman,[2] and Leon Edel.[3] Both my cousins have been admirable about what I wrote about their families. The one from Hollywood, whom I hadn't seen since sometime in the late 20's, turned out to be rather startling. She arrived with, among other baggage, a blond wig in a kind of hatbox, which she said had not gone over very well in Maine, where her husband has a camp. When Elena asked her how she managed to look so young at 55, she answered "arrested development" and when she was asked when she had taken to painting dogs instead of portraits of people: "When I got disgusted with people." The whole thing, however, has rather depressed me—going back into the past and exploring all the tragedies and scandals.

Alcohol has a different effect on me than you say it does on you. It usually slows things up. I wonder when people will ever go when it may only be 9 o'clock.

We'll be spending the winter in Wellfleet but shall get to New York from time to time. I expect to go early in October—probably the second week—as soon as I can get this book typed and revised.

Mary Pcolar at the present time is happier, I think, than I have ever known her. She has really gone into business with the man who runs her drugstore—what she calls the only "ethical pharmacy" in Rome, New York, which means that it sticks to prescriptions—with a superior lunch counter called a "coffee bar" and is not allowed to become a 5 & 10 cent store. Mary has organized three services which operate as branches of the business: a surgical appliances department, a School of Charm for Teenagers, and a Conversation Class for Older Women. The charm school has had great success. She keeps an album which shows the girls before and after the treatment. When I asked about the conversation class, she explained that the first step is to get them off the weather and the next to get them off their children. When I asked how this was done, she said that she would remark that she had just read an interesting book on child psychology and talk about that. I don't believe these ladies of Rome [N.Y.] really want to learn to converse; I imagine they are simply fascinated by her magnetism, good looks, and authority.

I am writing in a better mood than I have sometimes done. I enjoy this time of year: crickets and the summer over—all the young people gone away and everything perfectly quiet. I am sorry that you have been feeling "low-spirited." [A portion of this letter appears in Section IV.]

What is your daughter studying—ancient or modern Greek? I studied some modern Greek when I was in Greece but never got very far with it. I am just as glad I didn't because I am not under any obligation to read Cavafy[4] or Kazantsakis[5] (I'm not sure I'm spelling it right).

Do write me in an empty moment.

Love, / Edmund

[1]Lillian Hellman (1905–1984): dramatist, *The Little Foxes* et al., and memoirist, *Pentimento* et al.; her Stalinist views made her the implacable foe of Trotskyite Mary McCarthy, whose remarks about Hellman's "a's an's and the's" being lies "like everything she wrote" on the Dick Cavett Show started dueling libel suits that raged until both women were dead.

[2]Max Eastman (1883–1969): political writer and leftist friend from the 1930s.

[3]Leon Edel (1907–1997): celebrated biographer of *Henry James* (5 volumes, 1953–72), Wilson's choice to edit his posthumously published journals (he lived to do four of the five decades, beginning with *The Twenties*) and dedicatee of this volume.

[4]Constantine Cavafy (1863–1933): Greek poet ("Ithaca," "Waiting for the Barbarians").

[5]Nikos Kazantzakis (1883–1957): novelist, author of *Zorba the Greek* and *The Last Temptation of Christ*.

Oct. 20, 1966 / Wellfleet

Dear Clelia:

You speak of your Italian soul, and I had only learned quite recently that you had an Italian strain. This explains your name and your peculiar kind of attractiveness, neither of which I have been able to account for. Where does the Italian come in?—I have never seen *Tosca*. Have been playing the three different *Faust* operas. None of this is really first rate. Boito[1]'s is much the most interesting. He really tries to do something with Goethe. Neither Berlioz nor Gounod, apparently, knew anything but inadequate French translations. Gounod is rather corny; Berlioz flimsily romantic.

I enjoyed the animal book, as I always do books about animals. Lorenz[2] is much more serious. Some of the paragraphs of the translations are rather opaque, due to German technical abstractions imperfectly transposed into English; but it is well worth going through and clears up toward the end. I have read in the other book, which is entertaining, but, Clelia, don't expect me to read Gerald Kersh[3] at my time of life, I am trying, in the years left to me, to get through as many as possible of the famous books I have never read. By the way, have you been seeing the many booklets that Ted Gorey gets out about every three months? The last one, *The Adventures of Gremlin*, is not unamusing; has a text by someone else.

I saw the Epsteins twice in New York. Jason is much excited about his

Negro education project, says that in two years he will have every boy in Harlem reading Latin. I'm not sure that this is desirable. Barbara, as I told you, has been transformed by the *New York Review* and seems to look smarter and talk more sparklingly every time that I see her. They now have a regular sort of salon. I always go there intending to talk business with them, but then all kinds of stimulating people come in, and nothing ever gets settled. Truman Capote is giving a ball, to which he is supposed to have asked 1500 people. He tries to dictate the dinner parties that are supposed to precede it—also the dress of the guests, who are directed to wear masks. We have been assigned to the Epsteins, who are going to go through with it; but we are not going. I think that this use of the thousands he has been making out of that murder book is rather repellent, as is Capote himself—especially in the role of Elsa Maxwell.

[Greek sentence addressed to Cynthia, meaning "Good day and Good Luck."]

As ever, / Edmund

[1]Arrigo Boito (1842–1918): sometime collaborator as librettist with Verdi (*Otello, Falstaff*), and composer—his *Mefistofole* is one of several operatic versions of this subject.

[2]Konrad Lorenz (1903–1989): Austrian zoologist known for his work *On Aggression;* the topic was a Wilson obsession. See introduction to *Patriotic Gore* and its depiction of America as a devouring sea slug.

[3]Gerald Kersh (1911–1968): English writer of fantasy and mystery stories; in 1938 he wrote *Night and the City,* later a movie with Richard Widmark.

Nov. 28, 1966 / Wellfleet, Mass.

Dear Clelia:

We are back in our quiet, monotonous but very satisfactory routine. The evening we saw you, my precautions against being devastated at the Epsteins went so far that I left at nine, and as a result, neither of us was able to sleep all night. The next evening, we had dinner with Anita Loos,[1] and she and I gossiped about the twenties. She is doing a second volume. She is a curious, a unique person. Have you read the other books besides *Gentlemen Prefer Blondes?* I think that they are actually all about equally good, and have urged her to bring them out all in one volume. Ted Gorey's last book, *Cultural Slag,* with verses by Felicia Lamport, has some of his best drawings. He has created a race of little insects—like elves—that strike a more cheerful note than has been characteristic of him lately.

I have read another good book about animals: *Sexual Reproduction* by

Susan Michelmore, published in paperback, through Doubleday, by the Museum of Natural History. It is well and intelligibly written and describes the procedures of reproduction from mushrooms and jellyfish up to human beings. From our point of view, some very odd things take place.

I am going to get *Tosca* in order to see what you see in it. You ought to like *Traviata,* which is one of my favorite operas. There is what ought to be a good recording by Toscanini with Licia Albanese, but they had to make it much too fast to get it on two records when it really needs three. I now skip Violetta's scene with the father of Alfredo—*"Pura siccome un angelo"* [Pure she is as an angel] etc. I can't bear it that Violetta should give in so easily and can't bear the father's complacency when he keeps saying, "Piangi, piangi, piangi." [In effect, "Let your tears flow."] I have been twice through Strauss's *Die Frau ohne Schatten* [The woman without a shadow]—now current at the new Metropolitan. In spite of passages of discordant violence, it is full of Strauss's beer-y Bavarian gemütlichkeit, and the story itself is the greatest nonsense I have ever seen.

We had a Thanksgiving party, which everybody seems to have enjoyed except me. I had to talk to the French mother of a neighbor of ours who has been long separated from but is still quarreling with her husband, and getting a little dotty. Since the very nice and worried mother is as limited as most French bourgeois women, it is hard to know what to say to her, since the situation seems insoluble. Two old friends were visiting us, but I wasn't able to get to them till the next day. [A portion of this letter is in section IV.]

We very much enjoyed seeing you and wish it were possible more often.

As ever, / Edmund

[Postscript] This letter sounds like the *Saturday Review*—first books, than records.

[1]Anita Loos (1894–1981): satirist of the 1920s and '30s; author of *Gentlemen Prefer Blondes* and *The Better Things in Life.*

February 17, 1967 / *The New Yorker*

Dear Clelia:

We've been having quite a gay and interesting time; but it seems to me that the whole atmosphere is rather sinister. Norman Podhoretz[1] sounds dotty; Robert Lowell, the poet—a manic depressive—is in a Boston hospital and can only be seen when he is out "on parole," and another friend of mine seems in almost as bad a way mentally. One of Elena's Russian friends, an old lady, was mugged and seriously injured in front of a Russian church; another woman I know was raped in her apartment and has been shattered by the experience; the illegitimate son of an old friend has been killed in a motor accident, and his legitimate son strangled a woman and was got off on grounds of insanity. A great many of the taxi-drivers refuse to go out at night because so many of them have been mugged.

And the supposed entertainments we have seen here have only added to the general grisliness: Pinter's *Homecoming*,[2] the film called *Blow-Up*[3] and the new Metropolitan Opera House, which is a miracle of bad taste and ineptitude. The only attractive features are the Chagall murals, which are hung in a too narrow space, where it is impossible to get far enough back to look at them, and the Christmas tree ornament chandeliers donated by the Austrian government. But *The Apple Tree*[4] is the best show we have seen in years and about the only cheerful one—directed by Mike Nichols, who really has a magic touch. If you want to see something, you ought to see that. But avoid the matinees, when an understudy appears instead of Barbara Harris.[5]

I have been getting away from it all by going back to the Dead Sea scrolls. I am planning to go to Israel and Jordan in April in order to bring up to date a little book on the subject that I wrote ten years ago. It may be hard to believe but the problems of the scrolls and the situations created by the personalities and conflicting faiths of the people who work on them are extremely exhilarating. I have just seen two youngish men who are authorities on the scrolls and who seem to me to represent something new in this field. They are crack Semitics scholars who are less constrained by the fear of getting in trouble with their churches than the older Biblical scholars. One of them is what Roger Straus called "a Jesuit drop-out."

About my play:[6] I did not know when I wrote it that there was a real Hillsdale College in Michigan, and now I have had a letter from a graduate of the real Hillsdale in which he says that the characters in the play are so much like some of the people there that it can't be a mere coincidence. I have written him that there are types like that in practically every college in America.

The editor of *The New Yorker* has suggested having Ted Gorey illustrate my memoirs, but much as I admire Ted, I don't want him turned loose on my parents and my uncles and aunts.

Love as ever, / Edmund

[1]Norman Podhoretz: editor of *Commentary,* whose midlife crisis took the form of switching the magazine's political sympathies 180 degrees to the right, and writing an autobiographical book, *Making It,* in which he excoriated friend and foe alike—but more often friend. In fact, a recent volume 2 is called *Ex-Friends.*

²*The Homecoming:* Harold Pinter's version of the dysfunctional family, with lots of Pinteresque pauses.

³*Blow-Up:* Michelangelo Antonioni's first non-Italian film, set in Carnaby Street and other newly mod locales in London. Admirers of the auteur praised his break with old fashioned linear narrative—early in the then new mode of jumpy cuts.

⁴*The Apple Tree:* a musical comedy of Eden, based on stories of Mark Twain, Frank R. Stockton, and Jules Feiffer, starring a pre-Hawkeye Alan Alda as Adam.

⁵Barbara Harris: delicious as Eve.

⁶*The Duke of Palermo,* Wilson's send-up of academic foibles, set in what Wilson intended as an imaginary campus called Hillsdale College.

April 4, 1967 / Wellfleet, Mass.

Dear Clelia:

I hope that my piling-up of horrors in my letter from New York didn't make you despair of stopping in. [. . .]

I am flying from New York on the 27th and shall spend about a week there before I leave for Rome, Jordan, Israel, and Paris—for the purpose of bringing up to date a new edition of my book on the Dead Sea scrolls. By the way, I forget whether I told you that I think John Allegro's theories on the New Testament—you said you read his things in *Harper's*—entirely unreliable. I have just had a letter from him, and he sounds to me like one of those people who thinks he has discovered a cipher that shows that Shakespeare was written by Bacon.

The weather here was horrid all through March—heavy snowstorms. I rather dreaded another long trip involving hotels, taxis and airports, but am now looking forward to it.

Immersing myself in the antiquity of the scrolls I always find refreshing and cheering; it gets one entirely away from the worries of the modern world. My old friend Father D'Arcy, the Jesuit, from our winter at Wesleyan two years ago is coming to see us this weekend. Though entirely non-religious myself, I find it rather reassuring to see somebody as intelligent as he is who has himself the assurance of an unshakeable faith and the strength of an institution to which he has devoted his life. And having weathered a winter at Wesleyan is almost like being in the army together.

This letter is uninteresting, but I hope you will reply, I take a touching pleasure in hearing from you.

Love as usual, / Edmund

[Postscript] Have just acquired Verdi's *Otello* and Prokofiev's *War and Peace.* Did you ever get through the Ring? I have been through *Madam Butterfly,* which I had never heard before, and I like it even less than *Tosca*. I think you saw *Tosca* at just the right age.

[Illustration enclosed: both sides postcard from Israel]

Aug. 1, 1967 / Talcottville

Dear Clelia:

Your letter has just reached me. I am up here till some time in September. How long will you be in Nantucket? I may be back in the second week of September. There is a cultural explosion taking place here, and I am committed to taking part in a program.

Elena is still in Wellfleet with her son and his family and a Russian cousin is joining her later. [A portion of this letter, deleted here, appears in section IV.] This is a place no one wants to live. In my own case, though I used to be capable of spending part of the summer alone in order to get something written and though it still seems wonderful at first to get away to this freedom and quiet from the traffic and visitors of Wellfleet, it gets more difficult to live here.

Have you read the biography of Cole Porter?[1] I found it fascinating, though not everybody would; I saw a good many of those shows and knew some of the people, and now I can hardly believe that I really lived through that period and first saw Porter when he came to Princeton to perform with the Yale Glee Club. There is so much of my earlier life that I now can hardly believe in. Have you been reading Anais Nin's[2] diary? Some people think she is pretentious and silly, but she is an old friend of mine, and more amusing and attractive than she would seem to people who didn't know her. She has a very Latin comic sense which doesn't seem to come through in what she writes. When I last saw her, she gave me one of her novels—or whatever they are—and said, "This is my first <u>funny</u> book." But if you didn't know she meant it to be funny it would seem just like all her other books. I recommend Thornton Wilder's *Eighth Day*.[3] I think it's the best thing he ever wrote.

I do hope to see you in the course of this summer. If you're still there when we get back, we'd love to have you come to Wellfleet. Let me know. Regards to Philip.

As ever, / Edmund

[1] *The Life That Late He Led* by George Eells.
[2] Anaïs Nin (1903–1977): diarist and fiction writer who was strongly feminist in her themes and had a horror of Wilson's supposedly domineering way with women.

³*The Eighth Day:* a philosophical novel about destiny; the comment shows Wilson's soft spot for him, since the book is hardly one of Wilder's best.

August 2, 1967 / Talcottville

Dear Clelia:

I just had a note from you, postmarked July 26, telling me that you were going to be in Nantucket, which I answered yesterday. Then, this morning, I got a letter, postmarked July 27 but dated June 26. What happened? Did you forget to mail the first one?

About the points you raise: Perhaps it was just as well that the U.S., from whatever motive, didn't do anything about the Middle Eastern crisis. (There'll be an article by me about the Middle East in the *New Yorker* in a week or two, but it doesn't have much about the politics.)¹

In *Galahad*² the family and house of the friend were based on those of George Perkins. George and his sister were not much like my characters—his sister not at all like the girl in the story—but George's mother was like the friend's mother. The apartment that figures in *Daisy* was not like the one that Scott Fitzgerald visited. I did live for a summer in Bank St. in Elinor Wylie's³ apartment; but the experiences in the book are imaginary.

I missed the Ellison-Podhoretz correspondence.⁴ The prospect of reading anything of the kind so long did not tempt me to buy *Harper's*.

I don't know whether or not your daughter ought to go on with Greek, because I don't know what she's like or what she wants to do.

My Hungarian friend [Mary Pcolar] and her husband drove me over to Sodom, New York the other day. I had always been curious about this place: how it came to be called that and why the inhabitants hadn't changed the name. (Someone who has just bought a place there is trying to have it known as Peaceful Valley.) It turned out to be quite far away in a very wild part of the Adirondacks, with terrible roads and primitive people. There is, however, a motel for skiers, presided over by a very amusing Jewish woman from New York, who says that God had made a good job of it when he decided to wipe Sodom out and that what she liked to call Gomorrah was just down the road. I have had the idea of doing a piece on three strange places: Sodom, Bomarzo—but I can't think of a third. My daughter suggests Hershey, Pa., where everything is shaped—she says—like Hershey bars. Bomarzo is too long to explain in a letter.⁵

I see from this letter of yours that has just come that you plan to be away three weeks in Nantucket. I don't have much luck in making connections with you, and I have never so much missed talking with anyone I see so little.

As ever, / Edmund

¹An update on his *Scrolls from the Dead Sea* of 1955; it came out in book form as *The Dead Sea Scrolls 1947–1969* in 1969.

²*Galahad*: this early Wilson novel was brought out in a reprint edition with *I Thought of Daisy* by Farrar, Straus and Giroux, 1967.

³Elinor Wylie (1885–1928): a poet of the 1920s, she died young, never realizing her early promise, though Wilson was an enthusiastic supporter and friend.

⁴Ralph Ellison (1914–1994): his masterpiece, *Invisible Man* made him a prominent spokesman for the African American point of view.

⁵Wilson's essay on the Bomarzo monsters is in *The Devil and Canon Barham.*

Sept. 22, 1967 / Wellfleet, Mass.

[A portion of this letter, retained here for clarity, appears in *Letters on Literature and Politics.*]

Dear Clelia:

Yes: the upheaval is still in progress. My study has been enlarged, and my attic made into a decent room. But sorting out and reorganizing my library when the books have been brought down from the second floor (my part of the house is an independent unit) proves to be quite appalling. At the time I visited Russia and wrote a *Finland Station.* I acquired every book, pamphlet and periodical that threw any light on the subject. I had forgotten how much there was that I'll never look at again. And I've decided to give it to the Yale Library, which specializes in this sort of thing. And there's also a huge junk heap, which I'll sell. A good deal of my collection of old records which I haven't been able to get at for years turns out now to be rather impracticable because they are the old-fashioned kind of the days before record changers which you have to turn over after every side. Elena loves architecture and designed the whole reconstruction.

I'm glad that you are going to learn Italian. You must read *The Divine Comedy,* which seems to me—perhaps even more than Shakespeare—the greatest work of imaginative literature ever written. Yeats called Dante "the first imagination of Christendom." You won't get this at Berlitz, but you could probably take a course at Johns Hopkins, or just read it for yourself. It's not really very difficult. I wish I could read it with you. I haven't been all through it since college.

I don't know when we'll get to New York. We are supposed to attend the opening of Lillian Hellman's *Little Foxes* on October 26; but we're going up to Talcottville the 10th and had thought of going on to the Canadian expo. I doubt, however, that we'll make this.

I have arranged with a man at Utica College, who has written a book an the subject, for a celebration on the 19th in honor of the novelist Harold Frederic, the only really first-rate writer who ever came out of that part of the world. (He died in the late nineties.) Have you read *The Damnation of Theron Ware*? Our evening performance will be followed by a colossal party at my local club, which will be paid for by the college as public relations promotion but enable me to pay off social debts without having, as we used to do, an end-of-the-summer party in our house. The occasion has amusing aspects, because it follows a celebration for another illustrious Utican for whom we feel that extravagant claims are being made by a man who has just discovered him and has become fanatical on the subject. A competitive spirit has got into the thing, and we feel that we are running Frederic against this hitherto unknown other man. (Not that he may not have merit: he was a pioneer in the field of semantics, about which I know nothing. In his lifetime he was only known as a successful businessman and banker, who had married John Adams's granddaughter.) My coorganizer tells me with glee that the other celebration drew only about fifty people. We are hoping to do much better. [. . .]

It was a pity that you couldn't come here. Regards to Philip.

Edmund

Nov. 30, 1967 / Wellfleet, Mass.

Dear Clelia:

Thank you very much, but my Virginia cousin, who spends Christmas with us every year, always sends us a Virginia ham, which is delicious but sometimes takes a long time to eat. Two would be too much and might embarrass my cousin.

Our trip to [Utica] New York, followed by a visit to N[ew] Y[ork] City, proved to be something of an ordeal—especially since Elena did all the driving. Our cultural manifestation was successful, and we managed to see a lot of people there and in town, but Elena only lasted a week in New York, and I hardly two. To work at the *New Yorker* in the afternoon and then have a different person to dinner every night and go to some show or both is getting to be too much for me. For Thanksgiving we had planned to have the Epsteins and somebody else here, but, the week before, Helen got sick in New York and Elena went down to look after her, then brought her back here and collapsed herself, so we called our Thanksgiving party off—stayed indoors and saw no one during the horrible weather. Thanksgiving is also such a pointless holiday that I think the best thing, anyway, is to ignore it. [A portion of this letter appears in section IV.]

My new study here is finished, but I am still sorting out papers and books. Tons of the latter are going to be sold or given to the Yale Library. I get some satisfaction out of getting things in order, but it also makes me rather melancholy: so many deteriorated books that bring back phases of my life that are now deteriorated in memory. I am trying to brighten up this big book-lined room—have bought a sort of rich-orange Polish rug—I have only one tie that goes with it, and the only books that do are the J. Dover Wilson orange jacketed Shakespeare.[1] Am going to get a couch and chairs in Boston. The room is certainly more convenient than the old one, but I haven't got used to it yet and have fears that I am now too old to.

This letter must be just as boring as the ones that you say you abandon.

I am back at my playing operas. My phonograph, to my surprise, sounds infinitely better with the new acoustics of the room. This afternoon I am going to play *Lady Macbeth of Mtsensk,* Shostakovich's opera that was angrily suppressed by Stalin. I have just read Leskov's horrible story on which the opera is based, and I wonder whether Stalin wasn't worried by the series of brutal murders that the Russian Macbeths commit.

Norman Podhoretz's autobiography[2] has just come to hand—though I think it won't be out till January. He is amusing about the Looking Glass Library. He says that he caught a children's disease called roseola by reading children's books in the public library. The whole thing is amusing, but unconsciously. He sounds like some very queer kind of megalomaniac—which I shouldn't have suspected of him. Almost every review he has written is made into a major episode, and he recounts what he regards as the struggle for "power" among the editors of *Commentary* as if they had been Lenin, Trotsky and Stalin or a Roman triumvirate. He thinks that being editor of *Commentary* is the pinnacle of success.

Well, best wishes to all of you for the holidays, etc. / Edmund

[1]Wilson's rather peculiar ideas of interior decoration were the despair of Elena, according to Rosalind's *Near the Magician.* She nevertheless managed to prevail sufficiently to create a home in Wellfleet that Dorothea Straus, Louise Bogan, Glyn Morris, and others have described as the essence of old-world charm.
[2]*Making It.*

Dear Clelia:

Yes: I ought to have got some brown furniture to go with my orange rug, but instead, I bought in Boston, a long curving luxurious more or less gold couch, and two similar pale lemon upholstered chairs of a type known as "pivot rockers," on which you can both rock and rotate. I am looking forward to this.

You astonish me about Svetlana [Alliluyeva]. I knew that she and Mrs. Macmillan loathed one another and that the latter, in a TV interview, had behaved rather badly with her, but I hadn't heard that she had stolen the husband. Priscilla Macmillan did a terrible translation—see my article in last week's *New Yorker*.

I'm not doing much about Christmas this year, don't think I've even sent out cards, but I sent you from Cambridge Angus Wilson's latest novel.[1] It is, I think, one of his best—quite a dazzling tour de force—though there is a little too much, at the beginning, of the horrors of the horrible parents, and I can't accept the plausibility of some of the unpleasant incidents such as the aunts' and the grandmother's making them kill the kittens.

A bookseller in Cambridge has just come and removed cartons of books. Elena has just come back from Chatham, where she gave an informative speech about China to what she calls the League of Old Lady Voters. Do you belong to this organization? I am suffering from senile lassitude, really caused by my stalling off returning to the subject of the Dead Sea scrolls, which, since the war, has become more interesting but more difficult for me to deal with. I gather that Yadin, the big Israeli scroll scholar, went over to old Jerusalem and searched the premises of the Jordanian antique dealer who had been acting as a middleman between the Bedouin and the scholars, and found in the basement there a lot of material still unsold. It isn't clear whether he simply confiscated this as Israeli property, now. But he is known to have now in his possession the longest such document as yet discovered, which sounds extremely curious. It purports to be written by, or a message from, God, who with perfect insouciance mentions His own unmentionable name. I didn't know whether to put off my book till this text has been made available.

Well, we send you such good wishes as are possible for what seems to me this rather ghastly holiday season.

Edmund

[1] *No Laughing Matter.*

Dear Clelia:

The holidays flattened us out. We had so many friends and family here that I completely stopped work for the festivities, and there were moments when I was burning so dim that I wasn't sure I really existed or would ever function again. But now we are back again in our old monotonous comfortable routine.—I working on the Dead Sea scrolls and Elena doing taxes and instructing the Lady Voters on the situation in China. This otherwise blank season I find very satisfactory if I have something demanding to fill it with.—

The Epsteins spent New Year's with us, with their children and beloved family dog. The children were well behaved, the little girl very pretty and already a little coquette; but the dog is capable of snapping when his inclinations are crossed, and the dog situation had to be watched, creating constant confusion. Jason is very much involved with his educational project and Barbara with the *Review*—I don't know whether you see it nowadays. They have been going through a crisis lately on account of an article of Elizabeth Hardwick's,[1] which was extremely disagreeable about the recent production of Lillian Hellman's *Little Foxes*. I expect there is some Southern thing behind the bad relations between Elizabeth and Lillian. Also, Norman Podhoretz's book has presented them with a problem.[2]

I didn't know in advance about the shifts at the *New Yorker*. I am glad that Brendan rather than [John] MacCarten will be doing Broadway now. Penelope Gilliatt,[3] who will be doing the movies, is a terribly nice English girl, very goodlooking, with bright red hair that she says not even the beauty parlors can believe is real. She was married to John Osborne, the English dramatist, whom she has just divorced, and is at present the girlfriend of Mike Nichols. I have been reading her in the *Observer* for years, but never knew her till lately. She has been up to see us here, and I like her because she laughs at everything I say that is meant to be funny, besides being amusing herself. [A portion of this letter appears in section IV.]

My present plans are to try to get the scrolls off my hands by the 1st of April, then for us to go South. That is a bleak and raw season up here. There is sometimes no real spring, no modulation into summer. We used to make tours through your part of the world, taking in the people we knew in Wilmington, Baltimore, Washington, and Virginia; but I don't believe we're up to it any more. We'll certainly go to Charlottesville however, and, if we succeed in getting off, shall try to make some sort of connection with you.

How are you getting on with your Italian?

Don't have writing me on your mind. You don't have as much leisure as I do.

Love, / Edmund

[1]Elizabeth Hardwick (b. 1916): critic and novelist, former wife of Robert Lowell, a frequent contributor to the *New York Review of Books.*

[2]It posed a problem of what Wilson refers to as "tact"—Podhoretz wrote unpleasant things about *Review* contributors.

[3]Penelope Gilliatt (1932–1993): British short story writer, film reviewer for the *New Yorker;* wrote the screenplay of John Schlesinger's *Sunday, Bloody Sunday.*

May 1, 1968 / Wellfleet, Mass.

[A portion of this letter, retained for clarity, appears in *Letters on Literature and Politics.*]

Dear Clelia:

We were going to stop over to see you on our way from Charlottesville to Baltimore, but not having heard from you, I imagined you were away. I'm sorry you were put to so much trouble to try to locate me. We were disappointed to miss you. We didn't run into any riots, though they seemed to have been expecting trouble in Charlottesville, and the atmosphere of the hotel seemed rather tense. One change I particularly noticed was that the colored waiter and porters, who used to say, "Yassah" now say, "Yes sir." Those Virginians rather bore me nowadays that I'm not able to drink to keep up with them. One lady, whom I saw in the morning, said, "What do you like to drink after breakfast?" I said I didn't drink during the day. "Whisky sours are very nice on a hot day like this." They run on in their pleasant way about genealogy and local events and never seem to have any real curiosity about what is going on in the North or anywhere else. It seems to be inevitable at some point that you talk about dogs and cats. After that, my evening with old [W. F.] Albright was absolutely exhilarating. He is now 77—told me that I was a mere child. I don't think I have ever seen a scholar who reveled so continuously in his work. He is the great demiurge in this country, of Semitic archaeology, palaeography and scrolls interpretation as well as an Assyriologist and, I think, Egyptologist. His ex-students are everywhere in more or less key positions. He laughed and giggled like a demon as he talked about the aberrations of other scholars and gave me delighted gossiping digressions: one rather out-of-bounds Biblical scholar had "tried to date" the attractive wife of another extremely square one, and a veteran Bible man at Oxford, whom everybody in the field makes fun of, had succeeded in getting himself knighted by campaigning for Harold Macmillan. Albright has both glaucoma and cataract, and this makes it difficult for him to travel, but he says that he has "nothing to complain about because it gives him more time at his desk."

I'm going up to Talcottville next Thursday—you know my address, don't you?; Boonville, RED 1, Oneida Co., N.Y. Elena is flying to Chicago to see my son's baby. I'll probably go out there, too, after the hearing about the road in front of my house, which they are threatening to widen, cutting off part of my already shallow front lawn. I have been awarded $30,000 (tax free) by a foundation in Aspen, Colorado, established as a tribute to the "humanities" by one of their oil millionaires. They have a show that goes on a week, and I had intended to be there for the day they hand me the cheque, but have discovered that Aspen is 8,000 feet high, and that people sometimes have to be taken down in ambulances; so, on account of my "heart condition," I can't possibly go. I hope they don't give the money to somebody else who can put on a performance there—which is what they want.

Will you be at the Vineyard this summer at all? I'll be back at the end of June. We always seem to miss each other.

Love, / Edmund

May 27, 1968 / Talcottville

Dear Clelia:

They told me at the hearing that they did not like to touch the old houses and I expect that I'll save my stone steps, but they're planning a four-lane highway (two of them soft parking shoulders), which is entirely unnecessary, since there's already an almost finished highway running parallel to this only a few miles away. They say up here that this needless road building is a racket for the cement-making industry. The people on the other side of this country road will have to move their houses or have them demolished. A gentle plumber, whom I have known a long time, who got me a new furnace at a wholesale price and who refuses to send me bills, will have to lose his house because there is a slope just back of it to which he cannot move it and he wants to buy a piece of my property to build on. I think I will let him have it: remnant of old New York feudalism.

I was glad to get back here from Chicago, where I went to see my son and his family. I used to enjoy Chicago for a certain coarse grandeur and the dynamic efforts of the people to make it something important; but it is now very ugly and dirty and straddled by sinister-looking high buildings, and the people seem as sordid and stunted as any other city-dwellers. The Negroes have been erupting, and the Negro quarter on the South Side is full of broken windows and boarded-up stores. The air is polluted and the lake is polluted. It is quite claustrophobic. When you read the Chicago papers, you feel you are in the midst of a horrible civilization, and beyond it a horrible world. The only refreshing thing in Chicago is the tank of trained porpoises which perform incredible feats and seem as close to human beings as dogs.

The Aspen people have compromised on a dinner in New York on June 12. Elena will join me there, and we'll be there the whole of the week from Monday—in case you should be coming on.

It has been so pleasant here this spring that I haven't gotten much accomplished. I fritter away my time reading papers and magazines, making a daily trip to Boonville, writing letters and writing up my diary and playing solitaire and listening to the phonograph. Though I am alone, I have dined out or had someone to dinner almost every night, and the weather for this time of year here has been unusually delightful. All the rare Showy Orchids—do you know this marvelous wildflower—which I planted last autumn are coming up.

Apropos of Southern Womanhood, have you read Nancy Hale's novel about Charlottesville—*Dear Beast*? It is extremely funny—a New England woman adapting herself to the South. The "dear beast" to whom Nancy is married is an eminent bibliographer and a queer kind of academic monster. I am going to have to fight him in the *New York Review* on account of his noxious influence on the projects and productions of the MLA (Modern Language Association)—which makes it awkward because I like Nancy and have just seen them both in Charlottesville.

As ever, / Edmund

July 1, 1968 / Talcottville

Dear Clelia:

These transcriptions from my diary might amuse you. Please don't let them get back to anybody through whom they might be likely to get back to the people I tell about. Both these occasions seem to me odd, but I suppose because we don't get around much. You see me here at my most ungracious and cantankerous.

Yes, I always pass on to Elena information I have just read, and she does the same for me.

I am still here in Talcottville—on account of the proposed new road and other things, I am more involved here than I usually am. [A portion of this letter appears in section IV.] Elena is coming up presently. She'll probably be here till the middle of July—then back to Wellfleet. You won't be coming to Martha's Vineyard in August?

I am writing an attack on the publications of the Modern Language Association for the *N.Y. Review*.[1] It makes my blood boil and is rather a comfort because I don't feel it is any good to have my blood boil over any of the other things that disgust me.

Love as ever, / Edmund

[Enclosure from journal deleted]

[1] *The Fruits of the MLA* (1968.)

Sept. 26, 1968 / Wellfleet

Dear Clelia:

We have been burning rather low lately. Elena has been having the collapse that usually comes for her at the end of the summer, and I have turned up with shingles—which, it seems, comes from the Latin word for <u>girdle</u> and has nothing to do with the things that you put on a house—a horrid ailment which not only makes you uncomfortable but also makes you feel exhausted. I slept for two days and felt as if my mind had been erased like a blackboard and my personality had half melted away. We are better now, however, and I am going up to Talcottville tomorrow to perform at our annual regional cultural demonstration of Utica College—this year we are giving them the Iroquois Indians. I'll be there till after the middle of October.

Everybody is depressed by the current happenings. What is your opinion of Agnew? Very sorry about the disaster of your fire.

Have I ever written you about Bomarzo? I made a point of going there when I stopped off in Rome on my way to the Middle East—not far from Rome, beyond Viterbo. One of the Orsini dukes in the sixteenth century arranged on the steep side of a hill below his castle an extraordinary park of limestone monsters. There is nothing else like it in Italy, and the Italians, who like things to be pleasing, do not much care about it. The legend is that the duke was a hunchback and that his wife had an affair with his goodlooking younger brother—as a result of which he had the young man murdered and vented his bitterness in this park, where the unpleasant figures and animals, and the strange inscriptions on them, seem to represent some kind of poem which the duke was trying to write in this way. When I got back home, I discovered that an opera on this subject, written by the South American composer [Alberto] Ginastera, was just being done. It is still this winter in the repertory of the City Center Opera. I haven't seen it yet but have it on the phonograph. I recommend it to you. He has been called "the twelve-tone Verdi,"—is said to be most effective on the stage. All the possibilities of the twelve-tone system for the hateful, the macabre and the horrible—which turn out to be considerable—have been exploited in it: ballets of monsters, mummies, etc. (There is a mummy in the castle.) The musical technique is used to express the hunchback's distorted view, and the love scenes are frustrated and most unattractive. I'd like to go to Bomarzo again and eventually write something about it; but the hillside is hard, at my age, to climb, with its dirt paths and worn-down steps. It was a jungle till recently but is now partly cleaned out and you pay to go in.

The accounts of evenings I sent you were extracts from a notebook diary that I have been keeping ever since college. There are volumes of it but most of it can never be published till well after my death.

Love, / Edmund

March 31, 1969 / Wellfleet

Dear Clelia:

I hadn't known you sent me a Valentine. The only one I got from anybody but the family was a pretty little doily-type thing on a round piece of purple paper, with an accordion-type heart in the center. Was this it? I didn't send out any Valentines because there were none in Jamaica where we were, and when we found some in Kingston it was too late.

We lived in a vacuum in Jamaica in a little cottage on the water, and this was beneficial to us both. Our excursions to Kingston—a horrible place—and a visit to Canadian friends gave us some idea of what was going on. It is a miserable little country, rather at a loss since the British left and hoping to be taken over as a province of Canada. It is full of Canadians competing with us but I don't think we want them as another state, and I hope the Canadians do annex them. They have been fighting off American gangster gambling, which I guess is really the issue in Anguilla.

We came back to a number of depressing things—including a set of horrible murders here that almost beat the English "Moors murders." A friend who has spent years in Provincetown and Truro, where there is not usually much excitement, seems to have became obsessed by these murders. He said of the murderer, "He's twenty-five, you know. He's right up there on the top!" It was evidently a story of local boy makes good.

I am reading Svetlana's second book, which I am convinced is going to be of considerable historical importance. The first book, written mostly before she left Russia, is very guarded and concentrates on her mother's family. This one is something quite different. She tells the whole story—and it is as if she had suddenly said, in a kind of explosion part way through, "If you really want to know what it was like to be Stalin's daughter, this is it." The book is so painful and moving that it gave me a headache the other night. You must be sure to read it when it is translated. It will have terrible repercussions in the Soviet Union. She has been in the unique situation of having had more or less the status of a princess and at the same time having got to disapprove of and be humiliated by everything her father was doing. At his funeral, she even refused to do like everybody else and kiss his corpse on the forehead. She treats all the present incumbents in Russia very much de haut en bas, as if they were inferiors who had had no right to tell her what she could and couldn't do. It is going to make them furious. She spent two evenings with us here—our neighbor Paul Chavchavadze is translating her book. Everybody is enchanted by her—including Elena, who was prejudiced against her. The photographs and TV showings have given quite a wrong impression of her, that made her seem a big strapping woman when she is actually small (as Stalin was), very pretty and with a mesmerizing charm (I wonder whether Stalin had something of this). She combines being shy and well bred with a very firm will and confidence in her own opinions. The story in her book of her escape from the Soviet officials is absorbing and as she tells it, creates suspense. She strikes me, rather unexpectedly, as one of the most extraordinary people I have ever known.

About Brendan: I always see him when I go to New York, and I don't know what to make of him. He is always amusing and cheerful—perhaps unnaturally so, since you say he is despairing. I never understand intelligent people who don't have any ambition to do anything. I always assume that they are at work on something that they don't tell people about.

I hope that Philip has recovered. Did he go to the Caribbean? It is really a good part of the world in which to get away from everything that has been worrying you at home and to recuperate from illness; but I really don't much like the tropics. It gets to be hard to write or even think. I begin by giving up my work to write letters; then give up letters for postcards; then give up post-cards for swimming and bananas and cold drinks of gin and lime juice. In between, you go to sleep. The pretty rigorously segregated luxury hotels, with their vacationers, are awful in Jamaica: Canadians, Americans, and English, all exactly alike, having a boring holiday, and outside of them, the black na-tives living in poverty and filth, who resent the white vacationers, on whom their economy partly depends, and rob them when they can.

Love, / Edmund

I expect to be in New York again around the second week in July. Do let me know if you should be there then. I'm afraid that our correspondence is be-coming more and more disembodied.

June 6, 1969 / The Princeton Club / New York

Dear Clelia:

Jason [Epstein] <u>was</u> rather miffed because I hadn't asked him. He said that you were offended with him, and it was obvious that he regretted it. Of course, I told him that you were deteriorating. It was wonderful to see you, and Ted Gorey quite brought back the past. I wish it were possible more often. Jason has grown quite fat again. He gets more and more anti-Semitic, in re-sponse to my interest in Jewish history—seems only to have just discovered Deuteronomy and is indifferent at Jehovah's ferocious Threats to the Jews unless they heed his admonitions. He accuses God of being a fascist. Barbara has a new way of doing her hair which makes her hardly recognizable. Don't forget to write me from time to time. Your life is no more humdrum than mine, and your letters are vibrant and interesting.

Love, / Edmund

Sept 11, 1969 / Wellfleet, Mass.

Dear Clelia: I am going to New York for a week on Wednesday the 17th. Do let me know if you will be there: *New Yorker*, Princeton Club.

Haven't heard from you all summer, which has been rather rocky for me. I evidently brought back from Jamaica some malarial form of tropical disease and came back to Boston to try to find out what it was. I spent five days in the hospital being x-rayed and having all sorts of tests made and came out in much worse condition than I went in. They do not know much about tropical diseases in New England and upper New York. They tell me I ought to have gone to an army hospital. But my attacks since are very much milder, and I am now in much better shape.

Svetlana has been in Wellfleet again. Be sure to read her book, which will be out at the end of this month.[1] I thought it was such a bombshell for the Soviet Union, that they might decide to ignore it, but she says they are not bright enough for that, that they will probably say, as they did about the other book, that it was written by the CIA and circulate scandal about her personal life. I am very curious to see what happens.

Love, / Edmund

[1] *Only One Year,* translated by Paul Chavchavadze.

Dec 12, 1969 / Talcottville

Dear Clelia: Your card arrived this morning just at the moment when I was about to sit down and write you.—yes: I am alright except for the ravages of age. I tend to go to sleep when I sit down to read, and I find that I alternate now between thinking I've had enough of life and feeling, at other times, that I wouldn't mind a little more of it. Growing old, your mind and spirit seem to go on the same, but you discover when you try to do things, that you are irremediably debilitated.

Here is an errata list for the scrolls. They're mostly not serious, but they annoy me, because the book is just coming out in England, and they may give those British scholars I've been attacking a chance to retaliate.

We've been leading our usual monotonous life. We livened up Thanksgiving this year by inviting Penelope Gilliatt and John Hearn, the brilliant Jamaican novelist with his wife and little girl. It was very jolly, but afterward, we both collapsed with guest-fatigue. We don't know whether or not we'll get away anywhere this winter. What are you going to do? I see you have a different address. Are you not living at the manor?

Love as ever, / Edmund

Dec 24, 1969 / Wellfleet, Mass.

Dear Clelia: We are in the last convulsions of Christmas preparation. Elena, being Russian and German, puts on such celebrations as I haven't had since my childhood. She insists on filling a stocking for everybody in the house, which results in a clutter of candy, engagement calendars, Farmers' Almanacs, paperweights, ballpoint pens, and puzzles. The schedule now is:

8 to 9: breakfast and unpacking of stockings

11 to 12: champagne and distribution of presents from tree

5 to?: Christmas dinner, to which our old boring friends are invited

We have shifted the dinner from midday in order to avoid what used to be the inevitable letdown of depression and ill-humor that used to set in in the late afternoon. The main problem of Christmas, I think, is to avoid this reaction. Friends of ours here one winter solved the problem by giving a party in the evening which kept up people's sinking morale.

Thank you for the cheese—which hasn't yet arrived. I am going to send you a copy of a first novel that I have just been reading and that I think is quite remarkable. His name is so Finnish and hard to remember that I always call him "Woodwind."[1]

I don't know when I'll ever get to New York again. We are hard-up, too, and I don't know what we can do after New Year's. It is hard to take up here after that. There are hardly more than half a dozen people that we know, and they are all aging and crippled or dotty. We wait and wait for the spring, and sometimes it even comes.—Merry Christmas and all that to you both.

Love, / Edmund

[1]Larry Woiwode: Midwestern novelist whose first novel *What I'm Going to Do I Think*, was a considerable critical success. Wilson seems to be mistaken about his Finnish background: Woiwode himself believes the name is Romanian, though his people were German-speaking. See *What I Think I Did*, p. 6.

Dec. 26

Christmas has passed off more or less painlessly, but I am very glad it is over. Usual accumulation of trinkets. People think they have to give me little frogs and owls. I have enough things of this kind to set up a small gift shop.—Is Sarasota expensive? How is it possible to live there? Drop me a line after your visit.

I've finished the Woodwind book since I wrote the above. The end is rather disappointing, but I'm having it sent to you. Should be interested to know what you think of it. What is the matter with the hero? I couldn't make out.

Feb. 26, 1970 / Wellfleet, Mass.

Dear Clelia:

The mail seems to be fantastic. I mailed that Valentine to reach you Valentine's Day. You say you did not get it till the 24th.

We are going to New York for a week March 5—Princeton Club—wish there were a chance of seeing you.

Yes: the Woodwind is disappointing. Have you read *The French Lieutenant's Woman*, which people can't drop? Elena—what is rare with her—completely surrendered herself to it and did nothing else but read it for two days. I read it, too, and it lures you along, but you feel at the end that it is something of a swindle.

Our life up here has been a blank, except that I have gotten some work done—mainly based on my old diaries, which present many problems of tact.

Do come to New York and celebrate the liquidation of February.

Love, / Edmund

August 12, 1970 / Wellfleet, Mass.

Dear Clelia: Your letter arrived when I was ill and my mind a blank, and, in spite of its bad news, it revived me.

Yes: it is hard to write about one's family when some of them are still alive. I was fatigued by my exercise of tact, and since I have been back from New York state, have been taking a vacation by returning to a collection of Russian studies with the excuse that I have a Russian friend of Helen's who has brought a Russian typewriter and who has been acting as my secretary. I have been concentrating on the strange story of an old regime Russian dramatist who is supposed to have murdered his French mistress, one of those Russian mysteries that never gets cleared up; they are still arguing about it.—It diverts my mind from the news—and from the horrible hot weather, which seems to me worse and more unremitting than anything I remember in New Jersey at its worst. Last night there was a queer thunderstorm which sounded like a movie battle with shells exploding. You must be having some of this down there. I'm going back to Talcottville on the 16th and continue my researches into old houses. I wish the Historical Association would buy mine—and the remnants of the strange nineteenth-century halls that still survive up there.

My son and his wife are in Europe and have left their little boy with us. This relieves the congestion—Helen is in Maine at art school—but life, in this weather, is still rather sticky and messy. The Russian girl and Elena and Mabel Hutchins from Talcottville look after the little boy, while I sit in the back part of the house sweating and thinking about the life, luxurious and outrageous, of the Russian aristocracy before the Revolution.

Tania Letkovsky [the Russian girl] is very handsome, and the situation is further complicated by the young men who are always coming. When I emerge from my library and study, I play solitaire and it never comes out. I feel that this is one of the periods in life that just has to be crawled through and endured.

A pity that I see you so seldom. I suppose I may go to New York in the fall, but we so rarely make connections. Do write me from time to time. Address from August 16 till sometime in the middle of September: Boonville RFD I Oneida Co., New York.

Love, / Edmund

Sept. 2, 1970 / Talcottville

Dear Clelia: [Portions of this letter appear in *Letters on Literature and Politics.*] My researches have led me to explain the spiritualist community at Lily Dale, New York, which is a very queer place in every sense of the word: 80% of the mediums are women, and the rest homosexuals. The village is shut off from the rest of the world, and you feel that you are surrounded by a conspiracy of a different kind of creature. Did you ever read Algernon Blackwood's stories of the supernatural?

Have also been visiting old mansions, which, like mine, have become white elephants for the owners. They are all being sold as museums or institutions for feebleminded old ladies or something of the kind.

I'm going back to Wellfleet when I get near the end of my book. Chautauqua County where Lily Dale is, is very flat and unattractive. Even the thunderstorms are flat. The people seem on such a low level that you wonder that they are able to get to the point of mating and producing more of the same kind. Here we at least have mountains, and the inroads of the wild animals, which as the farms are being abandoned, seem now to be moving in on the countryside. [. . .]

Love, / Edmund

Dec 14, 1970 / Wellfleet, Mass.

Dear Clelia:

I saw the Epsteins in New York and they have just spent a weekend up here with their very good-looking daughter. I don't think they can be further from separating. He dedicated his book to Barbara, and they seem to be on the best of terms. Jason complains despairingly of what is going on in the US but he has always done a good deal of that. It may be that somebody has got their situation confused with that of the Lowells. Cal[1] went off with a Lady Somebody,[2] who was taking him to a villa in Italy, but he broke down mentally and ended in an English sanitarium. Elizabeth [Hardwick], as usual, was threatening to leave him, but I hear that he is coming back for Christmas.

We have just come back from an excursion to Boston, which is almost as bad now as New York, to do our Christmas shopping, and have at least got that behind us.

"Merry Christmas!" said old Scrooge. / Edmund

[1]"Cal": aka Robert Lowell, the nickname was short for Caligula in his days at St. Marks.

[2]Lady Caroline Blackwood, a Guinness Stout heiress and novelist, and every bit as unbalanced as Lowell..

Jan. 10, 1971 / Wellfleet, Mass.
Dear Clelia: Thanks for the [Johnny] Allegro [book], which I am glad to add to my collection. It is all nonsense, though. He is now a little crazy, I think. Don't be deceived by his display of learned languages.

I had a slight stroke the day before Christmas, which affected my right hand, as you can see from my writing. But it seems to be passing off.

Love, / Edmund

VI. Literary Business

Wilson's dealings with publishers and editors were legendary. In his half century of appearing in print, he never permitted himself to be bluffed, deluded, or brushed off. Authoritative and blunt with publishing house heads and top editors, he managed to get decent terms for his serious books and good treatment despite the trends that went against him and the demand for mass-market books. He went from publisher to publisher in the first half of his career, trying Scribner's, Doubleday, and Houghton Mifflin, among others; in Britain he continued to change houses, sometimes adding irascibility into the bargain. Each house got a piece of his mind about money matters, declining standards, and ineptitude. Nor did magazine publishers fare much better: Wilson managed to make a letter welcoming a new little magazine sound a cautionary note, and his letters to William Shawn at the *New Yorker*, though straightforward enough, are hardly deferential. By the 1950s he developed a congenial relationship with Roger Straus that lasted until the end. Straus is a hard-driving, no-nonsense businessman who is sophisticated enough to have been amused at Wilson's lapses into bullying and badgering. Reading Wilson's side of the exchange one has the impression that in Straus the crusty negotiator has met his match. Wilson's only "big money" books were *Memoirs of Hecate County* and *The Scrolls from the Dead Sea*, neither done for Straus. Wilson lived to prepare *The Devils and Canon Barham*, his last collection of miscellaneous essays, for Farrar, Straus, and Giroux. His massive journals also appeared under the firm's imprint.

The career as a writer of books went on simultaneously—even into the 1960s—with the work of a journalist. The Wilson formula for creation, explained in *Classics and Commercials*, was to start by reviewing, later build a larger essay from the review, and finally build a whole book—either a collection or a unified study—from the substantial essays and articles. He began the article writing with the old *Vanity Fair* in the early 1920s, wrote for the *Dial* and several other magazines of the period, and soon became an editor at the *New Republic*. This last magazine was home to Wilson the essayist through the 1920s and '30s, his great decades of reporting on contemporary American literature, political and social trends, and European ideas. After a break with the *New Republic* in 1940, caused by a conflict between Wilson's isolationist ideals and the magazine's pro-British interventionist policy, Wilson found his next journalistic berth with the *New Yorker*, first as book critic and then as steady contributor. The letters to William Shawn show Wilson's characteristic distrust of literary power blocks, rigidities, house rules, and entrenched interests. Forever seeking a culture of trust between editor and writer, he expressed disdain for both the illogic of bureaucracies and the arbitrariness of top editors.

We conclude this section with the cheerful evidence of a late-blooming literary collaboration Wilson formed in the 1960s with writer-illustrator Edward Gorey. Wilson came across Gorey during his stint as a consultant to the Looking Glass Library and gave him his first significant critical attention in the *New Yorker* in 1959. Though Gorey's books have had a steady and devoted following, most readers will know him best as the source of the animated illustrations for the public television series *Mystery*. The Edwardian lady swooning gracefully over a rooftop balustrade and the large stone urn sprouting a bouquet of red roses are a decent enough introduction, but only exposure to the grotesqueries of his other works—*The Fatal Lozenge, The Unstrung Harp, The Curious Sofa, The Doubtful Guest,* and so on—can account for why Wilson, aficionado of the grotesque, connected so warmly with Gorey.

TO JOHN HALL WHEELOCK OF CHARLES SCRIBNER'S SONS

New Yorker letterhead / December 1, 1947

Dear Jack:

I have absolutely no patience with these pleas that publishers are now making to authors to accept a reduction of royalties. Obviously, a few more volumes sold at the lower price would come to the same thing as a few less sold at the higher—so that the whole thing is simply an attempt on the publisher's part to jack his profits up when times are hard at the expense of the writer's profits. I do not understand how you people have the face to make these requests to be let out of the terms of your contracts when it ought to be plain to you that, if the publisher suffers from the high cost of production, the writer suffers even more seriously from the high cost of living and can usually less afford to take a loss.

I have refused to allow Doubleday to do what you are asking to do, and I do not see why I should let Scribner's do it. My answer is that I will not accept the reduction and that I expect Scribner's to bring out the book at a reasonable price—$3.75 seems about right. Otherwise, I will withdraw my introduction. Now don't tell me that by taking this stand, I am compelling you to put a higher price on the book and so limiting the circulation of John

[Bishop]'s work[1]. The responsibility is all on your side—since you want to get out of your contract and are trying to bring pressure by the threat that you will yourself limit this circulation by charging a higher price.

All the proof has not reached me yet, and as I am going to New Mexico next week to do an article for the *New Yorker* on the Zuni Indians and not coming back till just before Christmas, and as I must turn out two articles before I go, I don't see how I can get the proofs back to you till after Christmas. By the way, Allen Tate said that he would have galleys of the poetry volume sent to Margaret Bishop and me.[2] We ought to see them to check dates and things. Send us page proofs if they have gotten that far.

Please don't send me, about the other matter, a careful statement with figures provided by your production department. I have heard all the publishers' phonograph records ad nauseam.

Otherwise, friendly regards. This letter is directed not at you personally but at Mr. Charles Scribner's Sons.

Did you see the *New Statesman*'s review of the Isabel Bolton book?[3]

Sincerely, / Edmund Wilson

[1]Wilson edited *The Collected Essays of John Peale Bishop* for Scribner's. See Letters to Allen Tate in section II.

[2]Tate edited *The Collected Poems of John Peale Bishop* for Scribner's. Margaret Bishop was the poet's widow. See section II for further references to her.

[3]Isabel Bolton (1883–1973): author of *Do I Wake or Sleep?* And, along with Dawn Powell and Anaïs Nin, another of the women writers Wilson tried to boost.

TO CHARLES SCRIBNER OF
CHARLES SCRIBNER'S SONS

Wellfleet letterhead / September 13, 1954

Dear Mr. Scribner:

My letter a propos of royalty payments was not intended to be especially invidious to Scribner's. It was merely a protest on principle. I know that the payment of royalties four months after the accounting has been made and the statement gone out to the author has been standard publishing procedure; but I regard it as unfair to the author, since there is no reason he shouldn't be paid on the nail, and the publisher has, in the meantime, the advantage of disposing of the money earned by the author's books, and should really be paying him interest for the use of it. I have insisted, in my recent contracts, on getting my check at the same time as my statement, and I hope never to sign another which makes me wait for this payment till ten months after the book has come out.

By the way—quite apart from this—I do not feel that Scribner's, on your side, have been particularly obliging lately. You refused the request I made to include some of the chapters from *Axel's Castle* in a selection from my essays that Anchor Books was getting out, though Oxford allowed me to include four essays from the books of mine they publish, and I have assumed that it was hopeless to apply to you to let them get out a paperback edition of the whole book, which they would very much like to do and which, I should think, would be profitable for both Scribner's and me. It is true that I had refused before to allow you to reprint the book in a text book series; but you did not offer me a penny for this privilege, and I calculated that I should not stand to gain, but perhaps lose, with a clothbound cheap edition on the market. My book *To the Finland Station,* on the other hand, has been doing a good deal better in the paperbound Anchor Series, which is widely sold on the newsstands, than it ever did in the cloth edition.

Yours sincerely, / Edmund Wilson

TO KEN MCCORMICK OF DOUBLEDAY CO.

Wellfleet, Mass. / December 1, 1947

Dear McCormick:

Do you think that your accounting department could send me at the *New Yorker* whatever is due from my Europe book?

I still look in vain for ads. You have not, as far as I know, run a line about the book in any of the magazines whose readers would be likely to buy it: the *New Yorker,* the *Atlantic* and the *Nation.* Why on earth was it not included in your ad in the last *Atlantic,* which listed—I was glad to see—the Helen Muchnic book? It is silly to wait for quotes. I have a certain public that reads me and they ought to be told that I have published a book. If you will not announce the books of mine you publish and if you insist on publishing them at impossible prices that most of the people who read me cannot afford, it is ridiculous for you to publish them at all, from your point of view as well as mine, and it would be better for me to try and get, for the two books I still owe you, a publisher who has had some experience in handling books of this type. I'd like to talk to you about it next week when I come to town.

Sincerely, / Edmund Wilson

Wellfleet, Mass. / December 9, 1947

Dear McCormick:

Thank you for your letter. I was interested to see these pathetic specimens of Doubleday's feeble pretense to have advertised my book, and was fascinated by the select list of people to whom the book had been sent, a considerable number of whom are not reviewers at all but personal friends, to whom I sent it at my own expense. Your office tells me that you have not yet sold 3500 copies, though I thought you mentioned a larger number when I talked to you over the phone. This must set a new low. Oxford Press in two or three weeks time have already sold about half that number of a reprinted old book of mine.

Sincerely, / Edmund Wilson

TO FREDRIC WARBURG OF SECKER AND WARBURG CO.

July 22, 1954

Dear Mr. Warburg:

I had from you two years ago a characteristically curt note announcing that you were "dropping," I think the word was, due to its scanty sales, my book of verse, *Note-Books of Night*. Since then, Geoffrey Moore has included one of these poems in his *Anthology of American Poetry* and seems to have paid you a fee for it. Even assuming that you still regard yourself as the publisher of this book—I got the contrary impression from your letter—you owe me, according to our contract, 50% of this fee. I wrote somebody in your office (I haven't his name here) weeks ago, but have never had an answer. Will you please clear this situation up?

Sincerely yours, / Edmund Wilson

TO WILLIAM VAN O'CONNOR AT
AMERICAN QUARTERLY

New Yorker letterhead / December 15, 1948

Dear Mr. O'Connor:

Thank you for your letter. I have not yet got to the point of writing the book of which you have heard inaccurate rumors.

Good luck with your magazine.[1] I hope it will be less dreary than most of the other things of the kind. I think that a good principle in starting such a magazine would be that nobody was allowed to mention, during at least the first year, Melville, Henry James, Kafka, Kierkegaard or T. S. Eliot.

Yours sincerely, / Edmund Wilson

[1]Van O'Connor was founding out of the University of Minnesota a new journal of American Studies called *American Quarterly*.

TO WILLIAM SHAWN AT THE *NEW YORKER*

January 4, 1954 / Wellfleet, Mass.

Dear Shawn:

I don't know whether you will still feel that parts of this are too technical.[1] I have got to the point where I should have to have suggestions from somebody else, if anything is not clear. The part at the end about the Metropolitan is still unsatisfactory, because it has not been checked. Albright tells me that it is not true that somebody crept into the Chicago Museum and photographed his scrolls by infra-red rays. It seems he imagines things. I have to check everything he tells me by other people's evidence.

Thanks for the Christmas card— and Happy New Year.

EW

[1]Wilson is referring to his piece on the Dead Sea scrolls.

[Superscript] I am going back to Wellfleet after Labor Day.

August 30, 1954 / Talcottville

Dear Shawn:

This, in a still far from finished draft, is the first half of the Dead Sea Scrolls. I am sending it to you in this state mainly to report work in progress.

I haven't revised it obviously, because I want first to get it checked in this form by various people. I hope to deliver the whole thing in September.

E.W.

Nov. 1, 1962 / 12 Hilliard St. / Cambridge

Dear Shawn:

My tax case[1] was finally taken up to the top local man in Buffalo (who it seems, had read my Indian book), and who has offered to accept a settlement which is possible for me and better than anything I expected. I pay a certain sum down, and that clears me, so the liens and levies will be lifted.

Best regards, / Edmund W.

[1]Refers to Wilson's income tax problems and confusions about tax law. *The Cold War and the Income Tax* is his defense of himself, the non-filer.

Wellfleet, Mass. / December 5, 1971

Dear Shawn:

I have been trying for months to get from Mr. Mason's office an itemized report on my account. I don't doubt that it is all right but I didn't understand it. I have written and called them up any number of times, but I don't get any explanation. I assume that Mason's illness and absence may have made things difficult for them.

Yours sincerely, / Edmund Wilson

[Memo from Wilson to Shawn]

Unsolicited Comment from the Book Department
Protest against ostentatious lowbrowism.

Some weeks ago there was a "newsbreak" joke on a passage from a Russian grammar. This seems to me rather pointless. If you are going to go into technical works like grammars, you will certainly have no difficulty in finding statements that are unintelligible and may appear outlandish to people not studying the subject. In this case, the example chosen is arbitrary and perfectly non-comic. There are plenty of hair-raising anomalies in Russian; but that the first person singular of the present tense of iskat' should be ishchv would not appear at all abnormal to somebody who had been studying Russian, and to make fun of this fact would seem to a Russian no more amusing than it would to an Englishman to find a Russian magazine making a joke about the fact that the past tense of <u>ride</u> was not <u>rided</u> but <u>rode</u>. (By this standard, "I went" as the past of "I go" would be absolutely sidesplitting.) A further element of comedy had been provided in the *New Yorker*'s passage by the transposition of one of the Russian works into the international phonetic alphabet; but this alphabet has nothing to do with the peculiar features of Russian—it is now being used in American textbooks, and it certainly does not convert them into treasure-houses of laughs for the *New Yorker*.

It seems to me that the same principle applies to the foreword written by E. E. Cummings for an exhibition of his paintings last winter—which was also ribbed in the *New Yorker*. In the first place, again, I should think that if you were going to be funny about Cummings' queer way of expressing himself, you would pick some more sensational example: it is quite clear in this foreword what he is trying to say. But the truth is that Cummings is an eccentric writer who has become familiar and accepted to the point of being a classic. It might have been appropriate in the early twenties to reprint for comic effect one of his unconventional poems; but today it is as pointless to poke fun at him as it would be to quote a passage from Joyce. Everybody knows about Cummings and Joyce and either does or does not like them. (Louise Bogan wrote a favorable review in the *New Yorker* of Cummings' last book of poems, which were a thousand times more eccentric than this foreword, at just about the same time that this giggle over his foreword came out). But they are no more a fair field for newsbreaks than a foreign language grammar.

E.W.

TO ROGER STRAUS AT FARRAR, STRAUS

Mansgrove / The Little House / Princeton, N J / December 6, 1952
Dear Roger:

Here are several matters:

1.) The man at Doubleday, [Jason] Epstein, who is interested in bringing out a paperback *Finland Station,* thinks it would be a good idea to include at the end the little essay called "Marxism at the End of the Forties" which is in *The Shores of Light.* This was actually written as a summary just after I had finished the *Finland Station,* and I had intended to put it into a later edition, but as no new edition seemed to be coming, I decided to put it into *Shores.* I don't think it would do any harm to reprint it—with acknowledgements and a different title—in the *Finland Station* reprint, and, if you have no objections, I'll tell Epstein that it is all right.

2.) I am enclosing some further corrections for the new printing of *Shores.*

3.) I want to be sure to see a proof of the new foreword to *Daisy.* Are you able to reprint directly from the Allen English edition or will you have to change the English spelling? The point is that I want the revisions that I made for this and have no record of what they were.

4.) I am concerned about getting *Cyprian's Prayer* printed and have a new suggestion about it. Did you ever see my volume of plays, *This Room and This Gin and These Sandwiches*? Only one of them was done (though it attracted some attention) long ago in the twenties, and the book was published obscurely in the *New Republic* paper-covered Dollar Book series, and I have always regretted that it didn't get known, because it was written as a picture of the period and fills a place—in much the same vein—between *Daisy* and *Hecate County.* I sent a copy to Allen, and they have been toying with the idea of bringing it out. What I want to suggest to you, and am going to suggest to them, is that a volume be brought out by you, and exported to them, of these three plays plus *Cyprian* and a revised version of *The Little Blue Light.* It would be called Five Plays, by Edmund Wilson or This Room and This Gin and These Sandwiches, with Two Other Plays or, perhaps better, have an overall title that would not make the play idea so prominent. I could concoct little forewords and blurbs that would take the prospective buyer's mind off this and direct it toward my vivid portrayal of the period.

As ever, / Edmund W

April 1, 1953 / Mansgrove / Princeton, NJ

Dear Roger:

What about the play? I'd like to get this settled before I leave for the Cape (next Thursday).—I hope the royalties from *Shores* have been deposited at the Guaranty Trust. I expected them to be last Monday, after talking to you on the phone; but a telegram from your office says they will be sent today, explaining, however, that they are only $600 instead of $1000, as you said.— Before I leave home, I'll be sending back some extra copies of *Shores,*—shall simply address them to you.

Did you publish the Cabell[1] Smirt Trilogy? If so, I'd like to have it, have never read it. Please send it to Wellfleet, if you have copies, next week. We saw him when we were in Richmond—much the worse for a case of flu and an aureomyasin cure. He had had a heart attack and wasn't allowed to climb stairs, so his bedroom had been moved to the bottom floor.

I can't call on account of a phone strike here.

As ever, / Edmund W

[1]James Branch Cabell (1879–1958): author of *Jurgen*, wrote not one but three trilogies; this one, from the 1930s, particularly interested Wilson.

[postcard]
[Superscript] Do you publish a memorial volume about the Jewish scholar Rosenzweig? Or any translations of [S. Y.] Agnon[1] besides the one in the Schocken Library?

Oct. 22, 1953

Dear Roger:

I found your letter here when I got back. I didn't know the *N[ew] R[epublic]* had a new publisher. Isn't it still run by Michael Straight?[2] I have no objection to meeting Lou Harrison, unless he is an agent of the idiotic Straight; but I don't see that there'll be any opportunity in the immediate future.

As ever, / EW

[1]Winner of the Nobel Prize for literature in 1966; see letter to Stephen Spender in Section VIII.

[2]See May 14, 1950, letter to Betty Huling in section II.

Wellfleet letterhead / Dec. 1, 1953

Dear Roger:

Young Epstein of Doubleday come up here to see me, and I mentioned to him an idea that I was intending eventually to propose to you: a volume of my old political and social articles from the 20's and 30's . . . to the *Shores* (partly from two of my old books, partly from uncollected material). He was eager to have Doubleday do this and wants to sign me up, with a substantial advance, at once (book not to appear for a couple of years). I suppose that this won't break your heart. Any business I do with Doubleday will not prejudice my submissions of my projected work of fiction to you.—Epstein is sold

on my writings to an extent that is almost embarrassing. He is the only publisher I have ever met whom I have felt I have had to caution not to over
invest in my books. He claims that he is going to bring out a whole series of
them in Anchor Books.

Best regards, / Edmund Wilson

[Postscript] Thanks for the Agnon and the Rosenzweig. I've arranged to go to
Israel for the *New Yorker* on my way back from Salzburg.

[Superscript] Roy Barber is the man who did the Lincoln anthology. He is at
present at the Library of Congress.

Aug. 11, 1955 / Talcottville

Dear Roger:

My boy is coming back the 22nd, so I'll be at Wellfleet by then. The house
will then be full of family, so we can't offer to put you up but if you let us
know when you are coming, I'll get you reservations at the Holiday House.

Am here drinking champagne among the ancient Americana. I find that
the combination is good for my writing.

As ever, / EW

Wellfleet letterhead / May 17, 1956

Dear Roger:

I have been delayed in going to Talcottville because Elena caught her toes
in the electric lawn mower and hurt herself quite badly, but I expect to get off
on Saturday and shall be there by Monday afternoon. Telephone: Boonville
418K. The book[1] is all typed except the last chapter, and I am going to revise
it up there—about 60,000 words, I think.

I am going to write you now about the terms I propose, while I have
Elena to type the letter—but don't reply till you have read the MS.

I propose that you pay me a $1500 advance, of which you have already
given me $1000. Book to stand by itself—not on open account. Contract same
as for *Classics* (which is called Literary Essays in the actual document), except
that I want 12% for the first 3000, 15% thereafter. Price of book you will deter-
mine.

I have told John Peck the same format as before. I know that you don't
believe in this for moderate-sized books, but Oxford got out the *Scrolls* in that

format—though I hadn't necessarily meant them to—and I think it worked out remarkably well: it made a small clear compact volume that seemed easy to read and handle.

I expect to be in New York the 13th and 14th of June, and shall call you up then.

Elena sends thanks for the novel about Germany—which she says she read with much interest.

As ever, / Edmund

[1] *A Piece of My Mind.*

Hotel Vier Jahreszeiten letterhead / Aug. 27, 1956

Dear Roger:

I have just had a letter from Jason in which he speaks of having read my galleys. Please don't show them around. I always revise so much that, outside your office, I don't want them read in this form. And please don't offer the material to magazines without consulting me. You embarrassed me by giving the *New Republic* that preface to *I Thought of Daisy.*

Elena has gone back to Wellfleet, and I am spending twelve days here in Munich. I am enjoying it, but Germany is depressing. It is as if they had all been hit over the head. They still haven't recovered sufficiently from the Nazi regime to know what has been happening in the world. Young people have no interest in politics, I am told, want nothing but hot cars and radio sets—great awe of America, I gather. Enthusiasm to be found only in the Russian Zone, where many have been had by Communism.

Back in Paris at the Hôtel Lotti, September 5—sailing October 2—will see you in New York when I get in.

As ever, / Edmund W

Wellfleet Letterhead / Oct. 5, 1956

Dear Roger:

I don't want to come to New York at all this fall if I can help it. Our movements will all be directed to finding a place to live in Boston after the first of the year. Can't I just talk to Mrs. Pilpel on the telephone?

I am pleased with the jacket of *[A] Piece [of My Mind].*

You don't have the recent files of the *Spectator,* do you? I've been engaged in a kind of controversy in their correspondence columns, and understand I have missed a move—in the issue of August 20.

Please don't forget to send sheets of *[A] Piece [of My Mind]* to [W. H.] Allen.

As ever, / Edmund

Wellfleet letterhead / December 13, 1957

Dear Roger:

This letter of Sullivan's has made me laugh because it is so different from anything I could conceivably write—especially since I have barely met Walsh and do not address him as "Henry."

I'll write him, but I want to know first whether you are prepared—in the event of Oxford's not being willing to relinquish the Civil War book—to take on *Triple Thinkers, Wound and Bow, Scrolls* and *Red, Black* etc. I've been talking to Jason, who was up here for a weekend, and he seems to be ready to put them all into Anchor.

Thanks for the Eleanor Belmont book. The part about Shaw is interesting, but it seems to me she became awfully uninteresting after she retired from the stage.

As ever, / Edmund

Wellfleet letterhead / March 7, 1958

Dear Roger:

We'll be in New York from April 8th on for two weeks, and should love to come to dinner with you. We'll be in Jason's apartment: Susquchanna 7-4403.—I had wanted to talk to you about [William] Fenton before you saw him. He is the country's greatest authority on the Iroquois Indians—brilliant and quite free from anthropological jargon. He complains that the two publishers he has talked to—one of them Knopf—both wanted him to write some different kind of book. I told him that you were intelligent enough not to do this. He grew up among the Indians in southwestern New York and knows them intimately in a personal way.

As ever, / Edmund

12 Hilliard Street / Cambridge 38, Mass. / March 29, 1960

Dear Roger:

I am going to recommend to Fenton that the following revisions should be made in his contract with you for the Iroquois book:

Clause 8d (Translations): 85% to the author, 15% to the publisher. And the author must approve the translation arrangements (to guard against abridgement or alteration). [Clause] 7e, f, and g: These rights can only be granted by mutual consent of the author and publisher.

Clause 10 should end—as in my contracts—with the words, "it being understood that the term 'overpayment' does not apply to unearned advances."

Clause 13: make it five years instead of one year. This is to guard against the situation that might arise if you were to be shot by an envious competitor and the business fall into the hands of Pyke Johnson, who would not know that the book would have a limited regular sale for use in colleges, etc.

Fenton tells me that he has been examining your list and wonders—since it doesn't appear that you have published any book of this kind before—whether you will be the right publishers to handle a book which must partly depend on the academic market. I don't know what to say about this. I know that you are effective in pushing your books with the ordinary book-buying public, and I know from Fenton's other writings that he is readable and unusual among anthropologists on account of his human approach, so I don't think you are taking too great a risk on this; but how about the long-term textbook market? He is, in any case, quite enthusiastic at having at last undertaken to produce the book and is already launched on writing it.

Something that I want to discuss with you when you and I come to drawing up another contract is 7h. Why should the publisher have the right to sell at a discount what he regards as "overstock" a year after publication? The second sentence of this clause talks about "overstock or remainders sold below or near the cost of production" which "shall not be subject to payment of royalties." I don't have my Doubleday contract here, but, so far as I can see, this clause makes it possible for Farrar, Straus to do what Doubleday has been doing with Marboro[1]—give them books which they sell at so low a price that the publisher does not have to pay royalties. This takes all the force out of the remaindering clause, since the remaindering can be called overstock, and no notice be given to the author.

Best regards, / Edmund

[Postscript] You are mistaken, by the way, in thinking that anybody else could do better than I can in selling my books abroad. My experience in the past has been—before handling this myself—that the people in publishers' offices (I am not thinking of yours) who deal with these sales abroad simply accept anything that is offered them from the first foreign publisher that offers. I have just succeeded in getting from Einaudi an advance of $1000 for *Hecate*

County (Feltrinelli would not go beyond, I think, $200!), and have extracted from [W. H.] Allen for the *Iroquois* a sum far greater than they wanted to pay. I don't believe that any agent or publisher could have done for me so well as this. I do not, as you seem to think, let any opportunities slip but keep a chart with the estimated book-buying population of every country in Europe and have even conducted negotiations with Iceland, Finland, and Jugo-Slavia. I have, I fear, been outwitted by the Japs, who have succeeded in translating a book and an article of mine without paying me a penny.

¹A discount bookstore.

Dear Roger:

I am leaving with you to be microfilmed six more volumes of my journals. A good deal of this material now exists in two forms. One consists of the copybooks and loose pages, mostly written out by hand; the other is the typed version which I have edited to some extent, supplying a certain amount of explanation. I am planning in the immediate future to bring this typed and edited version through my trip to Russia in 1935. When I gave you the first installment of this material, you microfilmed two black-bound volumes that were very incomplete and in which the typescript was only partly revised and edited. These are now superseded by three volumes which I am giving you now. They cover January, 1930 to July, 1933. (I should prefer not to have the first two of these read by anyone till after my death.)

As you know, I want to make a third version, in which the whole thing is expanded and presented in a more literary way.

The fourth of the black volumes is the journal of Trip to Zuñi in 1947. You have not had this before in any form.

The two copybooks, XXII and XXIII, have also not been microfilmed. They bring the record up to date. A few gaps still remain to be filled in, and I'll later bring you another installment.

If I don't live to edit the whole thing myself, it will have to be done by my literary executor,¹ and I here want to put it on record that if he is dealing with the handwritten volumes that I shouldn't have got around to having typed, I don't want him to have them published in the strictly scholarly way that is getting to be the academic fashion. That is, I don't want him to reproduce my contractions and ampersands; misspellings and faulty punctuations.

If words have been dropped out they should be supplied in brackets. They ought, from this point of view, to be made as readable as possible. (The hand-written originals of everything are going to the Yale Library, where, in editing the typescript version, he could check any dubious passages.)

I may take this occasion to say that if I shouldn't live to get together another volume of miscellaneous literary essays, there is already enough material for one, and I hope that Farrar, Straus will publish it. A small book could perhaps also be made of the notes for my Comparative Literature seminar.

As ever, / Edmund

[1]Leon Edel functioned in the capacity of editor for the first four volumes, beginning with *The Twenties*; Lewis Dabney edited *The Sixties*.

Hôtel de Castille letterhead / Paris / Nov. 4, 1963

Dear Roger: Thanks for the clippings—though two that you mention you didn't enclose. The last sentence of Vidal's review,[1] about Tom Paine, could be used, I should think, for publicity. We are settled here comfortably at a moderate rate and expect to make it our headquarters all winter.

Regards, / Edmund

[PS] Who is the head of Scribner's now? I have got to make a fuss about something they have done. I tend to assume that there'll always be a Charlie Scribner, but am not sure that there is one now.

[1]Gore Vidal (b. 1929): American novelist and man of letters, author of the massive *United States;* he reviewed *The Cold War and the Income Tax* for the *New York Review of Books* and is an avid Wilson enthusiast.

Hôtel de Castille letterhead / Paris / February 28, 1964

Dear Roger:

I have no title for the book yet. I have done all but the last section of the Canadian piece, which will be about 40,000 words in all. This will be about current politics, but I want to go to Canada again before I write it—so much has been happening since my visit. The piece, on this account, can't appear in the *New Yorker* till fall, but we can synchronize things so that the book can come out immediately afterwards.

We are going to Rome on March 8th—Elena has sent you the Italian address—and very glad we'll be to leave Paris, which, with its air *vicieux*, as a taxi driver said to Elena, must be now one of the unhealthiest cities in the world.

I saw Lottmann the other day with two men for Schocken, to which, without my knowledge or consent, Doubleday sold *[To the] Finland [Station]* last May. After they left, Lottman and I had an amusing conversation about French publishers. He says that you have to behave as if you were dealing with a bank, and it is only very rarely that you are able to find out who the directeur général is.

Please tell them not to send me any more books over here. Books should be sent to Wellfleet. I've just received two copies of Podhoretz's book[1] and don't know what to do with them.

Best regards. / Edmund

[1] *Doings and Undoings.*

Wesleyan University letterhead / April 19, 1965

Dear Roger:

Would this picture be any use to you? It was taken by a student here, who would want $25 for it. I think it is not bad, except that he has the faculty of making everybody's face look as if it were made of granite or limestone.

What would you think of combining with *Daisy* that long short story called *Galahad*[1] that came out first in the *American Caravan,* then in a paperback called *First Love*? I had always wanted to do this if it ever got to the point of bringing out my complete works. You don't happen to have a copy of that paperback, do you? I don't believe I have.

You might send a copy of *Canada* to Leon Edel. It is possible he might review it. He spent most of his early life in Canada and was active in the literary life there.

As ever, / Edmund Wilson

[1] Appeared in *I Thought of Daisy and Galahad* (1967).

Talcottville / June 13, 1965

Dear Roger: (1). Here are some more [W. H.] Allen exhibits. Please return them when copies have been made. Also, my letters to Garnett. (2). Also, some photographs by that boy at Wesleyan. I don't see why you don't use that good photograph by Cartier-Bresson instead of these more or less lousy ones.

I think you said it was too expensive. How much do they want for it? I might buy the rights myself.

Thanks for the clippings. I don't seem to be getting much response in Canada. I don't think they know what to say about the book. There was one venomous attack—by an Englishman who has been there three years—which sounds rather like Wolfe on the New Yorker.

Regards, / Edmund

Oct. 13, 1965 / Wellfleet, Mass

Dear Roger: That copy of the Sherman Paul book[1] has never arrived. In the meantime, the author has sent me a copy, but I want to have another so that I can send it to him with corrections in the margins. I don't think it is too bad. It is the only attempt that has been made to deal with my work as a whole. I am particularly grateful to him for taking my plays seriously. Since he seems to think *Europe without Baedeker* a wonderful book, you can use quotes from him when you reissue it. Let me know when you hear from Doubleday. Have you thought about *The American Earthquake,* which they have issued in paperback? I don't know whether you would think it worth while to examine the MS mentioned in the enclosed letter (which I am not going to examine). Best regards,

Edmund

[1]*Edmund Wilson: A Study of Literary Vocation in Our Time.*

[Superscript] About the *Daisy* preface: I had intended to write a memoir about my experience of Greenwich Village, but have decided to save that for my memoirs proper.

March 1, 1966 / Wellfleet

Dear Roger: All the new material for *Baedeker* is now in the hands of John Peck. The material for *Daisy* will be as soon as I get it typed. I have had to make a pretty drastic revision of *Galahad*—otherwise, it would have been unprintable. I hope that they can be set up more or less at the same time, so I can get Betty Huling to come up here and check them with me. They should both, I think, be set in the C. &C. typeface rather than in the *Iroquois-Canada* typeface.

I haven't kept your letter about the *M[emoirs of] H[ecate] C[ounty]* you want me to autograph. Who did you say it was for?

Best regards, Edmund

[Superscript] About Mondadori: I have written them that a copy of *Prelude* will be sent them. You might send them a copy of the new *Daisy,* too.

Wellfleet, Mass. / January 20, 1967

Dear Roger: I thought that I wouldn't revise the text of *Daisy* and didn't re-read it before I gave it to you. But when I began to go through the proofs I realized that I could not let it be reprinted in the often inept form in which I wrote it in the twenties, so have had to revise it drastically, at the rate of only about ten galleys a day (but I'm sending it back today). I'll have to have a costly revise on this, too. I ought, of course, to have foreseen this, but I thought I could get by. Redoing it is a nuisance for everybody, but I am having a certain satisfaction in seeing my books republished in a better format and text.

I also cut the *Prelude* all to Hell and should be getting a revise on it in a week or so. As I get older I revise more and more and have been somewhat spoiled in this respect by the fact that the *New Yorker* allows any number of proofs—eleven on the *Dead Sea Scrolls*—and any amount of resettings. I suppose I'd hear the howl of the banshee if I suggested that, in the case of *Prelude,* Farrar, Straus and I should go halves on the cost of corrections.

I enclose a statement for publicity, which I'm also sending to John.

I've just had a letter from [Rupert] Hart-Davis, in which he says of *O Canada* that he understands "that arrangements had already been made to litho the New York edition for England." He has just read the Canadian book and says he thinks highly of it. I think that a copy of *Baedeker* should be sent directly to him—or has this already been done?

Best regards. Shall be seeing you in early February.

[Superscript] We shan't be able to attend the Clara Malraux affairs.

Wellfleet letterhead / June 12, 1967

Dear Roger: Thanks for the marionette book. Won't you have them send me a copy of John Berryman's sonnets?

Do you know about Lydia Chukovskaya's novel about the Stalin purges [title in Russian] (*The Abandoned House*)? Impossible to publish in Russia, and so far as I know, not yet translated into any other language. It is published in Paris by the Librairie des Cinq Continents. Lottman could get it for you. I am very much impressed by it. It was written at the time and is unique. How the purges looked to a woman in a typing bureau, who had been believing everything that the official press said.

By the way, I've settled down to work again, so please don't call me before about 3.

Regards, / Edmund W

August 11, 1967 / Talcottville, NY

Dear Roger: I am going to have to go back to Wellfleet at the end of next week (the 19th). My whole end of the house is being reconstructed, and I'll have to be on hand to supervise it. Back here for a while in October, when we put on our cultural demonstration.[1] In the meantime, we hope that you and Dorothea can come to see us in September.

I don't want to do business with Gallimard. I believe that Bourgeois will be able to publish anything translatable—as *Prelude* is certainly not. Thanks for the paperbacks that look like lollipops.

As ever, Edmund

[1] Wilson tells of arranging a celebration at Utica College in honor of Harold Frederic in *Letters on Literature and Politics*, p. 726.

Wellfleet letterhead / Nov. 6, 1967

Dear Roger: Thanks for the books, but I have John Berryman's sonnets. It was the other book of poems—not *Dream Songs*—I wanted.

Dorothea has written Elena that you are tied up for the two dates she proposed. Could you manage to come up any other time? We have no one else coming except at Thanksgiving.

What happened to the blast against me in *Commonweal*?[1] It has never reached me.

As ever, / Edmund

[1] "The Nerve of Edmund Wilson," a bad review of his book *A Prelude* by David Segal, ran in *Commonweal* October 27, 1967.

Wellfleet letterhead / January 10, 1968

Dear Roger: About my present plans: I am aiming to get the scrolls off my hands by the first of April; and after that, to go somewhere south, taking my plays along to work on them. (I'm going to include in the volume my Open Letter to Mike Nichols). I don't know whether or not the final publication of the scrolls book and article will be held up by the recent acquisition by the Israelis of a number of new scrolls, which it will take a little time to publish. I gather that Yadin, when they invaded the old city, went over and confiscated some manuscripts from the basement of Kando's antique shop—he has been the chief go-between between the Bedouin and the scholars—which he had been holding up for a very high price. One of them is the longest scroll yet found. It purports to be a message from God, who freely mentions/writes his own unpronounceable name—which had not otherwise yet occurred in any of the other manuscripts of the sect. Teddy Kollek[1] writes me that I ought to come back and hear about all this, but I am not going to go.

What, by the way, has happened to our friend Malachi Martin?[2]

If you and Dorothea ever have a chance to visit us, we would be delighted to see you any time.

As ever, / Edmund

[1]Mayor of Jerusalem 1965–1992; oversaw its growth into a great cosmopolitan city.
[2]Malachi Brendan Martin (1921–1999): Irish-born renegade priest, Biblical scholar, and author of thrillers with Catholic settings.

[undated]

Dear Roger: Sorry to miss you. I was glad to hear from Epstein that they are giving you the plates of *[The] Shock[of Recognition]* free. I have given the Nabokov MS to Mary McCarthy to read. She will soon return it to you. Am leaving for Wellfleet at 5 this afternoon—shall be at *New Yorker* till then.

Edmund W

Feb. 7, 1969 / Box 87, Runaway Bay / Jamaica

Dear Roger: Dick Lewis of Yale has written me that he is doing *Palermo* for the *Times*. Please insist that anyone who reviews it gets the published text. I went on tinkering with the endings of two of those plays even into the page proofs.

We are in a vacuum down here, and outside of our little villa, Jamaica seems a horribly dreary place, but it is a good way to get away from our worries and the rest of the world which hardly seems to exist. Back sometime not too late in March.

As ever, / Edmund W

[Postscript] Since this was written, your letter and statement have come. By the way, you have not yet sent me the cover—not jacket—of *Palermo*. It ought to be in line with my other books.

Feb. 16, 1969 / Box 67, Runaway Bay / Jamaica

Dear Roger: We are coming back either the first or the fourth of March, depending on what day we can get a flight. I expect to be in New York a week. Let us have lunch—I'll call you up. We came down here with the idea that Elena could swim and I could walk, but we haven't done as much of either as we hoped. We neither of us much like the tropics and Jamaica is a sad little country—on the one hand, dreary tourist exploitation, and on the other, utter poverty and squalor. We are lucky in having rented a little cottage on the water with a built-in maid and cook. I have been poisoned by the national fruit—appropriately named asker—and Elena has been suffering from having stepped on a bristling sea urchin. But the vacuum that we live in has been a relief.

As ever, Edmund

September 24, 1969

Dear Roger:

We were sorry to hear about your illness. I was glad to learn this morning from your office that you are now out of the hospital. I think you must face the fact that you can't excel at tennis and keep all your writers in order at the same time. [. . .]

TO EDWARD GOREY WITH NOTES
SUPPLIED BY ANDREAS BROWN

August 12, 1962 / Talcottville

Dear Ted: I have much enjoyed *The Willowdale Handcar*[1] and I was delighted finally, only a couple of weeks ago, to get from *Esquire* your illustrations for my rat poem.[2] They are so good and so much better than they were in the magazine that I wondered whether it would be a good idea to bring out a little Christmas book with both the poem and the pictures. I have suggested it to Roger Straus but since my book of verse which included this poem had a very slender sale, he thought there would be no point in it. I do think that the pictures are better than the poem; but do you think your present publishers would be interested in it?

Best Regards, / Edmund Wilson

[1]Edward Gorey's *Willowdale Handcar*, published 1962.
[2]my rat poem: *The Rats of Rutland Grange*, first published in *Esquire*, December 1961. Not published in book form until 1974 by Gotham Book Mart.

September 16, 1963 / Wellfleet, Mass.

Dear Ted: I understand that one of your books is dedicated to me?[1] Don't you think you ought to get your publisher to send me these?[2]

Best regards, / Edmund W

[1]*The West Wing* (a book of illustrations without text) was published as part of a three-volume set under the title *The Vinegar Works*.
[2]By this time Gorey had published fourteen books and Wilson was an avid collector.

Sept. 23, 1963 / Wellfleet

Dear Ted: Thanks very much for *The Vinegar Works*.[1] I think that *The West Wing* is the best of these, and am very proud to have it dedicated to me. It is obviously connected with *The Object Lesson*.[2]—What is the *Wuggly Ump*, which is listed among your works?[3] I aim at a complete collection.

Best regards, / Edmund

[1]A week later Wilson received *The Vinegar Works*, including *The West Wing*.
[2]*The Object Lesson* had been published in 1958.
[3]*The Wuggly Ump* had just been published (in 1963).

Wellfleet letterhead / December 29, 1966

Dear Ted: I was very much pleased by your drawings for my play.[1] You didn't put a crown on the skeleton's skull, and you made the Clown a jester with cap and bells, though he is meant to be simply a servant; but I don't hold you to literal accuracy.

I think, by the way, that your drawings for *Cultural Slag*[2] are among your very best. Those insect-like little elves introduce a cheerful note which has lately been lacking from your work.

I have framed your rat sequence for my Christmas poem,[3] and I wish that sometime when you are visiting your aunt,[4] you would come up here and sign it.

Best regards, / Edmund W

[1]Refers to the publication of Wilson's "The Lamentable Tragedy of the Duke of Palermo" in the January 12, 1967, issue of *The New York Review of Books*. Gorey had done a large cover-page title drawing for the play as well as five text illustrations. (When the play was included in Wilson's book of plays, *The Duke of Palermo and Other Plays* (1967), Gorey illustrated and designed the dust jacket).

[2]*Cultural Slag* was a witty and successful book by Felicia Lamport, illustrated throughout by Gorey and published in 1966.

[3]Gorey's thirteen illustrations for Wilson's *The Rats of Rutland Grange* had been given by Gorey to Wilson and were framed by Wilson and hanging in his Wellfleet home.

[4]Gorey frequently visited members of his family living in Barnstable, near Wellfleet.

Wellfleet, Mass. / January 16, 1971

Dear Ted:

Thanks so much for your Umbrella Book.[1] I think it is one of your best. From the graphic point of view, your use of the black against the otherwise pale drawings amounts to a brilliant discovery.

Best regards, / EW

[1]your Umbrella Book: Gorey's *The Sopping Thursday* (1970).

Wellfleet letterhead / January 5, 1971 [*sic* 1972]

Dear Ted: I was delighted to get your consignment of little books. I don't care much, however, for *Fletcher and Zenobia*,[1] which gets you out of your real vein. I loved *Cobweb Castle*,[2] though. You are charming when you work in color though not in *F[letcher] and Z[enobia]*. I have one serious criticism to make: the supposed witch could hardly hit anybody with that parasol, which is not even folded up.

Best regards, / Edmund W

[1]*Fletcher and Zenobia* (1967) was written by Gorey and Victoria Chess, with Chess illustrations. Many Gorey fans were disappointed that Gorey did not do the illustrations. However, the book received critical acclaim and generated a sequel four years later.

[2]Gorey illustrated Jan Wahl's *Cobweb Castle* in 1968 with exceptional watercolors.

VII. A Wilson Grab Bag

The following letters are samplings of Wilson's style that do not fall under any particular heading. Not every correspondent was a close friend, yet with each of them Wilson makes a strong connection based on sincere interest and personal involvement. Whether buoyant or dejected, pugnacious or quietly direct, Wilson makes his points. The first three items, though dated years apart, display his predilection for direct statement over pussyfooting, in politics, education, and religion as in anything else. He makes his Communist leanings clear in a 1932 letter to playwright Elmer Rice, a position that the horrors of the Stalin era and the changing situation in America and Europe caused him to abandon by the end of the decade. The second letter reveals, in an elegiac light, Wilson's devotion to the principles of what used to be called a classical education, of the kind he himself had been privileged to receive at the Hill School. Writing to one of his old teachers, Mr. John Lester, Wilson gives his imprimatur to Hill (as it once was) and denies it to most education then available even in the best schools in America—sadly, even at the modern Hill. A third letter forms the fullest statement to be found in any of these letters of Wilson's position on religion. His response to a professor of religion at Columbia makes it plain that, although his love of learning and his pursuit of excellence identify him as a humanist, he is definitely a humanist of the secular variety. Then comes a flurry of exchanges—mainly in the form of postcards—with the person who is perhaps his most unusual correspondent. Jacob Landau, a tavern owner from New Jersey, wrote Wilson about the scrolls and Judaica; they became epistolary friends and met once at the YMHA in Manhattan where Wilson was reading. The bond created by their love of the Hebrew language was cemented—perhaps one should say, lubricated—by generous offerings to Wilson of wines and liquors from Landau's tavern storeroom, and the relationship warmed over the years until Wilson felt comfortable making to Landau a most revealing statement about his feud with Nabokov. Wilson's earlier friendship with Nabokov was sparked by their enjoyment of each other's wit but complicated by a kind of sibling rivalry usually held in check. Here are three short missives that testify to the disintegration of that friendship. The first strikes the note of sibling rivalry in the not-quite-well-meant joke Wilson gets off at Nabokov's expense to Bill James, son of the famous William and nephew of the famous Henry. The beginning of Wilson's sense of estrangement was already present in 1948 in his distaste for *Bend Sinister* (see letters to Helen Muchnic in section II). It stems from what he has characterized (in *A Window on Russia*) as the note of *schadenfreude* he sensed in the novel. In 1959 he writes to V. S. Pritchett about *Lolita,* still championing its rights, but expressing a similar dislike for the later book. Then there is the outburst to Katharine S. White, considered by many to be the most influential editor in the *New Yorker* fiction department. The letter contrasts strangely with an earlier letter to White (in *Letters on Literature and Politics*) which casts Nabokov in the role of the wronged and interfered with writer and the *New Yorker*'s editing of him as deplorable and deleterious. By 1971, to Wilson, the reverse was true.

In letters of a decidedly mellower mood, Wilson engages poet John Hall Wheelock in a sonnet-writing tribute to Louise Bogan. Then comes a warm note of encouragement to another poet, John Berryman. Berryman and Wilson saw a good deal of each other when Wilson was at the Gauss seminar in Princeton in 1952 and Berryman was teaching at the university. Wilson's moving response to Berryman's poetry is one of many instances that give the lie to Stanley Edgar Hyman's idea, advanced in the first edition of *The Armed Vision*, that Wilson had no understanding of verse. A letter to Stephen Spender calls to mind the lovely practice of Wilson's of getting his poet house guests to etch a poem on panes of glass later installed in one of his two residences. Rallying to the aid of the blocked or embattled writer was another Wilson trait, and is here manifest in his letter to Robert Cantwell, who was evidently in the throes of a mid-life crisis, and in his letter of support for Newton Arvin, who was being pilloried at the time for activities associated with his homosexuality. Finally, the grab bag closes with an exchange that shows Wilson's ability, when his own cantankerousness and stiff-neckedness are pointed out to him, to laugh at himself. Surely a saving grace of sorts, it is on display in his correspondence with Henry D. Blumberg, president of the Herkimer County Historical Society in upstate New York.

TO ELMER RICE

Oct. 19, 1932 / Red Bank, N.J.

Dear Elmer Rice:[1] I'm sorry not to have answered your letter before, but had been up in Provincetown and thought I'd get hold of you when I came back to New York. When I arrived, I got news of my wife's death in California and have been unable to do anything.[2]

As for the Communists, I am aware of their shortcomings and don't agree in every respect with their present official policy—I'm not even sure that the revolution in America will be accomplished under Communist leadership. On the other hand, I'm convinced, as a Marxist, that they're fundamentally right and that they're the only party who are. Consequently I'm going to vote for their candidates. It will all come down to Communism in the long run, I believe—a new Communist revolution in Europe which would give the idea of world revolution a new impetus and get official Communism out of the control of Stalin would make the 3rd International the most formidable force in the world.

Sincerely, / Edmund Wilson

[1]Elmer Rice (1892–1967): proletarian playwright of *Street Scene* and other works, had long been involved in leftist causes and may have solicited this kind of letter from Wilson and others for recruitment or campaign purposes.

[2]Margaret Canby, Wilson's second wife, died in a fall after leaving a party in Santa Barbara.

TO JOHN LESTER

Wellfleet / Cape Cod, Mass. / November 20, 1950

Dear John Lester:

The Hill is celebrating a centenary this year. They have asked me to go there and speak, but it is too far from where I live, and there cannot be anybody I know left there—and in any case I have not had in recent years a very good impression of its standing. So it has occurred to me that the only appropriate thing that I can do to commemorate the occasion is to write to you, as the only survivor of the masters I knew at Hill, in acknowledgement of my great debt to you from my schooldays.

I have thought of you often, and the more I have seen of the inadequate training in English in this country, the more I have appreciated the training you gave us. The work you made us do, for example, in diagramming sentences gave me a grasp of the structure of language which I regard as one of the most valuable things I learned at school, and I can see how the lack of a sense of the architectonics of prose leaves a good deal of American writing so sloppy. I think it is a great advantage, at this stage of one's education, to be taught English by an Englishman, and I am not sure that things haven't reached a point where we ought to get teachers from England to teach English as a semi-foreign language, in which students have to be drilled from the ground up. What was remarkable, however, in your courses was the combination of this drill you gave us with a deep appreciation of the literature we were reading and a scholarly attention to the text. Your method of studying the Ancient Mariner still represents for me an ideal of knowing a work of literature inside out, and I have never read it since without thinking of our old classes.

I am struck, in looking back on the Hill, by the amount and the relatively high quality of the literary activity that went on there, and I don't know that I can quite account for it. It was largely, I suppose, due to you and Rolfe and Bement and the Bavertus, and you people, I suppose, were due to John Meigs—though, as you once later said to me, his ideas on education must have been otherwise rather dim—having set out to equip the Hill with top-notch masters in every department. But it may be that we students were unconsciously taking part in the general literary renascence that was going on in this country at that time. In any case, it seems to me curious to find in the colleges nowadays these composition courses designed to encourage "creative writing." In our time, we tried to do creative writing outside the college curriculum without any need for such courses and on the basis of the training and stimulus that we got out of the courses in literature. Though Hill did have what seem, as I look back on it, some rather depressing features, a boy with an interest in writing could certainly not, in this country at that time, have gone to any other school that would have given him so much help and inspiration.

I was sorry not to have seen you when I was at Haverford several years ago, and I wish very much that we could sometime meet to talk about the Hill and the problems of education generally. If you are ever in New York when I am there, I so hope we can get together. We may be there for a month or more sometime after Christmas.

It is a pity that, as it turned out, the Hill had to stand or fall with the Meigs family. It is impressive to see that Exeter and St. Paul's—both, I should say, inferior to Hill in its best days and both rather old-fashioned—have, in their respective ways, survived and kept up their standards through a long succession of administrations, whereas Hill, so far as I hear, is now more or less second rate. I haven't been able to make up my mind where to send my son. He is at present a day-scholar (in the Second Form) at St. George's in Newport, but I am not sure that I want him to finish there. I get the impression that St. George's, too, is not quite what it used to be. Is there any school at present that you would recommend for a boy who is already developing decided intellectual interests?

In the meantime, I am sending you two books of mine. There is an essay in one of them on Alfred Rolfe. When I first wrote it, I also had you and some of the other masters in it, but decided that it was better to concentrate on a single subject. Your imprint is, however, to be seen in everything I have ever written, for I first learned from you to pay attention to the mechanics of writing and to have some ideal of prose expression. Wasn't the great message of Buehler's <u>Rhetoric,</u> <u>cleanness,</u> <u>precision,</u> <u>ease</u> and <u>force?</u>

I hope that you are well and happy. I hear good reports of your son from Harvard. Please remember me to your wife, of whom I have pleasant memories.

Yours as ever, / Edmund Wilson

TO NORMAN GOTTWALD

August 6, 1954

Dear Mr. Gottwald:[1]

Thank you very much for your interesting letter, and for the von Rad translations.

I. Yes: I could not go deeply into the scholarly analysis of Genesis. My article was, after all, journalism. But I did not mean to give the impression that I did not consider the scribes "authors"—in fact, I meant to make the point that they were.

II. Nor did I mean to belittle the importance of the Hebrew "sense of vocation and destiny." I tried to bring it out at the end, but had no space then to develop the subject at length.

III. The question of Jewish intolerance and its paradoxical opposite I discuss in my second article, which will be out sometime in the autumn. In the meantime, I ought to say that I do not believe in God at all except in some sense that would transpose the conception into terms that no church would accept, and that I favor dropping the word—as handicapped by too many obsolete connotations—even for purposes of metaphysics.

Yours sincerely, / Edmund Wilson

[1]Department of Religion, Columbia University.

[postcard]

July 1, 1962 Wellfleet, Mass.

Dear Jack: Thanks for the clipping. I already have a Yiddish school grammar, thank you, but have never yet got the hang of it, because I've got Hebrew fixed in my mind, & lately I've been studying Hungarian.

Best regards, / Edmund W.

New Yorker letterhead / August 6, 1962

Dear Jack: I am sorry that I don't have the books you mention—though I know about Benjamin Tudela[1] and have thought I should like to read him.

I am sorry to hear about your wife.

I have come up here for the rest of the summer and hope to accomplish some more solid work than I did among the gayeties of Wellfleet.

Best regards as ever, / Edmund

[1] A late twelfth-century Jewish travel writer.

[postcard]

Oct. 5, 1962 / Talcottville

Dear Jack: I haven't read *The Slave* but intend to. I thought his *Magician of Lublin* was wonderful. Did I tell you I saw Singer in Cambridge?[1] He seemed to think himself that Yiddish would have to struggle to survive. I was very much impressed by him: he reads and talks so well that you don't notice his very heavy accent. I'm leaving for Cambridge Sunday. As ever, EW

[1] Isaac Bashevis Singer (1904–1991): Polish-born writer in Yiddish and English; author of *The Spinoza of Market Street*. This episode, described in a June 1962 article in *The Forward* by Singer under the pseudonym Isaac Warshawsky, is a complex bit of literary sparring by Wilson and Singer. Landau wound up translating the Yiddish article for Wilson—and helping the scrolls scholar keep up with the novelist. See Castronovo and Whitehouse, "Edmund Wilson: Combat and Comradeship," *Shofar* 26, no.3 (spring 1998): 132–38.

Aug. 21, 1963 / Talcottville

Dear Jack: Thank you very much for the Hertzolumes,[1] which I am glad to have—they are interesting. I have never seen haftorah[2] readings before.

I am sailing for Europe September 6. We are going to put our daughter in school in Switzerland and spend the winter there. I'll be doing some work for the *New Yorker*—including bringing my Dead Sea scrolls book up to date—a good deal has happened since I wrote it. I'm leaving directions for a copy to be sent you of a pamphlet[3] I wrote this summer.

Every morning I have to say to myself:

[Printed in Hebrew characters: Hazak, hazak,venit hazak, meaning Be strong, be strong, let us make ourselves strong.]

Best regards, / Edmund Wilson

[1]Hertzolumes: biblical passages from prophetic books, themed to weekly readings from the Torah in Jewish synagogues.

[2]Haftorah: the chants that follow the Torah readings; Bar Mitzvah boys and Bat Mitzvah girls chant haftorah.

[3]*The Cold War and the Income Tax.*

New Yorker letterhead / February 14, 1966

Dear Jack:

Thanks for the clipping, which I hadn't seen. Nabokov and I are now fighting on two fronts: *Encounter* and the *New York Review of Books*.[1] It is like that story of Gogol's about the quarrel between Ivan Ivanovich and Ivan Nikiforovich.[2]

As ever, / Edmund Wilson

[1]Wilson roughed up Nabokov in his review of the *Eugene Onegin* translation Nabokov had worked on for years (with commentary, it runs to four volumes)—he was not amused. Nabokov's riposte in *Encounter* found its mark also.

[2]"The Quarrel of the Two Ivans": a story often mistakenly seen by Russians as pure comedy, it in fact borders on the tragicomic as the two friends fall out over a silly name-calling incident. When one Ivan would make up, the other will have none of it and vice versa. Wilson wrote a prescient comment on it many years before his life and Nabokov's were to imitate art. His essay "Gogol: The Demon in the Overgrown Garden" appeared in the *Nation* on December 6, 1952 and is reprinted in *A Window on Russia.*

TO WILLIAM JAMES JR.

Talcottville / May 24, 1957

Dear Bill: Thank you for your paper. What you are dealing with is the whole unconscious part of our mind that actually does most of the work for us and, as you say, is sometimes at odds with our rational will.

What you say about Santayana reminds me of something he is supposed to have said about his religious position: "There is no God and Mary is his mother."

I have shifted to my New York state base, where I'll be for most of the rest of the summer. Am going over to Ithaca to see the Nabokovs this weekend. Volodya tells me that Pnin is going to marry Lolita—they meet in the University of Alaska.

Sincerely, / Edmund Wilson

TO V. S. PRITCHETT

February 17, 1959 / Wellfleet, Mass.

Dear Pritchett:[1] I don't want to say in print that I don't like *Lolita*—to which I may not have done justice, anyway. Of course I think it ought to be printed and would always back it from that point of view.

Was rereading your *Living Novel* the other night, and it seemed to me remarkably good. I don't think the English weeklies nowadays give enough space to literary articles to make it possible to treat on an adequate scale any subject of any large interest. Even these essays could perhaps stand to be somewhat longer; but they do manage to get into their subjects.

Yours sincerely, / Edmund Wilson

[1]V. S. Pritchett (1900–1997): English writer renowned for *A Cab at the Door*, for his literary essays, and for the text accompanying the photography book *London Observed;* Wilson is here praising him for essays on the novel.

TO KATHARINE S. WHITE

Wellfleet letterhead / December 27, 1971

Dear Katharine: Thank you for your letter and congratulations to Andy.[1] Now that he has got that prize, I don't think there is anyone left to give it to.

Nabokov has really become intolerable. He combines the pose of a big Russian liberal with that of a big Russian aristocrat. Actually, he is neither. I suspect that the language situation has a good deal to do with it (his present bad temper): he confesses in his postscript to his Russian version of *Lolita* that he finds he has partly lost his Russian and his English is getting to be more and more peculiar. You may have been able, as an editor, to straighten his English out.

Best regards to you both, / Edmund W

[1]E[lwyn] B[rooks] White (1899–1985), *New Yorker* essayist, author of *The Second Tree from the Corner* and of such children's classics as *Charlotte's Web*. E.B., as he signed himself, was married to Katharine S. White (1892–1977), fiction editor of the *New Yorker,* and was known to his friends as Andy. The prize was the 1971 National Medal for Literature, which Wilson was awarded in 1966.

TO JOHN HALL WHEELOCK

Jan. 18, 1955 / Welfleet, Mass.

Dear Jack:[1] I suggest that you and I compose a sonnet for Louise Bogan on her winning the Bollingen award—writing alternate lines, as Max Beerbohm and Edmund Gosse did when they paid their memorable tribute to Henry James.[2]

Here is my beginning:

I enjoyed your fire-winged bird

Edmund W

[1]John Hall Wheelock (1886–1978), a poet (*Bright Doom*, 1927) who spent part of his life as an editor at Scribner's (coming in for a drubbing at Wilson's hands over a bid to get Wilson to alter his royalties on the Bishop collection of essays he edited). Note that Wilson calls him Jack.

[2]See *The Fifties* where the James tribute is reprinted.

Wellfleet letterhead / Jan. 22, 1955

Dear Jack: Yes: an Italian sonnet. I think it is a good idea to exchange lines and then write them in afterwards. I'm going to be in New York from the first of February on, and we can get together and do this in time for Valentine's Day. Here is the next line:

August by Androscoggin's swollen tide
(Louise was born in Livermore Falls on the Androscoggin.)

As ever, / Edmund

Dear Jack: Yes: <u>august</u> is an adjective. Here is the next line:

> *Pensive she plucked the plangent strings of pain*

—In view of the turn that the poem is taking, I think it might be a good idea to change the <u>dallying</u> of the first line to <u>languishing</u>.

What would you think of the following for the design for the blank space on the front page of the valentine: two hearts (easily cut out of red paper), one above the other, each transfixed by an arrow, and each bearing the initials of one of us?—otherwise, the valentine to be unsigned.

We don't expect now to get to New York the first, so new lines—till further notice—ought to be sent me up here.

As ever, / Edmund

Princeton Club letterhead / [undated]
> *Or, deaf to Passion's piercing ophicleide.*

New Yorker letterhead / [undated]
> *Columbia brings the guerdon, dear Louise,*

I hope it is clear that applies not to the university, but to the Columbia that is the gem of the ocean.

EW

Princeton Club letterhead / [undated]
> *While we, your rapt admirers, on our knees,*

I consider it bad form, in an enterprise of this kind, to try to dictate one's collaborator's lines; but I might perhaps suggest that some reference now be made to the bottle of whiskey we are giving her—though I should hesitate to recommend such a phrase as "a bottle of Bourbony"

EW

TO JOHN BERRYMAN

Wellfleet / March 15, 1959
Dear John: I read your poems[1] through whiskey the other night, then instantly remembered them the next morning as though they must have been an out-of-this-world alcoholic dream—especially since the book had disappeared,

due to Elena's having taken it. We are both very much impressed by them. It is extraordinary how, beginning with the Bradstreet poem,[2] you have made yourself a new and ironic-lyrical style. Don't you want to go to the Peterborough Colony?[3] But I imagine that that kind of thing is not the way you work. I've been asked to do my Civil War at Harvard in their new Lowell lectureship—it is a good deal better now than when you heard it—so we'll be in Cambridge or Boston all next winter. Be sure to let us know if you should be there.—Really, I haven't admired any new poetry so much as these of yours since goodness knows when.—Elena sends love.

Edmund

[1]John Berryman (1914–1972): poet, teacher, critic, biographer of Stephen Crane; the poems he sent Wilson were probably some or all of his *Dream Songs*.

[2]Berryman's Pulitzer Prize–winning *Homage to Mistress Bradstreet*.

[3]An artists' colony in Peterborough, N.H., for those with residence grants, which Wilson evidently felt he could arrange—a place similar to Yaddo in Saratoga Springs. Not every writer or artist favored the enforced socializing after work hours.

TO STEPHEN SPENDER

Wellfleet, Mass. / September 16, 1960

Dear Stephen:[1]

You misunderstood what I said about the poem.[2] I meant simply that you oughtn't to want to think about your work as something that is "writ on water." But I seem to have misunderstood the poem, because evidently you didn't mean that. I am very much pleased with it in any case and am going to have it installed.

I did see traces of our conversation[3] in your article. There is a story about it in *Time* this week. What Pamela Johnson said was that in London you always knew, before you had written a word of a book, not only who was going to review it but exactly what they were going to say.

We are moving to Cambridge at the beginning of next week—12 Hilliard Street, Cambridge 38—and that will by my address all winter. Please have *Encounter*[4] send those Agnon[5] translations back to me if you haven't already sent them to the author and if you have already sent them, let me know his name and address, which I don't seem to have. I want to try to interest *Commentary* in them.

As ever, / EW

[1]Stephen Spender (1909–1995): poet, memoirist; part of the Auden-Isherwood set in the 1930s.

[2]See the journals of *The Forties* where Wilson describes his practice of asking his poet house guests to etch a poem on a pane of glass which he then installed at one of his two residences. See also the letters to Isaiah Berlin in section II.

[3]Evidently a dialogue comparing and contrasting the literary worlds of New York and London.

[4]Spender founded this respected and influential magazine of art and ideas with Irving Kristol in 1953.

[5]S. Y. Agnon (1888–1970), one of Wilson's favorite Jewish writers, author of *Bridal Canopy* (1968) et al. It was typical of Wilson to try to get the work of international literary figures he admired published (in translation) in an opinion-making organ such as *Commentary*.

TO ROBERT CANTWELL [FRAGMENT]

[undated, but may be 1946]

. . . This is often a difficult period for writers: they have to take stock seriously, and arrange for their future activities, and this is likely to involve adjustments that seem as painful as pulling teeth.[1] We are all full of ideas of things that we think we can do and ought to do that are absolutely irrelevant to our real purpose and value in life, and when we see middle age approaching, when our most serious work will have to be done, we are obliged to recognize this.—I am saying all this at a hazard, and I hope you will forgive me if it is beside the point in your case.

In any event, I can't help feeling relieved that you are going to be out of the *Time* office for awhile. You've always seemed to me misplaced there. I can imagine that such a job as you have had would keep you in a constant state of nervous excitement about the affairs of the world, to which, nevertheless, the relation of a journalist in your position is doomed to be fundamentally unreal, and I should think this would drive you crazy in the long run.—I wish there was some prospect of your sitting down quietly and writing another novel. I've always thought you were one of the only ones of the American writers of your generation who had genuine talent and brains; and I've always been convinced that you were so much a real writer that you never would remain a Luce journalist indefinitely.[2] I've been hoping that you'd emerge and do a novel about the Luce world and its inhabitants.

I wish you would come up here and visit us. We'd love to see you—so would Dos, who will be back here presently. It's very quiet and pleasant here this time of year.

As ever, / Edmund Wilson

[Postscript] Please pardon this letter if it is all off the track.[3]

[1]Robert Cantwell (1908–1978) wrote a proletarian novel, *The Land of Plenty*, in 1934. He worked on editorials staffs of *Time* and *Fortune*, rising to associate editor of *Time*, 1938–45. He then left to write a biography of Hawthorne. This may be the period of Wilson's letter.

[2]He took a job on a non-Luce publication, *Newsweek*, where he served as literary editor from 1949 to 1954. Then, however, after a two-year period of freelancing, rather than going back to writing novels as Wilson had earlier hoped he would, he joined *Sports Illustrated* (a Luce publication) in 1956, an association that lasted the rest of his life.

[3]Cantwell evidently did not take offense—there are several cordial exchanges between the two in 1957.

TO THE *NEW YORK TIMES*

September 12, 1960 / Wellfleet, Mass.

I regard Newton Arvin as one of the two or three best contemporary writers on American classical literature.[1] As a scholar, a literary critic and a master of English style, he has long been one of the most distinguished representatives not only of the English department of Smith College but of the whole cultural field in the United States. I have known him for many years and in my conversations with him have always been struck not only by his sensitivity but also by his excellent judgment and his obviously high principles in both his personal and professional life. I am unable to believe the charges against him which sound like a fantasy of the local police distorted by an incompetent reporter.

Edmund Wilson

[1]Meyers says that Wilson dashed off this letter between Arvin's arrest and trial—a police raid of Arvin's apartment had turned up a large stash of photographs deemed to be pornographic; he was arrested and charged with being "a lewd and lascivious person." Wilson's letter was never published. As for Arvin, he was given a suspended sentence and forced to retire from Smith on half salary. See Meyers, p.401.

TO HENRY D. BLUMBERG

[Letter from Henry D. Blumberg to Wilson:

July 12, 1968

Edmund Wilson / Boonville, New York
Dear Sir:

I wonder if you would be interested in addressing, for a fee, the Herkimer County Historical Society some time this fall. The topic should relate to Herkimer County or the Mohawk Valley but it is not essential that it do so. I believe that I can guarantee that there will be no obligations other than your talk except, perhaps, a few autographs.

Hoping that I may have the favor of a reply, I am.

Very truly yours, / Henry D. Blumberg /
President of the Herkimer County Historical Society]

[Printed card[1] to Henry D. Blumberg]

Edmund Wilson regrets that it is impossible for him to:

Read manuscripts,
Write articles or books to order,
Write forewords or introductions
Make statements for publicity
  purposes
Do any kind of editorial work
Judge literary contests
Give interviews
Conduct educational courses
Deliver lectures
✓ Give talks or make speeches
Broadcast or appear on television,

Contribute to or take part in
  symposiums or "panels" of any
  kind,
Contribute manuscripts for sales,
Donate copies of his books to
  libraries,
Autograph books for strangers,
Allow his name to be used on
  letterheads,
Supply personal information about
  himself,
Supply photographs of himself,
Supply opinions on literary or other
  subjects,
Take part in writers' congresses.

[1]The only handwritten addition to this printed postcard is the check mark beside "Give Talks or Make Speeches."

[To which Blumberg replied:

July 16, 1968

Dear Mr. Wilson:

From your List of Regrets I feel you have omitted: "Divulge old Family Receipts."[1]

Very truly yours, / Henry D. Blumberg, President /
Herkimer County Historical Society

[1]Receipts: an old-fashioned form of "recipes."]

July 29, 1968

Dear Mr. Blumberg: Your note has reminded me of the only secret family receipt I know. An old lady we have always known in Lewis County wanted to do something especially nice for my wife and communicated to her the secret of making a particularly delicious kind of icing for chocolate cake, which she was not to tell even to me. This receipt had been known to her sister-in-law who had promised to tell her on her deathbed. But when the sister-in-law came to die and our friend asked for the secret, the dying woman said, "No: I'm not a-gonta tell you!" Our friend, however, found it out from some other source. It proved to be simply that for this kind of icing she used canned condensed milk—a device which, in that dairy country, nobody would ever have been able to guess.—I hope that this may compensate you somewhat for my non-appearance in Herkimer.

Yours sincerely, / Edmund Wilson

VIII. At Talcottville

This corner of New York State provided Wilson with a quiet place for sustained work, a window on his family past, and a source of friends outside the literary establishment. While the Wellfleet, Cambridge, and New York of his later years supplied a dizzying round of parties with writers and intellectuals—and friends like Arthur Schlesinger, W. H. Auden, and Penelope Gilliatt on tap—Talcottville meant long hours of uninterrupted writing, reading about Iroquois and Civil War figures, savoring never-read classics, and visiting and dining with locals who were either year rounders or summer residents. He had made a trip to the Old Stone House at Talcottville in 1933 and written movingly of its pocket-of-the-past irrelevance: his famous essay about the place, written for the *New Republic* and republished in *The American Earthquake,* combines memories from childhood with dispirited reflections on the fate of an older America. When he claimed the house as his retreat in the early 1950s, after his mother's death and years of neglect, he galvanized it into life, put his career into a remote, baronial setting, and used an ancestral place as his last grand-scale subject in *Upstate.* The letters printed here, however, reflect Wilson's ordinary moods and contain no large themes. At work a good deal of the time, he nevertheless had the leisure and patience to make contact with new people and try to understand their lives. The Costas were genial hosts of the 1960s who understood his crotchets and physical limitations and could also provide talk and the kind of listening Wilson liked. Richard Costa, a professor and one-time journalist, held up his end on literary topics. Glyn Morris, a forceful Presbyterian minister and teacher, interested Wilson because he was intelligent, articulate, and a Welshman in an Anglo-Saxon setting. Mary Pcolar, one of Wilson's last loves, was his helper-secretary-chauffeur, not to mention his sometime Hungarian tutor. At a time when disillusionment with American culture threatened to make him bitter and depressed, Wilson had a not-so-ordinary neighbor to intrigue him with her exotic culture and looks. She also gave him the adulation and gentle, quasi-sexual affection that he craved.

There is an odd burst of nostalgia for his childhood evident at the end of Wilson's life. His letters to his old friend Margaret Rullman, together with one from a newly widowed Elena to her, provide a suitable last look at the old man in the old stone house, of whom Glyn Morris records that, in his last glimpse of Wilson alive, "he was reading away."

October 6, 1962 / Talcottville

Dear Professor Costa:

I am sorry that I can't give you an interview—I am leaving here next Sunday. I don't like to give interviews anyway, unless I can play the "straight man" myself, as in the one that you saw in the *New Yorker*. I should like, though, to meet the people at Utica College.

Yours sincerely, / Edmund Wilson

Oct. 29, 1964

Dear Costa: I'm afraid I didn't give them a very good show in your class the other night. I was tired and not prepared for it.

The Haitian friend of Lowry is Philippe Thoby-Marcelin, 3439 17th St. N.W. Washington 10, D.C.

I have been through Wells' *Marriage* and can't find the passage I told you about. I am mystified and am going to look in some of his other books.

Please remember me to your wife.

Best regards, / Edmund Wilson

March 17, 1965

Dear Costa:

I am going up there about the 25th and hope to get a chance to see you. I'm glad to hear that Mary is still taking her courses and doing well. I never see her when I go up there without regretting that I can't see enough of her to help her with her education.

Yes: I got Kurt Rolfe's pictures. Thank you. I look like hell in them, but I don't doubt I look like that.

Best Regards, / Edmund Wilson

April 12, 1965

Dear Dick:

Thank you for your letters. I'm sending the check for Mary.

In the country, I read a novel of George Meredith's that I hadn't read before: *Beauchamp's Career.* You know that Wells acknowledges a debt to Meredith's *One of Our Conquerors,* and I think that this must have influenced him, too—politics, English institutions, and a conflict of love affairs.

I very much enjoyed the other evening. Please thank your wife for me. I'm sorry I conked out so early, but nowadays I can't talk and drink as much as I once could.

Sincerely, / Edmund Wilson

July 23, 1965 / Wellfleet, Mass.

Dear Dick: I'm afraid I shan't be back till after Labor Day. I'll be sorry not to see you—I wanted to read you that Russian preface to Wells. There is an amusing passage in which the writer quotes Wells on his impressions of Russia before he had ever been there, from reading Russian novels, and registers his own Soviet horror. Apropos, Nabokov has replied with shrieks, having discovered two mistakes in my Russian and I have made a cool rejoinder.

I know the Brautingan Inn. The lake is nice, and I don't think you'll mind the people much. The little boy will love it. Would you like me to talk about your book with my publisher? But it might be better to talk about it with whoever publishes his books in New York.

Please remember me to your wife.

Edmund W

I look for a sensational improvement in Mohawk service—followed perhaps by the total demoralization of the personnel.

Nov 17, 1965 / Wellfleet, Mass

Dear Dick: I had forgotten that you had to get a Ph.D. Yes, I am still of that opinion about *Ulysses*—also, about *Finnegans Wake.* I don't believe that Maugham-Beerbohm story. I was never in Rapallo except that time in '54 that I tell about in *Bit,* and then there was no Somerset Maugham in the offing. And there was no real "library" in MB's villa—only his study on the roof. In my article on Maugham, I said nothing about his "undermining the principles of Christianity"—not being a Christian myself—and nothing to the effect that it would have been better if he had gone on with his medical career.

Best regards, / Edmund W

Wellfleet, Mass. / June 10, 1966

Dear Dick: Thanks very much for your letter. I left after the luncheon in Utica, but shall be back after August 7 and hope to see you then. Tom O'Donnell will tell you about the grandiose project with which we have been toying over the phone.

Best regards to you and Jo, / Edmund W

March 9, 1971

Dear Costas: Fortuna molto mi dispiace adesso. (Fortune is much displeasing to me now.)

I'm glad to hear that you're liking Texas, but should hate to have you sell your Utica house. Though physically somewhat shaken, I expect to get back to Talcottville in May. If only to see what is happening about the road in front of my house.

A part of my Upstate book will be coming out in *The New Yorker,* but I warn you not to read it there—wait till I send you the book. In order to cut it down to size, they have left out the historical and family chapters and omitted the most interesting episodes from the diary—so that it reads like *Walden, or Life in the Woods*—all about the birds and flowers. The people require so much explanation, which is contained in the early chapters, that they have mostly had to be omitted, and this leaves me practically a hermit.

I was finally bullied into reading *Middlemarch,* which is a good deal better than *Adam Bede* and *Silas Marner*—I had to read them at school and hated them. It is a good picture of English country life.

Lecturing is out of the question, thank you. I cannot really lecture but only read things I have written. At the present time, I haven't written anything appropriate and couldn't make the trip anyway.

Best regards, / Edmund

TO MARY PCOLAR

Feb. 28, 1962 / 12 Hilliard St. / Cambridge

Dear Mary: I was glad to hear from you. We have been having a dismal life here lately. Elena and Helen have been sick with the flu, have spent a week, mostly in bed, without going out of the house; but Elena is better now, and Helen went back to school today. I have had only minor ailments, gout and an annoying nose infection that I always get in winter here, so I have been able to get around. Out of doors everything is covered with gray snow, and the streets are ankle deep in water. We hope to get away at the end of next week, when Helen gets a three weeks vacation, and take a trip to New York and Washington.

My only cheerful spots lately have been my sessions with a Hungarian friend in Boston. She told me that the little conversations in the soldier's manual I was studying were so awful—such clumsy Hungarian—that I oughtn't to bother with them, since nobody ever spoke like that, so I have had the happy idea of reading one of Molnár's comedies.[1] This is delightful: she read all the woman characters, and I read all the men. Perhaps you and I can read one next summer. She says that that poem about the fog and the forest is as difficult as anything in Hungarian—she had to puzzle over it a little herself. Ady[2] created his own style, and even to some extent, it seems, his own language. I think that it is a wonderful thing, and someday I may try to translate it.

I have records of a lovely little opera by Kodály.[3] Hungary's great number two composer—now over eighty. I have also sent for one for you. It was made in Budapest, and the Hungarian libretto is in the album. I think your whole family ought to like it. It is called *Székely Fonó*—which, as I probably don't need to tell you, means The East Transylvania Spinning Room.[4] I hope you enjoy "a nagyorru bolha,"[5] who is one of the characters.

I don't know when I'll be coming over there again. I may have to make a trip fairly early in the spring. I have been done with the Civil War book for some time now, but it is not coming out till the last week in April. It is so long that they want the reviewers to get a chance to read it through. 850 pages for $8.50—a penny a word and cheap at the piece!

Please remember me to your family and Roy Kream, and take care of your invaluable self.

Szerelemmel [with love, as in "con amore"] / Feher Nandor[6]

[1]Ferenc Molnár (1878–1952), author of *Liliom*, source of *Carousel*.

[2]Endre Ady (1877–1919): a Hungarian poet influenced by the French symbolists.

[3]Zoltán Kodály (1882–1967): best known in the West as the composer of the *Háry János* suite. Wilson is evidently alluding to Béla Bartók, Hungary's number one composer.

[4]The Szekelys are a million-plus strong Hungarian people living in what is today Rumania.

[5]Wilson probably means the second word to be *baba*; the phrase would then be "a big-nosed witch."

[6]Literally "White Ferdinand"—Wilson carries his penchant for funny signatures over to Hungarian.

July 3, 1962 / Wellfleet, Mass.

Dear Mary: Can you tell me exactly when the Hungarian picnic is to take place at the end of July? If they really want to invite me, I'd like to get back by then though my son is coming in from California in the latter part of July, and I want to be with him here.

How are you? Has anything been done about the job you applied for?

As ever, / Edmund Wilson

12 Hilliard Street / Cambridge, Mass. / January 19, 1963

Dear Mariska: I was a little worried by your letter, and I hope that you are holding up. I thought after I had written you before that I shouldn't have suggested your dropping your job because you were probably dependent on it. I wish there was something I could do to help you. Call me collect if you ever want to or let me know if there's anything I can do. Did you pass your exams? I imagine you did.

I was glad to have the old grammar and have written something about it in an article called "My Fifty Years with Dictionaries and Grammars," which I'll send you when it comes out. The title page and some other pages are missing—they're not anywhere around the house, are they? Did you notice that in the grammatical part in the front a whole elaborate set of tenses and modes is given which really doesn't exist in Hungarian? It's a good thing I didn't try to memorize them when I had the book up in the country. One of my Hungarian friends here said she had never seen such forms in her life and couldn't account for them at all; but Zoltán Haraszti examined them and announced, "This part of the book was written by a dishonest notary from some provincial town, who had got in trouble and had to leave Hungary and had come to the United States." I was astonished by this feat of Sherlock Holmes detection. His reasoning was as follows: In Hungary till the 1830's, the language of the educated people was Latin, and it was still true up to the present century—and, for all I know, may still be true—that the legal documents were written in Latin. The contriver of the bogus conjugations in the grammar was trying to provide for Hungarian the whole structure of the Latin conjugations—hence the pluperfects, future perfects, passive mode, etc., which don't really exist in Hungarian. Only a notary who used Latin would have had the idea of doing this—and only one who was none too well educated would have tried to do anything so silly. And such a man—since his skill would have had no market abroad—would never have emigrated unless there had been some pressing reason. Zoltán said he had known several such people in his early days over here when he was working for a Hungarian newspaper. This notary in exile would have needed work, and some man who had been over here longer would have asked him to supply a section of grammar for a colloquial phrasebook for immigrants. The colloquial part, Zoltán says, is perfectly all right. I don't know how much this will interest you, but it seems to me very curious.

I think I told you that my mild angina had been giving me more trouble last autumn; but I get along all right now and am comfortable as long as I don't try to walk in the cold and don't make too much physical effort. The worst thing, from my point of view, is that I can't have more than one or two drinks without paying the price in heartstrain afterwards. I think that I am going to have an upstairs phone put in at Talcottville.

The medicine I take every day seems almost entirely to have killed off my gout. The tax problem is still not settled, and this is an immense nuisance.

I am including some more stamps for Eddie—Israel, Poland, Japan, India, Norway, Spain, Greece, etc.

Cambridge is terribly dreary. We'll never spend another winter here. The only compensations are theaters, concerts, bookstores, and a few friends. We saw the movie *Lawrence of Arabia* yesterday, and when it comes out to Boonville, I think you ought to be sure to go and take the children. It is really one of the very good films. We'll go down to Cape Cod in March, when Helen has her spring vacation.

Drop me a line when you have a moment.

Szcrctcttcl, [Affectionately,] / Edmund Wilson

[Translated from the Hungarian, with accompanying notes, by Francis Bethlen, who has approximated Wilson's errors for flavor.]

February 22, 1963 / Washington's Birthday

Dear Mariska: My Hungarian teacher told me that I have to write something in Hungarian and therefore I try to write to you a letter.

I am very happy that you have visited New York that you enjoyed it and that you like you work. Still I do not know what I will do next summer when I'll be in Talcottville. I would like to find somebody who could come every day so that we could talk and read Hungarian together. This you can not do anymore because you are excessively busy. Do you know somebody who would undertake this? Maybe Mr. Mihaly[1] might know somebody.

Last Friday was Helen's birthday. She became fifteen years old, developing into a pretty and tall girl. It is happening for the last time that we are spending the winter in Cambridge. Maybe next Fall we will enroll Helen in a school in Switzerland and we might stay in Europe until Spring.

Several foreign stamps are enclosed for your son. He wrote to me a very nice letter. Please read this letter out loud to your Mother and tell her that I am studying the Hungarian language only because of you. (Please forgive me for addressing you on a "thou" term. Next time I shall practice the "You" approach in my writing. Don't think that I can write Hungarian that good. My teacher corrected my mistakes . . .)

Well, I do hope that you not work so much as to become unduly tired. Write to me when you have the time.

I am writing with pencil on yellow paper because it is difficult for me to write on white paper with a ball-point pen. Sometimes the pen does not work well and the writing is not clearly visible.

Good-bye[2]—see you again. Affectionately,

Wilson Edmund[3]

[1]A real estate broker in the Adirondack Region of Hungarian origin.
[2]"Isted veled" means literally "God be with you." It is a traditional farewell.
[3]Wilson signed this letter in the Hungarian way, family name first, followed by a given name.

TO S. N. BEHRMAN

March 13, 1963 / Hilliard St. / Cambridge, Mass.
Dear Sam: Just read your interesting article about Molnár[1] in the Hungarian Album. I did not know that you write so well in Hungarian.[2] These days I am reading Molnár's comedies and I find that he is a better writer than I thought. Do you know the *High Class Prima Donna* which was translated into English with the title *Fashions for Men*, but was not successful on the New York Stage? I think that this is one of his best plays. Let us talk about Molnár when we meet next time in the White House or somewhere else. I am sorry that I did not see your work (play) *Lord Pengo* especially since I think the hero is a Hungarian. Molnár's third wife Lili Darvas[3] is here in Boston; she plays in Lillian Hellman's new dramatic work.[4] One evening we got acquainted and we have invited her for lunch to us. She is still pretty, too beautiful as I told her to

play an old dying Mother in Lillian's play. Believe it or not Lillian's play is very amusing but it is much too shocking for Boston: Every evening twenty or more ladies are getting up and leaving the theatre. [The above passages were written in Hungarian, translated by Francis Bethlen.]

Don't bother with this unless there's a Hungarian handy. I write letters in Hungarian for practice, and hope to get the *New Yorker* to send me to Hungary later on. Cambridge is dismal beyond belief—especially since Isaiah [Berlin] has gone back. I find it makes it a little better to try to think of Cambridge-Boston as Buda-Pest on the Charles. We are soon getting away for two weeks in New York. Since I composed the above paragraph, Lillian's play has closed its run and gone on to Manhattan. It was a great mistake to open it in Boston.

Best regards, / Edmund

[1]One of Molnár's plays was adapted and put on in English by the Lunts.

[2]Wilson was so enchanted with the idea of being able to practice his Hungarian he wrote to S. N. Behrman (1893–1973), the Broadway playwright who brought some of Pagnol's stories to the stage in the musical *Fanny,* and adapted his own profile of Lord Duveen for a Charles Boyer vehicle, *Lord Pengo,* as well as turning out a biography of Max Beerbohm called *A Portrait of Max*—see letters to Elena Mumm Thornton in section III. Behrman was so nettled by receiving the preceding letter (fully a half of which was in Hungarian) that he wrote back saying "That was very cruel of you! Had you written me in Russian or in Hebrew, I should have had resources— . . . it is so very tantalizing, the Hungarian part of your letter, because I gather you discuss in it Lillian Hellman's play about which I am curious, and who knows what else. However, I'll have my revenge on you. . . . [Y]ou must come and have dinner with me and . . . I will practice my Swahili on you. That will teach you a lesson!"

[3]Lili Darvas: see letters to Elena Mumm Thornton in section III.

[4]*Toys in the Attic.*

TO MARY PCOLAR

May 7, 1963 / Cambridge, Mass.

Dear Mariska:

Your letter has given me much happiness. (As you observe in this letter I am not addressing you in the intimate "te"-thou form but in the more formal pronoun "maga"-you as a matter of practicing.) I am hoping to go to Talcottville at the beginning of June and I am looking forward to seeing you. Now, I am healthier—my heart is better—my arthritis almost gone. My tax problem is also solved, but the darned Government has taken away the greatest part of my money.

My daughter Rosalind just told me that the Hubert home in Boonville burned down together with two stores, but I have not read any article in the paper about that. It's really terrible.

Several foreign stamps are included for your son.

When I described you in New York to a Hungarian friend of mine he said—using an expression—that in Hungary they would call you a "person-of-all-trades." Are you familiar with this word?

Good-bye—see you again.

Edmund Wilson

Hôtel de Castille, Paris, letterhead / Nov. 30, 1963
Dear Mariska: We have settled down in this hotel, probably for all winter. Paris is not very gay anymore. People are poor, and there is lots of unemployment. You almost never see well-dressed women even at the theater. We are living very quietly, almost the way we did in Cambridge—except that it's more interesting when you go out of doors. Next week I am going to make a break in my work, and Elena is going to hire a car and drive me up to the Vosges, where I spent over a year in the first war. I am curious to see it again. In the spring, I hope to get to Hungary. After the first of the year, when I've finished my piece on Canada, I'm going back to working on Hungarian; there is a Hungarian girl who takes care part time of Elena's Russian cousin's little daughter. She is a considerable scholar, they tell me, and I am going to try to get her to help me.

My *Protest*[1] got two or three nasty reviews, but, on the whole, has been more favorably reviewed than I expected. There was even an article about it in the financial section of the *N.Y. Times*. I was surprised to hear that Kennedy is supposed to have read *Patriotic Gore* and to have proposed me for that medal himself. It may be that he would have been glad to have that sort of thing said: Tax reduction, good relations with Russia. And he took more interest in literature than I had realized, more interest than I'm afraid Johnson will. Europe has really been hard hit by Kennedy's assassination. I've been surprised to see how much they counted on him.

Helen is coming here for the holidays and we are going to celebrate Christmas with Elena's Russian relatives. The Russians make a lot of Christmas, the French very little.

Love to all the family, and write me when you get a moment.

Szeretettel, [Affectionately,] / Edmund W

[1] *The Cold War and the Income Tax.*

Budapest / April 13, 1964

Dear Mariska: I am here in Budapest. Often having you on my mind. Just had lunch with Professor Orszag who wrote these dictionaries which I have used. He is a charming intelligent man of the world. I have talked to him about the possibility of you coming to Hungary for a short time. He said, that it is easy if you came on your own expense, but otherwise it is difficult. Now I am not sure, that if you want to come to Europe Hungary would be the best place for you—Italy might be a better country for you. We will talk about that later.

We spent Helen's Easter vacation in Italy. Rosalind joined us there and we all had an unusually good time. Now Helen is back in school in Switzerland. Elena is with her family in Germany. She might be back here before I leave on May 10th.

In the opera I have seen *Háry János.*[1] It was a matinee for children. Kodály himself was present in the opera house. I would have liked it very much that you and your children would have been there with me. Orzse, János' bride, had always red ankle-high boots on.

I am enclosing Hungarian stamps for your son.

Affectionately, / Edmund Wilson

[1] Kodály's popular comic-opera about a bragging soldier; the composer's method of teaching music to children is used worldwide.

Wesleyan University letterhead / Oct. 28, 1964

Edes Mariskam [My sweet Mariska]: The Areopagus was a hill in Athens where the big council and criminal court held its meetings. The Areopagitica was addressed to the English parliament, which was exercising a rigorous censorship, against which Milton was protesting. Areopagitica means matters having to do with the top council.—The parable of the talents is in Matthew 25. It might interest you to look it up in connection with Milton on his blindness. A talent was an ancient coin, but the word gradually got to mean a natural gift, as when we say a person is talented. The idea is that God has given us our talents as the Master in the parable gave the money to his servants. The servants who got five and two talents invested their money and doubled it;

the servant who got only one hid his and was rebuked by the Master, who, when he found out that nothing had been done with it, took it away from him and gave it to the man who now had ten.

My folder had been put in the safe at the club, and they quickly sent it on to me.

[Hungarian for: I thank you very much—

see you again in the Spring] / Edmund W

[Postscript] Your children are better looking than those photographs you gave me—you ought to have pictures taken of a family group.[1]

[1]Wilson's memoir *Upstate* contains a very good family group photograph of the Pcolars.

Dec. 4, 1964

Dear Mariska: I was very glad to hear from you and to know that you are still taking your courses. I had had a letter from Costa in which he said he was afraid you were going to give them up.

I have been thoroughly enjoying it here, but Elena has been a little lonely. However, we had Helen with us over Thanksgiving, and both the girls are coming for Christmas. We went to New York for Thanksgiving and had lunch with the young Hungarian that I met at Smith College, and who is now teaching history at Columbia. He was in Hungary last summer and told me a good deal that was interesting that I hadn't been told when I was there. He says that the collectivization of the peasantry was put through with such brutality that they will never forgive the administration, that the younger ones all move to the cities, and there will be no new generation to work the land. He thinks that it was a mistake of Kádár's which he probably recognizes but which now cannot be undone. The old ebullient kind of Hungarian, he tells me, hardly existed in his own generation, which had been through war and revolution. These old-timers that I know over here are now museum pieces. He is entirely not like that himself.

I discussed, also, with Istvan Deak[1] the problem of how to say you in Hungarian, and he made it seem ever more complicated than it had seemed before. He said that since I was so much older than he was, he couldn't call me either maja or te, but that if he felt I was well disposed toward him, he would eventually call me batgam. He said that he had a problem, when he was in Budapest last summer, as to how to talk to party history professors, who, he found, were not in the habit of using Kokeja with one another and who couldn't be addressed as us. In the office of a history department, they insisted on calling him elvtars (comrade); and when he said to the girl who ran the office, "I'm not elvtars—I'm from America," she answered sternly, "Everybody here is elvtars." He had been brooding about how to begin a letter to one of the men in this department and had worked out a formula but was dubious.

I think about you often and wonder how you are getting along.— Remember me to the family.

Love, Edmund W.

[1]Professor of Eastern European history at Columbia.

[Note: three boxes of letters to Mary Pcolar were acquired by the Beinecke Rare Book and Manuscript Library at Yale University for the Wilson collection when Mary and her second husband were tragically killed in a fire in Florida in 1982.]

TO GLYN AND GLADYS MORRIS

Wesleyan University letterhead / Oct. 29, 1964

Dear Glyn: Here is an interesting Catholic article about your favorite historical character. This priest has a better impression of him than I have; but I agree that it is a mistake to think of him as the constructor of a hard-and-fast logical system. The Institutes[1] are usually quite inconsistent.

Love to Gladys, and thank you for the other evening.

/ Edmund

[Postscript] . . . the Kindergarten poll, I am told, showed that the little children were almost 100% for Johnson.

[1]The Institutes of the Christian Religion: the doctrinal code of the Calvinists, including predestination and salvation by faith alone.

Sept. 19, 1966 / Wellfleet, Mass.

Dear Glyn: I was delighted to get the Hebrew slogan[1] and have put it up on the wall of my study.—We hope you will be able to come over here later on.

Love to Gladys.

As ever, / Edmund

¹The "Be Strong" slogan—see letters to Jacob Landau in section VII.

Wellfleet letterhead / Oct. 26, 1966

Dear Glyn:

Thanks for the Modern Language Association¹ material.—I am working on my mad Presbyterian minister,² which eventually I want to read you.

Love to Gladys.

As ever, / Edmund

¹*The Fruits of the MLA* may have been partially a result of this research. It came out in 1968.

²*Dr. McGrath*, a play in the print edition of *The Duke of Palermo;* it features a deranged Calvinist man of the cloth.

April 20, '67 / Wellfleet, Mass.

Dear Glyn: Yes: the oil has been a nuisance. People rescue the poor birds and take them to the Audubon Society to be cleaned off.—I am taking off for Jordan and Israel on the 27th in order to bring my Dead Sea Scrolls book up to date. (Am back plodding through the Hebrew bible again.) I'll be gone a month, and when I get back shall have to stay here till after the 4th of July in order to finish my manuscript—I have all my notes and other things on the subject here. But shall then go over to Talcottville where I look forward to seeing you.

The weather here has been horrible. We had snow a couple of days ago.

Love to you both, / Edmund.

[Postscript] If you have any time for such things, do read Thornton Wilder's new book *The Eighth Day.* I think it is the best thing that he has done. The review in the *New Republic* was incredibly stupid. [Stanley] Kauffman fell into all of the traps that Wilder has laid for the reader. I should be interested to know how you react to the religious element.

Wellfleet letterhead / June 27, 1967

Dear Glyn: I am disappointed to know that you will be coming over here just about the time I'll be going to Talcottville. I had been very much looking forward to seeing you.

But I may still be here after the 15th—so can hope to see you then. I am working on an article on Israel and the new edition of my book on the scrolls and have to be here, where I have my apparatus. Please call us up when you get to Bass River.

I had all my trip in May arranged in advance and a flight from Tel-Aviv for the morning just after the Consul called me up to say that he had had word from Washington to tell all Americans to leave. I had a most satisfactory time and have some things to tell you that may interest you.

As ever, / Edmund

July 18, 1967

Dear Glyn: Your departure[1] has left a gap and a blank. I am only now coming to realize how dull the life up here is. I have decided to try to sell this house, if I can find anyone who wants to buy it. Rosalind and Elena are with me now, but Elena and I are going back to Boston next Tuesday. I have had another of those malarial attacks since you left, and my doctor in Boston wants me to spend a few days in the hospital there. I'm hoping to get my new bridge put in today.—This is all the news, except that Barbara came in the other night. I had already heard from Bill Alexander about your difficulties in getting installed.—It has been horribly hot here, as I understand it has been with you.— Tell Gladys that I miss her excellent meals and her quiet, benign presence. I have conceived a horror of the restaurants with their invariable menu of lobster tails and liver and bacon. I have, except for Elena's lunches, subsisted almost entirely on soup and butterscotch sundaes.—Best of luck in your new milieu. As ever,

Edmund

[1]The Morrises briefly left Lewis County for the Appalachian region they had formerly lived in; as future letters show, they found it not to their liking and, much to Wilson's delight, returned to upstate New York.

Wellfleet, Mass. / March 12, 1968

Dear Glyn: I haven't read Mumford's book; but I am allied with him in a campaign against the Modern Language Association which we are carrying on in the *New York Review of Books*. I have been shut up here all winter with the late B.C. and the early A.D. centuries but hope to get my book more or less finished by early April.[1] Shall then go to N.Y. and Virginia and perhaps arrive in Talcottville by the first of May. Love to Gladys. I look forward very much to seeing you.

[1] *The Dead Sea Scrolls.*

New Yorker letterhead / November 21, 1968

Dear Glyn:

Thanks for your letter and the pamphlet. The methods for ending poverty proposed in the last paragraph are a pretty large order.

We were sorry not to see you again before we left—called you several times.

I've been spending a week in New York, and shall be glad to leave on Saturday.

Have you seen Kennan's book, provoked by his speech about the protesting young people? It is in paperback now and worth reading. I don't agree with his objections to fighting the draft.[1]

I miss seeing you people now. Love to Gladys.

As ever, / Edmund Wilson

[1] Wilson's review "Unscrupulous Communists and Embattled Democracies" ran in the *New Yorker* September 9, 1961 and was reprinted as "George F. Kennan" in *The Bit Between My Teeth.*

[Postcard from Jamaica, "Fishing in Jamaica"]

[February 1969]

Dear Glyn: Your letter reached me here. This card will give you an idea of what we are <u>not </u>doing. This is a miserable little country, with terrible problems since the British left; but we live here on the water in a kind of vacuum, which is really what we wanted—back the first of March. Talcottville sometime in May.—There is a non-education situation here which would haunt even you. Look forward to seeing you before too long. Love to Gladys.

Edmund

Wellfleet letterhead / August 16, 1969

Dear Glyn: I was interested to hear of your struggles in getting your house in shape—as contrasted with the procedures in Lewis County.

I forget whether I last wrote you before or after I went to the hospital in

Boston. They discovered nothing of interest, and I—what with extractions of blood and marrow and innumerable x-rays when I was suffering fearfully from gout—I came out feeling worse than when I went in. I am now more or less recovered, but I am still not doing much work—it is terribly hot here.—I read about a hundred and fifty pages of *Ada*[1] when I was in the hospital but did not really like it much. I suppose I shall eventually go on with it.

I hope to get back to Talcottville in the latter part of September. If you should be coming there, I could put you up.

We are living in a let-down discouraging time. I blame a good deal of it on Nixon and the idiots that elected him.

Love to Gladys,

As ever, / Edmund

[1]Another Nabokov novel that failed to please. See comments on *Lolita* in section VII.

Talcottville letterhead / Nov. 11, 1969

Dear Glyn: I'm up here again for the dentist and have been incapacitated by gout so that I can hardly get across the room. The weather has been so foggy ever since Saturday as I have ever seen it up here. When we came up from the airport, we couldn't see my house and drove past it without seeing it even though there was a light on.—I'm returning in a few days to Wellfleet.

I've done a book note on the Mencken and shall perhaps note your correction.— The poem of Ms. Reese's I tried to recite was not Rain, but Tears. See p. 99 Am. Poetry—Untermeyer.

Love to Gladys.

Yours at present very poorly, but hoping to recover, / Edmund

Dec. 15, 1969 / Wellfleet, Mass.

Dear Glyn and Gladys: I'm not sending out any regular Christmas cards this year—I'm bored with them.—No great news with us. We're leading our usual monotonous life. I've finally got around to writing my book about Talcottville and environs. Hope to be able to finish it when I go up there next spring. [. . .]—Later, I hope to be able to send you a copy of Flusser's little book on Jesus. Very interesting as the scholarly production of a pro-Jesus Jew who knows all the historical background. My scrolls book which did nothing at first, has now picked up and is selling.—I hope you are getting to know people down there and finding it a little more stimulating. Our circle of friends up here is becoming more and more depressing—aging and death—but I doubt if I am going to get away for long this winter.

Love from us both to both of you.

As ever, / Edmund

Wellfleet letterhead / Dec. 21, 1969

Dear Glyn: My cousin Susan is Susan Wilson, 2262, Ivy Road; telephone: Charlottesville 29–33724. I am going to call her up and shall tell her that you are coming. You will find her something of a museum piece.

I am really rejoiced to hear that you are coming back to Lewis County. I have missed you people acutely.—I have really got rolling now with my book on that part of the world. Hope to finish it up there next summer. My cousin Dorothy Mendenhall has written an autobiography which I hadn't known about and which I am now reading with fascination. It tells a lot about the earlier life up there which I otherwise should not have known. I now know where my Indian blood comes from—the Wampanoags in this part of the New England world.

Love to Gladys, / Edmund

Jan. 14, 1970

Dear Glyn: Do you know why the Mennonites did not believe in buttons?[1] I have looked it up in a huge 4-volume Mennonite encyclopedia, but it doesn't give any explanation. I am well into my upstate New York book and want to include this detail.—I hope that you will persist in your intention of coming back. You have left a gap which is hard to fill. I expect to go over in the middle of May. As ever,

Edmund

[1]Buttons: Morris notes that on page 19 of *Upstate* Wilson has written the answer to this question.

Wellfleet letterhead / April 6, 1970

Dear Glyn: I'm delighted about your getting your house back. I had really become attached to it, was depressed when you left and couldn't imagine you living anywhere else. I have hoped to get up there the second week in May;

but I had a heart attack when I went to New York, have spent some time in the Hyannis hospital, and my plans must depend partly on the reading of cardiograms. There is a new way to the hospital which, as a gadget laboratory, rivals yours. They do what they call, "monitor" your heartbeats. They wire you to a box and the action of your heart is projected, in jewel-like green or amber lights against a black background as little elf-like signs that hop downward. These are read on another TV box by the doctors and nurses in a separate room. Somebody has suggested that the next stop will be interpolated commercials. Since I have been back here at home, however, I have been thoroughly enjoying myself. My bed has been moved downstairs just across from the table where I write, and, since I don't have to do anything about anything else, I have been making great progress with my Talcottville book.[1] I am pleased with it, but don't know how far it will be possible to interest other people in my own and the local affairs. Lots of points I want to ask you about.

Love to Gladys, / As ever, / Edmund

[1] *Upstate.*

[Letter to Glyn Morris's secretary, Barbara]

Wellfleet letterhead / April 20, 1970

Dear Barbara: Thank you for your card. Since I got out of the hospital I have been enjoying all those luxuries; but now that I've been given a clean bill of health, I'm up and around again. I'm looking forward to seeing you all again—hope to get up there not later than May 11.—I've been working all winter on my Talcottville book and am now getting a little bored with it. It partly consists of a journal of twenty summers at Talcottville!—It is delightful and rather amusing that the Morrises can go back to their house. I never could imagine them in any other setting.

Affectionately, / Edmund W

[Postcard from Boonville postmarked June 10, 1970]

[Addressed to Mr. and Mrs. Glyn Morris]

Looking forward to your arrival.—Your house has been painted gray with yellow trimmings.—I'm still working on my upstate book—I don't know who outside my friends up here will ever read it. The police dog at The Perfect has had nine puppies— father a husky. This is all the news.

Edmund

[Postcard]

August 2, 1970, Wellfleet, Mass

Dear Glyn: I'll be coming back on the 16th—I shall call you up. Am eager to see you.—We've been having a hot spell here such as I've never known even in New Jersey; it is really rather hard to get through. A queer thunderstorm last night, like a movie battle with shells exploding. I think Javeh [Jehovah] is very angry.

Edmund

Wellfleet letterhead / Oct. 9, 1970

Dear Glyn: Thanks for the further information on the fisher and the educational services. I'm about to start on the last chapter of my book, and it better be good to justify all the perhaps boring stuff that has gone before.—I may possibly get up there for a few days again, but am not sure I'll be able to make it.

Love to Gladys and Barbara. / As ever, / Edmund

Wellfleet letterhead / Nov. 1, 1970

Dear Glyn; The curious thing is that I have never noticed—except perhaps once, when I had also had a little too much—your being much affected by liquor. If you were, I suppose my two highballs and some wine at dinner had made it imperceptible to me—I am extremely glad to hear that Ogdensburg has freed you up. I miss seeing you. The prospect here is bleak—everybody that we see is either very old or dotty. We have to import occasional life-enhancers from Boston or New York.—I am back to my Russian subjects again and find them rather a relief after Talcottville and environs, since they do not present any problems of tact.—Love from us both to Gladys.

As ever, / Edmund

Wellfleet letterhead / Nov. 8, 1970

Dear Glyn: I am back from six days in New York, which nearly finished me—I don't think I'll ever feel able to go there again. But my book has gone over well both with my publisher and with the *New Yorker* editor, who's running two installments of it. I regard this as the high point of my journalistic career—to induce the *New Yorker* to print an account of twenty years of Talcottville.—I saw *Conduct Unbecoming* which I understand you also saw. It preserves the suspense though a fairly long performance, but it seems to me the end is rather confusing and implausible. And somebody shouted too much.—New York is worse hell than ever. I really can't struggle with it any longer.

I hope you have recovered by this time. I am sending this to Lyons Falls in case you may be out of Ogdensburg. I know that it must be hard for you to adjust yourself to so relatively inactive a life, but I have great hopes of your book.[1] Would you like to have me read it in MS? My difficulty is the opposite one nowadays of adjusting myself, as in New York, to seeing and doing business with people. It fatigues me and my memory breaks down. When alone with one person and my work, I don't have to worry about other people—can always simply write them letters. I've decided not to sell Talcottville. That provides almost the only real story to my book. In the Prologue I'm deciding to give it up; in the Epilogue, not to.

Give my love to Gladys and Barbara. Barbara was kind enough to come and get me, and Gladys to give me a good dinner in your absence after you went to Ogdensburg. Don't forget the Hebrew motto which is still tacked up behind the oxygen tank in my bedroom-study.

As ever, / Edmund

[1]Morris did publish privately a memoir called *Less Travelled Roads*, which Wilson did not live to read. One chapter, chapter eight, is devoted to Morris's friendship with Wilson. He later expanded on that chapter to write a book-length memoir of Wilson's last years. It will eventually reside with Wilson's papers at Yale.

[Morris's handwriting: Probably Florida winter 1970–71]
Dear Glyn and Gladys;

The weather here is very mild, but Elena, who sends love, is in bed fighting off the flu, and Helen phones that she is arriving with it. I am getting over a prolonged allergy, perhaps caused by seeing pictures and TV views of Nixon.—Love and greetings from us all.

Edmund and Elena

Feb. 19, 1971 / Naples, Florida
Dear Glyn: I had already written you when I just got your letter.—I had forgotten you had lots down here. They will probably go up in value. The "developments" are going forward at breakneck speed.—When I read that story

about the White House dinner for the *Reader's Digest,* I at first thought of doing an article about it, but gave up the idea because I realized that it could only be abusive and that it wouldn't look well because the "Freedom Medal" that Nixon gave Wallace was the same thing that Kennedy gave me.—A man I know—not a writer but a banker—whose judgement I think is pretty good predicts that we are in for another mediocre president—"McGovern's too pure." The Americans won't do anything until they feel a severe economic pinch. I don't feel any enthusiasm for either Musky or Lindsay.—About the *Reader's Digest,* Harold Ross forbade his contributors to allow any article to be reprinted in it.—I think I wrote you before how boring this place is. It's largely populated by elder parties who are delighted to get away from the blizzards and winds of the Great Lakes and who are shocked and uncomprehending when you say you find it dull.—I hope to be back in May rather than April, but we are going to stop off in March to see my cousin in Virginia. Then the Cape, thank God.

As ever, / Edmund

Wellfleet letterhead / June 22, 1971

Dear Glyn: I am getting better, but slowly. It is exasperating to be so helpless in this beautiful weather. Thank you for the clipping. I am still reading *Wild Wales,*[1] which has a soothing effect on me. I look forward to getting back eventually. Please give my love to Gladys. Elena takes me out for a drive every day after lunch, as you did, but I miss our conversations.

As ever, / Edmund

[1] A kind of Welsh classic.

Wellfleet, Mass. / September 7, 1971

Dear Glyn: Thank you for your letter. This clipping might interest you. I don't want it back.

I believe I am getting somewhat better but nothing to make a fuss about. Love to everybody.

Edmund

Wellfleet, Mass. / November 16, 1971

Dear Glyn: I, too, have had to reconcile myself to a very limited activity. I am still more or less crippled and can't get around easily. We want to go somewhere for the winter but haven't decided where. When are you coming to see us? We may be here till the end of December.

About Jephthah:[1] I had forgotten about it and have just looked it up. It has, so far as I know, never been used for an opera or the subject of a painting—though I may be wrong about this last. I don't quite see its possibilities as you do. I should be interested to know how you used it for a sermon.

Elena sends love. Love to all the family.

As ever. / Edmund

[1]Jephthah: in the book of Judges, a Hebrew who vowed to sacrifice the first of his household he met on returning from victory over the Ammonites. His daughter was the sacrificial victim.

Wellfleet, Mass. / December 18, 1971

Dear Glyn: I am not sending out any Christmas cards this year but want you and your family to have our warmest holiday greetings.

We are just having our first heavy snowstorm—I suppose you are much further advanced in this respect.

We are going to Naples, Florida, for the winter after the first of the year. The address is 231 Second Ave. S.

You have probably finished *Wild Wales* by now. I read it with much pleasure, though it is rather monotonous. It is probably less so for you. I am still partly crippled— am hoping that the warmer climate will pick me up and that I can get back to Talcottville in the spring. Please drop me a line occasionally.

As ever, / Edmund

[Postcard of pelicans]

[Winter, 1972]

These are our only companions, along with a lot of retired business executives who are astonished when I say the place is dull because they think it is Heaven. You see all the most discouraging of well-off, middle-class America. They will elect Nixon or somebody like him.

Love to Gladys and Barbara, / Edmund

Wellfleet, Mass. / April 22, 1972

Dear Glyn: Rosalind has just sent me a notice of Gladys's death. It has made me very sad, and I know that it will be very upsetting for your whole life. Our dinners and conversations at your house are among my pleasantest memories of these last years. Gladys was able to add so much to them by her quiet and intelligent attention to us. Please believe in my sympathy for you during this trying period of your life. Elena sends all her condolences. I hope that you will now get back on your book.

I hope to get up there in May and shall be very glad to see you again.

Yours sincerely, / Edmund

TO MARGARET RULLMAN

Wellfleet, Mass. / January 1, 1962
Dear Margaret: I was very glad to hear from you and much interested in the photographs and other things. Of course I remember Verriker Farquhar—I think he spells his name like this—do give him my regards when you see him.— We almost never get to New York nowadays, spending the winter in Cambridge as we do. We have come to Wellfleet for the holidays—[A portion of this letter deleted here appears in section IV.]

The day before Christmas Helen unearthed all the family photographs that my mother used to have around. She cleaned them all up and they rather upset me by making me think about Red Bank. I had forgotten we had them in the house here. I remembered our old Christmas parties, with Uncle Win standing by to extinguish Christmas tree fires with a wet cloth on the end of a broomstick. It made a sad contrast with our thin Christmas this year, with only one of the children with us and some of our friends away. I thought about you the other day when I was going through the diary you gave me when we went abroad in 1908. My entries at that time were sketchy, but later on—in England in 1914—I began keeping a kind of journal—though not writing it up every day—which I've continued up to the present. I'm getting this in order to publish, filling it with new material so that it will make a kind of memoir. A good deal of it can't be published till after my death, but I think that a volume or two can be published now. Looking back, it seems to me today that you were the only friend in Red Bank that really interested me. I have finished the book on the Civil War that I have been working on, on and off, for about fifteen years. It is supposed to be out in April.

I am sorry that your life has been so difficult. If we ever get to New York for any length of time, perhaps you could come in and see us. Elena goes down occasionally to visit her son and his family on Long Island—they have twin girls whom she adores. I usually stay only long enough to do business with my editors and publishers.

Elena sends love and Happy New Year. I don't believe we can expect much that is cheerful. I think this country is in a mess right now, don't you?

Love as ever, / Edmund

Wellfleet letterhead / December 27, 1971

Dear Margaret: I don't know whether I told you but I broke a vertebra and have since been partly crippled. We are going to Naples, Florida for the rest of the winter: the address is care of Ganders, 231 Second Ave. S., Naples, Florida. I was glad to have the picture of you and the dog, collapsed.[1] I am feeling old and useless: I do a few hours of writing a day and that is all. I didn't send out any Christmas cards this year.

Love, / Edmund

[1] Evidently enclosed in a collapsible folder.

[Letter from Elena Wilson to Margaret Rullman]

Wellfleet, Mass. / June 22, 1972

Dear Margaret:

You were one of the few people I had meant to call that morning before I left for Talcottville and then in the rush and confusion, I didn't. I had been going to meet him the next day in Northampton—he said he was anxious to get back.

He had been very, very sick but he died quickly and easily and his mind was all there—all of it. . . .

With love, / Elena

CREDITS

Wilson letters from the Wilson Papers courtesy of the Beinecke Rare Book and Manuscript Library, Yale University.

Wilson letters to Burton and Hazel Rascoe provided from the Burton Rascoe Papers, courtesy of the Rare Book and Manuscript Library, University of Pennsylvania.

Wilson letters to Allen Tate provided from the Allen Tate Papers, Manuscripts Division, Department of Rare Books and Special Collections, Princeton University Library, published by permission of the Princeton University Library.

Wilson letters to Louise Bogan are provided from the Louise Bogan Papers (Box IV, Folder 8), Archives and Special Collections, Amherst College Library.

Wilson letters to John Dos Passos provided by the John Dos Passos Papers, courtesy of the Albert H. Small Special Collections Library at the University of Virginia.

Wilson letters to Morton Dauwen Zabel provided from the Morton D. Zabel Papers, courtesy of The Newberry Library, Chicago

Wilson letters to Lionel Trilling provided from the Lionel Trilling Papers, courtesy of the Rare Book and Manuscript Library, Columbia University.

Wilson letters to Dawn Powell provided from the Dawn Powell Papers, courtesy of the Rare Book and Manuscript Library, Columbia University.

Wilson letters to Betty Huling provided from the Edmund Wilson Papers, McFarlin Library, The University of Tulsa.

Wilson letters to Helen Muchnic provided from the collection Edmund Wilson Letters to Helen Muchnic, Manuscripts Division, Department of Rare Books and Special Collections, Princeton University Library, published by permission of the Princeton University Library.

Wilson letters to Cyril Connolly provided from the Cyril Connolly Papers, McFarlin Library, The University of Tulsa.

Wilson letters to Isaiah Berlin courtesy of Henry Hardy, Wolfson College, Oxford University.

Wilson letters to Mary McCarthy courtesy of Special Collections, Vassar College Libraries.

Wilson letters to Elena Mumm Thornton from the Wilson Papers, courtesy of the Beinecke Rare Book and Manuscript Library, Yale University.

Wilson letter to Rosalind Wilson (Ms. Am. 1017) provided from the Boston Public Library/Rare Books Department, courtesy of the Trustees.

Wilson letters to Clelia Carroll (Carey) courtesy of The Pierpont Morgan Library, New York, MA 5058.

Wilson letter to Charles Scribner provided from the Archives of Charles Scribner's Sons, Manuscripts Division, Department of Rare Books and Special Collections, Princeton University Library, published by permission of the Princeton University Library.

Wilson letters to Ken McCormick provided from the Edmund Wilson Papers, McFarlin Library, The University of Tulsa.

Wilson letter to Fredric Warburg from the Wilson Papers, courtesy of the Beinecke Rare Book and Manuscript Library, Yale University.

Wilson letter to William Van O'Connor provided from the William Van O'Connor Papers, courtesy of the Syracuse University Library Department of Special Collections.

Wilson letters to William Shawn provided from *The New Yorker* Records, courtesy of the Manuscripts and Archives Division of The New York Public Library, Astor, Lenox and Tilden Foundations.

Wilson letters to Roger Straus provided from the Farrar, Straus & Giroux, Inc. Records courtesy of the Manuscripts and Archives Division of The New York Public Library, Astor, Lenox and Tilden Foundations.

Wilson letters to Edward Gorey courtesy of the Edward Gorey Estate.

Wilson letter to Elmer Rice courtesy of the Harvard Theatre Collection, Houghton Library.

Wilson letter to John Lester from the Wilson Papers, courtesy of the Beinecke Rare Book and Manuscript Library, Yale University.

Wilson letter to Norman Gottwald from the Wilson Papers courtesy of the Beinecke Rare Book and Manuscript Library, Yale University.

Wilson letters to Jacob Landau courtesy of the Jacob Landau Estate.

Wilson letter to William James Jr. (bMS Am 1938 [138]) published by permission of the Houghton Library, Harvard University.

Wilson letter to V. S. Pritchett courtesy of the Berg Collection of English and American Literature, Manuscripts and Archives Division, The New York Public Library, Astor, Lenox and Tilden Foundations.

Wilson letter to Katharine S. White provided from the Katharine Sergeant White Papers, courtesy of Bryn Mawr College Library, Special Collections.

Wilson letters to John Hall Wheelock provided from the Archives of Charles Scribner's Sons, Manuscripts Division, Department of Rare Books and Special Collections, Princeton University Library, published by permission of the Princeton University Library.

Wilson letter to John Berryman from the Wilson Papers, courtesy of the Beinecke Rare Book and Manuscript Library, Yale University.

Wilson letter to Stephen Spender from the Wilson Papers, courtesy of the Beinecke Rare Book and Manuscript Library, Yale University.

Wilson letter to Robert Cantwell provided from the Robert Cantwell Papers, courtesy of the University of Oregon Library.

Wilson letter to Henry D. Blumberg from the Wilson Papers, courtesy of the Beinecke Rare Book and Manuscript Library, Yale University.

Wilson letter to Dick and Jo Costa from the Wilson Papers, courtesy of the Beinecke Rare Book and Manuscript Library, Yale University.

Wilson letters to Mary Pcolar from the Wilson Papers, courtesy of the Beinecke Rare Book and Manuscript Library, Yale University.

Wilson letter to S. N. Behrman provided from the S. N. Behrman Papers, courtesy of the Manuscripts and Archives Division of The New York Public Library, Astor, Lenox and Tilden Foundations.

Wilson letters to Glyn and Gladys Morris provided from the Edmund Wilson Collection, Manuscripts Division, Department of Rare Books and Special Collections, Princeton University Library, published by permission of the Princeton University Library.

Wilson letters to Margaret Rullman provided from the collection Edmund Wilson Letters to Margaret Rullman, Manuscripts Division, Department of Rare Books and Special Collections, Princeton University Library, published by permission of the Princeton University Library.

Wilson letter to Frances Steloff courtesy of the Berg Collection of English and American Literature Manuscripts and Archives Division, The New York Public Library, Astor, Lenox and Tilden Foundations.

Schiller, Friedrich von, 95
Schlesinger, Arthur, 129, 130, 130 n, 317
Schnitzler, Arthur, 148, 149 n, 186
Schocken Library, 282, 288
Schuman, Frederick, Lewis, 90
Scribner, Charles, 275–76
Scribner's, 45, 63, 64, 273, 274, 275, 276, 307
Scrutiny, 73 n
Seldes, Gilbert, 157, 158 n, 163, 164
Sellers, Peter, 181
Shakespeare, William, 250, 253, 255
Sharp, Malcolm and Dorothy, 180 n, 184, 185
Shaw, George Bernard, 22, 45, 66
Shawn, William, xii, 127, 127 n, 273, 278–80
Shelley, Percy Bysshe, 68
Shostakovich, Dmitri, 255
Silone, Darina, 188, 189, 190, 190 n
Silone, Ignazio, 189, 190 n
Singer, Isaac Bashevis, 304 n
Siphraios, Eva, 173
Smith, Logan Pearsall, 168, 170 n
Sophocles, 106
Soule, George, 36 n, 72
Spectator, 284
Spender, Stephen, 100, 107, 108, 188, 300, 309, 310 n
Sports Illustrated, 141 n
Spotlight, 35
Stafford, Jean, 132, 132 n
Stalin, Joseph, 90, 102 n, 112, 255, 263, 301
St. Bernard's School, 206, 207, 209, 211
Stein, Gertrude, 121
Steloff, Frances, 129 n
Stevens, Wallace, 62 n
Stewart, Donald Ogden, 50, 50 n
St. George's School, 218, 302
Stilwell, George, 19
Stockton, Frank R., 250 n
Stolberg, Ben, 113, 113 n, 114
Straight, Michael, 83, 83 n, 87, 282
Straus, Dorothea, 255 n, 292, 293
Straus, Roger, xii, 87, 103, 165, 172, 186, 249, 273, 280–94, 295
Stravinsky, Igor, 155, 215
Swinburne, Algernon, 94, 152, 152 n, 178, 178 n

Taft, Alphonso, 123 n
Taft, William Howard, 27, 54, 122
Taine, Hippolyte, 66
Talcottville, 84, 91, 131, 134, 154 n, 174, 184, 195, 204, 205, 229, 236, 237, 240, 254,

259, 260, 261, 267, 283, 317, 320, 323, 325, 330, 332, 333, 335, 336, 337, 338, 341
Tandy, Jessica, 77
Tate, Allen, 33, 40–43, 275, 275 n
Tel Aviv, xii
Thoby-Marcelin, Philippe (Phito), 160, 161, 161 n, 169, 318
Thoby-Marcelin, Pierre, 161 n
Thornton, Elena Mumm. *See* Wilson, Elena
Thornton, Henry, 65 n, 79, 83, 83 n, 85, 139, 139 n, 141, 146, 148, 171, 182, 191 n, 211, 214, 216
Thornton, James (Jimmy), 133, 137, 138 n, 139, 141
Time, 141 n, 311 n
Tolstoy, Leo, 107, 108 n, 151
Toscanini, Arturo, 248
Town and Country, 134, 138 n, 145 n
Trilling, Diana, 69, 69 n
Trilling, Lionel, xi, 33, 34, 66–74
Trotsky, Leon, 90, 116, 255
Turanos, Tom and Ann, 152, 152 n
Turgenev, Ivan, 101, 102, 102 n, 103, 103 n
Twain, Mark, 250 n

Udmark, John A., 15, 17 n, 18, 20, 21, 22, 39, 39 n, 42
University of Chicago, 111, 119
Untermeyer, Louis, 58 n, 333
Utica College, 239, 254, 261, 318, 320

Vanity Fair, 25 n, 273
Van O'Connor, William, 278
Vassar College, 19, 33
Verdi, Giuseppe, 250
Vidal, Gore, 288 n
Virgil, 39
Vogue, 122 n

Wain, John, 73 n
Walker, Charles (Charley), 122, 123 n, 126, 133, 145
Warburg, Fredric, 277
Waugh, Elizabeth, 145 n
Waugh, Evelyn, 99, 99 n
Wedekind, Frank, 148, 149 n
Weeks, Edward, 157, 157 n
Wellfleet, xii, 53, 66, 90 n, 92, 93, 98 n, 123 n, 130 n, 131, 134, 138, 154 n, 167, 170, 174, 195, 204, 209, 216, 226, 227, 239, 240, 245, 251, 255 n, 261, 265, 278, 283, 284, 288, 292, 317, 333

Wesleyan University, 250, 289

West, James, 131 n, 178 n

Wharton, Edith, 22, 112

Wheelock, John Hall (Jack), 274–75, 300, 307–8

White, E. B., 307 n

White, Katharine S., 300, 306–7

White, Newman, Ivey, 68

Wilde, Oscar, 168, 185

Wilder, Thornton, 114, 251, 330

Wilson, Angus, 96, 97 n, 129, 235, 256

Wilson, Caroline, 19, 19 n

Wilson, Colin, 56

Wilson, Edmund, "The Ambiguity of Henry James," 44 n; *The American Earthquake,* 25 n, 38 n, 141 n, 290, 317; *The American Jitters,* 38 n; *Apologies to the Iroquois,* 79 n, 87, 152 n, 287, 290; *Axel's Castle,* 34, 56 n, 58, 276; *Beppo and Beth,* 51 n; *The Bit Between My Teeth,* 34, 62 n, 96 n, 105 n, 106 n, 152 n, 182, 241 n, 332; *Classics and Commercials,* 64 n, 77, 139 n, 165 n, 273, 283, 290; *Cold War and the Income Tax,* 57 n, 66 n, 81 n, 188 n, 279, 288 n, 305, 327; *Cyprian's Prayer,* 281; "Dawn Powell: Greenwich Village in the Fifties," 34; *The Dead Sea Scrolls 1947–1969,* 253 n, 291, 332; "The Death of a Soldier," 3; "The Death of Margaret," 50 n; *The Devils and Canon Barham,* 165 n, 253 n, 273; "Dickens: The Two Scrooges," 39, 77; *Dr. McGrath,* 330; *The Duke of Palermo,* 242, 250 n, 293, 294, 296 n, 330; "Eisenstein in Hollywood," 38 n; *Europe Without Baedeker,* 88, 88 n, 96 n, 127 n, 290, 291; *The Fifties: Notebooks and Diaries of the Period,* 122 n, 307 n; *From the Uncollected Edmund Wilson,* 33, 73 n; *The Fruits of the MLA,* 330; *Galahad,* 252, 253 n, 289, 289 n, 290; "Give the Beat Again," 113 n; "Gogol: The Demon in the Overgrown Garden," 305 n; "Haiti: Landscape and Morale," 167 n; *The Higher Jazz,* 60 n; "The Historical Interpretation of Literature," 67 n; "Inaugural Parade," 50 n; *I Thought of Daisy,* 37, 45, 113 n, 165, 252, 253 n, 281, 284, 289, 289 n, 290, 291; "Justice to Edith Wharton," 112 n; "Koussevitsky at Tanglewood," 155 n; "Legend and Symbol in Doctor Zhivago," 106 n; *Letters on Literature and Politics,* 41, 61 n, 131 n; "Lieutenant Franklin," 3; *The Little Blue Light,* 51, 66 n, 77 n, 83, 281; "Marxism and Literature," 41 n, 43, 65 n; "Marxism at the End of the Forties," 280; *Memoirs of Hecate County,* 45, 60, 62 n, 69 n, 76, 90, 92, 100 n, 134, 135, 139, 140, 143, 145 n, 146, 273, 281, 286–87, 291; "Morose Ben Jonson," 152 n; "My Fifty Years with Dictionaries and Grammars," 322; *Night Thoughts,* 34, 95 n, 181; *Note-Books of Night,* 277; "Note on the Elegiac Meter," 95 n; *O Canada,* 81, 133 n, 188 n, 290, 291; "The Omelet of A. MacLeish," 157 n; *Patriotic Gore,* 66 n, 80 n, 131, 182 n, 183, 326; "Paul Rosenfeld: The Three Phases," 141 n; *A Piece of My Mind,* 29, 72, 87, 284, 285; *A Prelude,* 3, 5 n, 11, 17, 291, 292; "The Princess With the Golden Hair," 62 n, 145 n; *The Rats of Rutland Grange,* 242 n; *Red, Black, Blond and Olive,* 152 n, 167 n, 284; "A Reporter on Shalako," 152 n; *Scrolls from the Dead Sea,* 100 n, 174 n, 253 n, 273, 284; *The Shock of Recognition,* 61 n, 63 n, 293; *The Shores of Light,* 49, 53 n, 93 n, 112 n, 113 n, 114 n, 158 n, 171 n, 280, 281, 282; *The Sixties: Notebooks and Diaries of the Period,* 76, 132 n, 148 n; "Somerset Maugham and an Antidote," 77 n, 139 n; *The Thirties: Notebooks and Diaries of the Period,* 43 n, 50 n; *This Room and This Gin and These Sandwiches: Three Plays,* 281; *To the Finland Station,* 34, 44 n, 47, 253, 276, 280, 281, 288; *The Triple Thinkers,* 44 n, 67 n, 285; "Unscrupulous Communists and Embattled Democrats," 182 n; *Upstate,* 20 n, 317, 328, 334, 335; "Who Cares Who Killed Roger Ackroyd?" 29 n; *A Window on Russia,* 102 n, 107 n, 299, 305 n; *The Wound and the Bow,* 39, 48 n, 70, 112 n, 285

Wilson, Edmund, Sr. (father), 3, 6, 12, 18, 169

Wilson, Elena (Mrs. Edmund Wilson), xi, xii, 42 n, 49, 54, 65 n, 79, 84, 85, 86, 87, 93, 100, 101, 104 n, 128, 131 n, 133–91, 195, 196 n, 201, 204, 210, 211, 214, 215, 218 n, 224, 225, 227, 234, 235, 238, 240, 242, 243, 248, 251, 253, 254, 255 n, 257, 259, 260, 261, 263, 265, 267, 283, 284,